ECONOMICS OF THE ARTS

Selected Essays

CONTRIBUTIONS
TO
ECONOMIC ANALYSIS

237

ELSEVIER
Amsterdam – Lausanne – New York – Oxford – Shannon – Tokyo

ECONOMICS OF THE ARTS

Selected Essays

Edited by

Victor A. GINSBURGH
C.E.M.E.
Uni ersité Libre de Bruxelles
Brussels, Belgium

Pierre-Michel MENGER
Ecole des Hautes Etudes et Sciences Sociales
Paris, France

1996

ELSEVIER
Amsterdam – Lausanne – New York – Oxford – Shannon – Tokyo

ELSEVIER SCIENCE B.V.
Sara Burgerhartstraat 25
P.O. Box 211, 1000 AE Amsterdam, The Netherlands

ISBN: 0 444 82402 2

This book is printed on acid-free paper.

PRINTED IN THE NETHERLANDS

INTRODUCTION TO THE SERIES

This series consists of a number of hitherto unpublished studies, which are introduced by the editors in the belief that they represent fresh contributions to economic science.

The term 'economic analysis' as used in the title of the series has been adopted because it covers both the activities of the theoretical economist and the research worker.

Although the analytical methods used by the various contributors are not the same, they are nevertheless conditioned by the common origin of their studies, namely theoretical problems encountered in practical research. Since for this reason, business cycle research and national accounting, research work on behalf of economic policy, and problems of planning are the main sources of the subjects dealt with, they necessarily determine the manner of approach adopted by the authors. Their methods tend to be 'practical' in the sense of not being too far remote from application to actual economic conditions. In addition they are quantitative.

It is the hope of the editors that the publication of these studies will help to stimulate the exchange of scientific information and to reinforce international cooperation in the field of economics.

The Editors

Table of Contents

List of Contributors

Isabelle Busenhart, Institute of Empirical Economic Research, University of Zurich, Switzerland.

Peter Cannon-Brookes, Joint Editor of *Museum Management and Curatorship*, Oxon, U.K.

Olivier Chanel, GREQAM, Centre National de la Recherche Scientifique, Marseille, France.

Corinna Czujack, CEME, Université Libre de Bruxelles, Belgium.

Neil De Marchi, Professor of Economics, Duke University, Durham, U.S.

Renato Flôres Jr., Professor of Economics, UFRJ, Rio de Janeiro, Brasil and CEME, Université Libre de Bruxelles, Belgium.

Bruno S. Frey, Professor of Economics and Director, Institute for Empirical Economic Research, University of Zurich, Switzerland.

Louis-André Gérard-Varet, Professor of Economics, GREQAM, Ecole des Hautes Etudes en Sciences Sociales, Marseille, France.

Victor A. Ginsburgh, Professor of Economics, CEME, Université Libre de Bruxelles and CORE, Université Catholique de Louvain, Belgium.

William N. Goetzmann, Professor of Economics, Yale Scool of Management, New Haven, U.S.

William D. Grampp, Professor of Economics Emeritus, University of Illinois, Chicago, U.S.

Marc Gurgand, Département et Laboratoire d'Economie Théorique et Appliquée, Ecole des Hautes Etudes en Sciences Sociales and Centre National de la Recherche Scientifique, Paris, France.

Claudia Keser, Institut für Statistik und Mathematische Wirtschaftstheorie, Universität Karlsruhe, Germany.

William M. Landes, Clifton R. Musser Professor of Law and Economics, University of Chicago Law School, U.S.

Pierre-Michel Menger, Directeur de Recherche, Centre de Sociologie des Arts, Ecole des Hautes Etudes en Sciences Sociales and Centre National de la Recherche Scientifique, Paris, France.

John Michael Montias, Professor of Economics Emeritus, Yale University, New Haven, U.S.

Mark A. Olson, Senior Researcher, Center of Experimental Economics and Political Decisionmaking (CREED), University of Amsterdam, The Netherlands.

James E. Pesando, Professor of Economics and Director, Institute for Policy Analysis, University of Toronto, Canada.

Richard A. Posner, Chief Judge of the U.S. Court of Appeals for the Seventh Circuit and Senior Lecturer, University of Chicago Law School, U.S.

Pauline M. Shum, Associate Professor of Economics, Atkinson College, York University, Toronto, Canada.

David Throsby, Professor of Economics, Macquarie University, Sydney, Australia.

Ruth Towse, Lecturer in Economics, University of Exeter, U.K. and Joint Editor of *Journal of Cultural Economics*.

Hans J. Van Miegroet, Associate Professor of Art and Art History, Duke University, Durham, U.S.

Stéphanie Vincent, GREQAM, Université de la Méditerranée, Marseille, France.

Introduction

Economists often think that the economics of art markets constitutes a too specialized field to be worth of their attention. This volume is intended to contribute convincing them that, in fact, the domain is open to econometricians, theorists, economic (and, of course art) historians, labour economists, students interested in the economic analysis of legal problems.

In his recent review article in the *Journal of Economic Literature*, David Throsby (1994) suggests three lines along which research in cultural economics could proceed: (a) use the tools of positive and normative economic analysis to study theoretical and empirical problems; (b) construct better data sets; and (c) focus on wider horizons than those of conventional economics, by including into the analysis views taken from history, philosophy, aesthetics, sociology, etc.

The various contributions in this volume try to cover a large number of issues, ranging from auction anomalies, the management of museums, the excess supply of labour in the performing arts, the economic analysis of law, investment in artworks, to what we can learn from history on the behaviour of collectors and on prices of originals with respect to copies. It will become clear to the reader that each essay takes into account at least one, but often more than one of Throsby's three suggestions.

Some readers may perhaps find that the coverage of topics is unbalanced, since there are ten papers on artworks (including two papers on the management of museums), only three on the performing arts, and one that considers both issues. This was the outcome of our call for papers and reflects probably the expansion of markets for artworks during the 1980s, as well as the increasing number of discussions on the legal foundations and property rights of arts-related organisations. During the preceding decade, research on the economics of the arts was much more characterised by issues related to the organisation and the financing of the performing arts industry, with the seminal contributions by Baumol and Bowen (1966), Peacock (1969) and many others.[1] Though some important contributions are still being made to this more policy-oriented field, research has, as in many other domains of economics, shifted to less normative work.

[1]See also Blaug (1976) and Peacock's (1992) reminiscences as well as the recent volumes by Benhamou (1996) and Heilbrun and Gray (1993).

Artworks: markets, collectors and investors

Collecting (and the large amounts of money associated with it[2]) is as old as history. Art collections have started to build up as early as 700 BC,[3] and collectors have always valued art very highly. King Charles the First (1625-1649) buys paintings and Greek sculpture; his 1,400 paintings and 400 sculptures were put on sale (by the Parliament) between 1650 and 1653; this attracted many foreign collectors, including Mazarin and Philippe the Fourth, King of Spain. In 1625, Rubens sells his personal collection (which includes Roman sculptures) to the Duke of Buckingham for the price of Guilder 100,000. In 1612, Rodolph the Second, a German prince, dies; his collection is estimated to be worth Guilder 17 million. According to the 17th century diarist John Evelyn, even Dutch farmers pay high prices for paintings, which they resell at "very great gaines."[4] And, of course, nowadays, art has often be thought of as a possible asset in a financial portfolio. It is therefore not surprising that economists try to understand how and why markets value art and how art performs with respect to other assets.

In Chapters 1 and 2, John Michael Montias, Neil De Marchi and Hans Van Miegroet, who exploit the information available on 17th century art and art markets in the Netherlands, contribute to the first question.

Montias extracts information from probate inventories drawn up in Amsterdam, combines this with some ingenious quantitative techniques and from there on, draws inference on the life patterns of collecting – during which period in their life, do collectors acquire art –, on the productivity of artists – which more than trebled between 1610 and 1660 –, and on the ratio of copies to original works in art collections – which amounts to 66% for landscapes and 80% for still lifes. These contributions add to the already impressive amount of quantitative findings made by Montias on 17th century Dutch paintings.[5]

De Marchi and Van Miegroet are also interested in copies and originals,

[2]In this connection, see among many others Shell (1995), who also deals with how money becomes art.

[3]In Babylon, King Ashurbanipal (669-630 BC) constructs the famous library; Nebuchadnezzar (605-562 BC) collects objects. There even exists an inventory of his collection.

[4]Cited by Buck and Dodd (1991, p. 53).

[5]See Montias (1996) for an extensive overview of his and others' contributions.

but they concentrate on comparing prices. During the 15th century, factors such as the religious character of the work and costs of inputs prevail in valuing a painting; attribution and reputation of the artist are not neglected, but play a secondary role only, so that there was little difference between a copy and an original. The development of transactions and the increasing importance of art collectors and art dealers in the 17th century tends to widen the role played by the artist: works are more often valued for their originality and the inventiveness of the painter, signature becomes an important factor and originals are now valued at three times the price of copies. This is of course a very small ratio, compared with what happens today and shows that the formation of prices depends not only on the relative valuations of beauty, rarity, technical skill, etc., but also on the social context and on the various forms of labour division: a "copy" of a Rubens by one of his students had (and still has) a value, since the idea of "workshops" was prevailing and respected. In today's world of individualism, a copy or a painting "in the manner of" say, Picasso is valueless, even if the painter was closely connected to Picasso: creation, inventiveness and name of the artist[6] have become the main contributing factors to value.

There is obviously need to understand the relation that goes from aesthetic values to economic values (or, as some people argue, the other way round). Fashion and herd behaviour is one such factor, but certainly not the only one. There is also need to study the behaviour of the various actors on the markets, including the behaviour of artists themselves, some of which do contribute to the economic value of their works, while others do very little effort to promote their names.[7]

Anderson (1974) and Stein (1977) were among the first to look into the financial performance of art, using some econometrics. They were followed by Baumol (1986) and Frey and Pommerehne (1989). These various studies recognise that the difficulty in measuring returns (and constructing price indices) is due to the heterogeneous character of artworks. In order to ho-

[6]On the importance of the name, see e.g. Meyer (1989, p. 87). Though this paper deals mainly with forgery, most of the arguments apply to copies alike. See also the discussion by Grampp (1989, p. 131).

[7]Among recent contributions in both directions, see Heenk's (1995) dissertation on Van Gogh, Kendall's (1996) chapter on Degas and the market-place and Penders (1996) on the behaviour of earthartists.

mogenise, they base their computations on resales of identical works only (using, in one way or another, a repeat-sales regression technique[8]). This entails important limitations: (i) the number of resales is often small and represents a small proportion of total sales; (ii) resales may embody a sample selection bias; (iii) as pointed out by Guerzoni (1995), unobserved resales may also take place between observed sales at auctions[9] and if one takes these into account, returns may turn out to be very different from those usually obtained. Limitations (i)-(ii) are partly circumvented if, as suggested in Chanel et al. (1996), all sales are accounted for and hedonic regression is used instead of repeat-sales regression.

In Chapter 3, William Goetzmann points to an additional problem that is encountered when using repeat-sales regression,[10] the risk of obsolescence: many artworks are never resold because they disappear for natural reasons (fire, physical decay, etc.) or they are dumped because they are valueless or at least thought to be such.[11] Using simulated portfolios that embody a 20% rate of obsolescence, Goetzmann shows that rates of return can be seriously affected downward, though they remain much higher (5%) than what is suggested by Baumol, Frey and Pommerehne (0.5% to 1.5%).

Chapter 4 by Corinna Czujack, Renato Flôres and Victor Ginsburgh is (also) concerned with returns to investment in art. More specifically, they compare returns on paintings with returns on prints created by five well-known artists – Braque, Chagall, Ernst, Miró and Picasso. If returns turn out to be comparable, it may be wiser for investors to buy prints, which are cheaper, more liquid and probably less risky than paintings. They show that both media have a common trend, but that prints yield somewhat lower long-term returns (with the exception of prints by Picasso). A related question to which the technique (cointegration analysis) used to analyse the first issue can also provide an answer is whether one of those artists "leads" the market. Not too surprisingly, it is found that Picasso plays a leading role, though all five markets are pretty much interrelated.

---

[8]See Goetzmann (1990) and Shiller (1991) for very complete surveys on this issue.

[9]Guerzoni's findings are based on Reitlinger's (1960, 1970) data used by most researchers, since they go back to the 17th century.

[10]This is probably also the case with hedonic regressions, though it is less obvious.

[11]Schwartz (1994) estimates that of the 10 million works painted during the 17th century in the Netherlands, at most 1% have survived.

Art auctions

Chapters 5, 6 and 7 deal with anomalies that occur at auctions and show that auctions may suffer from many inefficiencies, that are usually not predicted by theoretical models. That this is, in fact, not surprising should be clear from the book by Smith (1989) who discusses the behaviour of auctioneers and salerooms.

It is difficult for the economist trained in price theory to accept that a commodity can be sold at different prices in the same location at (about) the same moment. The so-called "declining price anomaly," which was brought to the attention of a wider audience of economists by Ashenfelter (1989),[12] is one of the instances of market inefficiency: in multi-object auctions of the same commodity, prices for identical lots tend to decline over time. The anomaly is reported to occur in the papers by James Pesando and Pauline Shum (Chapter 5) for Picasso prints, and by Olivier Chanel, Louis-André Gérard-Varet and Stéphanie Vincent (Chapter 6) for jewellery. In both cases, some freedom is however taken to define "the same moment," "the same place" or "the same commodity." For Picasso prints, sales of the same print take place "at the same moment" and "in the same location" if they occur within one month, in any of the well-known salerooms dealing with prints (Christie's, Sotheby's, Kornfeld). For jewellery, sales occur during the same auction, but heterogeneous objects have to be made homogeneous.[13] Though the paper by Claudia Keser and Mark Olson (Chapter 7) does not deal with art auctions, it contributes to the understanding of the declining price anomaly. Indeed, by running experiments, the authors are able to (partially) control for a certain number of factors (risk-averse bidders who increase their bids for the first objects, bidders acting as agents, who buy at the possibly too high reservation prices set by their clients and do not wait for better bargains). They also find that declining prices are pervasive.

Declining prices is not the unique auction anomaly. Pesando and Shum report that prices for identical prints are higher in the U.S. than in Europe; this may perhaps be explained by differences in buying behaviour, but the fact that there is also a significant difference between Sotheby's and Christie's in New York can hardly be explained by the same argument. They also find that price differences across markets and auction houses were larger during

[12]The observation itself had already been made by Burns (1985).

[13]Ashenfelter reports on sales of identical wine lots during the same auction.

the boom of the print market (1984-1990) than otherwise. A similar "time dependence" result is obtained by Chanel et al. for jewellery: they show that prices are lower during the winter season.[14]

Because of these inefficiencies, there is room for manipulating the timing of auctions (e.g. late spring or summer instead of winter), the sequencing of lots within an auction, and the design of the auction itself (e.g. simultaneous v. sequential auctioning of multi-object auctions).

The theft of artworks

In Chapter 8, William Landes and Richard Posner take up the issue of property rights and disputes of ownership that arise when a stolen work is bought by a "good faith purchaser," i.e. a buyer who believes that the work is not stolen and takes "reasonable" information about former ownership. They construct a model in which they describe the behaviour of an original owner whose work is stolen, a good faith purchaser and the legal system and ask whom – the original owner or the buyer – the law should protect in order to maximise social welfare. There are basically two choices: the law can protect the original owner, by returning the stolen object to him (at some or at no cost) or it can favour the current good faith owner. Landes and Posner show that the optimal legal rule should almost always protect the original owner. They give examples of judgements in the U.S. that were indeed consistent with the prescriptions of their model. This is not so in many European countries, where the periods allowed for suits to recover stolen works are extremely short (3 years in France, 5 years in Belgium and Switzerland; a recent European directive suggests to extend this to 30 years). If a work is discoverd after this period, the good faith owner is entitled to keep the object or at least to get reimbursed for his purchase by the original owner if he has to return it to him.[15]

Landes and Posner's results are also consistent with the recent Unidroit proposal which suggests that illegally exported archeological finds or other stolen cultural objects should be returned to the country of origin. Notwith-

---

[14]It is interesting to point out that such anomalies are also noticed by professionals. See for example, a letter to the editor of the renowned wine review *Decanter* (May 1992, p. 7) "Fair bidding at auctions?" and the careful answer in the June 1992 issue by Michael Broadbent, Christie's wine specialist and auctioneer.

[15]See *Le Journal des Arts*, 26, June 1996, p. 12.

standing, several countries (Great Britain and Germany, in particular) have refused to sign the agreement, and a painting by Gino Severini, proved to have been stolen in Milano in 1992, will soon (at the time of the writing) be sold at auction in Germany. Such was not the case with a work by Dürer stolen in Germany from the castle of Schwarzburg, (probably) by an American soldier, just after the war. Though it took over fifteen years for American courts to decide, the painting was returned to Germany.

It will be interesting to see what happens to the artworks and the gold stolen by the Nazis that still sleep in the vaults of Swiss banks,[16] to works taken as "war booty" from Germany to the Soviet Union, and, why not, to the Elgin marbles, though they are probably better preserved in the British Museum than on the Acropolis hill.

The management of museums, special exhibitions and festivals

The number of museums has dramatically increased in the 1980s, and so has the number of visitors; the important cultural projects that are undertaken in many larger cities (Los Angeles, New York, Paris, Berlin, to cite only a few) include also the renovation and extension of existing museums. But the objectives of museums are also becoming more diversified, and as is stressed in the contributions by William Grampp (Chapter 9) and Peter Cannon-Brookes (Chapter 10), the question of "what should be maximised" is getting more crucial as organisations are becoming more complex. Increasing the number of visitors is certainly a legitimate objective, but involves new challenges: rooms may be congested; services aimed at specific audiences have to be developed, etc. The resulting choices have direct implications on entrance fee policies, on the amount and the diversity of funding (whether private or public), on acquisitions, on the presentation of permanent collections, on special exhibitions.

Museums are very "wealthy," given the value of the assets they hold; at the same time, they are poor, since their assets are frozen and that operating costs are growing. In many countries, museums are under permanent financial pressure: sources of financing are drying out, while costs are increasing

[16] Note that even in 1945, the Swiss government was not extremely keen to return stolen works for which the original owners had proofs of ownership. See Nicholas (1994, pp. 415-427).

and new acquisitions are almost out of reach.[17] Therefore, deaccessioning has become a major issue.[18]

Deaccessioning, together with establishing a hierarchy between the different functions of a museum (collecting, preserving, exhibiting and studying collections, but also promoting tourism, selling posters, postcards and books, providing visitors with coffee and lunches, etc.), finding financial means and satisfying their various types of customers, including trustees and funding public agencies, have induced wide (and wild) discussions concerned with the foundations of the activity of museums, as well as more academic research. The volume edited by Feldstein (1991) is a good example of this two-headed orientation. The contributions by Grampp and Cannon-Brookes included here, adopt the same two-headed approach.

In the form of a colloquy between a curator and an economist, Grampp, the economist, discusses how museums could be made efficient and why most of them are not. Cannon-Brookes, the curator, proceeds in the same way, but in complete opposition with Grampp. The role of museum manager is at the heart of the discussion. Grampp bases his analysis on public choice-theoretic arguments: the inefficiency of a museum reflects the utility function of its managers (agents), who take advantage of the weak degree of control exercised by trustees and public authorities (principals), and whose career and reputation is correlated with the size of the museum and its collections, much more than with efficient management. Cannon-Brookes argues that clarifying the legal status and the intellectual environment is an essential prerequisite to any cultural-economic analysis: these two factors condition the possibility for museums to change the definition of their functions. In that sense, common law countries offer better possibilities to adapt to changing conditions, but are, at the same time, subject to continuous erosion of the consensus about objectives, as is made clear by the controversy about deaccessioning and the emergence of the notion of "concept-based" museum.

Research on the performing arts as well as on museums has mainly concentrated on stable, permanent organisations; their number has increased, but the number of temporary ones has boomed.[19] Temporary organisations, such

---

[17]See Rosett (1991) and Feldstein (1991).

[18]Even Westminster Abbey sells off sculpture. See *The Art Newspaper*, 61, July-August 1996, p.1.

[19]Where are the times in which the Salzburg festival was created, shortly after World War I, to ensure jobs for unemployed Austrian artists during the summer season. See

as music or opera festivals and special exhibitions may provide a way to apparently escape from Baumol's disease (increasing wages and little possibility for efficiency gains) that is likely to plague museums, orchestras, operas, etc.: they provide much more flexibility both for organisers and artists. In Chapter 11, Bruno Frey and Isabelle Busenhart compare the incentives to creativity in both types of settings; the comparative advantage of temporary events in terms of artistic innovation and economic efficiency may paradoxically be eroded by their own success, in terms of number and regularity. Frey and Busenhart also study the complementarity relations between the two types of organisations. Special exhibitions, that are more linked to museums than music festivals to permanent orchestras and operas, are often viewed as one of the main promotional tools for a museum: they generate visitors and income, but they have also the adverse effects evoked by Cannon-Brookes.[20] Frey and Busenhart understress the positive dimension of this recent boom, but show that, by taking place in the premises of the organising museum, they may have ambiguous effects on its normal operations. In that, they differ from music festivals, which run much more like independent entities.

The performing arts

The last three papers (Chapters 12 to 14) deal with the permanent excess supply of labour in the performing arts. Artists are often cited as the example of risk-prone workers: expected income as well as psychic and social rewards are high in case of a successful career, but success is uncertain and the probability of lasting low wage income periods is significant. This apparently risk-prone behaviour of artists had already been pointed out by Adam Smith, Alfred Marshall and Milton Friedman.

Most survey-based studies show that, on average, artists fail to get enough monetary rewards to be compensated for the risk of discontinuous activity and recurring periods of unemployment. Nevertheless, the number of candidates for artistic careers is growing, and other explanations than the usual "compensating wage differential theory" are needed.[21]

Stefan Zweig, *Le Monde d'Hier*, Paris: Belfond, 1993, p.424.

[20] See also Blattberg and Broderick (1991).

[21] In addition to the surveys mentioned in the three contributions, see, among others, MacDonald (1988), Miller (1984) and Rosen (1981) for theoretical models of artists' labour supply decisions.

A key issue is concerned with the factors of success. Both Ruth Towse (Chapter 12) and David Throsby (Chapter 13) find that higher education plays only a limited, if any, role in determining income levels in the arts. Artistic skills may depend much more on on-the-job learning, as well as on talent and innate abilities, but talent as an independent labour supply decision and factor of success can hardly be measured. However, as Throsby argues, estimates of earnings functions are misleading if they are not based on the multiple job-holding decisions of artists. Human capital theory has some explanatory power if one takes into account the three types of labour markets (artistic, arts-related and non-artistic activities) in which many artists are simultaneously active: then, it can be shown that arts training and general education do exert a positive influence on earnings.

This, in turn, points to another direction which helps understanding why agents do take occupational risks. Unlike in most job situations, artists very often find in multiple-job holdings a way to insure themselves against uncertain career prospects. Among these portfolio-like bundles of activities and income sources, Pierre-Michel Menger and Marc Gurgand (Chapter 14) single out the possibility for French performing artists to "exploit" unemployment insurance benefits: those who meet some eligibility criteria, optimise their position by combining artistic fees and unemployment benefits. On the aggregate, and though demand for the performing arts expands, unemployment benefit payments are rising and play an increasing role in "subsidising" the performing arts industry, by reducing the cost to employers and keeping a large stock of workers with diversified skills on which art operators can draw.

Sharing the allocation of labour between a growing number of artists sheds light on a third dimension: the excess supply of artists. In Chapter 12, Ruth Towse argues that the oversupply of trained artists is probably the major cause of the disequilibrium and the fact that both the private and the social rates of return are low or negative raises questions about higher education policy in the arts. Throsby's findings partly clarify the paradox, since training positions turn out to be the main arts-related occupation that provides artists with additional income. For the policymaker, however, the challenging question is to make more efficient an educational system that has to deal with indeterminacy of talent, excess supply of labour and workers who may act as "rational fools" in order to learn whether they are well-suited for a career in the arts.

References

Anderson, R.C. (1974), Paintings as an investment, *Economic Inquiry*, 12, 13-25.

Ashenfelter, O. (1989), How auctions work for wine and art, *Journal of Economic Perspectives*, 3, 23-36.

Baumol, W.J. (1986), Unnatural value or art as a floating crap game, *American Economic Review*, 76, 10-14.

Baumol, W. and W. Bowen (1966), *Performing Arts: the Economic Dilemma*, New York: The Twentieth Century Fund.

Benhamou, F. (1996), *L'Economie de la Culture*, Paris: Editions La Découverte.

Blattberg, R.C. and C.J. Broderick (1991), Marketing of art museums, in M. Feldstein, ed., *The Economics of Art Museums*, Chicago: The Chicago University Press.

Blaug, M., ed., (1976), *The Economics of the Arts*, London: Martin Robertson.

Buck, L. and P. Dodd (1991), *Relative Values, or What is Art Worth*, London: BBC Books.

Burns, P. (1985), Experience and decision making: A comparison of students and businessmen in a simulated progressive auction, *Research in Experimental Economics*, 3, 139-157.

Chanel, O., L.-A. Gérard-Varet and V. Ginsburgh (1996), The relevance of hedonic price indices: the case of paintings, *Journal of Cultural Economics*, forthcoming.

Feldstein, M., ed., (1991), *The Economics of Art Museums*, Chicago: The Chicago University Press.

Frey, B.S. and W.W. Pommerehne (1989), *Muses and Markets*, London: Basil Blackwell.

Goetzmann, W.N. (1990), Accounting for taste: an analysis of art returns over three centuries, First Boston Working Paper Series FB-90-11, November.

Grampp, W.D. (1989), *Pricing the Priceless, Art, Artists and Economics*, New-York: Basic Books Inc.

Guerzoni, G. (1995), Reflections on historical series of art prices, *Journal of Cultural Economics*, 19, 251-260.

Heenk, L. (1995), Vincent Van Gogh's drawings. An analysis of their production and uses, Ph.D. Dissertation, University of London (Courtauld Institute).

Heilbrun, J. and C.M. Gray (1993), *The Economics of Art and Culture. An American Perspective*, Cambridge: Cambridge University Press.

Kendall, R. (1996), *Degas beyond Impressionism*, London: National Gallery Pulications.

MacDonald, G. (1988), The economics of rising stars, *American Economic Review*, 78, 155-166.

Meyer, L.B. (1989), Forgery and the anthropology of art, in D. Dutton, ed., *The Forger's Art*, Berkeley and Los Angeles: University of California Press.

Miller, R. (1984), Job matching and occupational choice, *Journal of Political Economy*, 92, 1086-1112.

Montias, J.M. (1996), *Le Marché de l'Art aux Pays-Bas; 15ème-17ème Siècles*, Paris: Flammarion.

Nicholas, L.H. (1994), *The Rape of Europa*, London: Papermac.

Peacock, A.T. (1969), Welfare economics and public subsidies to the arts, *Manchester School of Economics and Social Studies*, 37, 323-35.

Peacock, A.T. (1992), *Paying the Piper: Culture, Music and Money*, Edinburgh: Edinburgh University Press.

Penders, A.-F. (1996), An analysis of auction sales of earthworks over the past twenty years, Paper presented at the 9th International Conference on Cultural Economics, Boston, May.

Reitlinger, G. (1960), *The Economics of Taste: The Rise and Fall of the Picture Prices 1760-1960*, London: Barrie and Rockliff.

Reitlinger, G. (1970), *The Economics of Taste: The Art Market in the 60s*, London: Barrie and Jenkins Ltd.

Rosen, S. (1981), The economics of superstars, *American Economic Review*, 71, 845-858.

Rosett, R.N. (1991), Art museums in the United States: a financial portrait, in M. Feldstein, ed., *The Economics of Art Museums*, Chicago: The Chicago University Press.

Shell, M. (1995), *Art and Money*, Chicago: The Chicago University Press.

Schwartz, G. (1994), Figures and figuration: quantitative research on Dutch painting of the 17th century, Paper presented at the Congress on Cultural Economics, Witten, August.

Shiller, R.T. (1991), Arithmetic repeat sales price estimators, *Journal of Housing Economics* 1, 110-126.

Smith, C.W. (1989), *Auctions. The Social Construction of Value*, New York: The Free Press.

Stein, J.P. (1977), The monetary appreciation of paintings, *Journal of Political Economy*, 85, 1021-1035.

Throsby, D. (1994), The production and consumption of the arts: a view of cultural economics, *Journal of Economic Literature*, 32, 1-29.

Acknowledgements

We are very much indebted to Joop Dirkmaat from North-Holland-Elsevier who was very positive towards the idea of publishing a volume on the economics of the arts.

Each paper underwent a reviewing process by (usually) two anonymous referees who were, in most cases, other contributors to the volume. We also wish to thank five referees who are not among the authors, but we can hardly disclose their names without breaking the rule of anonymity.

Marlene Glinschi and Sheila Weyers made a great job in producing a hopefully homogeneous volume from a mosaic of non-normalised typed versions on all sorts of diskettes, produced by all sorts of computers.

The first editor acknowledges financial support from Services Fédéraux des Affaires Scientifiques, Techniques et Culturelles (under contract PAI 26) and from Université Libre de Bruxelles.

Economics of the Arts - Selected Essays
V.A. Ginsburgh and P.-M. Menger (Editors)

1

Quantitative Methods in the Analysis of 17th Century Dutch Inventories*

John Michael Montias
Yale University

1 Introduction

In this paper I first report some summary statistics (average numbers, values) concerning the works of art recorded in a stratified random sample of probate inventories drawn up in Amsterdam between 1600 and 1669 (Section 2). I then develop some elementary models to extract more information from these inventories. In Section 3, I use the dates at which inventories were taken, the marriage dates of collectors and the death dates of artists to whom paintings were attributed in their collections to make inferences about longitudinal patterns of collecting (whether paintings were acquired, on average, early or late in the life of collectors). In Section 4, I make comparisons of prices of paintings across time (also based on my random sample of inventories) to estimate changes in artists' productivity. In Section 5, I attempt to estimate the percentage of originals and copies in a subsample of inventories for which price data are available by comparing the distribution of these prices with distributions of prices of originals and inventories from contemporary auction records. All the model-based results in Sections 3 to 5 are grounded on strong assumptions (regarding the normality of distributions, the constancy of production costs etc..) which are very imperfectly realized in the data at my disposal. Some of my samples are also too small to bear the weight of the inferences I place on them. The results should therefore be considered tentative or illustrative rather than definitive or probative.

* I am very grateful to Neil De Marchi, Victor Ginsburgh and an anonymous referee for their substantive comments on an earlier draft of this article and for their detailed suggestions.

2 A stratified random sample of Amsterdam inventories

If we intend to study the inventories that have been preserved in Dutch archives as a reliable source of evidence regarding the goods that 17th century citizens possessed, we must be aware of three possible biases in the samples of inventories that can be extracted from the archives that limit the value of this evidence:

(1) Only a fraction of households had their goods "inventorized" in the 17th century; since better-off households were much more likely to undergo this process than poor households were, any sample of surviving inventories is apt to be biased.

(2) Of the inventories originally drawn up, only a certain proportion has been preserved to the present day; due to selective losses through time, surviving inventories may be a biased sample of the original set.

(3) A sample of inventories, unless it is drawn in such a way as to eliminate any systematic bias, will probably not be representative of all the inventories preserved in a particular archive.

Of the three biases, only the third can be rectified, at least in part, by choosing inventories at random, as I have attempted to do for Amsterdam inventories dated between 1600 and 1669. The second bias due to selective loss through time cannot be ascertained or corrected for; however, it may not be very significant, inasmuch as sources of destruction such as water or fire damage are likely to wipe out inventories in a more or less random fashion. There remains the first source of bias, the underrepresentation of poorer households, which presents a very serious problem. But the damage due to this bias can be limited if its causes are properly understood and if the uses to which the sample is put take it into account.

The sample of Amsterdam inventories that I will be reporting on is based on a random selection of the microfilms of notarial records dated 1600 to 1669 in the Amsterdam Municipal Archive. A quasi-random subsample, based on a running sequence, which picked up 40 percent of all the inventories in any microfilm selected at random, was retained. I ceased sampling in any decade when I had collected 120 inventories (except in the first decade of the 17th century for which fewer inventories were available; for this decade I only retained 60 inventories).

To get some idea of the extent to which the Amsterdam sample may have under-represented the inventories of poorer households, I compared some of the results in one decade (the 1640s) with a large sample of Delft inventories for that same decade, which I had reason to believe was less biased in this regard. This Delft sample, without being strictly drawn at random, is so comprehensive – I believe I was able to identify some 90 percent of the recorded notarial inventories of the 1640s in that city's archives – that it may serve as a tolerable basis of comparison. Delft's population, to be sure, was only about one sixth of Amsterdam around the mid-century point. It was far less bustling a center of business than the great metropolis, which presumably had more very rich citizens in proportion to its population. But the daily wages of the craftsmen living in the two cities were not very different – roughly one florin (henceforth abbreviated f.) or Dutch gulden per day for ordinary carpenters and masons. The higher cost of living in Amsterdam, particularly marked in the case of housing,[1] probably offset any difference in nominal wages. We would expect therefore that common laboring folk would have had roughly the same opportunities for accumulating movable property – furniture, apparel, clothing – over their life time in the two cities. If there were proportionately more people with a low value of assets in one city than in the other, we would seek the reason primarily in the broader coverage of the inventories recorded and preserved, rather than in the greater poverty of that city's population.

Let us consider first the direct evidence that we can assemble regarding craftsmen's inventories in the two cities. In the Delft sample for the 1640s, 26 percent of the owners of preserved inventories were identified as craftsmen or wives or widows of craftsmen (109 inventories in a total sample of 419 inventories). In the random sample of Amsterdam inventories for the same decade, 13 percent were so identified (16 inventories in a total sample of 120). Unless Delft notaries had a significantly greater propensity to associate the owners of inventories with their craft occupation[2] – which seems improbable, at least to the extent of the difference in the two proportions – we can only

[1]Because the housing market in Amsterdam was very tight, there had been a roughly 80 percent increase in rents from the 1600s to the 1660s, which was out of proportion with the modest increases in other items of consumption. On rents in Amsterdam in this period, see Lesger (1986).

[2]Internal evidence suggests that the craft occupation of owners was omitted in many inventories in both cities, particularly in later decades of the 17th century.

Table 1
Cumulative Distribution of the Value of Movable Goods in Amsterdam and Delft Samples (1640s)

Percentage of total number of owners with movable goods valued at less than:	Amsterdam (1640-1649)	Delft (1640-1649)
100 f. (gulden)	0	20.3
200 f.	3.7	35.7
300 f.	7.4	43.9
500 f.	24.1	64.2
1000 f.	61.1	80.5
5000 f.	100.0	97.6

Sources: Gemeentearchief Delft and Gemeentearchief Amsterdam, Notarial archives.

conclude that relatively more craftsmen were covered in the Delft than in the Amsterdam sample.

A more general type of evidence for the difference in coverage may be obtained from the percentages of inventory owners with a low total value of movable goods possessed in the two samples. This comparison is made in Table 1.

The proportion of "poor" inventories is clearly much greater in Delft than in Amsterdam: nearly half the inventories in the Delft sample contained movable assets valued at less than 300 f., whereas only 7.4 percent of the Amsterdam inventories were in this wealth category. But this does not imply that the proportion of "rich" inventories was greater in Amsterdam than in Delft. In Delft, there were 50 percent more inventories in which the total value of movable goods was assessed at more than 1000 f. than there were inventories in the 500-800 f. range.[3] In Amsterdam there were 43 percent

[3]Movable goods comprise, in addition to works of art of all sorts, furniture, clothing, silver, and jewelry.

more inventories in the first category than in the second, a difference from the Delft proportion that is unlikely to be significant statistically. It is apparent, therefore, that there is a deficit of "poor" inventories in the recorded sample for Amsterdam, whereas the coverage of inventories above the 500 f. range is about the same in the two cities.[4] Correcting the results drawn from the Amsterdam sample for the deficit in "poor" inventories on the basis of the Delft value distribution is a useful first-step adjustment, but it falls short to the (unknown) extent to which the Delft sample itself may have underreported such inventories.

The failure of the Amsterdam sample to capture anything like the proportion of poorer inventories that must have existed at the time does not invalidate all the calculations that can be made on the basis of the sample. The seriousness of the damage depends on the questions we wish to ask. If our interest lies in the average number of paintings per inventory – from which we could infer the total number of paintings in Amsterdam collections at any point of time – then the under-coverage makes a good deal of difference. The average number of paintings per inventory in a total of 34 assessed Amsterdam inventories of the 1640s was just over 10 (about one in five inventories were assessed). Maintaining the number of paintings found in each wealth interval but weighting the relative importance of the different intervals by the Delft distribution for the same decade lowers the overall average for Amsterdam to 5 paintings per inventory.

The statistics assembled in Table 2 help us to trace the source of fluctuations in the decade-to-decade averages in the number of paintings per inventory within the subsample of assessed paintings in the Amsterdam random sample.

The first column of Table 2 shows the average number of paintings in assessed inventories calculated over all intervals of "wealth" or, more precisely, of the total value of movable goods recorded; the second the number of paintings in the interval 50 to 500 f. (there were no inventories assessed at less than 50 f.); the third, the percentage of all assessed inventories in the decade represented by inventories in the 50-500 f. range; the fourth the number of paintings in inventories assessed at 1000 f. and over; the fifth the percentage

[4] I suspect that the difference in coverage of "poor" inventories is due mainly to the fact that the Orphan Chamber regulations which prescribed the inventorization of the assets of deceased parents of minor children were more comprehensive and/or more strictly enforced in Delft than in Amsterdam.

Table 2
Number of Paintings in Different Wealth Intervals in Assessed Inventories (Amsterdam, 1600-1669)

	Av. all wealth intervals	50-500 f.	Percent all inv's	1000 f and over	Percent all inv's
1600-1619	11.9	5.3	34.6	18.8	28.2
1620-1629	5.5	3.0	73.9	15.0	17.4
1630-1639	10.3	4.6	44.0	16.0	20.0
1640-1649	9.9	6.2	29.1	15.5	35.2
1650-1659	16.7	8.6	17.2	21.1	51.7
1660-1669	11.5	6.6	38.9	18.1	27.8

of all assessed inventories in the decade represented by inventories valued at over 1000.[5]

The average number of paintings per assessed inventory falls within a narrow range of 10 to 12 in all decades but 1620-1629 when it was unusually low (5.5) and 1650-1659 when it was unusually high (16.7). The low overall average for the 1620s can be explained by the fact that nearly three out of four inventories in that decade were valued at less than 500 f; the high average for the 1650s from the fact that more than half the inventories were valued at over 1000 f. It is also true that there were relatively few paintings (3.0) in the 50-500 f. interval in the first of these two decades and relatively many in inventories valued at over 1000 f. in the second (21.1), but an analysis of the distribution within these intervals shows that this too owed much to changes in distribution.

While the samples of assessed inventories are too small to rule out significant random fluctuations from decade to decade in the distribution of inventories by wealth intervals, they are probably adequate to support the

[5]The number of assessed inventories in each decade was the following: 1611-1619: 19; 1620-1629: 23; 1630-1639: 25; 1640-1649: 34; 1650-1659: 29; 1660-1669: 22.

Table 3
Number of Paintings per Inventory in a Random Sample of Amsterdam Inventories (1600's to 1660's)

	All invent's			Poor invent's	Rich invent's
	arith. av.	st. error	med.	arith. av	arith. av.
1600's	5.0	1.4	2	1	32
1610's	6.9	0.9	4	2	48
1620's	5.8	0.6	4	0	52
1630's	10.6	1.3	5	10	40
1640's	8.8	1.0	5	5	41
1650's	11.7	1.0	9	6	18
1660's	12.1	1.4	7	7	26

conclusion that decade-to-decade changes in the overall average of the number of paintings per inventory are likely to have resulted from changes in the wealth distribution rather than from changes in the number of paintings in each wealth interval. The statistics in Table 3, based on the entire sample of 120 per decade (except the first when only 60 were collected), give us a better idea of the trends in the averages.

In Table 3, "arith.av." is the arithmetical average of the number of paintings for all inventories in each decade, "st. error" is the standard error of this arithmetical average, "med" (median) the number of paintings in all inventories for each decade that is exceeded by half the inventories. "Poor invent's" relates to the number of inventories containing no more than two paintings in a decade. "Rich invent's" is the number of inventories containing 35 paintings or more in a decade.

These larger samples leave little doubt that the average number of paintings rose over time. This is confirmed by the much greater number of inventories containing over 35 paintings in later decades and the relatively small number of inventories containing two paintings or less in the last two decades. It is likely that these trends were due to the increasing wealth of owners or, to be precise, to the relatively greater number of sampled owners in the larger wealth intervals. But was this due to a real trend in the universe of existing inventories or to a sampling phenomenon ? For lack of corroborating evidence, I cannot exclude the possibility that notaries, over time, recorded a declining fraction of poor inventories and an increasing fraction of wealthier inventories. I will exclude this disturbing possibility *ex hypothesi*, while keeping it open for further research. Another source of error in calculating trends in the average number of paintings per inventory stems from the under-representation of inventories in lower wealth intervals. The data in Table 3 give some support to the hypothesis that the decade-to-decade shift toward higher wealth intervals was roughly of the same extent in the low (i.e. partly omitted) intervals as in the higher ones.

These tentative results underpin my calculations of the rate of increase in the total number of paintings in Amsterdam collections (3.8 percent per year), which I obtained by adding the rate of increase in the estimated number of Amsterdam households from 1600 to 1650 (2.1 percent per year) to the rate of increase in the average number of paintings per inventory in Table 3 (1.7 percent per year).

Another result that may be affected by the under-representation of poorer inventories in the Amsterdam sample is the "wealth elasticity" – the cross-section relation between percentage increases in the value of movable goods possessed by different owners and the value of the works of art that these inventories contained. My regression results for Amsterdam in the period 1600-1669 suggest an elasticity of 1.42, which is significantly larger than unity.[6]

---

[6]It should be noted that the average number of paintings per inventory is not perfectly correlated with the average value of the works of art per inventory. High numbers of paintings may be offset by low prices. Low numbers of paintings may be compensated by a higher value of prints and other works of art. It is possible that a slightly higher number of paintings in each wealth category in latter decades may have been nullified by decreasing prices (see below Section 4).

3 Life patterns of collecting

Inventories measure attributes (number of paintings in individual collections, the value of art works collected and of the total movable assets of collectors etc.) at a particular point of time; they say nothing about the behavior of economic agents *through* time. These variables represent stocks (snapshots taken at a point of time) rather than flows (variables measured over an increment of time). Consider, for example, the study of the relation between the total value of movable goods and the value of works of art possessed that I referred to earlier. This is useful information but it only provides an approximative answer to the question we would really like to answer, namely how individuals responded over time to changes in their incomes by increasing their purchases of works of art. This response is measured by the income elasticity, a relation between flows for which the wealth elasticity, a relation between stocks, that I was able to calculate is only a proxy (i.e., in this case, a rough approximation). This problem dogs us at every step in our analysis of inventories. The attributions and the subjects that we observe at the time an inventory was dated may reflect purchasing decisions that were made many years in the past. We usually have no information over the way a collection has been built up over time. Were the works of art owned by a collector inherited from his parents ? Were they bought twenty or thirty years previously at the time he married ? Did they accrue over his life time as his income rose ?

The only longitudinal information of this type that I know of is the history of the collection of Carel Martens (Knoester and Graafhuis (1970)), who jotted down his purchases of works of art at the time he made them. Martens's experience, which may or may not be typical of other collectors, illustrates the problem.

Martens lived from 1602 to 1649. In 1628, when he was 26 years old, shortly after his marriage, he ordered three portraits of members of his family. The next year he bought a copy after Honthorst for 6 f. In the 1630s, he acquired a number of prints, including six by Rembrandt, a painting of Bachus and Venus for 22 f., a vanitas for 17 f. and a few other inexpensive paintings. He begins to collect in earnest only in the 1640s: in 1642, he acquires two flower paintings by Ambrosius Bosschaert the Younger (60 f. plus 7 1/2 f. for the frame); in 1645, a Rembrandt portrait (54 f.); in 1646, two paintings by (Joost Cornelisz. ?) Droogsloot (32 1/2 f.), a landscape by

(Gillis or Gysbrecht) d'Hondecoeter (38 f.), a genre piece by David Teniers (170 f.), and a "kitchen" by Pieter Aertsen (36 f.). It emerges clearly from these diary entries that Carel Martens bought the most important paintings in his collection in the last few years of his life. Unfortunately, we do not have Martens's death inventory, which would have allowed us to learn whether he sold or otherwise discarded any of the works he had purchased in the course of approximately twenty years that elapsed between his marriage and his death.

The idea of the following model is to make use of extraneous information (on the date of marriage of collectors and the year of death of the artists represented in their collections), in connection with the date at which an inventory was recorded, to make inferences about the life pattern of collectors (i.e. whether they collected paintings early or many years after they first established a household, which I assume to coincide with the date of their first marriage). Only the year of death (or cessation of activity) of artists whose works are likely to have been bought when they were still alive are considered in this calculation. In Figure 1, which represents movement along a time axis, B stands for the year of birth of the collector, M for the date of his first marriage, P for the average year of purchase of the works of art in his collection, D for the year in which the inventory was taken (generally the year of death of the collector), and T for the average year of death of artists to whom works of art were attributed in a collection (T may of course lie to the left of P and D and even in some cases of M). The year of marriage M is generally known for the collectors in the sample, but if it is not, it can often be estimated from B, the year of birth (which is even more frequently available); D, the date at which the inventory was taken, is of course known; T, the year of death of an artist represented in a collection or of the cessation of his activity represented in a collection, is generallly ascertainable (or can be estimated with a small error). T can be averaged for all the artists represented in the collection. Only the variable P is unknown.

Figure 1
Life Patterns of Collecting

$$B \longrightarrow M \longrightarrow P \longrightarrow D \longrightarrow T$$

The procedure involves using known data about M, D, and T to make inferences about a critical ratio, denoted β, equal to $(P-M)/(D-M)$. The ratio β represents the ratio of the (average) number of years elapsed between purchase of works of art and marriage to the number of years elapsed between the date of inventory and marriage. If β is small, most works of art were acquired shortly after marriage, i.e. early in the collector's carreer, if it is close to unity, late in the collector's carreer. The estimation procedure relies on the assumption that the difference $(T - P)$ is invariant to the date of purchase and is therefore a constant. The rationale for this assumption is the likelihood that the life expectancies of artists remained more or less the same throughout the 17th century.

The reasoning is as follows. By adding and subtracting P and M from $(T - D)$, we may write:

$$(T - D) \equiv (T - P) - (D - M) + (P - M)$$

which can also be written:

$$(T - D) \equiv (T - P) - [1 - (P - M)/(D - M)](D - M)$$

or

$$(T - D) \equiv (T - P) - (1 - \beta)(D - M)$$

In a linear regression of $(T - D)$ on $(D - M)$, we may treat $(T - P)$, which we have assumed to be constant, as the intercept and $-(1 - \beta)$ as the slope. The data in Table 4 below, when they are graphed, are generally consistent with a linear relationship between $(T - D)$ and $(D - M)$.

Let us now consider the available information. Municipal archives in the Netherlands normally have baptismal, marriage and burial information on file about most of the town's residents that can at least help set the perimeters within which a collector's accumulations took place. (This is much more easily done for collectors whose last name is known than for the thousands of individuals designated simply as "Aeltje Jansdr." or "Jonas Jacobsz." whose last name isn't.) In the case of Amsterdam, many of the wealthy collectors who owned works of art that were attributed in their inventory are cited, along with the available biographical information, in Elias (1963). In my computerized sample of Amsterdam inventories, which consists mainly of inventories containing at least one attribution, I have information on the year of first marriage of 163 collectors. I assume, as a first approximation, that collectors began acquiring the works of art in the collections that they owned at the time when the inventory of their possessions was taken at this initial date. This implies the (rather doubtful) assumption that they did not inherit any of the works of art in their collection. The average time that elapsed between a collector's first marriage and the date when his or her inventory was taken was 21.4 years.[7] I augmented this sample by including a few inventories whose owners' date of marriage was unknown (or who never married) but whose date of baptism could be ascertained. On the basis of a sample of 48 collectors whose date of first marriage averaged 27.3 years after their baptism, I added 27 years to the year of baptism of collectors for whom I did not have a date of marriage to arrive at the approximate year of inception of their collections. I then extracted all the attributed paintings and drawings in the collections of the owners for whom I had an estimate of the total number of years during which they acquired their collections and took an average of the year of death (or the term of activity) of the artists represented in these collections. However, I excluded any painting or drawing by an artist who died more than two years before the presumed onset of his or her collecting activities (on the presumption that the collector had not bought the painting from a living artist).[8]

Before presenting the results of the regression of $(T - D)$ on $(D - M)$, I tabulate, in Table 4, the average values of the second difference on various values of the first, based on 88 inventories.

The differences $(D - M)$ and $(T - D)$ in Table 4 have already been defined above. As we would expect, $(D - M)$ is negatively correlated with $(T - D)$: the greater the number of years elapsed between the date of a collector's marriage and the date when his or her inventory was taken, the less contemporaneous the collection (the greater the algebraic difference between the average terminal year of the artists to whom works of art were attributed and the date of the inventory).

---

[7]Of the 163 inventories, 3 were drawn up in anticipation of marriage where the bride and bridegroom wished to keep their assets separate; 13 were dated within four years of first marriage; 16 between 5 and 9 years after first marriage; 21 between 10 and 14 years; 20 between 15 and 19 years; 23 between 20 and 24 years; 22 between 25 and 29 years; 16 between 30 and 34 years; 8 between 35 and 39 years; 7 between 40 and 44 years; 9 between 45 and 49 years; 3 between 50 and 54 years; and two 55 years after first marriage.

[8]From other data, analyzed in Montias (1996), I inferred that the bulk of paintings in collections were acquired from living artists.

Table 4
Years of Collecting and the Contemporaneity of Collections (Amsterdam, 1600-1679)

$(D-M)$	45-54	35-44	25-34	15-24	5-14	0-4
$(T-D)$	-12.7	-11.1	-5.8	+0.9	+4.1	+9.7

The ordinary least-squares regression of $(T-D)$ on $(D-M)$ yields:

$$(T-D) = 7.72 - 0.37(D-M)$$

The standard error of $(1-\beta)$ equals -0.109. The confidence interval around this coefficient, at the 99 percent level, is -0.261 to -0.479. The expected value of $(T-D)$ when $(D-M)$ is zero – that is, when the inventory is taken immediately after marriage or the onset of the collecting period – is 7.72 years.[9] This is our most likely value of the constant difference $(T-P)$.

Recall now that the coefficient of $(D-M)$ should be equal to $-(1-\beta)$, where β is the ratio of $(P-M)$ to $(D-M)$. Since $(1-\beta)$ turned out to be equal to $-.37$, our most likely value of β is 0.63. This fraction is a measure of the rate of accretion of the works of art in collections through time. It implies that the average number of years that elapsed between a collector's marriage and the average date of purchase of the works of art in his or her collection, based on our sample of 88 collections, was equal to nearly two thirds of the entire collecting period from marriage to the date of inventory. If we take into account the confidence intervals calculated for the above regression, this ratio could range from one half to three fourths. Our results strongly suggest that collectors bought more works of art in the second half of their period of collecting than in the first half. This conclusion is consistent with the history of the collection of Carel Martens, which provides the only available longitudinal information of which I am aware.

[9]In Table 4, the average value of $(T-D)$ for $(D-M)$ equal to 0-4 years is 9.7 years. This higher-than-expected value is due to sampling fluctuation and to the fact that the equation on which the regression is based is not a perfect representation of the data.

When we confront a new collection (one not included in the sample) with the Amsterdam averages, we can make a guess about whether the rate at which the works of art that entered it were "front-" or "back-loaded," that is, whether the rate of accumulation was greater in the early or the late years of the collecting period, as the following examples illustrate.

The two collections, dated in the same decade, are from Delft. I assume, for the purposes of illustration, that the regression obtained from the Amsterdam sample can be applied to Delft collections. The first collection belonged to Boudewijn de Man who died bankrupt in 1644, when he was in his late 60's or early 70's. The rich collection he had formed over the years was auctioned off shortly after his death. From the fact that his daughter was born circa 1602 (Salomonson (1988)), I deduce that at least 43 years must have elapsed between his marriage and the date of his inventory. There were 38 works of art attributed to artists whose terminal year of activity could be ascertained. The average of these terminal years was 1640.6 (25 artists, 38 observations). The inventory date subtracted from this average yields a difference of −3.4. We should have expected a larger negative difference for such a long period of collecting (−8.2 on the basis of the Amsterdam regression). Conclusion: Boudewijn de Man must have bought most of the works of art in his collection even more recently before his death than our sample of Amsterdam collections would have predicted.[10] The second collection, dated 1647, belonged to Johan van Hogenhouck who drowned in a Delft canal when he was about 40 years old. He had been married close to 15 years. There were 27 works of art (paintings, drawings or sheafs of drawings) in his collection attributed to 23 artists, for all of whom a terminal year of activity was known or estimated. The average of these terminal years was 1654.5 or 7.5 years more than the inventory date. This is a bit higher than we would expect (2.17 years). It is likely, therefore, that he also collected more intensively in the last few years preceding his death than did the collectors, on average, in the Amsterdam sample.

Needless to say, the inferences that I have made throughout this section

[10]The only information we have about Boudewijn de Man's actual purchases was that he owed 42 f. to the flower painter Jacob Vosmaer (for painting 21 tulips), according to Vosmaer's death inventory of 10 April 1642 (DGA, Weeskamerarchief no. 1847). A note next to this entry indicated that it was doubtful the debt could be recovered. It is likely, in any case, that it had been incurred not long before Vosmaer's death (in 1641) and thus late in the life of De Man.

are affected by chance. Among other things, the results are quite sensitive to variations in the life expectancy of individual artists. The purchase in 1605 of a painting by Abraham Bloemaert, who died very old in 1651, will raise the average $(T-D)$ of a collection, whereas the purchase of one by Karel van Mander, who died in 1606, will reduce it. The argument, though, is that this source of random variations is unbiased and should not affect significantly the averages on which we base our inferences. However, another source of random variation may be less benign. I have in mind the possible selectivity bias on the part of the inventory-makers who attributed a varying proportion of the works of art they contained. Sworn assessors, notaries and clerks, if not the guild experts, may have been more apt to recognize paintings and drawings by older masters whose reputation was already established than by younger masters who were only beginning to build up their career. On the other hand, as fashions in demand turned away from the older painters, they may have been apt to leave more of their paintings unattributed. It is not clear whether the net effect of these two selectivity biases would make collections as a whole appear older or younger than they really were. It is even less clear whether it would have any impact on the true relation between $(T-D)$ and $(D-M)$ (that is, on what that relation would have been if all the works of art in collections had been attributed).

4 Prices of paintings and the productivity of artists

We have seen that the contents of about one inventory in five or six of the random sample of Amsterdam inventories was evaluated. The estimates were generally made by women, called "sworn assessors." In the case of more valuable collections, however, members of the guild of St. Luke were called in to evaluate the works of art they contained. The common assessors were of limited competence to evaluate works of art, and they no doubt made mistakes, but I have found no evidence that they were systematically biased, upwards or downwards, in their evaluations, as compared to the market value of the works they assessed. In the following analysis of price trends, in any case, I will assume that the errors they made were distributed randomly around the true market values of the objects. I will call their evaluations "prices" as a sort of short hand, although I am aware of the inaccuracy of this designation.

For the purpose of the following analysis, I shall assume that paintings, at any point of time, were produced at constant average cost and that there were no special "unearned" profits or rents that sundered price from cost, either before or after an increase in productivity took place.[11] A condition that is nessary (but not sufficient[12]) for this assumption to be satisfied is that the market for paintings should be competitive, as I believe the Dutch market was, at least to a reasonable extent.[13]

[11] Artists' labor costs are of course geared to the opportunity wages or profits they could obtain if they devoted their labor to some other activity.

[12] As Neil De Marchi pointed out to me in correspondence the assumption that a given relative increase in average per-artist productivity translates into an equivalent decrease in the per-unit costs and prices of paintings produced, is strong and may well be unrealistic. Consider first a representative artist producing x paintings in a ten-hour day at a constant cost per painting. This is also assumed to be his capacity, defined as the number of paintings he can produce at constant per-unit cost v. (Beyond x, his unit costs rise). Let his productivity double. If his only costs consist of labor, his per-unit costs are cut in half, to $v/2$. His capacity doubles to $2x$. If all the artists in the industry are identical and exhibit the same increases in productivity, the capacity of the industry increases to $2x$ times the number of artists. Whether the price of a painting falls by half or less will depend on the elasticity of demand for the market as a whole. If the demand schedule is linear and demand is unit-elastic at the original equilibrium point (where the demand intersects with the supply schedule before the increase in productivity), the new equilibrium will occur at or near the point where the supply schedule is still infinitely elastic. If demand is more elastic, the demand schedule will intersect with the supply schedule at a point where the latter is rising, and the equilibrium price will be higher than $v/2$. Some artists will be induced to produce more than $2x$ to meet demand. In the period of 55 years covered by this study, there will also be shifts in supply (as more artists enter the industry) and in demand (as incomes rise and the demand for paintings shifts outward.) If demand increases faster than supply, as I believe was the case (the data supporting this hypothesis are marshalled in Montias (1996)), prices should decrease relatively less than productivity increased, even if demand were unit-elastic or even slightly less. This possibility leads me to conclude that my estimates of labor productivity increases based on observed changes in prices are likely to be downward biased (assuming these changes are themselves accurately measured.)

[13] An anonymous reviewer of the present paper raised doubts about whether I could assume the Dutch market to be "reasonably competitive." This inference is based on the commonly acknowledged fact that most works of art were produced for the market rather than for patrons. The Amsterdam market, from which my price data are drawn, was particularly free of guild-imposed restrictions on imports of works of art (nearly half the paintings in Amsterdam inventories were attributed to out-of-town artists.) It is

In my calculations of long-term changes in productivity, I infer from the above reasoning that the gains from technical innovations that raised artists' productivity were not retained by the artists who introduced them but simply had the effect of reducing the prices of their paintings. The only "rents" artists earned were those that resulted from the favor they enjoyed in the public's esteem (which were reflected in the opportunity costs of their labor).

I begin my analysis with a comparison of the prices of landscapes in the period 1600-1619 and in the period 1650-1659. In a modest sample of landscapes (size of sample $N = 64$) in randomly selected inventories dated between 1600 and 1619, the average valuation assigned to a painting of such a subject was 11.65 f. In a sample of inventories dated 1650 to 1659, the evaluation of a comparable painting was 6.1 f. ($N = 60$). This decline in current prices must have been matched by a comparable decline in real terms of at least the same magnitude if we consider that the cost of living rose (albeit slightly) during this period. To what should we attribute this precipitous drop (assuming that the samples at the two dates are sufficiently reliable for a meaningful comparison) ? The costs of items other than labor (canvas or panel, colors, frame) probably did not exceed 25 percent of price (Montias (1996)). There is no reason to believe that there was a marked reduction in these non-labor costs. The conclusion is inescapable that the drop in prices – if they were accurately measured – resulted from a diminution of labor costs. It must have cost less labor to produce a landscape in the second period than in the first. Equivalently, the average time needed to

---

remarkable that the innovations of landscape and still-life painters, such as Esaias van de Velde, Jan van Goyen and Pieter Claesz. who were active in Leyden and Haarlem, were soon imitated by artists in all the major centers of Holland. The originators of these innovations did command a (modest) premium in price in the market, but this was primarily due to their superior reputation rather than to any rents they could derive from their power in the market. The question of "quality" raised by this same reviewer is a delicate one. I argue in Montias (1987) that the productivity gains achieved by the new tonal school, particularly in landscape and still-life painting, were achieved without perceptible decline in quality, in the sense that rich and sophisticated collectors continued to buy these fairly inexpensive paintings, which they frequently exhibited in their homes along with the more finely painted products of the preceding generation (and sometimes even along with the paintings of the "fijnschilders" – the painters practicing a minute technique – of the generation of 1640-1680.) However, to the extent that any quality deterioration may have been perceived by collectors, the increases in productivity that I have calculated are overstated.

produce a landscape had fallen. This observation would seem to lend support to my speculations regarding an increase in artist's productivity, based on visual evidence, which I associated with the "process innovations" (tonal painting, drawing with the brush, more evocative than strictly descriptive approach) introduced in landscape and still-life painting in the first quarter of the 17th century (Montias (1987)).

A simple algebraic model makes clear the relation between changes in prices and changes in productivity between the first period and the second. I denote by W_1 and W_2 the average daily earnings of a landscape painter in the two periods.[14] It is obvious that if an artist earned W per week and produced y paintings in the same period, the cost of the labor he invested per painting was equal to W/y. Suppose that he produced y paintings per week in the first period but that, as a result of a gain in productivity, he raised his production to γy paintings in the second period (where γ is a number larger than 1). Labor costs per painting were W_1/y in the first period and $W_2/\gamma y$ in the second. Let the ratio of the labor costs per painting in the second period to the labor costs per painting in the first be denoted r. Then we can write: $r = W_2/\gamma y \div W_1/y$, from which we deduce that $\gamma = W_2/rW_1$. The ratio W_2/W_1 can be approximated by assuming that the earnings of master painters from the first to the second period increased in the same proportion as those of master carpenters and masons, or 27.5 percent, according to Jan de Vries (1982, p.73), over the 45 years from the midpoint of 1600-1619 to the midpoint of 1650-1659. Thus W_2/W_1 equals 1.275. The ratio r is easily derived from the price comparison to which I alluded earlier. I estimate non-labor costs per painting as 25 percent of 11.65 f. or 2.9 f. On the assumption that changes in productivity were minimal in the production of these inputs between the two dates (or were offset by the rise in labor costs), I take non-labor costs to be the same in the period 1650-1659 as in the period 1600-1619 or 2.9 f. Subtracting 2.9 f. from 11.65 f. in the first period and from 6.1 f. in the second yields estimates of labor costs per painting equal to 8.75 and 3.2 f. respectively. The ratio r of the second magnitude to the first equals 0.365. Substituting this ratio and the ratio of W_2 to W_1 in the expression for γ above yields our estimate of the change in productivity, equal to 3.49.

[14]For convenience, I write as if the artist were the same in the two periods. But the analysis is the same if two different artists are involved, provided that their daily earnings bear the same relation to the average earning of all artists in each period.

According to these calculations, the average artist's productivity per painting rose nearly three and a half fold over 45 years or at a yearly compound rate of 2.8 percent.

I need hardly stress that this estimate of productivity gain is extremely tenuous. For one thing, it is based on fairly small samples of prices, whose averages may deviate significantly from those that would be obtained from more representative samples. The method also relies critically on assumptions about the effects of productivity changes on prices that are unlikely to be fully realized. It would be safest to treat this result as an illustrative example based on empirical material of limited validity.

5 Originals and copies

Only very few inventories drawn up by sworn assessors or by notaries and their clerks specify whether any of the works of art they contained were originals ("principaelen") or copies. I shall try to show that a majority of the paintings that have neither been designated as originals or copies were probably in fact copies or "work by the dozen," multiples which were copies in all but name.

An analysis of the ratio of copies to apparent originals in inventories prepared by members of the guild of St. Luke, who were presumably more expert in distinguishing copies from originals than other people were, reveals that this ratio was significantly higher than in inventories prepared by non-specialists. This difference emerges from the data presented in Table 5.

In Table 5, the sample of inventories whose works of art were itemized by guild masters equaled 33; the sample of inventories prepared by other individuals (sworn assessors, notaries and their clerks) equaled 288. Dealers' inventories are excluded from both categories.

A χ^2-test applied to the statistics in Table 5 shows that the difference in the ratio of copies to originals in the two samples could be due to chance only in less than one out of 1000 replications. Yet the result seems to defy common sense, inasmuch as we would expect that collections that were fine enough to warrant calling in guild members for an expertise would have relatively *fewer* copies than collections that were not examined by connoisseurs. Even if we were to set the modest standard that the percentage of copies in inventories made up by non-guild members should have been as great as that in collec-

Table 5
"Originals" and Copies in Inventories Drawn up by Guild Masters and Other Individuals (Amsterdam, 1600-1679)

	Guild Masters	Other Individuals	Total
"Originals"	470	2,185	2,655
Copies	53	105	158
Total	523	2,290	2,813
Percentage ratio			
Copies/total	10.1	4.6	5.6

Source: DGA, Notarial archives.

tions expertised by guild members, there was an apparent understatement of the percentage of copies in the former exceeding 50 percent.

My strategy in grappling with this problem is to make use of distributions of contemporary prices of originals and copies that I presume to be reliable and, by means of a comparison of these distributions with the prices of paintings in inventories that were neither designated as copies nor as originals, determine which were most likely to be which.

An enormous auction took place in The Hague in April 1647 under the auspices of the Guild of St. Luke (Bredius (1915-1921), pp.426-520). The sellers were almost all members of the guild who were either selling their own paintings or those of other artists. The names of 235 different buyers, including at least five art dealers, some of whom lived outside The Hague, were noted by the "venduemeester" Joris Bock. Given the large number of buyers who came from all over the Netherlands and the presence of dealers, it is very likely that the prices of the works of art that were auctioned off represented accurately their competitive market value in Holland at the time. Altogether 850 paintings were sold at prices that ranged from 1.8 to 75 f. The unusual feature of the sale is that a fair number of copies were put up for sale along with a majority of originals. Since the painter-sellers themselves designated the paintings they sold either as originals or as copies (virtually no paintings were neither designated as one or the other), I would suppose they knew which was which. I would also expect that the control of the "venduemeester" and of the dealers present would have made it difficult for them to cheat in their classification. I have assumed accordingly that the classification was correct. One drawback of the records of the sale is that the subject of most of the paintings sold was left unspecified. However, the specialization *qua* landscape, still-life, genre and "history" painters of most of the artists to whom paintings were attributed in the sale was so pronounced that samples of paintings that are likely to have represented these subjects can be reconstructed from the records of the sale. Landscapists dominated the sale (Frans de Momper 121 pictures, Mathijs de Bus 51, Pieter Croost 33, Dirck Dalens 33, Willem Swinderwijck 32, Johannes Schoeff 31, Jan van Goycn 30, etc...). Still life painters were next in importance (Abraham Hennis 22, Jacques de Claeuw 20, Johannes Cuvenis 19, Pieter de Putter 18, Cornelis Lelienberch 14, etc...). I have limited my experiment to these two categories (landscapes and still lifes) because the samples that I was able to assemble for genre and other painters were too small, particularly with respect to the number of copies, to carry out the intended comparison. The average price of an original landscape was 10.1 f. (319 paintings), of a still life 7.9 f. (109 paintings). The average prices of copies in these two categories were 4.6 and 3.0 f. (20 and 12 paintings respectively).[15] Neither the distribution of prices of originals nor those of copies were precisely normal, even when we allow for the fact that all four distributions were truncated at zero (since prices cannot be negative).[16] I will make the somewhat unrealistic assumption in

[15]Among the copies of landscapes, one brought an auction price between 1 and 1.99 f., 6 between 2 and 2.99 f., 6 between 3 and 3.99 f., 2 between 5 and 6 f., 1 between 6 and 6.99 f., 2 between 8 and 8.99 f., and one between 10 and 10.00 f. Among the copies of still lifes, 2 brought prices between 1 and 1.99 f., 7 between 2 and 2.99 f., 2 between 5 and 5.99 f. and 1 between 6 and 6.99 f.

[16]Auction prices of landscape originals had a peak (the mode) between 8 and 8.99 f., a median beween 8 and 8.99 f. and an arithmetic average equal to 10.1 f. This is not inconsistent with a truncated normal distribution. However, there was an excess number of observations between 3 and 3.99 f. (about 50 percent). The failure to control for the size of paintings may account for these discrepances (it is likely that there were many small paintings in the 3 to 3.99 f. range). From the preceding note on the prices of copies, it can be seen that there was slight excess, compared to what we would expect in a normal distribution, in the number of paintings between 8 and 8.99 f., but this excess, in a small sample, could easily be due to chance. The mode and the median of the distribution of prices of original still lifes both lay between 6 and 6.99 f., the arithmetic average was 7.85 f. These statistics are also consistent with normality for a truncated distribution.

the following exercise that the distributions of auction prices were samples drawn from normal distributions, although I am well aware that this is only a rough approximation.

The probability distributions of the auction prices of originals and copies are summarized by the density functions f_1 and f_2. The probability distribution of the inventory prices, denoted f_3, is taken to be a combination of f_1 and f_2 with unknown probability weights p and $1-p$ respectively. The idea is to find the value of p (as well as the averages and standard deviations of all three functions) that maximize(s) the value of the likelihood function made up of f_1, f_2, and f_3. The value of p that maximizes the likelihood function is identical with the probability that a painting in the inventory sample happens to be an original. p is then also the most likely fraction of originals in the inventory distribution.[17]

However, there was a moderate excess number of observations between 2 and 2.99 f. and between 4 and 4.99 f. These excesses may, as in the case of landscapes, be due to the bunching of paintings around certain sizes. The distribution of prices of copies of still lifes showed no conspicuous deviations from normal, but the very small size of the sample (12 observations) is hardly conducive to confidence in this regard.

[17]More technically, the maximum likelihood function is constructed as follows. The prices in the 1647 auction cited in the text of the n_1 original paintings are denoted $(R_1, \ldots, R_i, \ldots, R_{n_1})$, or the vector r for short, those of the n_2 copies $(C_1, \ldots, C_j, \ldots, C_{n_2})$ or the vector c for short. The prices of the n_3 paintings in the randomly selected Amsterdam inventories (dated in the periods 1650-1659 and 1660-1669 respectively) are denoted $(Y_1, \ldots, Y_k, \ldots, Y_{n_3})$. We assume that the prices r of the originals and the prices c of the copies are identically and independently distributed with probability density functions $f_1(r, \mu_1, \sigma_1)$ and $f_2(c, \mu_2, \sigma_2)$ where μ_1 and μ_2 are the respective means of the prices of the originals and of the copies and σ_1 and σ_2 are their standard deviations. The probability density function f_3 of the prices in the Amsterdam inventories Y_k are assumed to be a convex combination of the densities f_1 and f_2 with weights p and $1-p$. Accordingly, we write: $f_3 = pf_1(r, \mu_1, \sigma_1) + (1-p)f_2(c, \mu_2, \sigma_2)$.

The maximum likelihood function for the three samples of prices $(R_1, \ldots, R_i, \ldots, R_{n_1})$, $(C_1, \ldots, C_j, \ldots, C_{n_2})$, $(Y_1, \ldots, Y_k, \ldots, Y_{n_3})$ is as follows:

$$\prod_{i=1}^{n_1} f_1(R_i, \mu_1, \sigma_1) \cdot \prod_{j=1}^{n_2} f_2(C_j, \mu_2, \sigma_2) \cdot \prod_{k=1}^{n_3} [pf_1(Y_k, \mu_1, \sigma_1) + (1-p)f_2(Y_k, \mu_2, \sigma_2)].$$

In order to estimate $(\mu_1, \mu_2, \sigma_1, \sigma_2, p)$, we assume that the probability functions f_1 and f_2 are normal. However, since prices cannot be negative, the normal distributions must be truncated at zero. This requires an adjustment in the formulae of the normal distributions. The adjusted maximum likelihood function is finally maximized with respect to p, μ_1, μ_2, σ_1 et σ_2. The values of these five variables are tabulated in the text. I am grateful to

Table 6
Hypothetical Proportion of Originals in Amsterdam Inventories (1650-1669)

	1650-1659 p (percent)	1660-1669 p (percent)	1650-1669 p (percent)
Landscapes			
Actual inventory prices	34.2	33.1	34.2
Raised 25 percent	42.5	46.9	46.3
Raised 50 percent	48.3	62.5	56.2
Still lifes			
Actual inventory prices	23.2	13,6	19.9
Raised 25 percent	27.8	14.8	23.1
Raised 50 percent	37.3	18.2	28.8

The objection may be raised that the prices or evaluations in inventories tend to be systematically lower than at auction (because the contents of inventories are "second hand" and/or because works of art are relatively illiquid). To offset this bias, the maximum likelihood calculation was repeated after *all* inventory prices were raised by 25 and 50 percent successively. The results of all three calculations are shown in Table 6.

The proportion of copies to originals that emerges from these simulations is extremely high: in the pooled sample of inventories dated between 1650 and 1669, about two thirds of the landscapes in the random sample of inventories seem to be copies as do some four fifths of the still lifes when comparisons are made with actual inventory prices.[18] When inventory prices are raised

Donald W.K. Andrews who helped me formulate the problem and to Paul Willen who executed the procedure, using Gauss software.

[18]The proportion of copies among the still lifes seems inordinately high. This suspected error may be due to the unrepresentativeness of the small sample of copies of still lifes from the 1647 auction and to their significant deviation from normality.

by 50 percent, the percentage of copies falls only to 44 percent in the case of landscapes and 71 percent in the case of still lifes.[19]

These results may be less surprising if a "copy," among the works of art recorded in an inventory, is broadly interpreted to mean a painting produced "by the dozen," probably by apprentices and journey men, possibly but not necessarily after an original. It may also be that small, routinely executed panel paintings that were sold for one to four gulden cannot be dissociated from "copies" in these calculations, even though they may have been produced by guild masters.

6 Concluding remarks

After analyzing the sources of bias in the selection of inventories culled from the Amsterdam and Delft archives, this paper explores various ways in which the information contained in inventories can be supplemented to answer important questions about patterns of collecting: the rate of accumulation of collections (on the basis of biographic data about collectors and artists), increases in productivity of artists (on the basis of prices or evaluations of paintings), and the ratio of originals to copies (on the basis of inventory assessments and extraneous auction prices). The data at my disposal suggest that (1) collectors tended to purchase paintings toward the end rather the beginning of their collecting career, (2) the productivity of landscape artists rose significantly during the period 1600-1619 to 1650-1659, and (3) the proportion of copies among landscapes and still lifes in randomly selected (assessed) inventories may have been as high as one half to three quarters. The reader may well question whether the samples (random and non-random) that I have used in making inferences about these three subjects were sufficiently large and reliable to draw such strong conclusions. Whether or not they meet this test, I shall be satisfied if the methods I propose turn out to be useful for further research.

[19] Bok and Schwartz (1991, p. 193) estimated that at least 50 percent of the *surviving* paintings of the seventeenth century were copies. Considering that the proportion of copies that have disappeared over the last three centuries is likely to have been greater than the proportion of originals that have disappeared (because more care and expense was presumably lavished on preserving the more expensive paintings from destruction), I would conclude that my estimates are broadly consistent with theirs.

7 References

Bok, M.J. and G. Schwartz (1991), Schilderen in opdracht in Holland in de 17e eeuw, *Holland Regionaal-historisch Tijdschrift*, 23, 183-195.

Bredius, A. (1915-1921), *Künstler-inventare; Urkunden zur Geschichte der Holländischen Kunst des XVIten, XVIIten, und XVIIIten Jahrhundert*, The Hague: Martinus Nijhoff.

Elias, J. E. (1963), *De Vroedschap van Amsterdam*, 2 vols., Amsterdam: N. Israel.

Knoester, H. and A. Graafhuis (1970), Het kasboek van Mr. Carel Martens, *Oud Utrecht*, 154-217.

Lesger, C. (1986), *Huur en Conjunctuur. De Woningmarkt in Amsterdam, 1550-1850*, Amsterdamse Historische Reeks no. 10, Universiteit van Amsterdam, Amsterdam.

Loughman, J. (circa 1993), *Paintings in Public and Private Domain: Collecting and Patronage at Dordrecht 1620-1749*, Ph.D. Thesis, Courtaud Institute, London.

Montias, J.M. (1982), *Artists and Artisans in Delft; A Socio-economic Study of the Seventeenth Century*, Princenton, N.J.: Princeton University Press.

Montias, J.M. (1987), Cost and value in seventeenth century art, *Art History*, 10, 455-466.

Montias, J.M. (1994), Works of art in a random sample of 17th century Amsterdam inventories, paper presented to the International Congress of Economic History, Milan, September 1994.

Montias, J.M. (1996), *Le Marché de l'Art aux Pays-Bas; 15ème-17ème Siècles*, Paris: Flammarion.

Salomonson, J.W. (1988), The officers of the white banner: a civic guard portrait by Jacob Willemsz. Delff, *Simiolus*, 18, 13-62.

Vries, Jan de (1982), An inquiry into the behavior of wages in the Dutch Republic and the Southern Netherlands from 1580 to 1800, in M. Aymard (ed.), *Dutch Capitalism and World Capitalism; Capitalisme hollandais et capitalisme mondial*, Cambridge, London and New York: Cambridge University Press.

Economics of the Arts - Selected Essays
V.A. Ginsburgh and P.-M. Menger (Editors)

2

Pricing Invention: "Originals," "Copies," and their Relative Value in Seventeenth Century Netherlandish Art Markets*

Neil De Marchi and Hans J. Van Miegroet
Duke University

In 1664 the Antwerp art dealer Matthijs Musson sold a group of six works to the son of the mayor of Bruges. The group included two sketches by Rubens and a wolf hunt by Frans Snyders. A year later the buyer, Ignatius de Muelenare, wrote a sharp letter to Musson accusing him of false attribution. He had shown his hunt and the two sketches to someone from Antwerp knowledgeable about paintings, only to be told that what he had bought were no "principals" (originals), but simply copies. The Antwerp connoisseur (*kenner*) had added that the Dean and sworn valuers of the Painters' Guild "will always favor the painters [sic], never the copy" (Denucé (1949, p. 37), Duverger (1969, p. 130)).

Musson's client was miffed because he realized that he had paid too much. Copies were mostly priced at just a fraction of originals. Indeed, what De Muelenare had bought for *f*66 (the hunt) and *f*200 (the Rubens sketches, together) were in fact worth, he had been told, around a third to a quarter

* We have benefitted immensely from, and are grateful for, a large number of careful and challenging suggestions received from Svetlana Alpers, Joost Vander Auwera, David F. Bell III, Marina Bianchi, Marten Jan Bok, Zirka Zaremba Filipczak, Walter Gibson, Martin Kemp, Joseph Koerner, Chris Wood, Michael Montias, David Chioni Moore, Keith Moxey, Jeffrey Muller, Peter Parshall, Walter Santagata, Gary Schwartz, and an anonymous referee. The comments of seminar participants in Canberra, Oxford, Cambridge, Venice, and the London School of Economics, as well as exchanges after papers in the Royal Museum, Antwerp, the Sixteenth Century Conference, San Francisco (1995), and the Renaissance Society of America, Bloomington, Indiana (1996) have also helped clarify aspects of the argument. Friso Lammertse kindly supplied an important reference. A section entitled "The Price of Inventiveness" in Zirka Zaremba Filipczak's *Picturing Art in Antwerp, 1550-1700*, initially piqued our interest in trying to measure the value added by what we have decided, after all, is better thought of as invention.

of those prices (Denucé (1949, p. 37)). But why was there this difference? Or, to ask the question another way, what arguments justified subtracting value from an original in order to arrive at the lesser value of the copy?

Such questions may seem superfluous today, because it is accepted that originals can sell at auction for hundreds of times the value of copies (see the indications in Schwartz (1993) and Nijstad (1995, pp. 77-78)). In the first half of the seventeenth century, by contrast, we have found and report here some evidence (Table 2 below) that originals often sold for only two or three times the price of a copy – not much different from what De Muelenare's adviser estimated. This was most reliably so when both original and copy were done by the same master. The price difference could be more when the copyist was another, lesser master, or remained anonymous; but even when one is dealing with unattributed works, many of which probably were copies, it is not uncommon to find a price ratio – named original to unattributed work – of 2 or 3 to 1 (Montias (1982, p. 259 and Table 8.6)).

These findings show that a great change has occurred in the way creative origination is now viewed, and they give us a reference point from which to start explaining the change. Our purpose in this chapter, however, is simply to place our findings in the context of contemporary thought and practices in the Netherlands, both north and south. We argue that the basis for the price difference observed even when the same master made both original and copy was invention. As an economic category invention was not widely recognized prior to the seventeenth century. Our task involves identifying the contexts in which invention could find acceptance. Apart from pure cases where the same master made both original and copy, invention tended to get mixed up with other factors contributing to value: scarcity, authorship and reputation, for example. Moreover, for paintings at large, invention could find its place only within existing practical rules for identifying an "original." These, in turn, rested on hierarchies such as those governing the relations, and conventional reward differentials, between masters and assistants. Accordingly, we examine guild attitudes to what counted as an original; whether special "touch" sufficed to qualify a painting as a work of invention; early evidences of a concern with authorship (attribution) as a way to exploit reputation, which could give rise to strange phenomena such as originals masquerading as copies in the manner of a master whose work was in demand; artists' own efforts to create a differentiated product, and dealers' practices, which show originals being treated as income-generating assets. We shall discuss first the basis for there being any price differential between originals and copies, then move on to examine the several contexts just listed, before reporting and discussing our numerical findings in some detail.

1 Introducing a value for invention

Two, three, or even five times the price of a copy might not strike us as much of a premium to pay for an original. Yet that there was any difference at all in the seventeenth century remains puzzling, given that masters freely copied their own work; or acted as copyists for others; and copy and original were not always distinguishable, even by experts.

In the tradition which viewed painting as a form of rhetoric it had long been accepted that a fine painting is one which embodies a well-chosen subject and elements, and combines these in an appropriate and compelling way. But no real distinction was made between this work, which might be said to be conceptual and to reflect learning and skill in design, and the work of execution. Differences between artists were of course recognized, as attested by different rates of pay. Designs, drawings and sketches as such, however, whilst preeminently part of the conceptual side of producing a painting, and regarded as an important element in the record of what had been contracted for, were not accorded value as distinct objects. Any value they might have as inventions was subsumed in the contract price for the finished art work.[1] Early (fourteenth century) Italian contracts, moreover, at times specified that a work of art was to be, in part or wholly, a copy of another (Goldthwaite (1993, p. 135)), while fifteenth century workshop practice for the production of paintings frequently involved copying (Thomas (1995, ch. 10 passim)). Indeed, prior to the sixteenth century, it has been plausibly suggested, novelty and invention simply were not seen as indispensable artistic qualities (Wackernagel (1981, p. 336)).[2]

[1]See Thomas (1995, p. 110) on designs as legal documents in fifteenth century Tuscany, and p. 182 for contract price, which covered materials and the artist's "expertise" – an inclusive descriptive category. The ease with which owners of originals made them accessible for copying, and the circulation of drawings (ibid., pp. 221-226)), support the notion that there was not as yet a distinct value ascribed to designs. This appears to have changed, for prints at least, by early in the sixteenth century (Landau and Parshall (1994, esp. pp. 297, 299)).

[2]The case of Titian is illustrative. Summoned by Charles V to attend him on a visit to

This absence of an artistic or an economic distinction between the work of origination or invention and the work of execution probably characterised early northern painting production as well. By the seventeenth century, however, an economic distinction at least was being drawn in the Netherlands. By then a value was considered to attach to an original painting that copies could not share; that is the implication of the price differential favouring originals noted already.

We suggest that it is reasonable to regard this differential as a payment for invention, meaning by that term the labor of creative origination.[3] Our argument has to be circumstantial, however. The term invention does not often occur in the descriptions of paintings or discussions between artists and dealers, or dealers and buyers, which we have seen. A notable exception is to be found in a letter from Jan II Brueghel to Chrisostomus Van Immerseel, where Brueghel contrasts works of "father's invention" to "common copies" thereof (Denucé (1934, p. 70)). Mostly, however, one finds terms such as "singular" (*raer*), "attentively done" (*curieux geschildert*), "proper" (*fatsoenlijk*) (Denucé (1949, pp. 13, 15, 42, 172)); and, somewhat closer to invention, expressions that refer to the complexity and amount of labour involved, particularly the number of animals or human figures: for example, "full of work and special detail" (*vol werx, heel curieus*) (Ertz (1979, p. 543, entries 76, 79, 80)).

It is no surprise that "invention" was not part of market talk about paintings. The term belonged to the rhetorical tradition and was appropriated rather by art theorists than by craft practitioners. Strikingly, there was no change in art theoretical ideals to match the change we observe in the form

---

northern Italy in 1532-33, the artist was asked to make two portraits of the Emperor. One of these was to be a copy of an existing portrait, by the German court painter Seisenegger. There is no indication that either patron or artist viewed this commission as in any sense demeaning; indeed Charles rewarded Titian by creating him Count Palatine and Knight of the Golden Spur, titles higher than any previously bestowed on an artist (Humfrey (1995, p. 164)).

[3] We distinguish between invention, which had to do with concept, design and composition, and inventiveness, which might be displayed at any stage of an artistic production. Inventiveness could affect the prices of both originals and copies; we shall see below how "formulaic" painters in the seventeenth century undertook creative differentiation of their products, which were basically copies. Invention, on the other hand, could only be part of an original. We are grateful to Chris Wood for prodding us to be clearer about this distinction and its implications.

of an economic distinction between originals and copies. Karel Van Mander, for example, in his *Den grond der edel vry schilder-const* of 1604, viewed invention in painting as it was viewed in classical rhetorical theory. Essential to the "invention" of a painting, in other words, was the choice of subject and its key elements, plus the pictorial ordering of the material (*dispositio*). Van Mander also valued highly working from memory, but he stressed most the importance of disposition or ordering, even using that term interchangeably with invention in his chapter on organization and "invention" in histories (Van Mander (1604, fols. 15-22); see also Miedema (1995, pp. 125-126)). Franciscus Junius, writing three decades later, chose somewhat different emphases, but remained firmly attached to the traditional categories. Proper choice, he insisted, could only be exercised within an appropriate (i.e., classical) educational background; this made "invention" inseparable from learning, decorum and discretion. Being true to nature was also part of this set of qualities (Junius (1638, pp. 232, 240-3) and Levesque (1994, esp. p. 91), for a recent exploration of Junius's ideas in the context of Haarlem landscape prints).

Amid the terminological complexities, usefully untangled and, along with the rhetorical scope of "invention," discussed by Melion (1991), one thing stands out clearly: invention in the early seventeenth century Netherlandish art-theoretical literature was not associated with individual creative genius. That is a more recent narrowing, though traces of a connection between "genius" (*ingegno*) and invention are visible in sixteenth century Italian writings (Miedema (1995, pp. 204 et sq.), Kemp, citing Vasari on Donatello, in Murray (1993, p. 46)). Even as an economic entity invention was not treated as the same as the contribution made to value by individual genius. In the marketplace talent continued to be rewarded, as it always had been, by unusual payments being made to artists whose work seemed special. Nor was there any general rush to attach the name of the artist to paintings; attribution did not become common for several decades after the market distinction between originals and copies had been accepted.

But what of the circumstantial grounds justifying our inclination to call the originals/copies price differential a reward for invention? We rely on parallels between the notion that value could be imparted to an original painting by invention, and certain merchant modes of thinking and behaving that are encountered in Antwerp and Amsterdam, sometimes among artists, and which amount to the same thing. Familiar examples occur in the area of print production. Thus Rembrandt can be found modifying his engraved plates, so that basically the same original could serve to sustain buyer interest in a series of variant prints. Here, clearly, the initial invention was viewed as capable of generating income through the prints. Rubens, for his part, as is well known, carefully chose engravers and supervised the making of prints after many of his paintings. The prints, of course, sold for very much less than the original paintings – mostly just one or two guilders; but, by creating a wider audience familiar with his style and works, the prints both sustained higher prices for his paintings and realised, print by print, each time a little of the differential value due to his original creations. Perhaps less familiar, dealers in art, such as Matthijs Musson, and others, made a practice of buying or gaining access to originals which they then had copied repeatedly, or copied before reselling, allowing further copies (of the copy) to be made. This too was a way of realizing the special value attaching to an original.

Such attempts to realize value added are exactly analogous to the franchising of an idea, a process or a product line, and they stand in place of having a patent on these inventions. Rubens, of course, did secure copyright (*privilegien*) on his prints (Orenstein et. al. (1993, p. 174)); and it is not accidental that in the last decade of the sixteenth century and the first two of the seventeenth, there was a surge in patents secured in Amsterdam as that city began to compete industrially as well as in the role of a trade entrepot (De Vries and Van der Woude (1995, p. 408)). The city's regents were presumably aware that there were social gains from invention, and were happy to swap some of these for limited patent protection to private inventors.

In another area, only seemingly more remote from art, recall that the Jesuit scholar Lessius, in Antwerp, was among the very first to make a convincing case for granting interest on loans of money. The case turned on the idea that there is always a greater number needing loans than there are individuals willing to make their money temporarily available, so social good is served – the analogy with the case for granting patents on inventions is complete – by giving a privilege to "originators" who made loans available (De Marchi and Harrison (1994, p. 55), Van Houdt (1995)). If it seems stretching language to think of powers of origination as somehow belonging even to cash, remember that exactly one of the tasks of those who wanted to challenge the prohibition against interest on ordinary loans was to dislodge the notion that money is barren. The counter argument for some time had been made in terms of opportunity cost. Those who might be expected to lend money could instead invest it productively in some business venture; why, then, should they not receive the equivalent in interest? Lessius simply expanded this argument to cover money loaned whether or not an alternative productive opportunity was forgone. Paintings are not excluded from the opportunity cost argument. Because of substitutability, or the rule that investible funds are fungible, not only uncommitted cash, but even cash temporarily invested in something like an original painting, had to answer to the demand that its present use compare favorably with alternatives which yield a flow of income. An owner might be happy to replace a cash flow by a flow of enjoyment; but so long as resources were limited a painting had to submit to the claims implicit in the notion that it could be sold off and the money used for another purpose. There is a strong hint that this was indeed how contemporaries construed things in the fact that in the seventeenth century Netherlands the word used by dealers and collectors alike for an original painting, "principal", meant, as in English, both "main" and capital sum. The practice of dealers such as Musson, outlined above, of generating income through copies, confirms that they regarded originals as capital assets.

To this point we have introduced what we have called the work of invention and claimed that this particular labour was seen as the economic basis for a distinction between an original and a copy. But there is a problem. An exact replica is, of course, a copy, but it will display all the features which qualified its original model as an invention. Handling, and overall quality might not match up to the original; on the other hand, a copyist, even if not exactly replicating the model, might in some cases produce what is indisputably a superior painting. There had to be practical criteria one could apply for selecting originals and, if necessary, for overruling what one's eyes told one about relative quality. A single guideline served both ends: the guild structure was used to assign the work of making originals to masters, and distinctions between Masterwork, which embodied the prevailing standard of excellence, master's work, which meant only that the hand of an assistant was not involved, and originals, were allowed to be fuzzy. Payment for invention, in short, was in practice not separable from the context in which originals were made and recognized.

This meant that there was series of oppositions posed, with fairly free substitution occurring among the terms on each side.

Work of a master	Work of an assistant
Original	Copy
Expensive	Cheaper
Superior	Lesser quality

Thus, reading from left to right, "superior" might be opposed to lesser quality, but also to plain copy; or, reading from the right, lesser quality might be opposed to expensive, but also to the work of a master. According to local context and historical moment, we find different specific combinations being stressed.

The Amsterdam Painter's Guild, when it suited, emphasized the quality-originals link, with originals understood as the work of masters. Part of the reason for this combination is that master painters were sensitive about their relative social standing, not least because rank tended to be linked to income differentials. Rank, in turn, meant, not only how a master stood relative to paid assistants, say, within the craft of artist, but how artists stood within the overall hierarchy of crafts. Hence, that originals were priced above copies might be explicable by invention, but invention in that case was also being used as an aspect of a double claim by master painters: about the role and value of art, on the one hand, and about their worth relative to that of assistants, on the other. Masters certainly had more experience and presumably more skill than assistants; nonethelesss, skill and quality being difficult matters on which to secure general agreement, it was convenient to foster a convention according to which masters were the ones who did creative, inventive work. Attempts to bypass the convention and judge merit directly would have been viewed as a challenge to the underlying hierarchies that gave practical and social meaning to such notions as quality. Something like this appears to lie behind the otherwise odd comment De Muelenare got from his Antwerp adviser: "the Guild's officials will always favor the painters, never the copy."

By contrast, there are cases in which invention is measurable in isolation from the socio-economic context. The diary of the painter Jan II Brueghel records such cases; they are to be found too in purchase agreements between the Antwerp merchant Chrisostomus Van Immerseel and various artists. These are cases where the original and a copy is made by the same artist or artists; the higher price of the original here can have nothing to do with reputation, or scarcity; nor need materials, support costs, size or complexity differ between the original and the copy. The price difference captures, instead, invention pure and simple. Several of the cases in Table 2 below are of this – for our purposes – ideal type.

It seems then that "original" may have had multiple meanings, each with somewhat different implications for valuation. We focus in the discussion which follows on production-related, or craft aspects, though clearly imputation of value came from the demand side as well: the same painting tended to be higher-priced when bought by a buyer of note.

2 Four views of the originals-invention connection

The results we obtain and will discuss more fully below for the price ratio between originals and copies seem fairly robust. This robustness leads us to think that the notions original, copy, and value of invention had acquired a relatively stable content by the early seventeenth century – speaking always only of the Netherlands. In principle this conjecture should be tested against earlier observations. We do not have the desired set of comparable observations, so we resort to a complementary way of judging our impression; we set our results against a discussion of some of the more fluid attitudes towards originals, and practices relating to inventorship, that are discernible over the course of the sixteenth century.

As noted earlier, we shall discuss four aspects of practice and attitudes which affected the way originals were viewed and valued and in which we see a difference between the seventeenth century and preceding centuries. First, there is the now familiar interest of the artists' guild in maintaining superior status and income for its masters, which meant that masters were the ones who determined the standard for quality work. In practice, as we have noted, quality was identified with originals, not copies. These things were conventional and required no debate. In the seventeenth century, however, we see renewed efforts by artists to have themselves distinguished from the other crafts with which they were bundled in a single guild; these efforts can be plausibly interpreted as part of a desire to establish a claim to superior creative status. Second, although the finishing "touch" of a master had always added value to work done principally by students or assistants, there is a distinction drawn in the seventeenth century between that added value and the value added by invention. Documentary evidence to this effect, including legal depositions carefully distinguishing between original, copy, and copy-of-copy, seems to multiply in the seventeenth century. Third, fifteenth and sixteenth century ambiguity about, or general indifference to, naming the author of a work survived alongside a perhaps growing and certainly at times extravagant tendency in the latter part of the sixteenth century to ascribe value to (claims of) authorship. This could produce bizarre effects, such as originals being sold, falsely, as copies after a famous master – the reverse of the usual problem. Finally, we point to a number of other such elements that suggest a lack of clarity in preceding centuries about what, if any, separate significance to give to invention in valuation. Full-time art dealers, who began to play a distinctive role in the seventeenth century, clarified that significance in the following way. Dealers could not always expect a large profit on an already-expensive original, so they treated originals as milch-cows, drawing off profit from repeated (though always limited) copying. As already indicated, this can be viewed as a way of realizing the value of invention.

2.1 A Guild perspective

In 1608 the Amsterdam Painters' Guild complained to the mayors about certain sellers who were importing paintings from "Antwerp, and other enemy territories," and selling them illegally and "far above their value;" for these paintings were said to be "mostly ordinary copies" (*meestendeel slechte copien*, Obreen (1880-81, p. 165)).[4] It is left vague whether the paintings were *slecht* and happened to be copies, or the fact that they were copies was enough to call them *slecht*. The issue is settled in a second complaint, lodged in 1613. There it is said that the importers reserved "the good or principal paintings" for themselves, actually selling only "copies and other poor rags," which is a polite translation of *copyen en andere slechte vodden* (ibid., p. 167)).

This was no fortuitous conflation of ordinary painting with copy, and of good work with original, as can be seen from various legal documents in which paintings are declared to be either an original or a copy, the distinc-

[4] Depending on the context, *slecht* could mean ordinary or poor, bad.

tion clearly being of some economic consequence for the makers, dealers and buyers involved. One such document, from 1615, notarised in Bergen-op-Zoom, has Ambrosius Bosschaert stating that a flower piece sold to Hans de la Tour in Amsterdam was his work, and his alone. A second, from the same year, but notarised in Amsterdam, has Bosschaert declaring that a St. Jerome sold four years earlier as by the Utrecht master Abraham Bloemaert, and recently resold for the not inconsiderable sum of *f*60, was in fact a copy (Bol (1960, pp. 7-8)). In the first of these two documents Bosschaert and his brother in-law Balthasar van der Ast also testify that a second painting was made by Balthasar's brother Hans, but retouched and over-painted by Bosschaert.

That detail introduces a third category, between copy and original: the pupil's or assistant's work, re-touched by the master. In 1618 we find Peter Paul Rubens, who was then negotiating the sale of some of his paintings to Sir Dudley Carleton, English Ambassador at The Hague, describing one of his own works as falling into this category. Rubens argued that the touched-up work "will pass for an original," yet he priced it as if it were a copy. We return to this in the next section.

Examples of a new emphasis on such distinctions could be multiplied. There is the complaint against Musson with which we began. There were two very public disputes which erupted in the 1660s and 70s involving authorship and price class (original or copy). These concerned, respectively, works by Van Dyck and his students, and some alleged copies sold by the Amsterdam dealer Gerrit Uylenburg as original Italian old masters (Un procès... (1868), Dudok van Heel (1982, p. 81)). We might point also to the caution shown by collectors who were offering important old masters for sale; they are to be seen making comments like: "all are true originals except two which are retouched by the masters named" (Denucé (1949, pp. 178-179)). Or, to look in another direction, there are letters from dealers such as Michel Picart in Paris, a major customer of Musson, in which he expresses interest in having works by various old masters, but only if they are "genuine originals" (*rechte princepalen*) (Denucé (1949, pp. 252, 362)).

Finally, there is a document from Antwerp, dated 28 November 1654, in which yet another sub-category made an appearance, the copy of a copy. Musson was involved here in attesting that two paintings by Thomas Willeboirts Bosschaert were made, not after well known originals (Van Dycks), but from copies done by Joan Meyssens after the originals. This degree of refinement in distinguishing the objects was necessary because one master, having seen Willeboirts' copies, found it hard to believe that they were not in fact made from the originals (Denucé (1949, p. 137)). All this careful categorization can only have been for economic reasons, since in this instance a master could not tell copy-of-a-copy from copy-after-an-original. Differences which the eye couldn't discern nonetheless were made the basis for a difference in price.

These documents might be supposed to prove nothing about differences between the seventeenth and preceding centuries, since they could be available to us merely because the fortunes of survival have favored the later century. We prefer to regard them as pointing to a burgeoning interest in the originals-copies distinction, and sub-variants thereof. Our reading seems warranted by independent evidence in the form of the behavior of artists within their guilds over the course of the seventeenth century. Starting in Antwerp in 1595, there is a series of recorded attempts by the artists to have themselves regarded in some sense as distinct from their guild brethren. Their claims owe something to the acknowledgement by the fifteenth century humanist Alberti that there are three arts with a dual character, theoretical, as well as practical. Architecture, sculpture and painting lend themselves to theorizing, whether or not their practitioners actually go on to make images or construct anything (Miedema (1995, pp. 122-123, 186-189), Binski (1992, p. 24), Goldthwaite (1993, p. 146)). Conceptualization, and the articulation of ideas in words, but above all in drawings or designs, lies at the heart of their theoretical aspect. Hence the artist's craft, for example, may be said to be marked by abstract invention in a way that the beating out of copper plates was not, though the two might be bundled into a single guild. Earlier, certain individuals had argued that, if they were designers only they should be free from guild membership, which was required for practitioners of a craft (Miedema (1995, pp. 189 et sq.)). Artists who both designed and painted could not make this argument, but they might still try to cultivate a separate standing. This might mean recognition in a separate guild, though more often it meant tacit acknowledgement of their status as inventors. One way to translate tacit recognition into a market price for invention was to insist on differences in pay between masters and assistants, and to apply these or roughly comparable differences to rates charged when the same master acted as originator and as copyist. Evidence on these differences is presented below. In charging less when acting as a copyist a master was in effect acting as, and charging like, an assistant.

Probably the last distinguishing move within the seventeenth century occurred in Amsterdam in 1699. The painters there set up a gallery in which to display and from which to sell their work. A year later they asked the mayors to recognize their gallery. Official recognition, they urged, would help them see to the business of "obstructing the bad and maintaining the good." Art lovers (*liefhebbers*), they argued, have a right to guarantees; but of what? Of quality presumably. Yet what we find the artists urging is that liefhebbers must be given "the truth," the truth as to "what is good, what is beautiful" and – lest their eminences the mayors miss the point – the truth about "what is a copy and what an original" (Bille (1961, vol. 1, pp. 155, 176)).

Why does this double conflation, of original with the good and the beautiful – in a word, the superior – and simple, or ordinary with copy, occur and recur? It was not confined to the Amsterdam guild. De Muelenare's Antwerp adviser suggested that the guild there shared it fully. It was in the interest of masters that their guild representatives maintain a rule which said that masters' work is more costly than that of pupils or assistants. That was of long standing. To reach the conflation from this position it is only necessary to add that it was the accepted province of masters to make originals. That was old as well. What was new in the seventeenth century was an insistence on translating the link between masters' work and originals into an argument that might survive a certain evident erosion of guild authority; the argument said that originals involve the work of invention, which must be rewarded.

2.2 Touch alone does not an original make

Certain masters had an exclusive touch. This had been a cause of higher price for centuries, and it was again crucial in the 1618 negotiations between Rubens and Sir Dudley Carleton, mentioned above. The story is well known, but some of the details are worth recounting, for what the episode reveals takes us beyond the long accepted notion that special talent had to have its reward. It shows, in addition, that even a work touched up by a master of special talent was regarded in our period basically as still a copy. As such it had to be priced below its model, the original. By implication, too, there was a payment reserved for the separate work of invention that characterized an original in a more essential way than "touch."

Michael Montias supplies striking evidence of this from a different set of circumstances. He compares two legal depositions, one in 1621, the other in 1644, both notarised in Delft. The former involved a bet whereby an artist accepted a challenge to produce a copy superior to an original painting. The other instance involved a wager that a painting carrying a signature could be shown not to be by that person. Montias notes that in the first situation the authorship of the original did not enter into the case, though quality clearly did, while in the second authorship was everything, to the exclusion of any artistic merit the painting in dispute might have. This last captures Rubens' problem. His touch would create a work of art in appearance indistinguishable from a Rubens original, but it would remain at best a Rubens copy, not a creative original. An authentic Rubens original involved not just "signature" (touch, in this case) but everything that went into the initial invention, here merely re-used. Montias (1982, pp. 234-235) observes that the switch to a focus on authorship was a seventeenth century phenomenon; we would add that the line connecting attribution with that which is seen as an original passes through invention.

To return to the Rubens-Carleton negotiations, Rubens wanted to acquire selected antiquities in exchange for some of his paintings. Among the antiquities were sculptures, part of a larger collection Carleton had bought in Venice from the Flemish dealer Daniel Nys for the Earl of Somerset. He got stuck with them when Somerset was arrested (see Muller (1989a, p. 57 and Appendix C) for inventories of the collection of ancient sculptures, Magurn (1955, pp. 59-60)). His goal was to sell again in "a good mart," and he presumably thought paintings by Rubens more vendible than the sculptures. The two men agreed on a total value for the sculptures, and it was then a matter of identifying pictures of equivalent value.

Initially, twelve paintings were discussed. Rubens offered them, along with summary information about subject, size, authorship and price. "Original," as we have seen, meant the work of a master, but that did not necessarily apply in reverse. Hence in specifying "authorship" Rubens found himself sending noisy signals. For instance, there was a *Daniel in the Lions' Den* valued at *f*600, said to be "an original entirely by my own hand" (*Originale tutto de mia mano*, Rooses and Ruelens (1887-1909, vol. II, p. 136)). Yet the following entry, a *Leopards with Satyrs and Nymphs*, also set at *f*600, was described as "original, by my own hand, except for a beautiful landscape, by the hand of a worthy master of that genre" (*Originale de mia* *mano, eccetto un bellisimo paese fatto par mano di un valenthuomo in quel mestiere*, Rooses and Ruelens (1887-1909, vol. II, p. 137)). This did not cause difficulties, since, as we might now predict, an original by two masters is still an original. Another entry, however, was problematic. Rubens listed a *Last Judgement*, which he valued at *f*1200. It had been, he said: "begun by one of my pupils, after a very large one which I did for the Most Serene Prince of Neuberg, who has paid me 3,500 guilders cash for it; but this, not being finished, would be entirely retouched by my own hand, and therefore will pass for an original".[5] That the price in this instance was set lower is not surprising; it may have been smaller, but in any case it would not pass for an original according to the market test. It involved copying, not fresh invention, and Rubens' hand could do no more than prevent the price of the copy from being still lower, as it would have been had he not intended to intervene.

Carleton was unimpressed by Rubens' claims on behalf of the to-be-touched-up work. He wanted paintings solely by Rubens himself. His concern was whether he could make a profit on the re-sale to a buyer whom he may already have had in mind, the King of Denmark (Muller (1989a, p. 57)), and he probably feared that the King would judge as he did, that this work was a copy and as such a less desirable asset. The issue here was not appearance; there was little doubt that the finished work would pass for a Rubens. The issue was whether it was a Rubens original, whether it embodied the design properties and invention expected of a true original. Touch was not a substitute for invention.

Rubens took the point, albeit with some reluctance. He not only believed strongly in the power of his brushwork but – this seems to be the meaning of somewhat obscure language in a reply to Carleton of 12 May 1618 – if he were to supply "unmixed" (*meri*) originals, which he could do, Carleton would have to accept a larger number of works (presumably of smaller size) to reach the agreed total value for the exchange (Roosens and Ruelens (1887-1909, vol. II, pp. 144-145)). One senses Rubens' resistance. Why should a substantial work like the *Judgement* – complex, powerful, surely *vol werx*, as the original in the Alte Pinakothek, Munich, attests – somehow be devalued relative to

[5] *Cominciato di un mio discepolo appresso uno chio feci in molto maggior forma per il Sermo Principe de Neuberg che me lo pago tre mille cinquecento fiorini contanti ma questo non essendo finito si ritoccarebbe tutto de mia mano et a quel modo passaria per originale* (Rooses and Ruelens (1887-1909, vol. II, p. 137)).

small, straightforward, "mere" originals (mere is the literal translation of *meri*), just because it is a touched-up version? Yet that was precisely the message of the market which Carleton had imbibed.

2.3 Reputation effects and phantom copies

The rule linking originals to masters, and both to higher price, even where no quality difference is discernible in the product, inevitably had to be extended and modified to cover the case where invention had become mixed up with the reputation of the originator and could no longer readily be judged, and valued, in and of itself. Where the same master makes both original and copy, we have argued, any price difference can in principle only be due to invention. But when the master and the copyist differ widely in talent, then both invention and reputation help to determine any price difference. If master and copyist are contemporaries and we can calculate a day wage equivalent for each of them, then once again we are able to isolate invention; but if the master is dead and the copyist living the two causal factors will tend to remain confused. In that situation "authorship," meaning naming or attribution, but covering both reputation *and* invention, may be invoked as a convenient way to justify a price difference between original and copy while hiding the fact that invention cannot be separately assessed.

Something like this probably happened over the course of the seventeenth century. As the number of surviving paintings in the category of "old" masters increased, questions of attribution and authentication necessarily became more pressing. At a certain point it was bound to happen that false claims would be made, as artists and dealers sought to exploit some of the price potential in the name of a famous master, no longer living. Unsurprisingly, the Rotterdam-born essayist Bernard de Mandeville, writing in the early eighteenth century, could introduce in the space of a single comment both the hoary problem of an objective standard of quality and the importance of name and reputation. He wrote in 1723: "the best Pictures bear not always the best Prices," adding that "a noted Original will be ever worth more than any Copy that can be made of it by an unknown Hand, tho' it should be better" (Mandeville (1924, p. 326)). This opinion is remarkably close to the judgement of the Antwerp *kenner* of 1665, when he spoke of the painters always being prized above the copy. Grammatically that may not read well, but the implication is clear, as is Mandeville's message: merit has something to do with price, though less than one might expect. More important is that a painting be attributed. The anonymity of a copy detracts from its worth, compared to the original. Copying emancipates an image from any aura of uniqueness that may surround its original,[6] and which often owes something to the person of the originator. Equally, however, in shedding that uniqueness, copies lose some of the appeal of originals. To the table of opposites above therefore we should add "signature or attributability" on the left, and "unknown authorship" on the right.[7]

Invention, in other words, if it cannot be captured separately from reputation, will be captured under reputation which, as a rule of thumb, is indicated simply by naming the author. Attributing a work thus becomes a way of appropriating some of the aura of an original, independently of whether it really is an original, or really was made by the author named. We draw attention here to a particularly odd consequence of trying to exploit authorship (more accurately, reputation) for economic gain, in a context of imperfect information. In such an environment, where attribution is uncertain, a clever copyist might make his or her own originals and attribute them to a master whose work is widely known and in demand. Such originals behave as copies, even though no corresponding original ever existed. They are, in short, phantom copies.

---

[6]Walter Benjamin (1963, pp. 20-21, 53; see also the well known translated essay on reproducibility in Arendt (1968, p. 220)) speaks of the link between *Einmaligkeit* and *Kultwert*. Benjamin raises separate issues, but among other things, he addresses the question posed, on our reading at any rate, by Rubens. Rubens was troubled that a striking, if touched-up work should be dismissed as a copy. We draw attention repeatedly to the fact that there was a difference in the market value of copy and original, but we do not enter into the question whether and why the excellence of an invention should not in certain cases, or in some degree, transfer to the copy.

[7]Attribution in Mandeville's time was undoubtedly more important than in the first decades of the seventeenth century. The change can be traced in inventory and sales records. Filipczak (1987, p. 44) cites Antwerp inventories from the late sixteenth century published by Denucé in 1932, to the effect that "a minority of collectors were concerned with the authorship of the works in their possession, but [...] all were interested in the subjects represented." This was no longer true after the middle of the next century. Montias (1982, p. 227) notes a significant rise in the rate of attribution in Delft inventories, for the 1640s through the 1660s; and Loughman (1992, Table 1, p. 46) finds something similar for Dordrecht, starting in the 1650s and continuing into the 1690s. The Musson-Fourmenois firm's sales records for Antwerp reveal an even more dramatic rise in attribution, also starting in the 1650s.

Reversals of role, including originals playing the part of copies, were common in the visual culture of the sixteenth century, and indicate that long before the pressures we have drawn attention to were widely felt, notions of inventorship and authorship were beginning to complement older factors adding to value. Though authorship and inventorship were sporadically acknowledged even in the fifteenth century – think of Jan Van Eyck or Rogier van der Weyden – the more usual elements adding value to the costs attributable to size, complexity and the time put in by an artist, were the sacredness of the subject (a holy icon) and materials costs (expensive pigments such as ultramarine; oil painting on oak panel versus tempera on linen). During the sixteenth century inventorship and authorship were progressively added to the older factors, and sometimes fused with them to make new combinations. One such is subject-based inventorship, to be examined in the next paragraph. In fact a phenomenon like phantom copying, painting "in the style of," or even forging, can only gain popularity in an environment where art is becoming more individualized or regarded as embodying invention; in other words, where invention and authorship are considered important and valued. The question still to be clearly formulated was, what relative weight should be assigned these various factors?

When we encounter a practice such as the copying, paraphrasing, and even forging on a large scale of, say, Bosch or Metsys (who died, respectively, in 1516 and 1530), it is clear that a section of the audience is placing more weight on recognizable, often subject-related inventorship, for their attributions, at the expense of other criteria. Jeffrey Muller (1989b, p. 142), commenting on the phenomenon of fraudulent Boschian originals, quotes Felipe de Guevara to this effect. De Guevara (1788, pp. 41-44) noted that copyists only imitated superficial elements of Bosch's style, without understanding the context of Boschian subject matter. But Guevara's own notion of authorship, as Muller points out, was defined purely in terms of invention, ignoring handling as an element defining authenticity. Not only, we infer, were the criteria for attribution not settled, but the fact that Bosch's copyists were able to take advantage of a hybrid standard, what we have labelled subject-based inventorship, suggests that nor was there a fixed terminology for defining the factors which contributed to value.

De Guevara thought in terms of Bosch originals and imitations, falsely inscribed. More than likely, however, among the so-called imitations were many originals, masquerading as copies. Part of the incentive to make such phantom copies, to be sure, was that it was less risky for a beginning or aspiring artist to work in the idiom of an already famous master, than to insist on working in a style of his or her own. But the phenomenon of phantom copying involves more than this. It also involves laying claim to a larger-than-actual range of copyable originals. This enhances the asset value of the original stock by adding novelty to established brand appeal.

Phantom copying works for paintings or prints. Indeed, the subterfuge can be carried out with even greater ease in the case of prints, where an explicit acknowledgement of inventorship can be added to a plate even though no corresponding original ever existed. Van Mander (1994, vol. 1, fol. 218 verso, pp. 132-133) mentions an illegitimate son of the famous Pieter Coecke, by name Pauwels van Aelst, whose own work was less notable than his talent for copying after the work of Jan Gossaert. It would have been a short step for Van Aelst to have created originals in the manner of Gossaert. The successful publisher and print maker, Hieronymous Cock (see Riggs (1971), Gibson (1978)) is widely suspected of having taken that step. Cock, as we shall illustrate in a moment, made use of attribution and name recognition, without necessarily observing niceties such as whether inventions for which he gave credit had ever been made.

Pieter I Brueghel is one who, in his late twenties and early thirties, took the route of producing designs which were in the style of a more famous artist, Hieronymus Bosch. This is true, for example of the designs for prints such as *Big Fish eat Little Fish* (1556), *Allegory of the Seven Deadly Sins* (1556-57), *Elck* (1558), *The Alchemist* (1558), and *Allegory of the Seven Virtues* (1559) (see Gibson (1977), pp. 44-64)). Moreover, the first of these, the *Big Fish eat Little Fish*, was taken by others and put through various states and altered copies which suggest consciously commercial, even political strategies, exploiting a public taste for attribution with respect to particular authors, without much respect for true proprietorship. When Brueghel made his drawing of the *Big Fish eat Little Fish*, only his name and the date were written in the lower righthand corner. No reference to Bosch was on the sheet.[8] In the first state engraved by Pieter van der Heyden for Cock, however, the inscription "Hieronijmus. Bos. inventor" appears above Van

[8]216 × 302 mm, pen and grey-black ink on spotted paper; signed and dated below right: "1556 Breughel." Vienna, Albertina, inv. no. 7875. On this see Gibson (1977, pp. 44-45) and Marijnissen (1988, pp. 81-82).

der Heyden's monogram in the lower left corner of the print. At lower right there is a reference to Cock and the date 1557; but Brueghel's name, initially on the Vienna drawing, has quite disappeared.[9]

There has been much speculation as to what occasioned these changes, a good deal of it based on the assumption that some elements of the composition were borrowed from a lost work by Bosch (see Riggs (1971, p. 322)). But perhaps Brueghel simply produced a Boschian composition, a phantom copy, that Cock decided to sell as a Bosch invention. It cannot be shown that a Bosch original never existed, but the subsequent history of the print certainly suggests a fairly free prevailing attitude towards attribution. When, in 1619, a reworked copy in mirror image of *Big Fish* was published in The Hague by Hendrick Hondius, "H. Bos inv." was still mentioned at lower left.[10] But in subsequent states (E-F) of Hondius' plate, published by Claes Jansz. Visscher somewhat later in Amsterdam, Bosch's name had disappeared and "P. Bruegel inven." was now engraved over traces of the date 1619 (Van Bastelaer (1992, p. 192)). As one might expect, this change occurred in a period when Bosch was no longer in high demand. Bosch had been overshadowed by a thriving cottage industry in Brueghel copies, phantom copies, variations, and imitations, originating from Antwerp, where these were produced and marketed with focussed energy by the Brueghel family (see exh. cat. on the Brueghel dynasty (1980)).

This seventeenth century "restoration" of Brueghel's inventorship may have been commercially motivated. Yet it should also be viewed against the background of fifteenth and sixteenth century ambiguity about attributions, which clashed with a growing tendency to ascribe value to a signature. Albrecht Dürer was involved in several lawsuits against engravers who were pirating his compositions, among which one of 7 February, 1506 against

[9]229 × 296 mm. This version, according to Van Bastelaer, is state A (one of three States A-B-C of the original plate). Lebeer (1969, p. 59) suggests that Bosch's name was added after the plate was completed since it is incised over already existing hatchings.

[10]Unlike the three states (A-B-C) of the original plate, mentioned in note 9, this state is the second of the copied plate of a series of six (States A-F). Van Bastelaer mentions a first state with "Hh [Hendrick Hondius] excud." and "H. Bos. inv.", but Lebeer doubts the existence of this first state. On the second (?) state there appears "Hh excud." and "H. Bos. inv.". The third and fourth states had by this time become political broadsheets, for which Hondius received 24 guilders from the States General. They targetted the pro-Remonstrant faction of Johan van Oldenbarnevelt, who was executed on 13 May 1619 at the insistence of stadtholder Maurits of Orange.

Marcantonio Raimondi in Venice and one in 1512 against a foreigner who sold prints in Nuremburg with a forged Dürer monogram (Koerner (1993, p. 209)). In the latter instance the notion attributability via monogram, inscription or signature is crucial, since the crime of the forger was not in copying the composition, but Dürer's "mark," a legal entity deriving its importance from mercantile practice.[11] Though, as we have seen, notions of attributability and reputation existed at this time, the issues of spiritual property and copyright had barely begun to be confronted (Bowker (1912, pp. 10-20)).

Attribution itself is applied differently according to context; for it reflects shifting attitudes toward collecting, invention, as to whether an atelier piece can count as an original, and so on. One of the central themes in art theoretical writings over the centuries is the struggle with naming, and always central seems to be: who is doing the attributing and for whom? In the seventeenth century there appeared a more differentiated buying public, and not all who wanted to own paintings brought to their selection of works the presumptions and learning of a classical education (Miedema (1995, pp. 106 et sq.)). This led, paradoxically, to an increased demand for attributed works (see note 7 above). But attribution for some of the new collectors meant that value could be attached to a painting (or a print) based on the reputation of its creator; that has been the thrust of the preceding discussion.

A single image, even if it is not an artist's best work, can share in the value of his or her work as a whole. Without an author's name attached, a painting or a print stands alone and must be judged by its merits, a notion which makes practical sense only for particular valuing groups who share a common knowledge of paintings, as well as a common terminology and ranking of works by genre and according to technical standards and art theoretical ideals. The applicability of such judgements will tend to be narrower than the judgements of the market, to which all groups must submit if they wish to transact in paintings. An illustration of this comes in the form of a letter of

[11] Dürer's own notion of spiritual property and invention is revealed in the Latin colophon printed on the final leaf of the 1511 complete editions of his *Life of the Virgin, Large Passion*, and *Small Passion*: "Beware, you envious thieves of the work and invention (*laboris et ingenii*) of others, keep your thoughtless hands from these works of ours. We have received a privilege from the famous emperor of Rome, Maximilian, that no one shall dare to print these works in spurious forms, nor sell such prints within the boundaries of the empire..." (quoted from Koerner (1993, p. 213)).

1671 from Musson's erstwhile angry client De Meulenare. Now penitent, he states that he was wrong earlier to have attacked Musson's attributions. He was satisfied that he had bought true originals and had even found a buyer for the two Rubens sketches; however, to be certain of getting a satisfactory price he would be obliged if Musson would supply him with a certificate of authenticity (Denucé (1949, p. 380)). De Meulenare's vacillation between the opinions of connoisseur and dealer is, after all, secondary; his unchanging standard was the market.

The importance to market value of attribution and reputation also helps explain why patent (copyright) privileges were sought by artists who felt they had some claim to distinctive merit. Rubens attempted to obtain general privileges in all the countries where prints after his work might be sold. Dürer, a century earlier, was one of the very first to exercise such privileges but, as his lawsuits suggest, his role was also part of a complex and evolving interpretation in the sixteenth century of notions of original, copy, protection, attribution and the value of invention (see Hughes (1990, esp. pp. 41-43)). Recall that one of his complaints was about the pirating of his monogram (as distinct from his composition); yet his personal general warning to would-be copyists (see note 11 above) was: "hands off my labor and invention." Was invention valued, then, or was it not? Yes, in a sense,[12] but in a consistent economic manner, no. These things took on a sharper cast only in the seventeenth century, with the growth of an extensive market.

2.4 Creative differentiation, and originals as capital

Prints, as we have seen, created wonderful opportunities for blurring origins. In some ways too division of labour served similar purposes. Where the

[12]Binksi (1992, pp. 21-22) notes that in products such as stained glass and tapestries, the role of the designer – in practice, the artist – had been recognized and accorded special (intellectual) standing, by the late fourteenth century. But the first market valuation of invention, it seems, may have occurred in print production; as certain collectors began to value inventive nuances, which engravings could record in greater intricacy than a drawing of the same size, so artists began to see a need to assert ownership of their designs (Landau and Parshall (1994, pp. 297, 299, 322)). Landau and Parshall mention an application for privileges in Venice, in 1504, in which the "labor of invention" was used as an argument (p. 300). Pirating could not be prevented by privileges but, as publishers began to assert control over artists' blocks and plates, privileges, monograms and even re-engraving (as a counter assertion of ownership) all became more common.

tasks of design and execution were separated, individuality of style and touch could be compromised. Sixteenth century prints, it is well known, often contained a distinction between *invenit* and *fecit* or *sculpsit*, roughly, between the one whose idea is shown and the one who actually engraved the plate. This artist-engraver relationship, the division of labour between the one who designs and orders the composition (*inventor*) and the one who engraves it (*sculptor*), is generally thought to have been of Italian origin, adopted in the Netherlands in the mid-sixteenth century.[13] By then, certainly, the older practice of the *peintre-graveur* à la Lucas van Leyden or Dürer, both of whom designed, executed, and signed much of their own graphic work, seems to have been replaced by a division between professional designers and professional engravers. The roles were less clearly separated for cheaper woodcuts. Dürer, for example, generally made no distinction between woodcuts executed by others according to his design and those completed by his own hand (Hughes (1990, p. 42)), though nor is there any evidence that he or any other painter or woodcut designer ever undertook the duties normally performed by a professional *Formenschneider* (Hutchison (1990, p. 58)).

Ironically, in the production of paintings, workshop practice probably helped foster recognizability and hence attributability. Division of labour could cause friction between assistants and master, by requiring that individual freedom submit to the patterns necessary for an audience to be able to associate a particular work with a master's name or workshop; but such tensions may also have led masters to adopt clearer means of identification. These include distinctive finishing touch and handling, as well as particular subject matter. The many versions of a particular composition, such as the *Butcher's Stall* from the atelier of Pieter Aertsen,would suggest that subject-based inventorship was a viable strategy in the middle of the sixteenth century.[14] For a known, desired master, the commercial advantage

[13]Silver (1993, pp. 2-3) gives Maarten van Heemskerck credit for propagating this division of labor in the Netherlands, after his visit to Rome in 1532-36, where he became thoroughly familiar with the creative and marketing possibilities of the Raphael-Marcantonio Raimondi artist-engraver relationship. For an invaluable contribution to the history of early print-making practices, see Landau and Parshall (1994).

[14]For Aertsen, see Moxey (1974), Craig (1982), Kloek (1989) and Kavaler (1989). Charlotte Houghton is preparing a dissertation (Duke University: Van Miegroet) employing a new conceptual frame for interpreting the *Butcher's Stall* in its respective versions, along with their social and political implications and subsequent reception.

from simplifying identification, in the midst of a still-prevailing confusion about originals and copies, is evident. Presenting collaborative works and atelier copies as original work by one master would increase the number of marketable "originals" of the desired sort. Masters also added marks and signatures, signifying origin as well as authenticating the work. Yet leading workshops may not have favored over-zealous signing, especially once – notably in the seventeenth century – buyers began making legal problems over atelier products presented as originals. Other, less legally binding means of authentication could be employed, including handling. Rubens systematically avoided signing the works from his very productive atelier, while at the same time adopting a very recognizable range of subjects, style and finishing touch. Withholding his signature may have been less a sign of modesty than a preemptive measure to avoid legal complications.

Rubens had a great deal to say about originality and the value of invention, though he stressed somewhat different aspects in different contexts (Magurn (1955, pp. 61-62, 76, 77)). His comments help us make connections between humanist ideals of painting and assigning value to invention in the marketplace. To see the marketplace at work, however, we must observe how undistinguished artists sought to create a niche for themselves, and how dealers and traders in paintings approached originals.

Throughout the fifteenth and sixteenth centuries there was what Alpers and Baxandall (1994, p. 21) have called a "prevalence of repetition." Their context is Italy, but the expression applies more widely. Subjects over a wide geographical area were quite standard, and originals, though they were the work of masters, represented in many cases only trivial reworkings of borrowed ideas and compositions. In such paintings, the price reflected size, materials, and the time and skill of the painter(s) (Wackernagel (1981, pp. 338-339), Thomas (1995, p. 182)). But for many artists too, the very givenness of the subject and model treatments posed a challenge to create a clearly differentiated version. Where an original, though loosely based on previous compositions, had a character of its own, value could be ascribed separately to the creativity displayed by the artist.

We find precisely this sort of acknowledgement in the sales records and correspondence of the business of Matthijs Musson and his wife Maria Fourmenois.[15] This is true even in the improbable case of what might be called

[15]Musson was, strictly speaking, the art dealer. From the time of his marriage to Maria

formulaic paintings, or works done according to a conventional recipe. These were mostly devotional in purpose and drew on established subjects and treatments. They were frequently ordered as series or sets, standardized by subject, type of handling, and often size: twelve Passion of our Lord, for example; or six Life of Moses; eighteen devotional landscapes with saints; and so on. These were unlikely candidates for displays of creativity. What we see happening, however, under the influence of competitive pressures, is fairly run of the mill artists, not employed in the first instance for their distinctive style, producing works which bear their mark in recognizable degree.

This manifested itself in two ways. First, from mid-century there is a dramatic rise in the practice of naming artists – even these artists. This did not necessarily mean signature; it certainly did mean that the initial buyer knew who had authored a particular piece. Preliminary counts, subject to revision, suggest that the order of change was from fewer than ten percent of works handled by the Musson-Fourmenois firm being attributed in the 1640s and 1650s, to somewhere closer to seventy percent in the 1670s. Less dramatic, and perhaps less sustained rises in the rate of attribution have been recorded for Delft, 1640s through the 1660s, and Dordrecht, 1650s through the 1690s (see note 7 above). These may not represent the same phenomenon; in any event, work in progress shows that from Musson's stable of artists there appears to have come a claim, supported by the dealer himself, for recognition, and for the rewards of distinctiveness, either in the form of more regular employment, or higher prices for their work, or both. The nature of this distinctiveness can be seen too in letters sent to Musson by dealers ordering from him. This is the second of two ways in which recognizability showed itself. Musson's client dealers can be observed favoring a particular artist whose work has sold readily, and stopping orders for others whose work has shown itself to be less vendible. Moreover, these clients – Picard especially – issued instructions suggesting ways in which their preferred artists might

Fourmenois in 1647, however, the business was noticeably shaped and in other ways influenced by her. Maria also kept the books and did most of Musson's correspondence, as well as facilitating a new partnership in the commissioning and, especially, shipment abroad of paintings with Cornelis de Baillieur, her brother-in-law by her previous marriage. So far we have mentioned mostly details involving Musson in particular, and it is appropriate to refer to him as the art dealer; nonetheless, the business was joint and, where the firm is involved rather than particular activities of Matthijs, we shall speak of the Musson-Fourmenois business.

render their productions still more acceptable.

Differentiation of product among artists producing works that have the character of "derivatives" involves inventiveness rather than invention, and inventiveness was certainly not new in the seventeenth century; but the fact that it seems to have been consciously pursued, and from an economic motive, makes it at least distant kin to acknowledged and rewarded invention.[16] When we see dealers and traders in art in the seventeenth century treating "true" originals as income-generating assets, however, it seems undeniably clear that we have to do with a separate economic entity, invention.

We have referred already to Musson's practice of making copies of originals, and copies of copies. He tends not to reflect openly on why he does this. As we have noted elsewhere, however (De Marchi and Van Miegroet (1994, pp. 452-53)), the brothers Goetkint and the merchant Christostomus Van Immerseel, as early as the 1620s and 30s, were discussing originals they had managed to acquire in terms of the paintings serving as models for limited "reproduction." Van Immerseel, for example, in 1634, wrote to his wife in Seville that he had obtained some Jan II Brueghel originals. Since they were "well painted," he told her, he would keep them to have them copied: "The principals will serve here as a shoemaker's last..." (Antwerp Stadsarchief, Insolvente Boedelkamer, IB 204, letter dated 11 October 1634). This, along with the differentiation later practiced by painters employed at first only to produce standardized works, is compelling evidence that invention had begun to be recognized as a distinct economic entity.

We turn now to the actual measurement of the value of invention. That there are cases available at all from which to take the measurement we want supports the idea that there had emerged a separate economic status for invention; that the measurements vary within the same narrow range in cases spanning the years 1618 to 1663 is consistent with our impression that invention had also acquired a relatively stable meaning.[17] Before presenting

[16]Creative differentiation, as we noted earlier, is the display of inventiveness, rather than invention; nonetheless, it is relevant in this instance. Our concern is with the price difference between originals and copies. Mostly we focus on the reason for there being a premium paid for originals, but in the case of creative differentiation affecting copies, this narrows the price difference, albeit from below, and thus forms part of our subject.

[17]The cases presented in Table 2 below fall within the period 1626 to 1636, but Rubens' dealings with Carleton in 1618 also yield a case, to be discussed presently, while an ex-

and interpreting the cases, however, it may be useful to summarize in tabular form some of the main factors causing value to be added to size and the artist's time over the early modern period. The factors indicated within each century are meant to suggest a growing sense of complexity and ongoing change, nothing more (see Miedema (1993)). Occasional exploitation of attribution, and special rewards for creative origination, we acknowledge, are to be found well before the seventeenth century. The difference seems to be that in that century concerns with attribution, and invention, and what they added to value became both widely shared and widely applied in transactions affecting paintings. The market, its categories, and its rationale for valuation, began to affect paintings and their authors at every level of quality.[18]

At the risk of over-simplification, then, in the fifteenth century the added worth of a painting still derived largely from subject and materials, not radically different from what popular criticism and valuation in antiquity drew on. Three major criteria affected the value of a work of art in antiquity: realism, miraculous qualities, and costliness.[19] Throughout the sixteenth century authorship and invention were on occasion exploited, but they neither displaced the older criteria nor was their role considered in isolation, and measured. Invention, in the seventeenth century, appears to have been both more widely acknowledged and more explicitly treated as an economic entity, as evidenced by creative differentiation by artists for economic reasons, a fairly robust price difference between originals and copies that were the work of the same master, and dealers treating originals as a capital asset.

---

tended set of cases, not shown here, includes an instance in which Abraham Willemsen, in 1663, both painted an original and made a copy of it himself.

[18]As Chris Wood put it in criticism of a more bland earlier version of the table, these concerns "got associated with ever more ordinary paintings and painters," not just "great" art and artists.

[19]Criticism in antiquity was not expressed as a coherent theory any more than was the case in the fifteenth century. However, realism appears to have meant that the boundaries between art and life were broken down, as the often-quoted story of Zuexis and Parrhasius, and the triumph of trompe l'oeil – paintings not only looking very real, but becoming reality – amply demonstrates. "Miraculous" included technical properties. See Pollitt (1974, pp. 63-66).

Table 1
Factors Causing Value to be Added to Size and Time
in Netherlandish Paintings

15th century	16th century	17th century
		invention
		naming at sale
	attribution/reputation	attribution/reputation
	subject-based inventorship	subject-based inventorship
subject	subject	subject
materials	materials	materials

3 The price ratio of originals to copies: some evidence from the period 1626 to 1674

In this section we address the question, what was the relation between the price of an original and a copy, as determined by producers in the first instance, and in secondary (resale) markets at some later point in time?

Table 2 summarizes a basic set of observations. Since a number of causal factors could be involved in any one observed ratio – size or support difference between original and copy, differential talent of the artists (unless they were one and the same), scarcity and reputation, if one of the artists is dead – we have looked for cases for which as much as possible is known about the product and the circumstances of its production and/or sale. The main information lacking is size, and support and medium. For a small sub-set, however, we can more or less control for size; as to support and medium, where nothing special is said, we assume there is in fact no difference between original and copy. Table 2 draws on extracts from the diary of Jan II Brueghel, and pertinent correspondence (Denucé (1934), Ertz (1979)). An Appendix presents the cases in greater detail. A few additional cases from Brueghel's workshop (not presented here) extend the time period covered to the 1650s, whereas Table 2 covers just a ten-year period, 1626 to 1636. A comparison set involving mostly different artists, and extending the time period to 1674, is discussed below. Both the enlarged set for the Brueghel workshop and the comparison set are available on request.

Table 2
Originals and Copies, Antwerp 1626-1636

Case	Original	Copy	Offer/sale of original to	copy to	Price ratio original/copy
1.	Jan II + van Balen	Jan II + van Balen	Dealer	Dealer	2.1 (sale)
2.	Jan II + van Balen	?	No sale	?	4.0 (est.)
3.	Jan II Brueghel	?	Dealer	?	2.5 (sale)
4.	Jan II + van Balen	?	Collector	Artist	3.3 (sale)
5.	Jan II Brueghel	Jan II Brueghel	Dealer	Dealer	3.0 (sale)
6.	Jan II Brueghel	Assistants	Collector	*Liefhebber?*	2.7 (sale)
7.	Jan II + Snayers(sic)	Jan II + assistants	?	?	2.4
8.	Jan I + Rubens	Jan II Brueghel	No sale	Dealer	2.7 (est.)
9.	Frans Francken	Frans Francken	Dealer	Dealer	2.6 (sale)
10.	Jan II Brueghel	Assistants	Dealer	Dealer	1.9 (sale)
11a.	Jan I + Rubens	Jan II Brueghel	No sale	Dealer	2.0
11b.	Jan I + Rubens	Assistants	No sale	Dealer	4.0 (offer)
12a.	Jan I + Rubens	Jan II Brueghel	Collector	Dealer	3.2 (sale)
12b.	Jan I + Rubens	Assistants	No sale	Dealer	6.4 (offer)
13.	?+ Rubens	Jan II Brueghel	Dealer	Dealer	2.5 (est.)
14.	A. Staelbempt	A. Staelbempt	Dealer	Dealer	2.0 (sale)
15.	S. de Vos	S. de Vos	Dealer	Dealer	2.0 (sale)

Summary statistics and other features

1. The mean price ratio for these seventeen observations is 2.9 to 1 (standard deviation 1.11). Adding four fairly secure cases from our enlarged set reduces the mean a little, to 2.8 (standard deviation: 1.15).
2. We have also calculated the average price ratio using three sets of assumptions which select for slightly different sub-sets of cases. None of the changes significantly affects the mean ratio.
(i) In three instances (cases 4, 6, 12a) the sales price of the original was almost certainly raised by the fact that the sale was to a known collector of stature. Of actual sales these three produced the highest price ratios, with the single exception of (5), which involved Jan II Brueghel's main accomplishment, the making of copies after his father's well-known *Five Senses* (Prado). Excluding the former three cases, the average is 2.86 to 1 (N = 14).
(ii) In two other cases (2, 8) no sale occurred of the original, the price recorded being only an estimate by Jan II Brueghel. Excluding these cases, but retaining those with a sale to a known collector, we are left with fifteen observations, for a mean of 2.84 to 1.

(iii) If we exclude both the no-sale-of-original and sale-to-known-collector cases, the average for the remaining twelve cases is 2.78 to 1.
3. Sundry features of the cases are worth noting, bearing in mind our basic purpose, to understand the value added by invention.
(i) Jan II Brueghel set his price as a copyist at exactly two times that of his assistants (cases 11, 12).
(ii) Jan II Brueghel also set his own charge for making a copy well below the price of an original, whether by his own hand or that of another, or combination of other, masters (cases 5, 8, 11a, 12a, 13).
(iii) Where the original is by one or more masters, and the copy by the same master or combination of masters (cases 1, 5, 9, 14, 15), the ratio is 2.34 to 1. These cases generate exactly what we are trying isolate, the amount subtracted from the value set on the original when it is reproduced in the form of a copy. As a percentage share of the value of the original, this loss is: (price of original - price of copy)/price of original $\times$ 100.
4. There are three cases where we can be reasonably confident that size difference between original and copy was not a factor (8, 9, 10). The ratio for these cases alone averages 2.4 to 1.

In sum, though the number of cases is few, we find that, controlling for size where possible, and not excluding the influence of sale to a collector, which biases upwards the sales price of the original, the price ratio varies mostly between two and three to one.

Comparison with other observations

How do the relative prices of originals and copies in our basic set of observations compare with the results of other, similar inquiries? First, still for the Southern Netherlands, we constructed our own comparison set. A search of the Musson-Fourmenois business records yielded 21 additional cases, for the period 1654 to 1674 (but mostly 1660s), and extended the range of artists to include eight not initially covered. The mean was slightly higher, 3.4 to 1. Only one of the new cases definitely involved the same artist (Abraham Willemsen) making original and copy, and the ratio in that instance was three to one. Most of the copyists in the new set were not named. Some, it seems likely, were assistants in the workshop of Frans Snyders, worked under his supervision and, possibly, had their work touched up by him. This set of circumstances comprises eight of the twenty one new cases, and for these the ratios are 3.0 or 2.5 to 1, so within the range for the earlier set. The remaining cases, which push the average ratio up, mostly involved unnamed copyists, and it seems almost certain in several cases that the copy was noticeably smaller than the original. In three instances where the copyist is named it is an artist who, we know with some assurance, stood lower in the hierarchy of day rate wage equivalents than the creator of the original.[20] Thus there is a strong presumption that quality and size differences account for much of the higher average.

Moving to the Dutch Republic, we can compare our results with information drawn from three sources: inventories, a very large public sale, and a lottery. Montias (1988, p. 253) reports the average prices of 278 originals and 20 copies by unknown painters after named masters, from Amsterdam inventories of the period 1630-49. The price ratio, originals to copies, is 2.4 to 1. Bredius recorded a large public sale which took place in The Hague in 1647; it involved some 850 paintings, including 68 copies after designated artists. The ratio for this record is 2.25 to 1 (summary report in Montias (1990, p. 69)). In the same range is the price list of a lottery held in Wijk bij Duurstede in 1649. This list yields a ratio of 2.2 to 1, for six instances (Kosse (1992, pp. 110-114)).

The data from the Republic are more anonymous than the cases we have collected for Antwerp. On average, nonetheless, they seem to fall squarely within the range we find for both our basic and the extended sets from Antwerp. The exact range is not of great significance, and further research will no doubt modify our results. It is of some interest that the premium paid for originals seems frequently to have been much less in the first half of the seventeenth century than we know it today, though if we add to invention other factors such as scarcity, relative talent, reputation and size, the price ratio then too could climb quite high.[21] The particular finding on which we

[20]Work is proceeding on the construction of a table of day rate equivalents for as many as possible of the artists who worked for Musson.

[21]Three examples of well known originals by Rubens illustrate this: *The Rainbow* (several versions, possibly closest, that in the Hermitage, 81 × 129 cm); *Meleager and Atalanta* ("small" version, Alte Pinakothek, Munich, 199 × 153 cm); *Adoration of the Three Kings (Magi)* (version in Musée des Beaux Arts, Brussels, 384 × 280 cm). In 1654 Musson was trying to sell *The Rainbow* for *f*700. Three years earlier a copy had been made by Abraham Willemsen, one of the artists who worked frequently on commission for Musson. Willemsen's copy was on a large copper plate, probably not much smaller than the version of the original now in the Hermitage; but it cost a mere *f*24 (Denucé (1949, pp. 116,

do place some weight is the price ratio when both original and copy are done by the same master(s). The ratio here, admittedly for just six cases – the five from Table 2, plus one from the extended set – averages 2.45 to 1, and the range is from two to three. A seventh instance is supplied by Rubens' own *Last Judgement*, the touched up version of which he wanted to sell to Carleton. The original had sold for *f*3,500, the copy was offered for *f*1200, a ratio of 2.9 to 1. This raises the average to 2.5 to 1. That all the cases we have found seem to fall within a quite narrow range might support the idea that "invention" had acquired, by the early seventeenth century, a certain stability of weight among the factors contributing to value.

To gain a clearer sense of how much was contributed by invention, take the price of an original to be 1. Some fraction of this value is lost in the copy, where invention is not present. We found the average price ratio for all those cases where original and copy were done by the same master to be 2.5 to 1 (= 1 to 0.4); thus 60 percent of the value is lost, on average, in moving from original to copy. This 60 percent is the average contribution of invention to the value of an original.

4 The wages of skill, status, and invention

Finally, we return to an earlier proposition, that invention had to receive its recognition within the guild structure, and within its associated socio-economic hierarchies, if conflict was to be avoided. The guild in effect made it the province of masters to create originals, and any tacit or open (i.e., market)

136)). Musson also tried to sell (a larger version of) the *Meleager and Atalanta*, offering it to Stadtholder Frederick Hendrik of the Republic in 1645 for *f*1,000. This may be the same as a "life size" version, sold for *f*800 from the estate of Frans Snyders. A copy was made, "after Rubens," in 1661, by Cornelis de Baillieur, Musson's relative by marriage and a trading partner as well as a modestly talented artist, for *f*21. Size was a factor here, but reputation, scarcity and talent also contributed to the price difference (Denucé (1949, pp. 41, 189, 248)). Finally, there was a *Three Kings*, also offered by Musson to Frederick Hendrik in 1645 – another instance of a work "completely over painted by Rubens and as good as the original" – for *f*500 (Denucé (1949, p. 41)). Many copies are recorded in the Musson-Fourmenois books. De Baillieur made two, in 1660 and 1661, for *f*34 and *f*21. Size was an important factor here; the original was probably something like eight or nine times the size of the copies. But talent also counted heavily: another copy, made by a better artist than De Baillieur, dates from 1652; the artist, Victor Wolfvoet, charged *f*54 (Denucé (1949, p. 112)).

value placed on invention had to be consonant with conventional differences in pay between masters and assistants. Thus we might expect that the price ratio between an original and a copy made by the same master, would be roughly comparable to the ratio between the daily wage rate equivalent of a master and the day rates paid to his or her assistants. Furthermore, if the claim of master artists to be recognized for the theoretical component of their craft – their design and invention skills – was ratified by the market, we would expect that the same, or similar, differences would be observed between the day wage equivalent of master artists and the rates paid in other skilled (but "a-theoretical") crafts. We did not expressly set out to investigate these hypotheses, and have only a few pertinent observations to offer; they are presented as a way of stimulating further discussion on the issues involved.

Assistants, like masters, were not all of the same experience and skill, and were paid various rates. Jan II Brueghel paid some of his at the rate of 24 and 25 *stuivers* a day (1.2 and 1.25 guilders), some at 1.8 guilders, and some even at 2.4 and 3.0 guilders (Denucé (1934, pp. 82, 83, 146)). The range, then, was 1.2 guilders to 3.0 guilders. Masters, unlike assistants, were not often paid by the day, but Chrisostomus Van Immerseel reckoned, in one back-of-the-envelope calculation, that Brueghel's services could be had for a day rate equivalent of 5 or 6 guilders (Denucé (1934, p. 93)). We have a few indications of day rates for other artists less highly regarded than Brueghel. These yield a range of rates for masters, which we can compare with the range for (Brueghel's) assistants:

Justus Daneels (1657)	*f*4 (Van der Stighelen (1989, p. 305))
one Gaspar de Wit (1674)	*f*4 (Duverger (1969, p. 190))
Van Neeck, as yet unidentified (1665)	*f*3 to 4 (Duverger (1969, p. 176))
Abraham Snellinck (1657)	*f*3 (Van der Stighelen (1989, p. 305))
Mattheus Van de Put (1665)	*f*3 (Duverger (1969, p. 176))
De Bruyn, as yet unidentified (1665)	*f*2.4 (Duverger (1969, p. 176))

Adding in Brueghel, the range for masters, from this set of observations, varies from 2.4 guilders to 6.0 guilders (allowing Brueghel the higher rate estimated by Van Immerseel). Comparing the two ranges, the ratio of daily rates for masters relative to assistants, is 2 to 1. That happens to be, as noted above, exactly the rate charged by Brueghel, compared with his own assistants, when he himself acted as copyist. This exact equivalence probably means little;[22] moreover, the important comparison is between the ratio of masters' to assistants' rates, on the one hand, and the average ratio for the price of an original and a copy done by the same master(s), on the other. The latter, recall, is 2.5 to 1. Given that the masters for whom we have day rates were by no means the very best – the difference with assistants would surely be greater than 2 to 1 for top masters – the ratio of masters' to assistants' rates is possibly on the low side, but of the right order of magnitude.

Turning to other crafts, the rate received by Breughel's lowest paid assistant was the same as the daily wage in Antwerp of a master carpenter or an interior refurbisher: 24 *stuivers*, or 1.2 guilders for all three.[23] We also have an observation from Antwerp on the day rate received by a registered master cabinet maker, a more skilled trade; in 1676 Matthijs Musson paid 1.6 guilders a day (Duverger (1969, p. 195)). From this rather skimpy set of observations, the range for less theoretical crafts than artist emerges as 1.2 to 1.6 guilders per day. The range among artists themselves, recall, was 2.4 to 6.0 guilders per day. At the lower end, then, a ratio of 2 to 1 (artists to other skilled crafts) might have prevailed; at the upper end, however, there was apparently a larger difference (and we would expect it to be even more for top masters). Our measure of the payment for invention, averaging 2.5 to 1, falls within the range of artists' rewards compared with those enjoyed in skilled but a-theoretical crafts. Since it is almost certain that those relative rewards were a well-established convention in different guild-regulated trades, a market payment for invention in the seventeenth century within the limits of that differential was probably, as we have suggested, in the nature of a new argument to help justify and perhaps sustain the conventional differential in an age of declining guild authority.

Do these results transfer to the Republic? Michael Montias (1990, p. 64) concluded, on the basis of his study of archival evidence from Delft, that master artists in the north may have earned "considerably more" than did skilled

---

[22]Binski (1992, p. 17) finds, however, in fragments of documents relating to the artists employed at Westminster Palace between 1290 and 1300, that the rate received by the master artist was also exactly two times that paid his assistants. Rubens, too, implied that something like 2 to 1 was a conventional differential (Magurn (1955, p. 76).

[23]Musson paid the decorators Carel de Kuster and Jan Hest for refurbishing a room with gold leather and curtains 24 *stuivers* per day each (Denucé (1949, p. 91)). The rate for a master carpenter in Antwerp varied little from 24 *stuivers* per day throughout the seventeenth century (De Vries (1982, esp. Table 1, p. 54)).

craftsmen. From information touching five artists in various locations in the north, and drawn from the seventeenth and the first half of the eighteenth centuries, plus assumptions about artists' costs and the average number of working days per month, Montias (1990, p. 66) felt he could specify the difference more precisely: "a typical workaday artist might have been able to earn above or between 2.2 to five times as much as a carpenter's wage [...] or 4 to 4.5 times the wage for a decorator (*faiencier*)." For carpenters at least, our tidbits of information from Antwerp approximate Montias' estimated range of differences rather closely.

5 Conclusion

We set out to account for the higher value ascribed to original paintings. Observations for Antwerp in the early to middle years of the seventeenth century show that originals often were valued at two to three times the copy, though differential talent between originating master and copyist, as well as differences in factors like size, and scarcity, could drive up the range. Our basic finding – a narrow range, in many cases not exceeding three to one – is in line with scattered sales and inventory data for the Republic. We made the supposition that the premium favoring originals was a payment for the labor of invention, and should be consonant with the relative status of masters and assistants. Our measure of the value contributed by invention to an original is the price difference between original and copy in instances where the two were made by the same master(s). This measurement turns out to approximate closely the differential rewards enjoyed by masters and assistants, and it is within the range of differences, in both north and south, for payments received by master artists as compared with other skilled but a-theoretical crafts. The value thus apparently placed on invention by the market fit, as it needed to, to avoid conflict, the guild-dominated context within which creative origination had to express itself. We argued separately that the acknowledgement of invention as an economic entity became widespread in the seventeenth century. Evidence for this comes from artists' efforts to differentiate their products; dealers' treatment of originals as capital; master artists' attempts to secure acknowledgement of the role of invention in their particular craft; and legal distinctions that began to appear between original and copy, as well as a distinction the market appears to have made between touch and invention.

Needless to say, our numerical results, and the interpretation we place on them, may be challenged by further research. A quietly expressed claim that is part of our interpretative framework is that we could not have drawn for earlier centuries even so tentative a set of conclusions as we have for the seventeenth century. Not only was the terminology original/copy more fluid, but it is not clear from observed practices that transactors in paintings (makers, dealers, buyers) thought in terms of a sharp distinction between the two. Confusion about the economic status of original was, moreover, deliberately maintained by the workshops of leading masters in the fifteenth and sixteenth centuries (and sometimes even later). As a result, evidence of how distinct components, including attribution, reputation, and invention, contribute to value, is not so obviously to be found. Focussed historical research for the earlier period may qualify this claim. A satisfactory analysis of the concepts of original and copy prior to the seventeenth century, however, seems likely to require careful examination of the process by which special creativity came to stand alone, as something that could, in Michael Baxandall's (1980, p. 117) phrase, be "bid for." Complementing such analysis must be a close examination of the records of dealers in the seventeenth century, since it is within the more pervasive scope of the market and in the sophisticated economic behaviors displayed there during that century that we should find more sharply defined notions of original, copy and the value of invention. Some of those behaviors have been touched on here; their careful elaboration is the next step in our own program.

6 References

Alpers, S. and M. Baxandall (1994), *Tiepolo and the Pictorial Intelligence*, New Haven: Yale University Press.

Bastelaer, R. (1992), *The Prints of Peter Bruegel the Elder. Catalogue Raisonné*, translated and revised by S.F. Gilchrist, San Francisco: Alan Wofsy Fine Arts.

Baxandall, M. (1980), *The Limewood Sculptors of Renaissance Germany*, New Haven: Yale University Press.

Benjamin, W. (1963), The work of art in the age of mechanical reproduction, in H. Arendt, ed. (1968), *Walter Benjamin. Illuminations*, New York: Harcourt, Brace.

Bille, C. (1961), *De Tempel der Kunst of het Kabinet van den Heer Braamcamp*, Amsterdam: De Bussy.

Binski, P. (1992), *Schilders*, Series Middeleeuwse Ambachtslieden, Kampen: J.H. Kok.

Bol, L.J. (1960), *The Bosschaert Dynasty. Painters of Flowers and Fruits*, Leigh-on-Sea: F. Lewis.

Bowker, R. (1912), *Copyright, its History and its Law*, Boston: Houghton Mifflin.

Bruegel. Une Dynastie de Peintres (1980), Exh. cat., Paleis voor Schone Kunsten, Brussels.

Craig, K.M. (1982), Pieter Aertsen and the meat stall, *Oud Holland*, 96, 1-15.

De Guevara, F. (1788), *Commenatrios de la Pintura que Escribio Don Felipe de Guevara*, Madrid: Don Geronimo Ortega, Hijos de Ibarra y campanie.

De Marchi, N. and P. Harrison (1994), Trading 'in the wind' and with guile. The troublesome matter of the short selling of shares in seventeenth century Holland, in N. De Marchi and M.S. Morgan, eds., Higgling. Transactors and their markets in the history of economics, *History of Political Economy*, 26, 47-65.

De Marchi, N. and H.J. Van Miegroet (1994), Art, value, and market practices in the Netherlands in the seventeenth century, *Art Bulletin*, 76, 451-64.

Denucé, J. (1932), *De Antwerpse "Konstkaners", Inventarissen van Kunstverzamelingen te Antwerpen in de 16e en 17e Eeuwen*, Antwerp: De Sikkel.

Denucé, J. (1934), *Brieven en Documenten Betreffende Jan Breughel I en II*, Antwerp: De Sikkel.

Denucé, J. (1949), *Na Peter Pauwel Rubens. Documenten uit den Kunsthandel te Antwerpen in de XVIIe Eeuw van Matthijs Musson*, Antwerp: De Sikkel.

De Vries, J. (1982), An inquiry into the behavior of wages in the Dutch Republic and the Southern Netherlands from 1500-1800, in M. Aymard, ed., *Dutch Capitalism and World Capitalism*, Cambridge: Cambridge University Press.

De Vries, J. and A. van der Woude (1995), *Nederland 1500-1815: de Eerste Ronde van Moderne Economische Groei*, Amsterdam: Balans.

Dudok van Heel, S.A.C. (1982), Het 'schildershuis' van Govert Flinck en de kunsthandel van Uylenburgh aan de Lauriergracht te Amsterdam, *Jaarboek Amstelodamum*, 74, 70-90.

Duverger, E. (1969), *Nieuwe Gegevens Betreffende de Kunsthandel van Matthijs Musson en Maria Fourmenois te Antwerpen tussen 1633 en 1681*, reprint of *Gentse Bijdragen tot de Kunstgeschiedenis en de Oudheidkunde*, 21 (1968), 5-273.

Ertz, K. (1979), *Jan Brueghel der Altere (1568-1625)*, Koln: DuMont Verlag.

Filipczak, Z.Z. (1987), *Picturing Art in Antwerp, 1550-1700*, Princeton: Princeton University Press.

Gibson, W.S. (1977), *Bruegel*, New York: Thames and Hudson.

Gibson, W.S. 1978), Some Flemish popular prints from Hieronymus Cock and his contemporaries, *Art Bulletin*, 60, 673-81.

Goldthwaite, R.A. (1993), *Wealth and the Demand for Art in Italy 1300-1600*, Baltimore: Johns Hopkins University Press.

Hughes, A. (1990), The cave and the stithy: artists' studios and intellectual property in early modern Europe, *Oxford Art Journal*, 13, 34-48.

Humfrey, P. (1995), *Painting in Renaissance Venice*, New Haven: Yale University Press.

Hutchison, J.C. (1990), *Albrecht Durer. A Biography*, Princeton: Princeton University Press.

Junius, F. (1638), *The Painting of the Ancients*, London: R. Hodgkinsonne; transl. of *De Pictura Veterum*, 1637.

Kavaler, E.M. (1989), Pieter Aertsen's meat stall. Diverse aspects of the market piece, *Nederlands Kunsthistorisch Jaarbock*, XL, 67-92.

Kemp, M. (1993), The 'super-artist' as genius: the sixteenth century view, in P. Murray, ed., *Genius. The History of an Idea*, Oxford: Blackwell.

Kloek, W. (1989), Pieter Aertsen en het probleem van het samenstellen van zijn oeuvre, *Nederlands Kunsthistorisch Jaarboek*, XL, 1-28.

Kosse, R. (1992), *Een Rare Lotereye. Het Verloten van Schilderijen in de Zeventiende Eeuw*, Ph.D. Dissertation, Rijksuniversiteit Utrecht.

Landau, M. and P. Parshall (1994), *The Renaissance Print, 1470-1550*, New Haven: Yale University Press.

Lebeer, L. (1969), *Catalogue Raisonné des Estampes de Bruegel l'Ancien*, Bruxelles: Bibliothèque Royale Albert I.

Levesque, C. (1994), *Journey through Landscape in Seventeenth Century Holland. The Haarlem Print Series and Dutch Identity*, University Park, PA: Pennsylvania State University Press.

Loughman, J. (1992), Een stad en haar kunstconsumptie: openbare en prive verzamelingen in Dordrecht, 1620-1719, in *De Zichtbaere Wereld. Schilderkunst uit de Gouden Eeuw in Holland's Oudste Stad*, Exh. cat., Zwolle: Waanders.

Magurn, R. (1955), *The Letters of Peter Paul Rubens*, Cambridge: Harvard University Press.

Mandeville, B. (1924 [1723]), A search into the nature of society, in F.B. Kaye, ed., *The Fable of the Bees: or, Private Vices, Publick Benefits*, Oxford: Clarendon Press.

Marijnissen, R.-H. (1988), *Bruegel*, Antwerp: Mercator Fonds.

Melion, W.S. (1991), *Shaping the Netherlandish Canon. Karel van Mander's Schilder-Boeck*, Chicago: University of Chicago Press.

Miedema, H. (1993), The appreciation of paintings around 1600, in *Dawn of the Golden Age*, Exh.cat., Rijksmuseum, Amsterdam.

Miedema, H. (1995), *Kunst* historisch, Leiden: Primavera.

Montias, J.M. (1982), *Artists and Artisans in Delft. A Socio-Economic Study of the Seventeenth Century*, Princeton: Princeton University Press.

Montias, J.M. (1988), Art dealers in the seventeenth century Netherlands, *Simiolus*, XVIII, 244-56.

Montias, J.M. (1990), Estimates of the number of Dutch master-painters, their earnings and their output in 1659, *Leidschrift*, 6, 59-74.

Moxey, K. (1974), *Pieter Aertsen, Joachim Beuckelaer and the Rise of Secular Painting in the Context of the Reformation*, Ph.D. Dissertation, University of Chicago.

Muller, J.M. (1989a), *Rubens: the Artist as Collector*, Princeton: Princeton University Press.

Muller, J.M. (1989b), Measures of authenticity: the detection of copies in the early literature on connoisseurship, in *Retaining the Original. Multiple Originals, Copies, and Reproductions*, Washington, D.C.: National Gallery of Art.

Nijstad, S. (1995), *De Kunsthandel*, Haastrecht/Baarn: Tableau Fine Arts Magazine/Tirion.

Obreen, F.D.C. (1880-81), Het Sint Lucas Gilde te Amsterdam, *Archief voor Nederlandsche Kunstgeschiedenis*, 3, 12-196.

Orenstein, N., H. Leeflang, G. Luijten and C. Schuckman (1993), Print publishers in the Netherlands, 1580-1620, in *Dawn of the Golden Age.*

Pollitt, J.J. (1974), *The Ancient View of Greek Art: Criticism, History, and Terminology*, New Haven: Yale University Press.

Un procès pour une vente de tableaux attribués à A. van Dyck (1868), *Annales de l'Académie d'Archéologie de Belgique*, 24, 561-606.

Riggs, T.A. (1971), *Hieronymus Cock (1510-1570): Printmaker and Publisher in Antwerp at the Sign of the Four Winds*, Ph.D. Dissertation, Yale University.

Rooses, M. and Ch. Ruelens, eds. (1887-1909), *Correspondance de Rubens et Documents Epistolaires concernant sa Vie et ses Oeuvres (Codex Diplomaticus Rubenianus)*, Antwerp: Veuve de Bakker.

Schwartz, G. (1993), Discounting quantum shifts in the perception of Dutch art, mimeo.

Silver, L. (1993), Graven images: reproductive engravings as visual models, in *Graven Images: The Rise of the Professional Printmakers in Antwerp and Haarlem, 1540-1640*, Exh. cat., Mary and Leigh Block Gallery, Chicago.

Thomas, A. (1995), *The Painter's Practice in Renaissance Tuscany*, Cambridge: Cambridge University Press.

Van der Stighelen, K. (1989), De (atelier-)bedrijvigheid van Andries Snellinck (1587-1653) en co, *Jaarboek Koninklijk Museum voor Schone Kunsten Antwerpen.*

Van Mander, K. (1604), *Den Grondt der Edel vrij Schilder-const*, Haarlem: Van Westbusch.

Van Mander, K. (1994 [1603-4]), *The Lives of the Illustrious Netherlandish and German Painters*, from the first edition of the *Schilder-boeck*, Doornspijk: Davaco.

Van Houdt, T. (1995), Money, time and labour. Leonardus Lessius and the ethics of lending and interest taking, *Ethical Perspectives*, 2, 11-27.

Wackernagel, M. (1981), *The World of the Florentine Renaissance Artist*, Princeton: Princeton University Press.

Appendix: Description of cases in Table 2.

Case No.1, 1626 (Denucé (1934, p. 146), Ertz (1979, p. 542, nos 8, 9)). Jan II Brueghel sold to Antoon Goetkint, dealer, a painting of his own making, "daer haer Flora sidt en ontkleedt voor een fonteyn..." with figures by Hendrik van Balen. Van Balen was paid *f*20 for this work and the figures in a copy.
Original *f*150
Copy *f*70

Case No.2, 1627 (Denucé (1934, pp. 148-149), Ertz (1979, pp. 543, 544, nos 79, 178)). Jan II Brueghel records in his diary: "Ghemact een groot Pineel, daer den Somer sidt in synen fleur, den Prima-Vere (of Lente-tyd), met syn bloemen, den Herfst met alle soorten van vruchten, vol figurkens, Nimfen, Engeltiens en Herders..."
Original (estimate) *f*400
For a Copy ("van't stuc, synde Somer met alle syn vruchten en bloemen") *f*100

Case No.3, 1627 (Denucé (1934, pp. 148, 149), Ertz (1979, pp. 543, 544 nos 80, 83, 179)). Jan II Brueghel made "Een stuxken daer Flora haer versiert met alle Bloemen, vol werx, heel curieus...." Sold to Antoon Goetkint.
Original *f*150
Copy *f*60

Case No.4, 1628 (Denucé (1934, p. 150), Ertz (1979, pp. 544, 545 nos 153, 185)). Jan II Brueghel sold to Jacques de Gheyn (possibly for the Prince of Orange), "een groot stuc, synde de somer, de figurkens van Hendrik van Balen."
Original *f*500
Copy, sold to Hans van Mechelen (artist) *f*150

Case No.5, 1628 (Denucé (1934, p. 151), Ertz (1979, p. 545 nos 187, 188)). Jan II Brueghel made and sold, to Goetkint, originals and copies after his

father's *Five Senses* *f*1,200 [*f*900]
The copies, based on another, single copy to Goetkint for *f*60, probably came to *f*300 (*f*60 × 5) , making the originals together worth *f*900.

Case No.6, 1630-31 (Denucé (1934, p. 154), Ertz (1979, pp. 542, 543 nos 94, 19)). Jan II Brueghel sold to a nobleman of the Court of the French Queen four pieces, "synde de historie van het boek Genesis, oft Adams-leven."
Originals *f*600
Sold to Bonnecroy, blanket merchant, copies plus "een begonst pineel van patroon saliger," for *f*280.
Another set of copies was made by Brueghel's assistants (*gasten*) (Denucé (1934, p. 85)). Brueghel wanted for these the same as he had charged Bonnecroy for work by the same assistants, namely *f*60. This would make the copies *f*220.

Case No.7, 1631 (Denucé (1934, p. 154)). Four pieces, *Adam's Life*, by Jan II Brueghel ("figures by Snayers (sic)").
Originals *f*350
Copies, with ebony frames *f*144

Case No.8, 1631 (Denucé (1934, p. 69)). Jan II Brueghel offered to Chrisostomus Van Immerseel a *Vanitas* by his father (Jan I), with figures by Rubens (for which Rubens was paid *f*100).
Original (estimate) *f*400
Copy by Jan II Brueghel, with same frame (worth *f*52) *f*150

Case No.9, 1632 (Denucé (1934, p. 79)). Van Immerseel orders six originals, the *Life of Our Lady*, by Frans II Francken.
Originals, exclusive of cost of plates and frames *f*187
Copies of same, by Francken *f*72

Case No.10, 1632-34 (Denucé (1934, pp. 83, 84, 86, 88, 90)). Another set of the *Five Senses*, by Jan II Brueghel.
Sold to Van Immerseel for 12.5 Flemish pounds a piece. Total *f*375
Copies of same, for 6.5 Flemish pounds a piece. Total *f*195

Cases No.11a-b, 1632 (Denucé (1934, p. 81)). Jan II Brueghel offers to make Van Immerseel a copy of an expensive *Vanitas* (same work as in Case No.8), by his father and Rubens.

The copy to be done by himself at half what he estimated the original to be worth *f*200
Copy, if done by assistants *f*100

Cases No.12 a-b, 1632 (Denucé (1934, p. 81)). Jan II Brueghel offers to Van Immerseel a copy of a large *Fruit Guirland*, by his father, figures by Rubens, said to be the best and most labor-intensive work his father had ever accomplished.
Original had sold to Prince of Poland for *f*1,600
Copy, if by Jan II Brueghel, offered for *f*500
Copy, if by Jan II's assistants *f*250

Case No.13, 1632 (Denucé (1934, pp. 69, 81)). Jan II Brueghel offers his copy of an original by Abraham Janssens (?), with figures retouched by Rubens, *Christ appearing as a Gardener.*
Original estimated at *f*300
Copy by Jan II *f*120
Note: according to Joost Vander Auwera, who is preparing a monograph on Janssens, Denucé's identification of "den Patroon" with Janssens is improbable (letter to the authors, 13 April 1995).

Case No.14, 1632-35 (Denucé (1934, pp. 97, 98, 105)). Van Immerseel buys from Adriaen Staelbempt 75 Histories, originals, for *f*7 each.
Originals, together *f*525
Copies of the originals also by Staelbempt. Total *f*262-10

Case No.15, 1636 (Denucé (1934, pp. 103, 108)). Antoon Cossiers, acting as agent for Van Immerseel, reports that he paid Simon de Vos for 2 originals and 2 copies, a total of *f*100. In reply, Van Immerseel states that he has already paid De Vos and that "the copies cannot be more than half the price of the originals."

Economics of the Arts - Selected Essays
V.A. Ginsburgh and P.-M. Menger (Editors)
1996 Elsevier Science B.V.

3

How Costly is the Fall From Fashion? Survivorship Bias in the Painting Market*

William N. Goetzmann
Yale School of Management

1 Introduction

The single largest source of risk for the art investor is taste – the possibility that a work of art will fall from fashion and become worthless. Grampp (1989 p. 68) argues that a substantial percentage of art executed in the past is doomed to obsolescence, and that this disappearance is due to the unique characteristics of the demand for art. Despite this obsolescence factor, most studies of returns to art investment use transactions data that is potentially biased by changes in taste. Anderson (1974), Baumol (1986), Buelens and Ginsburgh (1993), Frey and Pommerehne (1990) and Goetzmann (1993) all use repeated sales of paintings culled from auction data in order to estimate the return to art investment. In the databases used by these authors, typically less that 10% of the observed sale prices are for works with a previous auction record. In fact, the use of repeat-sale data implicitly conditions upon artworks being in demand, and thus understates the risk of obsolescence.[1]

The approach in this study is to simulate the returns to random purchases of paintings over eight decades of the twentieth century. Using auction records from *Art Prices Current* which records the prices of paintings

* Thanks to Stephen Ross for helpful discussions on this topic. Thanks to Anne-Marie Logan and the Yale British Art Center for resource support. Thanks to Michael Montias for helpful suggestions, Victor Ginsburgh and two anonymous referees for helpful comments and to Cathy Conger for data collection.

[1]An alternative to repeated-sales is the hedonic estimation procedure applied by Chanel, Gérard-Varet and Ginsburgh (1993), which employs all auction prices, but necessitates the measurement of time-invariant "prices" for hedonic characteristics which the authors show to be changing through time.

at major auction houses, we create eight hypothetical portfolios of paintings, drawn each decade from 1907 through 1977. We then use sales data for comparable art works to "appraise" the pieces as of 1987. Works by painters whose pictures did not show up at auction over the period 1977 to 1987 are deemed to be obsolete, and assigned a small residual value. The appraisals provide the basis for total return calculations for each picture.

The results of the strategy suggest that paintings bought in the twentieth century before 1987 typically achieved a 5% annualized real rate of return. This estimate is below the 13.3% real rate of return to art investment estimated in Goetzmann (1994) and above the real rate of return of .55% estimated by Baumol (1986) and above the real rate of return of 1.5% estimated by Frey and Pommerehne (1989). Even accounting for survivorship bias, the simulated portfolios of paintings yielded returns that exceeded inflation, U.S. government bond investment and the capital appreciation rate of common stocks in six of the eight periods sampled. These results were obtained with portfolios that typically suffered a 20% rate of obsolescence. In other words, the big winners in the portfolio more than made up for the losers. An important caveat is that these returns do not take into account the transactions costs, insurance costs and cleaning costs of art investment. In the section that follows, we describe our methodology in more detail. Section 3 reports the results and section 4 concludes.

2 Methodology

The simulated portfolios were drawn from the auction transactions reported in *Art Prices Current*, published in Great Britain over the period of our analysis. This annual purports to be a record of sale prices at the principal London, Continental and American auction rooms during the auction season, from August to July. It typically records tens of thousands of art sales from dozens of major auction houses.

Ten pictures were selected randomly with replacement from the "pictures" section of the index. The selection procedure is critical because of the potential bias of the researcher towards familiar artists. For each painting, two uniform [0,1] random numbers were generated. The first one was multiplied by the number of pages in the section, and rounded to an integer value. This referenced a page in the section. The second number was multiplied by the number of lines per page, and rounded to an integer value. This indicated which line to find on the page, and thus which transaction to select.[2] The particulars of the sale were looked up. These typically included the artist's name, a title for the picture, the size of the picture and a price in pounds sterling. For non-British sales, the price in the local currency is also recorded. This procedure yielded eighty pictures, of which four were thrown out because they were not identified by artist.[3]

The goal of the appraisal was to establish a market value for the selected pictures as of 1987. This date was chosen because it represents the end of the sample period for which repeat-sale data is available for comparison. In addition, stopping in 1987 avoids most of the boom in art prices that peaked in 1990. Extending the study to 1994 might result in higher estimates of returns, although art prices in 1994 were at or near their 1987 values. The appraisal procedure relies upon the on-line database of auction records maintained by Art Quest, Inc. in Great Britain. No "bought-in" sales are recorded, so the Art Quest data represents transaction prices. Art Quest is commonly used by appraisers for identifying sales of comparable artworks, and the service maintains a database of all auction sales at major houses around the world for which the price exceeded some minimum. For each artist in the sample, we obtained a print-out of all auction sales since 1977. In cases for which numerous sales were available, we restricted our attention to the sales in 1987 of comparable size. When a close match could not be made using 1987 data, we took the average price per square inch obtained for paintings by that artist in that year and multiplied by the dimensions of the selected picture.[4] In the few cases for which we had limited sales information for the year 1987, we used data from the years surrounding 1987, and factored in the annual average rate of return on paintings[5] to control for annual market-wide fluctuations in prices. Sales prices were converted to U.K. currency,

[2]This procedure implicitly weights by the volume of sales by that artist brought to auction in the year, and thus fairly represents the kind of return that might be obtained by random purchases.

[3]In each case, these were only identified as "English School." While sales from the "English School" were also found in the decade 1977-1987, there was insufficient information about the pictures to appraise them.

[4]Studies by Chanel and Gérard-Varet (1990) and Frey and Pommerehne (1989) both find size to be significant variable in an hedonic specification of the painting price function.

[5]For Sotheby's Art Index, provided by Ibbotson Associates, Chicago.

regardless of where they took place. Thus, some return calculations may incorporate exchange rate effects. For paintings by artists whose works did not appear at auction in the 1977-1987 period, we assigned a residual value as of 1987 of £26.5 ($50). Total compound returns were calculated as the sale price divided by the purchase price less one, and annualized by taking the n-th root of the price ratio, where n is the number of years between purchase and sale dates. These are deflated by a price index of U.K. consumables used in Goetzmann (1993).[6]

How representative are the auction records? There are certain potential biases in the sample which must be considered. The fact that we are drawing from major auction houses each decade implies that we are only choosing works deemed important enough to draw active bidders. Auction houses are selective about the works they will put up. Minor pieces, or works that do not fit clearly into the category of the sale are refused, or referred for private sale. Thus, we begin our analysis of returns to art investment by eliminating the possibility of a big profit through buying the works of relative unknowns. For example, *Art Prices Current* for 1961-62 contains no sales records for the well-known giants of Abstract Expressionism Jackson Pollack and Mark Rothko. Many major artists have little or no auction record. This is because it is not uncommon for a dealer to control most of the primary and secondary sales of an artist's work, and allow only minor or unrepresentative pieces to appear at auction. Thus, the auction records generally do not reflect the big profits from rising stars, but instead indicate the return to speculation in the secondary market for a sample of established artists' works.

Another caveat on the auction sales is that it is not known whether the *Art Prices Current* records include "bought-in" sales, that is, paintings that failed to meet the seller reserve price. When pictures are "bought-in" the highest bid may be recorded as a sales price. Art Quest, while it excludes "bought-in" sales has its own potential biases. It reports no sale prices below a minimum level which fluctuate over the period we gathered data. This lower bound means that some return estimates could be biased upwards. Interestingly, implicit upper bounds may also exist, and work in the opposite direction. Most masterworks by "Old Masters" find their way into museum

---

[6]It may not have been necessary to "appraise" these works as of the current date. Knowing that 20% of the painters, disappeared into obsolescence provides a rough heuristic: simply discount the rates of return conditioned upon survival by 20%. I thank an anonymous referee for this suggestion.

collections, and typically do not reappear at auction, due to museum policy against deaccessioning. For example, one of the artists selected in the sample is Jan Vermeer. Very few Vermeers remain in private hands, and the secondary market for them is, to say the least, thin. While some Vermeers have appeared at auction in the last decade, they have typically been minor works.

Thus, the sizeable (18" by 13.5") Vermeer painting "Young Man in Black Dress" which sold for £46 4s in 1937 is valued today at only £2,984 if sales of "comparable works" are used.[7] We must question whether recent auctioned pieces by masters such as Vermeer are truly comparable. There is no way of knowing how significant this type of survivorship bias in appraisals might be. In sum, the selection procedure we used and the assumptions we made about the residual value of works by "obsolete artists" tend to err on the conservative side, when used to estimate the typical return to a collector speculating in the auction market for paintings. In the next section, we analyze the returns obtained via the selection procedure for what they tell us about the risk and return of art investment.

3 Analysis

Appendix 1 shows the selected paintings. There are some great painters in the list: George Romney, Sir Peter Paul Rubens, Gustave Courbet, Jan Vermeer, Childe Hassam, René Magritte and Jean-François Millet, for example. Others are not so famous. Archibald Webb, Theodore Gerard, Laurent De La Hire and Martin Rico Ortega must have been famous enough to have their works auctioned by a major house at one time in the past, but they have not appeared at auction in more than a decade. The big winners were currently well-known artists. Rubens, De Hooch, Cross, Inness, Magritte and Millet all generated double-digit annualized real returns. Not surprisingly, most of the big losers were by currently little-known painters. There also appears to be no relationship between relative price and relative return – a regression of

[7] I thank Michael Montias for providing information regarding this painting. It is apparently of questionable authenticity itself. Thus, the return estimate associated with the picture in all likelihood is not a good estimate of the appreciation of an investment in a true Vermeer over the period, but might actually capture the return to an estimate of a "school of" or "after" Vermeer.

year-adjusted returns on year-adjusted prices yielded nothing. Apparently, the high-priced pictures had just about the same return as the low-priced pictures. It is interesting to find so little difference between returns for artists contemporaneously recognized as "Great Masters." This is useful for studies seeking to draw inference from tracking high-priced, as opposed to low-priced paintings. We find no basis for a "regression towards the mean" in painting values. One cannot say that the works by the masters of yesteryear systematically decrease in value as fashions change. While key examples of such fate stand out, e.g. Bougereau, Bierstadt and Alma-Tadema, the evidence for such declines remains anecdotal, and fails to manifest itself in our sample.

The lack of a systematic relationship between price and future return may also be of interest to current art investors. Purchasing a work by a well-known artist is just as likely to provide high returns as purchasing a work by a lesser-known artist. This accords well with the recent analysis by Ginsburgh and Jeanfils (1995), who considered the relationship between returns to investment in Impressionists, Modern and Contemporary painters, and lesser-known artists. One major concern of art buyers is that they will buy yesterday's winners rather than tomorrow's winners. Our study of random purchases suggests that this is not a problem.

Figure 1 shows the distribution of annualized inflation-adjusted returns to painting investment, aggregated across the decades. The obsolete pictures typically yielded between −10% and −20% per year. The best investment in the sample exceeded a 20% annual return. The median annual return was 8.24% (in nominal terms) or 2.42% (in real terms). The typical painting was a winner. In fact, only ten of the seventy-six paintings lost money in nominal terms, and only fourteen lost money in real terms. Fourteen of the seventy-six pictures were "obsolete," falling so far out of fashion that were could only ascribe a residual value. Curiously enough, the lowest rate of obsolescence is associated with the paintings selected in the early decades. Painters current in 1916 and 1927 were all current in 1987, however five of ten painters selected in 1937 were not found in the recent auction records, and twenty percent remained the typical rate of obsolescence in the decades following the Depression. One might speculate that the low rate of obsolescence associated with pictures drawn from the early years might be due to a revival of interest in early twentieth century arts and crafts, however it might be due to chance, and the small size of the sample.

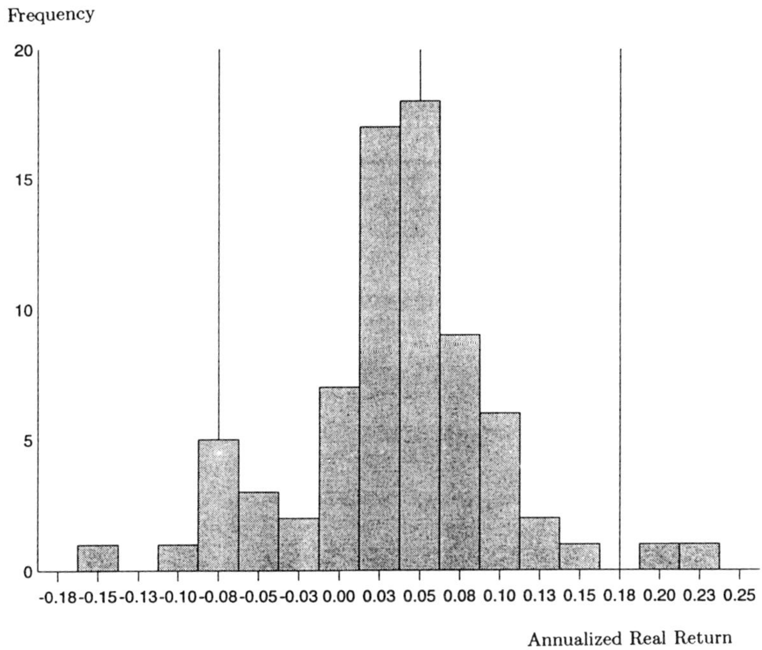

Figure 1: Painting Investment Returns (Real)
Annualized Appreciation 20th C.

Figure 1 also shows the dispersion in annualized returns. While the art market is typically considered a risky one, the standard deviation of annualized nominal returns is 8.00% and the standard deviation of annualized real returns is 7.47%. While there are a few dramatic outliers, the dispersion of annualized returns is surprisingly small, suggesting that, at least for holding periods greater than a decade, the risk is modest. This risk not only reflects the risk of the art market as a whole, but it includes the idiosyncratic risk of individual works, to the extent that it is not diversified away completely through inclusion in a portfolio.

How great is the potential survivorship bias due to conditioning upon repeated-sale? Figure 2 compares the mean return estimates given by the simulated portfolios to estimates obtained from repeat-sales data.[8] Note that

[8]The repeat sales estimates are taken from an annual repeat-sales regression described

the compound return estimates for the repeat-sales regression are greater for each holding period. Given the sample sizes of our simulation, however, we cannot reject the null hypothesis of equal mean returns for any holding period. The repeat-sales estimates typically fall within one standard error of the mean annualized return. It is important to stress that the simulated portfolios are based upon extremely conservative assumptions, and small sample sizes.

How do the painting portfolios compare to other assets as an investment? Total return data for the U.K. suggests that stocks had about 13% expected return over much of the twentieth century (see Goetzmann and Jorion (1995)). The capital appreciation of stocks was about 5% in this century, and the rate of returns on bonds was 5% to 10%. Table 1 compares the rates of return on our art portfolios to rates of return on financial assets. Art typically beats inflation, bond investment, and the capital appreciation of common stocks.

Table 1
Decade-by-Decade Results of Art Investment
Annualized Over Period to 1987 (in %)

Year	Return	RSR Return	Stock C.A.	Bond Return	Inflation
1907	5.75	8.15	3.47	4.80	4.13
1916	7.15	10.04	3.89	5.57	3.55
1927	9.20	9.62	4.22	5.61	5.21
1937	5.23	12.38	5.59	5.61	6.71
1947	9.87	15.02	5.95	6.13	6.52
1957	9.42	16.62	5.60	8.37	7.55
1967	7.69	13.44	3.89	11.59	9.97
1977	11.13	24.22	12.51	15.72	7.99

RSR estimates as well as stock and bond returns are described in Goetzmann (1993).

---

in Goetzmann (1993).

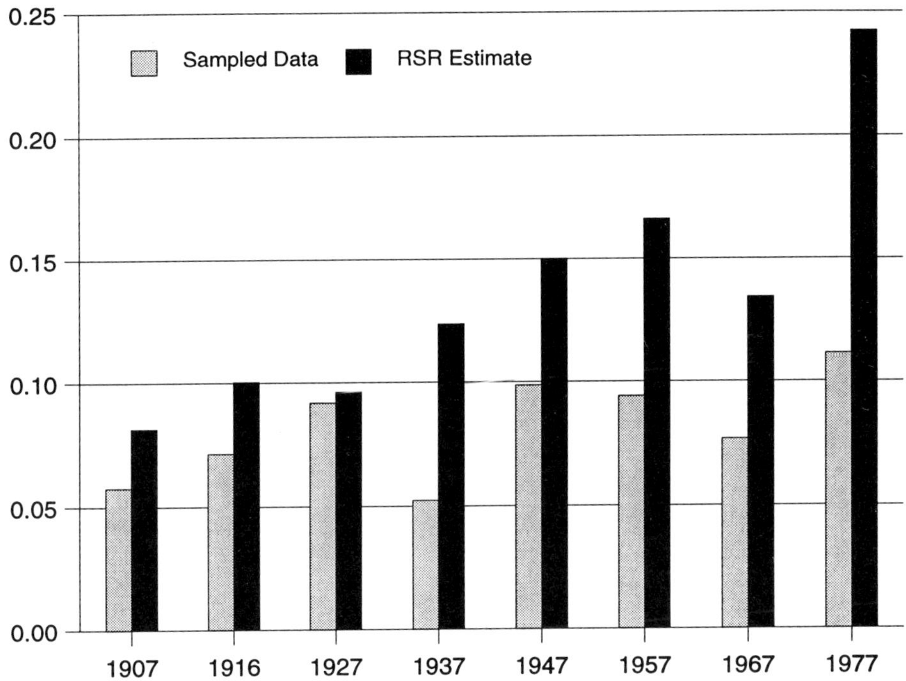

Figure 2: Rates of Return on Art Purchases
Annualized, held until 1987

4 Conclusion

Studies based upon repeat-sales data, as well as studies which base returns upon first differences in average current painting sales, are likely to be biased due to survivorship. One way to mitigate this bias is to simulate an investment portfolio using properties that the typical art investor might have purchased in the past, without the advantage of knowing which artists and art styles would be popular in the future. Using auction records from several decades in the twentieth century, and an exhaustive database of current auction sales, we have been able to approximate the returns obtained through art investment over the period 1907 to 1987. Real returns to these portfolios are not, as Baumol (1986) and Frey and Pommerehne (1989) suggest, between .5% and 1.5%. This comparison is not entirely fair, however, since both of these authors estimate returns over a far longer period than the 20th century. Painting returns are not as high as studies by Buelens and Ginsburgh (1993) and Goetzmann (1993) would seem to indicate, however. These authors have found double digit annualized growth in the twentieth century. Our results suggest that some of this may be due to shifting fashion. While this particular simulated art investment portfolio kept pace with stock prices, it did not beat the stock market when total returns are considered. The survivorship bias appears to be about 3% to 4% annually.

Because of the subjective nature of aesthetics, one might expect that once-popular artists would fall from public grace with great regularity. No decade has seen such profound changes in taste as our own, and yet the rate of "obsolescence" is not huge. While nearly all of the artists we selected during the first three decades of our sample are still represented in showrooms, it would be safe to say that only a few of the corporations extant during that time have survived. Tastes are more persistent that we might have thought. Given the attrition rate of corporations over the same period, we might even speculate that tastes in art evolve more slowly than production technology and preferences for consumer goods, durables, and services. Considering that we are only able to sample from the auction market, and have no access to private sale records, the chances are that the obsolescence rate for paintings is even lower than we have documented in this study.

While the relative valuation of an artist may decline as time passes, remarkably, there seems to be a market for most works. This would seem to imply that the appraisal-based returns calculated here, and the repeat-sales index estimate should be approximately equal. This is not necessarily the case. Estimators of return indices, such as the repeat-sales regression or hedonic regression rely upon observed transactions. These transactions themselves might be conditioned upon whether the work increased in value. In another study (Goetzmann (1994)), I show how a seller reserve based upon personal tastes and/or past market values may lead to positive biases in observed returns. The current methodology, while based upon observed prices of similar works, is less susceptible to such a bias, since we are not conditioning the disposition of the specific work in the simulated portfolio.

5 Directions for future research

Due to the constraints of time and cost, the current study is limited to a random sample of less than one hundred paintings. While investment in dozens of paintings represent a sizeable portfolio and is sufficient to draw inferences about the rate of obsolescence and the average rate of return over the period, the same methodology can actually be extended to the construction of a year-by-year index. If a researcher were able to draw one hundred pictures per year through the twentieth century, and value them currently using the hedonic methodology, annual rates of return can be well estimated by adapting the repeat-sale methodology. Future research may also take advantage of databases for valuation that have lower limits for inclusion into the sample, and those that include images. The newly-created ArtNet, Inc. database, for example, is well-suited to such a study. While expensive and time-consuming, this would virtually eliminate all the survivorship biases inherent in the hedonic and repeat-sales regression methods.

6 References

Anderson, R.C. (1974), Paintings as an investment, *Economic Inquiry*, 12, 13-25.

Art Trade Press (1907, 1916, 1927 ... 1977), *Art Prices Current*, Havant: The Art Trade Press, Ltd.

Baumol, W.J. (1986), Unnatural value or art as a floating crap game, *American Economic Review*, 76, 10-14.

Buelens, N. and V. Ginsburgh (1993), Revisiting Baumols' unnatural value or art as a floating crap game, *European Economic Review*, 31, 1351-1371.

Bryan, M.F. (1985), Beauty and the bulls: the investment characteristics of paintings, *Economic Review of the Federal Reserve Bank of Cleveland*, first quarter, 2-10.

Chanel, O. (1990), Du nouveau à propos de la rentabilité des placements en oeuvres d'art. Approches alternatives, in L.A. Gérard-Varet, ed., *For-*

mation des Prix des Peintures Modernes et Contemporaines et Rentabilité des Placements sur le Marché de l'Art, GREQE, Marseille.

Chanel, O., L.-A. Gérard-Varet and V. Ginsburgh (1993), The relevance of hedonic price indices: the case of paintings, *Journal of Cultural Economics*, forthcoming.

Frey, B. and W.W. Pommerehne (1989), *Muses and Markets*, London: Basil Blackwell.

Ginsburgh, V. and P. Jeanfils (1995), Long-term comovements in international markets for paintings, *European Economic Review*, 39, 538-548.

Goetzmann, W.N. (1991), Accounting for taste: art returns over three centuries, Working Paper, Columbia University, Graduate School of Business, New York.

Goetzmann, W.N. (1993), Accounting for taste: art and the financial markets over three centuries, *American Economic Review*, 85, 1370-1376.

Goetzmann, W.N. (1994), The effect of seller reserves on market index estimation, Working Paper, Yale School of Management, New Haven.

Goetzmann, W.N. and P. Jorion (1995), A longer look at dividend yields, *Journal of Business*, 68, 483-508.

Stein, J.P. (1973), The appreciation of paintings, Ph.D. Dissertation, University of Chicago.

Stein, J.P. (1977), The monetary appreciation of paintings, *Journal of Political Economy*, 85, 1021-1035.

Appendix: Paintings Selected by Random Draw from Auction Data.

Year	Artist	Purchase Price	Appraised Value	Annualized Return	Annualized Real Return	Sales in 1980's ?
1907	Jones, Charles	51.45	3,457.89	5.40%	1.22%	
1907	Schleich R.	37.80	12,962.07	7.57%	3.30%	
1907	Romney, George	39.90	7,703.41	6.80%	2.56%	
1907	Stevens, Albert	5.25	3,066.54	8.29%	3.99%	
1907	Ward, E.M.	2.10	26.50	3.22%	−0.88%	No
1907	Reinagle, P.	5.78	813.57	6.38%	2.16%	
1907	Webb, Archibald	1.75	26.50	3.46%	−0.65%	No
1907	Cave, J.	31.50	1,467.04	4.92%	0.75%	
1916	Nichol, Erskine	17.85	1,014.83	5.86%	2.23%	
1916	De Tauney, N.	157.50	83,929.02	9.25%	5.51%	
1916	Goodall, F.	36.75	783.55	4.40%	0.83%	
1916	Stanley, Stanley	4.20	112.19	4.74%	1.15%	
1916	Egley Maw, W.	25.20	787.05	4.97%	1.37%	
1916	Rubens, Sir Peter Paul	5.78	32,105.41	12.91%	9.05%	
1916	Jamieson, Alex	8.40	2,027.25	8.03%	4.34%	
1916	Wouverman, P.	50.40	2,360.67	5.57%	1.95%	
1916	Romney, George	31.50	11,554.72	8.67%	4.95%	
1927	Vincent, George	11.55	1,968.67	8.94%	3.54%	
1927	Wolstenholme	21.00	9,200.95	10.67%	5.18%	
1927	Northcote, J.	23.10	726.69	5.92%	0.67%	
1927	Faes, Peter	178.50	10,519.44	7.03%	1.72%	
1927	Herbert, John Rogers	18.90	4,596.37	9.59%	4.16%	
1927	Santa Croce, Francesco	46.20	5,379.69	8.25%	2.89%	
1927	Bennett, F.M.	29.40	2,307.62	7.54%	2.21%	
1927	Del Garbo, Raffaellino	23.10	10,773.84	10.78%	5.29%	
1927	Courbet, Gustave	147.00	22,268.38	8.73%	3.34%	
1927	De Hooch, Pieter	75.60	260,958.75	14.54%	8.86%	
1937	Longhi, Alessandro	44.00	56,178.58	15.38%	8.12%	
1937	Monfallet, A.F.	13.13	1,895.44	10.46%	3.51%	
1937	Stanton, Sir H. Hughes	6.30	26.50	2.91%	−3.56%	No
1937	Lesrel, Adolphe Alexander	44.00	1,594.04	7.44%	0.69%	No
1937	Gerard, Theodore H.	5.50	26.50	3.19%	−3.30%	No
1937	Mieris, Frans van	102.90	6,043.73	8.49%	1.66%	
1937	Watts, Fredrick	48.30	26.50	−1.19%	−7.41%	No
1937	Bogdani, James	110.25	26.50	−2.81%	−8.92%	No
1937	Mooy, P.	30.45	26.50	−0.28%	−6.55%	No
1937	Vermeer, Jan	46.20	2,983.73	8.69%	1.86%	
1947	Hoefnagle	22.00	26.50	0.47%	−5.68%	
1947	Pozzoserrato, L.	72.00	26.50	−2.47%	−8.44%	No
1947	Cross, Henri-Edmond	60.42	850,408.32	26.97%	19.20%	
1947	Spencelayh, Charles	36.00	4,637.24	12.91%	6.00%	

Year	Artist	Purchase Price	Appraised Value	Annualized Return	Annualized Real Return	Sales in 1980's ?
1947	Maufra, Maxime Emile	225.00	30,576.00	13.07%	6.15%	
1947	Jacque, Charles Emile	175.00	1,858.11	6.08%	-0.41%	
1947	Peeters, Bonaventura	180.00	3,416.58	7.64%	1.05%	
1947	De Greef, J.	793.75	37,350.00	10.11%	3.37%	
1947	Hardy, Heywood	68.00	13,021.94	14.04%	7.06%	
1957	Molenaer, Jan Miense	73.50	3,183.69	13.38%	5.42%	
1957	De La Cruz	70.00	26.50	-3.19%	-9.98%	No
1957	Vlaminck	2,855.78	22,122.94	7.06%	-0.45%	
1957	Hassam, Childe	716.85	24,091.68	12.43%	4.54%	
1957	Inness, George	250.90	31,796.82	17.52%	9.27%	
1957	Molenaer, Claes	100.00	26.50	-4.33%	-11.05%	No
1957	Cuyp, Benjamin Gerritz	82.53	6,639.20	15.75%	7.62%	
1957	Verelst	71.40	2,434.35	12.48%	4.59%	
1957	Soest, Gerard van	147.00	5,880.06	13.08%	5.15%	
1957	Albano	57.75	1,012.58	10.02%	2.29%	
1967	Magritte, René	3,942.65	59,700.47	14.55%	4.17%	
1967	Callow, William	400.00	442.66	0.51%	-8.61%	
1967	Luce, Maximilien	892.50	11,707.49	13.73%	3.42%	
1967	Millet, Jean-François	600.00	219,084.03	34.31%	22.14%	
1967	De La Hire, Laurent	840.00	26.50	-15.87%	-23.50%	No
1967	Ortega, Martin Rico	1,050.00	26.50	-16.80%	-24.35%	No
1967	Bylert, Jan	367.50	10,845.69	18.44%	7.70%	
1967	Villon, Jacques	1,050.00	5,412.61	8.55%	-1.30%	
1967	Jaenisch, Hans	346.15	2,759.65	10.94%	0.88%	
1967	Hulk, Abraham Sen.	399.00	2,044.26	8.51%	-1.33%	
1977	Soutine, Chaim	10,344.83	32,673.55	12.19%	3.89%	
1977	Carrier-Belleuse, Pierre	442.53	2,995.22	21.07%	12.11%	
1977	Girardet, Eugène-Alexis	358.62	1,191.07	12.75%	4.41%	
1977	Masson, André	1,724.14	11,094.62	20.46%	11.55%	
1977	Marko, Andreas	531.03	1,831.68	13.18%	4.81%	
1977	Serveau, Clement	2,450.57	886.08	-9.67%	-16.36%	
1977	Boggs, Frank	1,494.25	10,763.92	21.83%	12.82%	
1977	Klenczynski, Pierre	107.47	208.13	6.83%	-1.07%	
1977	Gallet, Helene	29.89	26.50	-1.19%	-8.51%	No
1977	Cockx, Philibert	675.86	2,463.29	13.81%	5.39%	

All prices are converted to pounds sterling. Appraised Value as described in text. Annualized real return compounded from date of purchase to 1987. Annualized Real Return is net of U.K. inflation index for the period. Sales in 1980's indicates whether artist's work appeared at auction in Artquest database in the 1980's.

Economics of the Arts - Selected Essays
V.A. Ginsburgh and P.-M. Menger (Editors)

4

On Long-run Price Comovements between Paintings and Prints*

Corinna Czujack, Renato Flôres Jr. and Victor Ginsburgh
Université Libre de Bruxelles

1 Introduction

The art market is the result of complex interactions, most of which can hardly be explained by economic theory. Signals such as the name of an artist, specificities of different media, reactions of art galleries, critics, museum directors, collectors and investors exert a large variety of influences on prices and values, which are difficult to model with accuracy.

It is however possible to address interesting questions, using sales prices as the basic information on values and relative scarcities. Indeed, if prices can be taken as synthesizing all the effects just mentioned, their dynamic interactions across artists and media may reveal some common patterns or, on the contrary, call attention to divergent behaviours. Both may turn out to be explainable by art history or aesthetical judgements in which case, further evidence would have been provided by a more quantitative analysis; otherwise, new directions for research could be opened.

In particular, if one accepts the idea of "a global market" for say, post-impressionist paintings, one may ask whether artists like Braque or Picasso lead or follow this global market. One may also examine whether prices of prints and paintings for a given artist follow a common pattern. If so,

* A previous version of this paper was presented at the conference Approches Comparatives en Economie de la Culture, Paris, May 1995. We thank Ruth Towse and other participants for comments. We also thank William Goetzmann and James Pesando for very useful remarks on a previous version. Financial support from the Belgian Government under contract PAI nr. 26 as well as from Université Libre de Bruxelles is gratefully acknowledged.

one could construct portfolios of prints, which are cheaper, more liquid and probably less risky than portfolios of paintings.

In this paper, we try to answer questions of this type, using the information contained in price indices for global markets and for some individual artists who have been active both as painters and as lithographers or etchers – Braque, Chagall, Ernst, Miró and Picasso.

The analysis is carried out by estimating vector autoregressive models under the error-correction representation (using the techniques developed by Johansen (1988, 1991) and Johansen and Juselius (1990, 1992)), which makes possible:
(i) to estimate steady-state relations between prices and isolate long-run from short-run behaviour;
(ii) to test for exogenenous behaviour within the setting of the model.

Though this methodology is known to many economists, it is much less widespread in the field of cultural economics.[1] Therefore, Section 2 is devoted to an intuitive overview of the basic framework and of the key concepts used in the paper. Section 3 briefly discusses the construction of the price indices on which our study is based. In Section 4, we analyze three kinds of relationships which may exist:
(i) between the market for paintings and the market for prints (Section 4.1);
(ii) between the market enjoyed by a specific printmaker and the global market for prints (Section 4.2);
(iii) between the print markets of the five artists whom we study (Section 4.3).

The discussion is kept informal, though more technical details can be found in the Appendix.

Our conclusions are the subject of Section 5. They can be summarized as follows. First, we find that prices of prints and paintings have a common trend, but prints yield lower long-run returns. Second, relations between individual artists and the global market for prints vary across artists, but again, prices have common trends. Third, though each of the five artists is unique by himself, a separating line can be drawn between Braque and Ernst on the one hand, and Chagall, Miró and Picasso, on the other. In particular, Picasso, as expected, plays a major role and Chagall, in spite of being very connected to the others, behaves somewhat differently.

[1]See however Ginsburgh and Jeanfils (1995).

2 Theoretical concepts

In this section, we give an informal discussion of the key concepts that will be tested in this paper. The interested reader should go to the papers cited for a rigorous view on the subject,[2] as well as to the Appendix.

2.1 The model

Assume that we are interested in studying the relation between 2 time series of prices $y_{i,t}, i = 1, 2; t = 1, 2, ..., T$. If the series are nonstationary, regressing say, the first on the second will usually lead to a high correlation, but this correlation may just be spurious and merely due to the strong upward (or downward) trend which drives both series. Regression coefficients will have little if any economic meaning, and no firm conclusion can be derived from their standard deviations. Therefore, the usual practice is to detrend both series (for example, by taking first differences of both series) before regressing one on the other. Then, however, one deals with the short-run and neglects the possible long-run equilibrium relation. Davidson et al. (1978) suggested to combine both the long-run and the short-run within the same framework, making for what is now called the "error correction model." An example of such a model is:

$$\Delta y_{1,t} = \alpha_1(y_{1,t-1} - \beta y_{2,t-1}) + \gamma_{1,1}\Delta y_{1,t-1} + \gamma_{1,2}\Delta y_{2,t-1} + e_{1,t}, \qquad (1)$$

where first-order differences of the first series ($\Delta y_{1,t}$) are regressed on lagged first-order differences of both series ($\Delta y_{1,t-1}$ and $\Delta y_{2,t-1}$) and on lagged values ($y_{1,t-1}$ and $y_{2,t-1}$) of both series. These values appear under the very special form of $(y_{1,t-1} - \beta y_{2,t-1})$, assumed to represent the long-run equilibrium relation between the two variables.

Note that along an equilibrium path, movement ceases and $\Delta y_{1,t-1} = \Delta y_{2,t-1} = \Delta y_{1,t} = 0$, so that, apart from a hopefully small error term, $(y_{1,t-1} = \beta y_{2,t-1})$. On the other hand, variations in $\Delta y_{1,t}$ can be due to variations in $\Delta y_{1,t-1}$, or in $\Delta y_{2,t-1}$ or to a disequilibrium in period $t-1$, i. e. to the fact that $(y_{1,t-1} - \beta y_{2,t-1}) \neq 0$, even if $\Delta y_{1,t-1} = \Delta y_{2,t-1} = 0$. If

[2] Davidson et al. (1978), Engle et al. (1983), Engle and Granger (1987), Granger (1969), Johansen (1988, 1991), Johansen and Juselius (1990, 1992). Chapters 2 and 3 in Urbain (1993) also provide a good insight on the issues.

$\alpha_1 < 0$, this will imply that any overshooting or undershooting of $y_{1,t-1}$ with respect to its equilibrium value $\beta y_{2,t-1}$ will be (partially) corrected in period t, and the two series will not move too far apart from each other, for too long. This is the essence of an error-correction mechanism (ECM).

The full model will include a second equation which explains the short-run behaviour of $y_{2,t}$:

$$\Delta y_{2,t} = \alpha_2(y_{1,t-1} - \beta y_{2,t-1}) + \gamma_{2,1}\Delta y_{1,t-1} + \gamma_{2,2}\Delta y_{2,t-1} + e_{2,t}. \tag{2}$$

Observe that in (1) and (2), all the parameters, including the error-correction coefficients α_1 and α_2 are allowed to be different, but that the long-run equilibrium relation between y_1 and y_2, i.e.:

$$z_{t-1} = y_{1,t-1} - \beta y_{2,t-1} \tag{3}$$

must be the *same* in both (1) and (2). Equation (3) is often referred to as the cointegrating relationship.

The terms:

$$\gamma_{i,1}\Delta y_{1,t-1} + \gamma_{i,2}\Delta y_{2,t-1}, i = 1, 2 \tag{4}$$

which appear in both equations describe the short-run dynamics.[3]

There are several ways to estimate the coefficients in (1) and (2),[4] but this does not concern us too much in this paper. It is however important to notice that it would make little sense to regress say in (1), a stationary series $\Delta y_{1,t}$ on nonstationary series $\Delta y_{2,t}$ or $(y_{1,t-1} - \beta y_{2,t-1})$. Therefore, one has to make sure that both time series $\Delta y_{1,t}$ and $\Delta y_{2,t}$ have "similar patterns" and that the "errors" $z_{t-1} = y_{1,t-1} - \beta y_{2,t-1}$ also have that pattern. Moreover, for the error-correction mechanisms to be meaningful, one should have $\alpha_1 < 0$ and $\alpha_2 > 0$, so that deviations from equilibrium are corrected in a reasonable way.

Special cases of model (1)-(2) can readily be obtained; in particular, it may happen that:

(a) no cointegrating relation exists,

(b) some or all of the α_i coefficients are zero,

[3]Clearly, these terms can be made more sophisticated by introducing a larger number of lags, as well as a coefficient for an intercept.

[4]See Engle and Granger (1987), Johansen (1988, 1991) and Johansen and Juselius (1990, 1992).

(c) some or all of the $\gamma_{i,k}$ coefficients are zero.
These special cases will be discussed in Section 2.2.

Estimating model (1)-(2) for price indices of painters or media, allows us to obtain an insight on the joint short-run dynamics of the series. As pointed out, the long-run or steady-state term z_{t-1}, present in these equations, acts in correcting the short-run deviations back to the "ideal" long-run equilibrium. Finding cointegration, say between paintings and prints created by a specific artist, is a nontrivial fact because it implies that, in the long-run, the prices for the two media do not diverge and also that their short-run variations are influenced by this long-run equilibrium. In other words, this means that the series have a common nonstationary movement, which is eliminated in the cointegrating relation.

2.2 Exogeneity and causality

The issues of exogeneity and causality often appear in econometric modelling involving several variables. Though intuitively simple, the concept of exogeneity can have different shades, as pointed out in the seminal paper by Engle et al. (1983).

In the case of the ECM-model, the concept is easy to understand. Consider a given equation, say (1). It may happen that α_1 is not significantly different from zero; then, the corresponding cointegration relationship z_{t-1} does not play any role in explaining the behaviour of the (differenced) price index $y_{1,t}$. If this is the case, we say that the behaviour of $y_{1,t}$ is "weakly" exogenous[5] with respect to the long-run relationships and (1) can be written as:

$$\Delta y_{1,t} = \gamma_{1,1}\Delta y_{1,t-1} + \gamma_{1,2}\Delta y_{2,t-1} + e_{1,t}. \tag{5}$$

In other words, the equilibrium relation does not (stochastically) condition the behaviour of $y_{1,t}$. As a result, the system can be separated into two subsystems.[6] The first comprises the equation(s) corresponding to the weakly exogenous variable(s), while the second is formed by the remaining one(s). Making the link with the informal definition of weak exogeneity stated above, as far as the long-run relationships are concerned, we can condition the second subsystem with respect to the first one, i.e. we can study the behaviour

[5]This idea has received a finer treatment by Mosconi and Gianini (1993).

[6]In our example, there is only one equation in each subsystem.

of the index(es) in the second subsystem for each "fixed" set of values of the weakly exogenous variable(s).

The concept of causality builds on ideas from common language and philosophy. In our context, causality will be defined in the lines of Granger (1969): x_t will (Granger-)cause w_t if and only if the past of x_t influences w_t, but the opposite is not true. The "past" is here understood as the collection of lagged values of x_t, influences being measured in terms of linear regressions.

Weak exogeneity plus Granger causality makes for what Engle et al. (1983) suggested to call "strong exogeneity." It is evident that a group of variables may be weakly but not strongly exogenous. This is easily seen if one remembers that lagged differences of all the indices appear in principle in the short-run part of the equations in (1)-(2). For weakly exogenous variables to be strongly exogenous, it must be that the short-run behaviour of the other variables do not Granger-cause them, i.e. that they do not appear in their equations. For example, $y_{1,t}$ will be strongly exogenous, if equation (1) can be written as:

$$\Delta y_{1,t} = \gamma_{1,1} \Delta y_{1,t-1} + e_{1,t}. \tag{6}$$

No other variable than the past of $y_{1,t}$ itself contributes in explaining $y_{1,t}$.

In our context, the series describe price indices for artists, some of which may turn out to be "important" and influence other prices, while some are less important and are absent from the long-run or even from the short-run part of the equations. One immediately sees that the concepts discussed in this section open up a rich spectrum of testing alternatives.

2.3 Efficiency and returns

If, in addition to exogeneity of say, $y_{1,t}$, we find that in (6), $\gamma_{1,1}$ is not significantly different from zero, we are left with the following equation:

$$\Delta y_{1,t} = e_{1,t} \tag{7}$$

and the $\Delta y_{1,t}$ series is a random walk.

Given that $y_{1,t}$ is a price series, the equation means that the underlying market is "weakly efficient:" in the context of the model, no other variable (contemporaneous or past) has an influence on $y_{1,t}$ and the price in $t-1$ is the best forecast for the price in t, since (7) can also be written $y_{1,t} = y_{1,t-1} + e_{1,t}$.

If the price series are expressed in logarithms, the differenced series $\Delta y_{1,t}$ represents returns, so that weak efficiency also means zero expected short-term returns. In the case of a two-equations system, there is also an interesting financial interpretation of the long-run relation. Taking the expectation of the first-difference of (3), we have: $E\Delta y_{1,t} = \beta E\Delta y_{2,t}$, which gives a relationship between the two expected returns. If $\beta > 1$, (long-run) returns from $y_{1,t}$ are higher than those generated by $y_{2,t}$. Since riskier assets yield higher returns, $y_{1,t}$ should probably relate to an asset that is riskier than $y_{2,t}$. Note that if $\beta = 1$, the expected returns of the two assets are equal.

Finally, consider a two-equations ECM in which the first price series is weakly efficient, while in the second equation, the long-run term is present:

$$\Delta y_{1,t} = e_{1,t},$$
$$\Delta y_{2,t} = \alpha_2(y_{1,t-1} - \beta y_{2,t-1}) + \gamma_{2,1}\Delta y_{1,t-1} + \gamma_{2,2}\Delta y_{2,t-1} + e_{2,t}.$$

This means that differences in the first series are white noise, while for the second one, some short-term forecasting is possible. It is then reasonable to expect that the first asset should provide higher returns, since it is riskier (i. e., "less forecastable") than the second one. This hypothesis can be tested on the β coefficient, which should then be larger than one.

3 The data

3.1 Principles of construction of the price indices

The price indices used in our calculations have been computed through hedonic regressions, as suggested in Chanel et al. (1992). One estimates the following equation:

$$p_{i,t} = \sum_{k=1}^{m} a_k x_{ik,t} + c(t) + \xi_{i,t}. \tag{8}$$

In this equation, $p_{i,t}$ is the (logarithm of the) price of a collectible i sold at time t, $x_{ik,t}$ is a time-variant idiosyncratic attribute of collectible (i,t); $c(t)$ is the market-wide price effect and $\xi_{i,t}$ is an error term. Model (8) can be given a convenient interpretation if one isolates in the right-hand side the time effect and the random error. The left-hand side can then be thought of as representing the price of a work i sold in t, freed from the implicit prices of its characteristics. This "characteristic-free price" is assumed to include the effect of time and a random error only; by averaging the characteristic-free prices of all works i sold in t (or, equivalently, by regressing these prices on time dummies), one obtains the average price of a "standardized" work at time t. The specification of $c(t)$ considered in that case is:

$$c(t) = \sum_{t=\tau_0}^{\tau_T} \phi_t \delta_t, \tag{9}$$

where $[\tau_0, \tau_T]$ is the time interval over which observations are available; δ_t is a dummy variable which takes the value *one* if work i is sold in period $t \in [\tau_0, \tau_T]$, and *zero* otherwise; the ϕ_t's are parameters to be estimated. The sequence $[\phi_{\tau_0}, \phi_{\tau_1}, ..., \phi_{\tau_T}]$ is used to construct the price (or the value) index y_t.

Most of the work carried out in order to compute returns on art, uses repeat sales regressions (i.e. regressions based on observations of collectibles sold at least twice) rather than hedonic regressions. The pros and cons of both methods are discussed in Chanel et al. (1992) and Ginsburgh (1994).[7] Here, we merely note that it would be impossible to construct yearly (or half-yearly) indices for paintings using repeat sales only, since the number of resales for which prices are observed is quite limited.[8]

3.2 Original data available

The data used to calculate value indices are taken from Mayer's *Annuaire des Ventes* (1963 to 1993). These yearbooks of public auctions are available since 1963 (sales of 1962); we thus cover the years 1962 to 1992. Two databases were compiled, one for paintings and one for prints. The first contains 25,073 sales for 84 well-known artists.[9] The database for prints contains 10,028 sales for 25 artists.

In addition to global price indices based on the 84 and 25 artists respectively, we also constructed indices for five artists for whom the number of

[7] See also Goetzmann (1990, 1993).
[8] This is much less so for prints. See Pesando (1993).
[9] For more details, see de la Barre et al. (1994).

works sold was large enough: Braque (359 paintings and 681 prints), Chagall (341 and 1,943), Ernst (435 and 280), Miró (288 and 1,708) and finally, Picasso (826 and 3,132).

In Mayer's compendia, each sale is described by a certain number of characteristics (see below) and by a sale number, corresponding to a specific auction describing the location and the date of the sale. It is therefore possible to construct semi-annual, quarterly or even monthly price indices. The relatively small number of sales[10] made us opt for semi-annual indices, taking the years 1962 to 1965 as base period.

The characteristics of the artworks are different for paintings and for prints. Those that describe paintings are rather limited; beside the name of the artist (and the title of the painting), the yearbooks provide only a very rough description: the size of the work (height and width), the year in which it was painted, the medium used, the place of the sale (saleroom, country) and the year of sale. Such a simple description is however hardly comprehensive enough to explain the price differences between artists and one is necessarily led to include some measure of the repute of the painter. We chose to work with dummy variables for artists.

The characteristics for prints are more numerous. Beside the name of the artist, the size of the work, the year of production, the medium used, the place of the sale (saleroom, country), and the year of the sale, Mayer provides information concerning the technique used (etching, lithography, etc.), the type of paper (Arches, Chine, etc.), the fact that the print is black and white or coloured, the signature, some specials (épreuve d'essai, épreuve d'artiste, etc.), the total number of copies and the number of the copy sold.[11]

Moreover, for the five individual artists considered and given that the year of production is (very often) available, it was possible to introduce dummy variables for the different "creation" periods (e.g. for Picasso, the "blue," the "pink," the "cubist" period, etc.), which are usually priced very differently.[12]

---

[10]Especially for the period 1962-1972, during which there are sometimes less than ten observations per year for a given artist.

[11]See also Table 1, for more details.

[12]It is obviously difficult to define these periods (painters have seldom changed their style suddenly: changes occur gradually, and painters may also simultaneously paint in different styles) so that the indications given in the various art history books do not necessarily coincide. We have used Laclotte and Cuzin (1989). The authors are respectively Chairman and Chief Curator of the paintings department at the Musée du Louvre.

Prices are given in current French francs by Mayer, who uses the exchange rate prevailing during the day of the sale.

3.3 Indices constructed

The model we use combines (8) and (9) and is estimated on the full sample of sales and resales. Regressions were thus run for all artists together to obtain the "market" index as well as individually for Braque, Chagall, Ernst, Miró and Picasso. The indices are then deflated, using the French consumer price index. They are reproduced in Figure 1.

3.4 Overall quality of the regression results

We illustrate the results with two regressions (one for paintings and one for prints), run on the full sample. These are the regressions used to obtain the "market indices." As can be seen from Table 1, the fit is quite good in both cases. All the coefficients (with the exception of the "paper" medium for prints, which should probably be negative) have the expected sign.

4 Empirical results

The analysis is split into three parts. First, we look for the relation between prices of prints and of paintings for the market as a whole, as well as for each of the five artists individually. We then examine the market for prints only and test whether prices for each artist are related to the global price index. Finally, we construct a system including the price indices for prints by the five artists. Before setting up these models, we tested whether (the logarithms of) the price series used are integrated of order one, so that their first differences are stationary. The results of these tests, given in Table A1 in the Appendix, indicate that all series, with the exception of the global indexes can be considered as integrated of order one, at the 5% level. The global indexes also show evidence of a single unit root at the 10% level.

Table 1
Some Results from the Hedonic Regressions

Paintings			Prints		
Characteristic	Coefficient	St. dev.	Characteristic	Coefficient	St. dev
Height	.01704	.00042	Height	.00925	.00061
Width	.00482	.00031	Width	.00116	.00030
Surface (x 100)	-.00400	.00030	Surface (x 100)	-.00030	.00060
Canvas	.00000	-	Etching	.00000	-
Collage	-.49946	.04203	Lithography	-.17682	.02071
			Silkscreen	-.40097	.09507
			Mixed techn.	.04434	.10077
			Arches	.00000	-
			Chine	-.18289	.13971
			Japon	-.19990	.05032
			Ord. paper	.09572	.10602
			Bl. and white	.00000	-
			Coloured	.18603	.02361
			No special	.00000	-
			Epr. d'essai	.07445	.34833
			Epr. d'artiste	.21308	.08293
			Bon à tirer	3.16567	.77890
			Hors commerce	.23987	.10018
			Total nb. of prints	-.00040	.00004
Artists	84 var.*		Artists	25 var.*	
Salerooms	24 var.*		Salerooms	24 var.*	
Semesters	54 var.*		Semesters	54 var.*	
R^2	.82		R^2	.72	
No. of obs.	25,073		Nb. of obs.	10,028	

* For obvious reasons, we do not give the coefficients here. F−tests have been run and show that the coefficients within groups (artists, salerooms and semesters) are not equal.

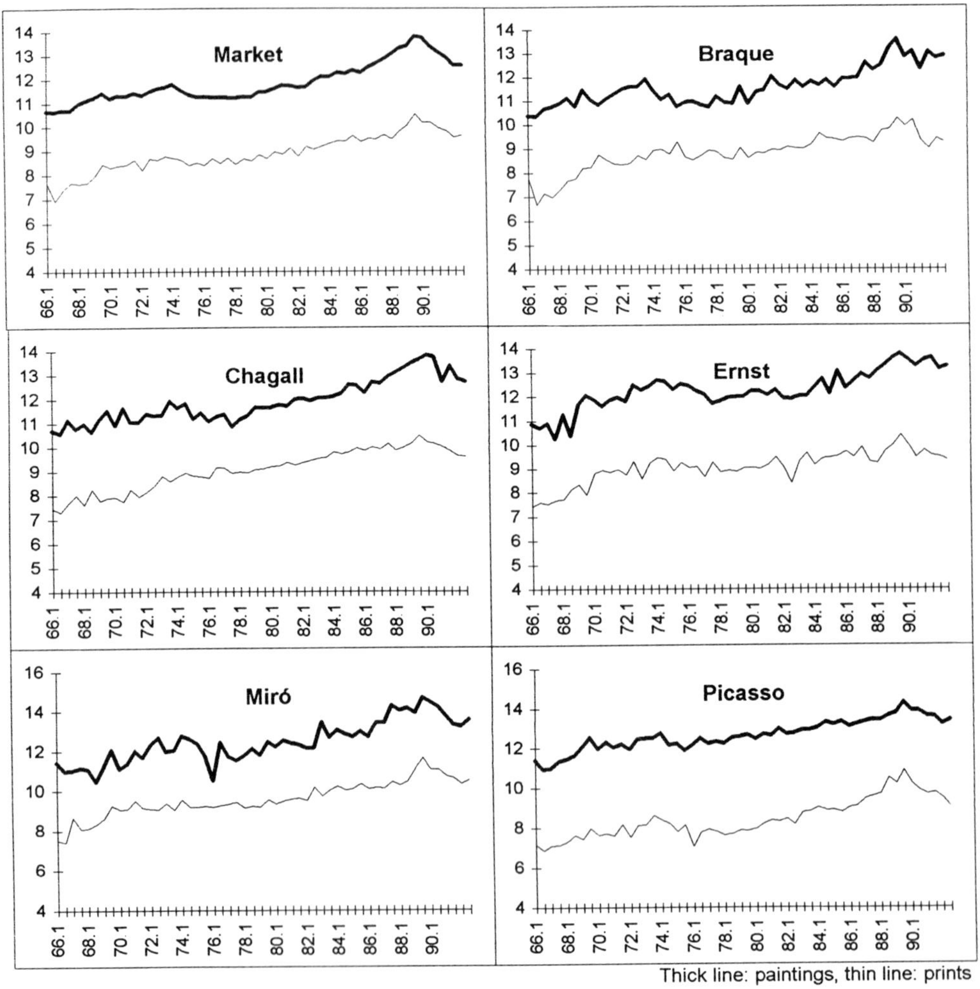

Figure 1: Price Indices for Paintings and Prints

4.1 Relations between prints and paintings

We investigate the conjecture that the markets for paintings and prints – both globally and for each artist individually – move together in the long-run. We estimate in each case the following two-equations system (see equations (1) and (2)):

$$\Delta y_{i,t} = \alpha_i(y_{1,t-1} - \beta_2 y_{2,t-1}) + \sum_{k=1}^{K} \sum_{i'=1}^{2} \gamma_{ii',k} \Delta y_{i',t-k} + \gamma_{i0} + e_{i,t}, i = 1, 2,$$

where now, different values for K, the number of lags for short-run effects (including no lag at all) have been tried out.

The first equation concerns paintings, the second one concerns prints. The results are summarized in Table A2 in the Appendix, where a more technical discussion can also be found. The main findings follow.

The global market

For the global market, i.e. the one represented by the price indices pooling together many artists, the fitted model is:

$$\begin{aligned} \Delta y_{1,t} &= e_{1,t} \\ \Delta y_{2,t} &= 0.37(y_{1,t-1} - 1.24 y_{2,t-1}) + e_{2,t}. \end{aligned}$$

This shows that, with respect to prints, paintings are weakly efficient: their short-run returns follow a white noise process. Therefore, as expected, their long-run returns are almost 25% higher than those of prints. Short-run returns for prints are corrected by the cointegration relationship: whenever the price for prints is higher than 0.81 (i.e. 1/1.24) times the price for paintings, the print index falls – on average – by 37% of the difference between $y_{1,t-1}$ and $1.24y_{2,t-1}$.

Individual artists

For individual artists, the results follow either of two patterns. In the case of Braque and Ernst, prices of paintings are also weakly exogenous, but short-run lags appear in both equations, so that weak efficiency of paintings does not apply.

For Chagall, Miró and Picasso – though no short-run lags were found to be significant –, no index is weakly exogenous with respect to the long-run relation. For Chagall, the model is:

$$\Delta y_{1,t} = -0.35(y_{1,t-1} - y_{2,t-1}) + e_{1,t}$$
$$\Delta y_{2,t} = 0.14(y_{1,t-1} - y_{2,t-1}) + e_{2,t}$$

indicating that long-run returns for prints and paintings are identical.

For Picasso, long-run returns for prints are even higher than for paintings, as shown by the equations:

$$\Delta y_{1,t} = -0.39(y_{1,t-1} - 0.71y_{2,t-1}) + e_{1,t}$$
$$\Delta y_{2,t} = 0.46(y_{1,t-1} - 0.71y_{2,t-1}) + e_{2,t}.$$

This result is probably a consequence of the very high prices that are already obtained for paintings by Picasso.

4.2 Prints: relations between individual artists and the global market

In this section, we are interested in the relations between prices of prints for individual artists and the print market as a whole. We estimate a system similar to (1)-(2), where now the first equation is related to the artist and the second to the global market. Detailed results are given in Table A3 in the Appendix.

In Braque's and Ernst's cases, the global market is weakly efficient. Prints by these two artists have a lower long-run return than the one given by a portfolio, identical to the one used to construct the global index. In the case of Braque, for example, the model is:

$$\Delta y_{1,t} = -0.51(y_{1,t-1} - 0.87y_{2,t-1}) + e_{1,t},$$
$$\Delta y_{2,t} = e_{2,t}.$$

For Chagall,[13] Miró and Picasso, the long-run relation influences the global index, and their long-run returns are higher than those of the index. Pi-

[13] According to the λ_{max}-test, there is no cointegration at the 5% level.

casso's prints are weakly efficient, and the final model fitted for him is:

$$\Delta y_{1,t} = e_{1,t},$$
$$\Delta y_{2,t} = 0.20(y_{1,t-1} - 1.39 y_{2,t-1}) + e_{2,t}.$$

Picasso prints can be thus considered as "leading" or "pushing" the market. Their long-run returns are 39% higher than those of the print portfolio.

4.3 Prints: relations between individual artists

We now consider the system of five equations in which only prices of prints for the five artists appear. The order is Braque (subscript B), Chagall (C), Ernst (E), Miró (M) and Picasso (P). Given our previous findings, we assume that Picasso's prices are weakly exogenous and we set to zero the $\alpha_{P,j}$ coefficients in Picasso's equation. We then try to determine:
(i) who are the artists contributing to the long-run relationship(s)[14] and who are the weakly exogenous ones;
(ii) are there artists who are strongly exogenous;
(iii) what is the most parsimonious model that describes the short-run behaviour of the five price series.

A technical discussion is provided in the Appendix, together with Tables A4 and A5. The findings are as follows.

Chagall and Miró may be left out from the long-run cointegrating relationship. They thus follow long-run trends which are different from those concerning Braque, Ernst and Picasso. Therefore, it was interesting to check whether Chagall's and Miró's short-run lagged values could also be left out of the three other artists' equations. If so, this would indicate that neither the long-run nor the short-run of the former exerts any influence on the group of the latter, so that Braque, Ernst and Picasso would be strongly exogenous. This happens to be the case for Braque and Ernst, but not for Picasso, whose prices are partly explained by those of Miró.

The final, more parsimonious fitted model is:[15]

[14] Since we deal with a five-variables model, there may exist up to four long-run relationships. See Appendix.

[15] This parsimonious representation is based on the model of Table A5, dropping the short-run coefficient which are not significantly different from zero.

$$\begin{aligned}
\Delta y_{B,t} &= - 0.33 z_{1,t-1} - 0.49 z_{2,t-1} + e_{B,t} \\
\Delta y_{C,t} &= - 0.17 z_{1,t-1} + 0.06 z_{2,t-1} - 0.58 \Delta y_{C,t-1} + 0.26 \Delta y_{M,t-1} + e_{C,t} \\
\Delta y_{E,t} &= 1.02 z_{1,t-1} - 0.08 z_{2,t-1} + e_{E,t} \\
\Delta y_{M,t} &= 0.05 z_{1,t-1} - 0.26 z_{2,t-1} + e_{M,t} \\
\Delta y_{P,t} &= - 0.41 \Delta y_{B,t-1} + 0.40 \Delta y_{M,t-1} - 0.36 \Delta y_{P,t-1} + e_{P,t},
\end{aligned}$$

where $z_{1,t-1}$ and $z_{2,t-1}$ represent deviations from the long-run relation to which Chagall and Miró do not contribute.The relations are thus far from simple and each artist contributes in some way to the price behaviour of the others.

5 Conclusions

The analyses performed reveal that the prices of the five artists studied behave differently. We first have the Braque and Ernst group, who follow the market: the global prints index is, in both cases, weakly exogenous. The same holds if the global prints index is replaced by the paintings index of the artist.

The other three artists stand out as special individualities. For all three, paintings and prints are interrelated. Chagall is perhaps the most singular case. The other four artists are strongly exogenous with respect to him, in the joint, five artists model. Moreover, his prints index is the only one that presents weaker evidence of being cointegrated with the global index. Everything seems to indicate that Chagall has a market of his own, in which prints as well as paintings are equally rewarding in the long-run.

Picasso is, naturally, the other singularity. He alone seems to be weakly exogenous in the prints market. Indeed, his price index is weakly efficient with respect to the global index, and he is the artist whose prints generate higher long-run returns than paintings.

Miró's prints are interrelated with the market, and their formal interrelationship with those of Picasso seems to corroborate a well-known historical fact.

Finally, in financial terms, investing in prints whose prices are weakly efficient would be a bad choice for speculators. They should go for prints whose price changes can be forecasted by exogenous variables which may signal – as fundamentals do – the direction of the changes. On the other hand, the closer the indices are to efficiency, the higher is their (long-run) return, given that they constitute riskier assets. As a consequence, buying prints by these artists is a good choice for long-run investors.

6 References

Anderson, R.C. (1974), Paintings as an investment, *Economic Inquiry*, 12, 13-25.

Chanel, O., L.-A. Gérad-Varet and V. Ginsburgh (1992), The relevance of hedonic price indices: the case of paintings, *Journal of Cultural Economics*, forthcoming.

Davidson, J.E.H., D.F. Hendry, F. Srba and S. Yeo (1978), Econometric modelling of the aggregate time-series relationship between consumers' expenditure and income in the United Kingdom, *Economic Journal*, 88, 661-692.

de la Barre, M., S. Docclo and V. Ginsburgh (1994), Returns of Impressionist, Modern and Contemporary European Paintings, 1962-1991, *Annales d'Economie et de Statistique*, 35, 143-181.

Engle, R.F., D.F. Hendry and J.F. Richard (1983), Exogeneity, *Econometrica*, 51, 277-304.

Engle, R.F. and C.W.J. Granger (1987), Co-integration and error correction: representation, estimation and testing, *Econometrica*, 55, 251-276.

Ginsburgh, V. (1994), Objective properties of art and its price, paper presented at the Annual Meeting of the Midwest Economics Association, Chicago, March.

Ginsburgh, V. and P. Jeanfils (1995), Long-term comovements in international markets for paintings, *European Economic Review*, 38, 538-548.

Goetzmann, W.N. (1990), Accounting for taste: an analysis of returns over three centuries, First Boston Working Paper Series FB-90-11, November.

Goetzmann, W.N. (1993), Accounting for taste: art and financial markets over three centuries, *American Economic Review*, 83, 1370-1376.

Granger, C.W.J. (1969), Investigating causal relations by econometric models and cross-spectral methods, *Econometrica*, 37, 424-438.

Johansen, S. (1988), Statistical analysis of cointegration vectors, *Journal of Economic Dynamics and Control*, 12, 231-254.

Johansen, S. (1991), Estimation and hypothesis testing of cointegration in Gaussian vector autoregressive models, *Econometrica*, 59, 1551-1580.

Johansen, S. and K. Juselius (1990), Maximum likelihood estimation and inference on cointegration – with applications to the demand for money, *Oxford Bulletin of Economics and Statistics*, 52, 169-210.

Johansen, S. and K. Juselius (1992), Testing structural hypotheses in a multivariate cointegration analysis of the PP and the UIP for the UK, *Journal of Econometrics*, 53, 211-244.

Laclotte, M. and J.-P. Cuzin (1989), *Dictionnaire de la Peinture*, Paris: Librairie Larousse.

Mayer, E. (1963-1994), *Annuaire International des Ventes*, Paris: Editions Mayer.

Mosconi, R. and C. Gianini (1993), Non-causality in cointegrated systems: representation, estimation and testing, *Oxford Bulletin of Economics and Statistics*, 55, 399-417.

Pesando, J.E (1993), Art as an investment. The market for modern prints, *American Economic Review*, 83, 1075-1089.

Urbain, J.-P. (1993), *Exogeneity in Error Correction Models*, Berlin-Heidelberg: Springer Verlag.

Technical Appendix

Model (1)-(2) discussed in Section 2 can be generalized to take into account more than two variables (and equations). If there are I variables $y_{i,t}$, one can show that there will exist at most $J \leq I-1$ cointegrating relationships. The i-th equation of the model will then be written:

$$\Delta y_{i,t} = \sum_{j=1}^{J} \alpha_{ij} z_{j,t-1} + \sum_{k=1}^{K} \sum_{i'=1}^{I} \gamma_{ii',k} \Delta y_{i',t-k} + \gamma_{i,0} + e_{i,t}, \quad i = 1, 2, ..., I, \qquad (A1)$$

where:

$$z_{j,t-1} = \sum_{i=1}^{I} \beta_{ij} y_{j,t-1}, \qquad j = 1, 2, ..., J \leq I-1 \qquad (A2)$$

is one of the $I-1$ long-term relationships, while the other terms in (A1) (lagged differences with up to a number $K \geq 1$ lags) explain the short-run.[16]

One of the conditions for being allowed to write such a system is to check whether all the differenced variables $\Delta y_{i,t}$ are stationary. This is achieved by using so-called unit root tests.

The other condition is that the $z_{j,t}$ variables in (A2) also be stationary. This can only be checked by estimating the model, and is referred to as testing for cointegrating relations, using the λ_{max} and the *Trace*-tests. There may exist up to $I-1$ cointegrating relationships, but it may also happen than there is none.

The model can of course be estimated with different number of lags involving the $\Delta y_{i,t-1}$ variables. In practice, the number of lags, K should be such that the error processes $e_{i,t}, i = 1, 2, ..., I$, are Gaussian white noise.

Once the model is estimated, it is possible to run a certain number of hypothesis tests.

Excluding variables from the long-run relationship. This is a test on the β's in relations (A2). We shall test two types of assumptions: either $H_0 : \beta = 0$ to test for exclusion of a variable; or $H_0 : \beta = 1$ in the two-variables model[17]

[16] In (A2), one of the β_{ij} coefficients can, without loss of generality, be normalized to unity.

[17] Recall that since one of the $\beta's$ can be normalized to unity, relation (A2) can be written $z_{j,t-1} = y_{1,t-1} - \beta_2 y_{2,t-1}$.

to test whether returns on prints and paintings are equal.

Weak exogeneity. Here, one tests whether one or several α_{ij}'s are zero, so that some or all the long-run relationships in (A1) have no influence on some of the variables.

No influence of the short-run. This is a straightforward test on the $\gamma_{ii'}$ coefficients in (A1).

Strong exogeneity. This is a joint test on both the $\beta_{i'}$ coefficient in the long-run relationships (A2) and on the short-run $\gamma_{ii'}$ coefficients in all relations i. If they are all zero, then variable i' has no influence on any variable $i \neq i'$, and i can be considered as strongly exogenous, since it has no influence on the rest of the system.

Weak efficiency. Here one tests whether all the coefficeints in a given equation i are zero, so that the equation can be written as $\Delta y_{i,t} = e_{i,t}$.

Unit root testing

Table A1 presents the results for the augmented Dickey-Fuller and the Phillips-Perron tests. At the 5% probability level, the first test accepts the unit root null hypothesis in all cases, except for the global prints index. The second test rejects the null hypothesis in several cases. When applied to first-order differences, the Phillips-Perron test clearly rejects the second unit root in all cases; this root is however accepted for both global indices by the Dickey-Fuller test. At the 10% probability level, the unit root null hypothesis is accepted in all cases by the ADF test.

Relations between paintings and prints

Table A2 presents the results, which are now also briefly discussed.

Cointegration relationships. At the 5% probability level, cointegration is accepted by both tests in all cases. We may conclude that there exists a long-run relationship and that prices move together.

Number of short-run lags. The "optimal" number of lags is based both on the Jarque-Bera test and the existence of cointegration. As can be seen, K varies from one case to the other, but in four instances it is zero and the relationships are then:

$$\Delta y_{i,t} = \alpha_i(\beta_1 y_{1,t-1} + \beta_2 y_{2,t-1)} + e_{i,t}, i = 1, 2.$$

Weak exogeneity of paintings. To check this hypothesis, we ran a test H_0 : $\alpha_1 = 0$. If this assumption is accepted, the equation for paintings can be written:

$$\Delta y_{1,t} = \sum_{k=1}^{K} \sum_{i'=1}^{2} \gamma_{1i',k} \Delta y_{i',t-k} + \gamma_{10} + e_{1,t}.$$

The hypothesis is accepted for the market as a whole, for Braque and for Ernst. It is rejected in the case of Chagall, Miró and Picasso.

Error correction mechanisms. In order for the equations to represent error correction mechanisms, we must have $\alpha_1 \leq 0$ and $\alpha_2 \geq 0$. This is verified in all cases in which α_1 is significantly different from zero and means that, in the short-run, any over- or undershooting of prices is corrected.

On the proportionality of comovements. If the hypothesis $H_0 : \beta_2 = -1$ is accepted, the ratio of prices is equal to unity and expected long-run returns are the same. This assumption is accepted only for Chagall. For the global market, as well as for Braque, Ernst and Miró, prints have smaller returns than paintings. Picasso, is an exception to this rule, and significantly so, since his β_2 is much smaller than one.[18]

Weak efficiency of the market for paintings. For the global market, (i) prices of paintings are weakly exogenous (i.e. $\alpha_1 = 0$) and (ii) there are no lags in the short-run part of the relation; moreover, $H_0 : \gamma_{10} = 0$ is accepted, so that the global market for paintings is weakly efficient.

Returns on prints vs. returns on paintings. For the global market as well as for Braque and Ernst, the equation for prints includes the error-correction

[18]Note that if $H_0 : \alpha_1 = 0$ is accepted, we run a joint test $H_0 : \alpha_1 = 0, \beta_2 = -1$; otherwise, we only run a test $\beta_2 = -1$.

term, while for paintings it does not, so that, as discussed in Section 2.3, prints should have a smaller return than paintings and this is actually the case. Prints also have a smaller return than paintings for Chagall and Miró, while for Picasso, the opposite is true.

Prints: relations between individual artists and the global market

Table A3 gives the results for the five pairs. Cointegration is rejected at the 5% level for Chagall by the λ_{max}-test, but accepted by the *Trace*-test. Cointegration is accepted at the same probability level for all other artists. For the remainder, the interpretation of the results can be made along the same lines as in in the preceding section.

Cointegration between the five artists

As can be checked from the results of Table A4, both tests accept cointegration.

The long-run relationship(s). The long-run cointegration relationships read:

$$z_{j,t} = \beta_{Bj}y_{B,t} + \beta_{Cj}y_{C,t} + \beta_{Ej}y_{E,t} + \beta_{Mj}y_{M,t} + \beta_{Pj}y_{P,t}, j = 1, 2, ..., J,$$

with $J \leq 4$. Both the λ_{max} and the *Trace*-tests show that there are at most two cointegrating relations (at the 5% level), for $0 \leq K \leq 3$, where K is the number of short term lags. For $K = 4$, there is only one such relationship.

We are interested in relationships that are parsimonious, and contain a number of individual artists that is as small as possible. We tried all combinations excluding three artists from the above long-run relationship. As is seen from Table A4, the hypothesis is strongly rejected at the 5% probability level, whatever the number of lags in the short-run part of the relations. We then turned to test the exclusion of all possible couples of artists and found that, for $K = 1$, the hypothesis $\beta_{Cj} = \beta_{Mj} = 0$ could not be rejected at the usual 5% level.[19]

[19]Note that when three artists are excluded, there can be at most one cointegration relationship, so that the χ^2 variable used to test the null hypothesis for exclusion of three artists has 3 d.f. When two artists are excluded, there may be one or two cointegrating relations, so that the χ^2-test has 2 or 4 d.f.

This leads to accepting the following two long-run relationships:

$$z_{1,t} = y_{B,t} - 1.32 y_{E,t} + 0.04 y_{P,t}$$

and

$$z_{2,t} = y_{B,t} + 0.09 y_{E,t} - 0.59 y_{P,t},$$

in which Chagall and Miró do not contribute.

The short-run relationship(s). In Table A5, we give the short-run behaviour for $K = 1$. Recall that Picasso is assumed to be weakly exogenous from the start. Given that only Braque, Ernst and Picasso enter the long-run relations, we tested for strong exogeneity of these three artists. Table A5 shows the complete results for the short-run part (with $K = 1$). Though Chagall's and Miró's lagged price differences are not significant in the equations for Braque and Ernst – and for Miró himself – (as can be seen from the last column of Table A5, $H_0 : \gamma_{iC,1} = \gamma_{iM,1} = 0$ is accepted), Miró's short run behaviour influences Picasso's – which is not too surprising, given the connection between their works. This means that the four other artists are strongly exogenous for Chagall.

Table A1
Unit Root Tests for the (logged) Price Series

	H_0: I(1)		H_0: I(2)	
	A.D.F.	P.P.	A.D.F.	P.P.
Paintings				
Global	-2.67	-3.78	-3.03	-35.55
Braque	-2.55	-22.81	-6.71	-78.31
Chagall	-1.91	-24.30	-6.35	-78.71
Ernst	-1.80	-22.98	-6.49	-80.81
Miró	-2.77	-31.34	-7.54	-73.24
Picasso	-3.45	-22.11	-4.52	-70.75
Prints				
Global	-3.76	-22.86	-3.43	-74.50
Braque	-2.31	18.36	-5.81	-68.46
Chagall	-0.95	-14.64	-6.44	-78.84
Ernst	-2.63	-26.49	-8.01	-74.12
Miró	-3.39	-26.95	-6.91	-73.71
Picasso	-1.70	-16.37	-4.56	-75.32
Crit. value	-3.50	-19.80	-3.50	-19.80

A.D.F. = augmented Dickey-Fuller; P.P. = Phillips-Perron.
All tests include a constant term and a time trend.
The critical values shown refer to the 5% probability level.

Table A2
Cointegration between Paintings (Rel. 1) and Prints (Rel. 2)

	Global	Braque	Chagall	Ernst	Miró	Picasso
No. of lags	0	1	0	2	0	0
λ_{max}-test						
$r = 0$	15.57	14.65	15.57	14.06	28.08	25.28
Trace-test						
$r = 0$	16.91	15.42	17.87	16.80	22.94	16.27
$r \leq 1$	1.33	0.77	2.30	2.75	2.10	1.74
Parameters						
β_1	1.00	1.00	1.00	1.00	1.00	1.00
β_2	-1.24	-1.84	-1.08	-1.73	-1.25	-0.71
α_1	0.07	0.00	-0.35	-0.03	-0.65	-0.39
α_2	0.37	0.20	0.14	0.53	0.16	0.46
Hyp. tests (χ^2 val.)						
$H_0 : \alpha_1 = 0$	0.75	0.00	10.47	0.05	15.47	7.10
$H_0 : \alpha_2 = 0$	-	-	-	-	-	5.26
$H_0 : \beta_2 = -1$	-	-	0.24	-	4.89	11.48
$H_0 : \alpha_1 = 0; \beta_2 = -1$	6.21	7.40	-	11.01	-	-
Jarque-Bera (χ^2 val.)						
Rel. 1	2.94	0.43	1.82	0.16	0.39	0.88
Rel. 2	1.23	0.79	0.10	0.97	0.85	0.33

The critical values at the 5% probability level are:
14.04 for the λ_{max}-test and 15.20 and 3.96 for the *Trace*-test.
3.84 and 5.99 for the χ^2-test with 1 and 2 d.f.
5.99 for the Jarque-Bera test (χ^2 with 2 d.f.).

Table A3
Cointegration between Individual Artists (Rel. 1)
and the Global Market (Rel. 2)

	Braque	Chagall	Ernst	Miró	Picasso
No. of lags	0	0	0	0	0
λ_{max}-test					
$r = 0$	18.48	13.14	26.89	59.33	17.55
Trace-test					
$r = 0$	23.35	16.82	31.05	62.14	20.90
$r \leq 1$	4.87	3.69	4.16	2.81	3.35
Parameters					
β_1	1.00	1.00	1.00	1.00	1.00
β_2	-0.87	-1.22	-0.67	-1.11	-1.39
α_1	-0.51	-0.11	-0.82	-0.70	-0.23
α_2	-0.09	0.26	-0.08	0.46	0.20
Hyp. tests (χ^2 val.)					
$H_0 : \alpha_1 = 0$	-	-	-	-	1.90
$H_0 : \alpha_2 = 0$	0.41	6.47	0.42	9.77	4.05
$H_0 : \alpha_2 = 0; \beta_2 = -1$	3.44	-	11.50	-	12.74
$H_0 : \beta_2 = -1$	-	1.93	-	12.94	12.74
Jarque-Bera (χ^2 val.)					
Rel. 1	3.08	0.33	0.97	3.65	2.09
Rel. 2	1.03	1.32	1.21	0.71	0.54

The critical values at the 5% probability level are:
14.04 for the λ_{max}-test and 15.20 and 3.96 for the *Trace*-test.
3.84 and 5.99 for the χ^2-test with 1 and 2 d.f.
5.99 for the Jarque-Bera test (χ^2 with 2 d.f.).

Table A4
Cointegration between the Five Individual Artists and Exclusion Tests for Two and Three Artists

No. of lags	0	1	2	3	4
λ_{max}-test					
$r = 0$ vs $r = 1$	47.00	51.96	43.31	44.11	43.58
$r \leq 1$ vs $r = 2$	30.15	30.52	35.70	33.54	21.17
$r \leq 2$ vs $r = 3$	17.10	15.91	9.58	19.52	9.76
$r \leq 3$ vs $r = 4$	7.05	4.89	5.86	6.18	1.62
$Trace$-test					
$r = 0$ vs $r \geq 1$	101.29	102.39	94.45	103.34	76.12
$r \leq 1$ vs $r \geq 2$	54.30	50.43	51.14	59.24	32.54
$r \leq 2$ vs $r \geq 3$	24.15	19.91	15.44	25.70	11.38
$r \leq 3$ vs $r = 4$	7.05	4.89	5.86	6.18	1.62
Excl. tests (χ^2 val.)					
$\beta_B = \beta_C = 0$	17.74	25.31	24.02	27.60	21.39
$\beta_B = \beta_E = 0$	44.48	47.66	45.06	41.36	14.01
$\beta_B = \beta_M = 0$	42.25	42.93	37.61	37.32	29.44
$\beta_C = \beta_E = 0$	30.08	36.88	38.55	34.43	21.52
$\beta_C = \beta_M = 0$	15.72	7.75	20.23	28.71	26.73
$\beta_E = \beta_M = 0$	52.13	50.81	40.84	37.91	32.62
$\beta_B = \beta_C = \beta_E = 0$	23.85	22.55	18.03	23.97	21.64
$\beta_B = \beta_E = \beta_M = 0$	23.01	19.32	9.96	19.40	29.44
$\beta_C = \beta_E = \beta_M = 0$	31.07	26.58	19.35	21.24	33.82
$\beta_B = \beta_E = \beta_M = 0$	39.49	46.09	36.04	27.65	37.16
Jarque-Bera (χ^2 val.)					
Rel. 1	0.64	0.35	0.11	2.87	11.79
Rel. 2	0.87	1.38	0.71	1.00	0.82
Rel. 3	0.58	0.69	1.52	2.75	4.89
Rel. 4	1.87	5.62	5.48	23.55	2.54
Rel. 5	1.86	0.44	0.61	0.74	0.26

The critical values at the 5% probability level are:
33.18, 27.17, 20.78, and 14.04 for the λ_{max}-test
68.91, 47.18, 29.51, and 15.20 for the $Trace$-test.
5.99, 7.81 and 9.49 for the χ^2-test with 2, 3 and 4 d.f.
5.99 for the Jarque-Bera test (χ^2 with 2 d.f.).

Table A5
Cointegration between the Five Individual Artists
Model Coefficients ($K = 1$)

Relation	α_{i1}	α_{i2}	$\gamma_{iB,1}$	$\gamma_{iC,1}$	$\gamma_{iE,1}$	$\gamma_{iM,1}$	$\gamma_{iP,1}$	$H_0 : \gamma_{iC,1} = \gamma_{iM,1} = 0$
Braque	-0.33	-0.49	-0.02	-0.19	-0.23	0.02	0.01	
			(-0.15)	(-1.06)	(-1.86)	(0.17)	(0.10)	0.54
Chagall	-0.17	0.06	0.07	-0.58	0.05	0.26	-0.02	
			(0.06)	(-4.29)	(0.55)	(2.67)	(-1.79)	9.93
Ernst	1.02	-0.08	-0.11	0.10	-0.12	0.23	0.02	
			(-0.52)	(0.43)	(-0.69)	(1.30)	(0.15)	1.30
Miró	0.05	-0.26	-0.15	-0.32	0.08	0.16	0.11	
			(-0.85)	(-1.47)	(0.54)	(-1.04)	(0.80)	2.49
Picasso	0.00	0.00	-0.41	0.11	0.03	0.40	-0.36	
	(-)	(-)	(-2.66)	(0.48)	(0.22)	(2.52)	(-2.52)	4.19

t-statistics are given between brackets, under the coefficients.
The statistic in the last column is an F-variable with 2 and 45 d.f. Its critical value at 5% is 3.21.

Economics of the Arts - Selected Essays
V.A. Ginsburgh and P.-M. Menger (Editors)

5

Price Anomalies at Auction: Evidence from the Market for Modern Prints*

James E. Pesando
University of Toronto, Toronto

Pauline M. Shum
Atkinson College, York University

1 Introduction

Ashenfelter (1989) and Ashenfelter-Genesove (1992) have documented the declining price anomaly, at auctions for wine and for real estate. The declining price anomaly is the tendency for a lot offered for sale later in an auction to sell at a lower price than an identical lot sold earlier in the same auction. Pesando (1993) has found systematic differences across auction houses and across international markets in prices realized from the sale of modern prints, another violation of the law of one price. In addition, Pesando has documented the substantial noise that exists in prices realized at auction for modern prints. These contributions are part of an expanding literature that uses data from auction markets to establish a series of "stylized facts." These results serve as self-contained contributions to our understanding of these markets, including their efficiency. In addition, these stylized facts serve as inputs into theoretical work on the economics of auctions, as evidenced by the recent contribution of McAfee and Vincent (1993).

Prints, as multiples, are unlike other segments of the art market. This unique feature makes the print market a natural laboratory in which to explore price anomalies at auction. Impressions of modern prints – the prints of artists such as Picasso, Chagall, Miro and Matisse – do vary in quality and

* We thank Mark Flanagan for valuable research assistance, and William Goetzmann and Victor Ginsburgh for helpful comments.

condition, although such variation is far less than the variation in the quality and condition of the "old master" prints of Rembrandt, Durer, etc.. The unobserved variation in quality and condition, in turn, represents a potentially important caveat to the findings in Pesando (1993). The higher prices for modern prints realized at Kornfeld in Switzerland, for example, might simply reflect the ability of this auction house to attract especially fine impressions of the prints that are offered for sale.

In this paper, we test the robustness of these earlier findings by studying a narrower and more homogeneous segment of the market for modern prints. We do so by focusing on the prints of a single artist, Picasso. Impressions of the prints of Picasso – unlike those, for example, of Toulouse Lautrec – tend to be of similar quality and condition. Hence, the contribution of these non-observables to the noise in auction prices and to the systematic price differences should be minimal.

Our analysis proceeds in the following order. First, we study all of the prints of Picasso to look for systematic price differences across international markets and across auction houses. Second, we repeat the exercise for the 100 prints that comprise Picasso's *Vollard Suite.* There is less variation in quality and condition within this subset of Picasso's prints than in his graphic work as a whole, so that this exercise should provide an even cleaner test of the law of one price. Third, we disaggregate the sample period to determine if systematic differences in realized prices are confined to the period of rapidly rising prices, or whether such differences also occur in more normal market conditions. Fourth, we use the market for Picasso prints to provide an additional test of the declining price anomaly. Different impressions of a print are not truly identical, unlike, for example, different cases of the same wine. Subject to this caveat, we find that the declining price anomaly also exists in the market for Picasso prints.

This paper is organized as follows. Section 2 provides background information on the print price data and on Picasso's Vollard Suite. This section also updates to 1993 the index of print prices estimated by Pesando (1993). Section 3 contains extensive tests of whether the market for Picasso prints satisfies the law of one price. Section 4 examines the market for Picasso prints for evidence of the declining price anomaly. Section 5 concludes the paper.

2 Background

2.1 The print price data

Our data are drawn from *Gordon's Print Price Annuals*, published since 1978. The *Annuals* contain a detailed record of the prints sold at the world's major auction houses in the previous year. The information on each print includes the artist, title, number in the catalogue raisonné (reference catalogue) of the artist's work, price, location, date of sale, and whether the print is signed by the artist. The price of the print is inclusive of the buyer's premium, which is typically around 10 percent, and is recorded in the currency of the country in which the auction took place. If the auction was not conducted in the United States, the price is translated into U.S. dollars using the *Wall Street Journal*'s daily conversion rates. Data are available for the period 1977 to 1993, and this full data set is employed in our analysis.

2.2 The Vollard Suite

The Vollard Suite is a set of 100 etchings, aquatints, engravings and drypoints executed by Picasso during the period 1930 to 1937. The set is named after the art patron and publisher, Ambroise Vollard, to whom Picasso gave the 100 copper plates in 1937 (and the right to publish them in an edition), in exchange for several paintings. Prominent in the subject matter of the Vollard Suite are the themes of the artist's studio, with the artist working on or surrounded by classical-style sculptures and canvasses, and the Minotaur.

The Vollard Suite was published in 1939 in an edition of 300: 250 impressions on small format paper; 50 impressions on paper with larger margins; and 3 impressions on vellum (Bloch (1968)). Because of Vollard's accidental death in 1939 and the impact of World War II, most of the prints were not released to the commercial market until the 1950s. A significant number, but not all, of the individual impressions were ultimately signed by Picasso.

The vast majority of prints sold at auctions are from the edition of 250. There is relatively little variation in the quality of the impressions, and most impressions are in good condition. The prints are published in black and white, so that the attenuation of colours – a potentially important source of variation in price – is not a concern. There is a slight premium for impressions from the edition of 50, although these prints rarely come on the market.

Impressions from the edition of 3 in vellum are very rare, and command a substantial premium when offered for sale. For this reason, we have excluded impressions on vellum from the sample.

2.3 The print price index

We begin our analysis by first identifying the overall movement, from 1977 to 1993, of the prices of the prints contained in the data base. This exercise, of interest in itself, serves as a necessary prelude to our analysis of the behaviour of print prices in periods of sharply rising prices as distinct from more normal market conditions.

To this end, we estimate a semiannual price index for all the prints of Picasso. (There are not sufficient observations to permit us to obtain a reliable estimate of a similar price index for the Vollard Suite.) It is natural to work with a semiannual index since auction sales are clustered around May/June and November/December. As in Pesando (1993), the repeat-sale regression is employed to estimate the price index. A repeat sale occurs whenever the "identical" print (same catalogue raisonné, signed or not) is sold on two different occasions. For each pair of sales, the log-price relative is calculated: the log of the price on the later sales date less the log of the price on the earlier date. The log-price relatives are then regressed on a set of dummy variables, one for each time period in the log-price index, except for the first. For each observation of a log-price relative in the regression, the dummy variable is set equal to +1 at the time of the second sale, −1 at the time of the initial sale, and 0 at all other times. Econometrically, this procedure is equivalent to regressing the price of each repeat sale on a corresponding time-period dummy, whose coefficient is the estimated value of the index, and an individual "print" dummy.[1]

[1]The regression model is:

$$r_{itt'} = \sum_{j=1}^{T} b_j x_j + u_{itt'}$$

where $r_{itt'}$ is the log-price relative of print i, with the initial sale at time t and final sale at time t'; x_j is a dummy variable which equals +1 at the time of the final sale, −1 at the time of the initial sale, and 0 otherwise; b_j is the value of the log-price index in period j (to be estimated); and $u_{itt'}$ is a disturbance term. The log of the initial value of the index (b_0) is normalized at zero, and the T subsequent values of the log-price index are estimated by the regression.

The semiannual log-price index for all the prints of Picasso, from 1977 to 1993, is presented in Table 1. During this period, there are 6,446 repeat sales of Picasso prints, and thus 6,446 observations in the repeat-sale regression.

The first difference of the log-price index ($b - b_{-1}$) is the return to prints in each time period. The price index (antilog of b) is graphed in Figure 1. Shown too, is the corresponding real index of print prices. For the period 1977 to 1992, Pesando (1993) has shown that the Picasso price index is quite representative of the overall price movements in the market for modern prints. For this reason, the price index presented in Table 1 can also be interpreted as a measure of the behaviour of prices in the print market as a whole.

Figure 1 indicates that the prices of Picasso prints rose steadily starting in 1983, accelerated in the late 1980s, and eventually collapsed in the spring of 1990 (as did the entire print market). The "bubble-like" behaviour of the prices is immediately apparent. Between the peak of the market (1990:1) and the last observation in our data set (1993:2), nominal prices of Picasso prints fell by 43 percent. Real prices fell by 49 percent. In 1993, the additional year in our sample period, print prices continued to decline, but at a more modest pace than earlier in the 1990s.

Case and Shiller (1987) argue that the variance of $u_{itt'}$ is likely to increase with the length of time between sales, and propose a three-stage procedure to lessen the weight assigned to repeat sales that are widely separated in time. First, the index is estimated by ordinary least squares (OLS). Second, the squared residuals are regressed on a constant term and the time between sales. Third, the index is reestimated by generalized least squares (GLS) with each observation divided by the square root of the fitted value in the second stage. Pesando (1993) finds that GLS and OLS estimates of a price index for modern prints are very similar, and presents only the OLS results. The price index for the prints of Picasso is estimated using OLS. For additional examples of the use of the repeat sales regression technique, see Case and Shiller (1989) and Goetzmann (1992).

Table 1
Picasso Print Price Index: Semiannual, 1977-1993

Year	$b = \log \text{index}$	$SE(b)$	$b - b_{-1}$	$SE(b - b_{-1})$
1977:1	0.00000	0.000000	-	-
1977:2	-0.14160	0.039519	-0.14160	0.039519
1978:1	0.11313	0.035618	0.25472	0.037794
1978:2	0.23245	0.042576	0.11933	0.038426
1979:1	0.33640	0.034757	0.10394	0.036527
1979:2	0.42092	0.036989	0.08453	0.029542
1980:1	0.50476	0.033953	0.08384	0.027107
1980:2	0.63647	0.037195	0.13171	0.025441
1981:1	0.62340	0.035434	-0.01307	0.025983
1981:2	0.52336	0.039144	-0.10004	0.027298
1982:1	0.48293	0.037656	-0.04043	0.028625
1982:2	0.37937	0.041649	-0.10356	0.031931
1983:1	0.42983	0.039489	0.05046	0.033621
1983:2	0.41850	0.040226	-0.01133	0.031680
1984:1	0.48736	0.038884	0.06886	0.030576
1984:2	0.53959	0.039178	0.05223	0.028656
1985:1	0.54347	0.038167	0.00388	0.027275
1985:2	0.61528	0.041293	0.07181	0.029290
1986:1	0.78311	0.038808	0.16783	0.028962
1986:2	0.84187	0.040741	0.05876	0.028003
1987:1	1.11600	0.038649	0.27413	0.027573
1987:2	1.09438	0.042894	-0.02162	0.029891
1988:1	1.32260	0.039548	0.22822	0.030913
1988:2	1.45445	0.041011	0.13185	0.026821
1989:1	1.55865	0.040912	0.10419	0.027245
1989:2	1.63554	0.041348	0.07689	0.025449
1990:1	1.64016	0.040452	0.00462	0.023834
1990:2	1.53625	0.043058	-0.10391	0.026071
1991:1	1.39745	0.042732	-0.13880	0.028245
1991:2	1.30190	0.046653	-0.09555	0.032199
1992:1	1.25195	0.043942	-0.04995	0.033029
1992:2	1.15961	0.047949	-0.09234	0.033777
1993:1	1.10346	0.046181	-0.05615	0.036016
1993:2	1.08120	0.050354	-0.02226	0.038238

b is the value of the log-price index; $SE(b)$ is its standard error; $b - b_{-1}$ is the first difference in the index (the semiannual return).

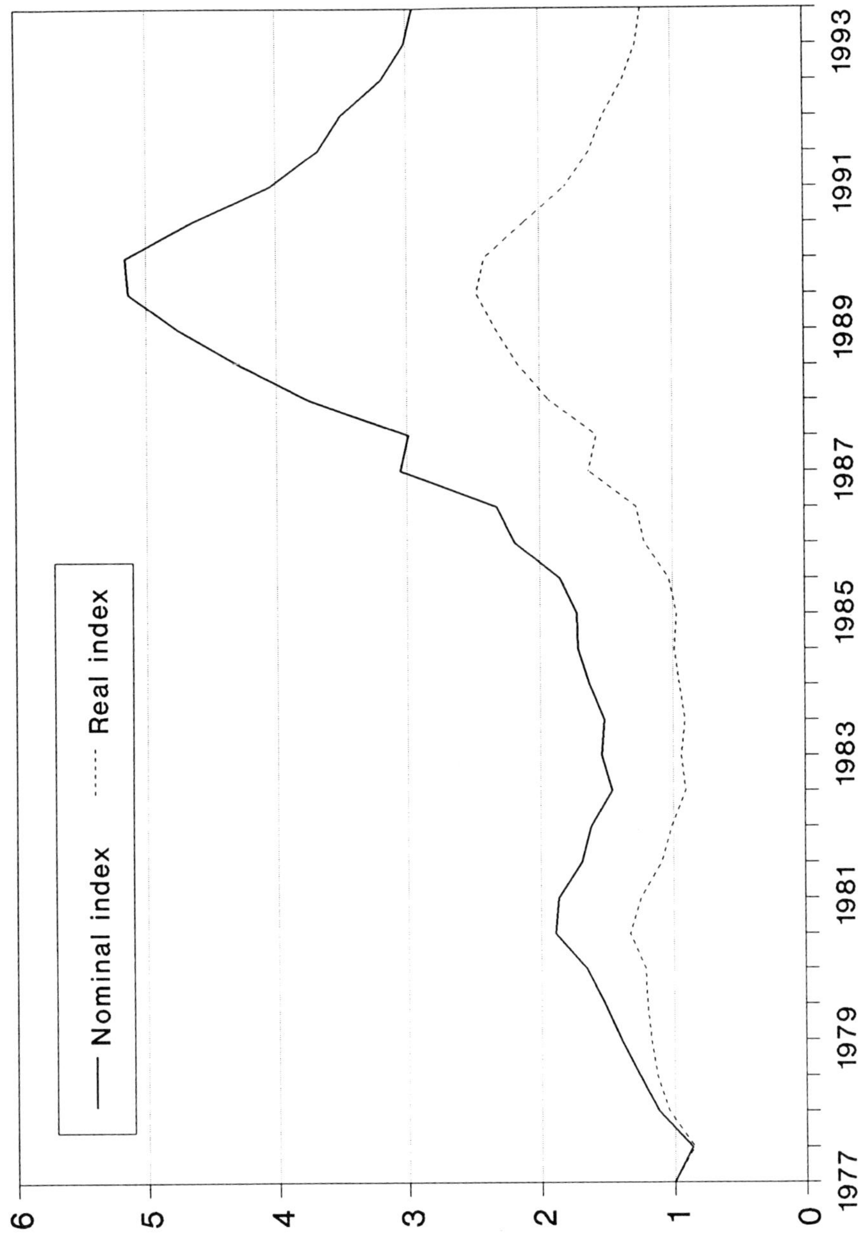

Figure 1: Picasso Print Price Indexes
(semiannual, 1977:1 - 1993:2)

3 The law of one price

As documented in Pesando (1993), there are often systematic differences across international markets and – especially – across auction houses in the prices realized from the sale of identical prints. For example, for identical prints sold within 30 days of each other, prices for the aggregate data set of 28 artists[2] are 10 percent higher in the United States than in Europe (excluding London). Prices are 22 percent higher at the auction house of Kornfeld in Switzerland than in the rest of the world, and 14 percent higher at Sotheby's than at Christie's in New York. These price differences are all statistically significant at the 5 percent level. The higher prices realized at Sotheby's than at Christie's in New York are particularly puzzling since the two auction houses are located in the same city. In addition to the evidence of systematic prices differences, Pesando (1993) notes the surprisingly large magnitude in the variations in price of the contemporaneous sale of identical prints. For prints sold within 30 days of each other, the mean *absolute* price difference is typically in the order of 30 percent of the average price. This fact suggests that there is a great deal of "noise" in auction outcomes.

In this section, we re-examine the evidence for systematic price differences by focusing on all of the prints of Picasso as well as the subset of prints that comprise the Vollard Suite. We compare the prices of identical prints that were sold in two different international markets or auction houses within 30 days of each other. If there were two or more sales of the print in the same market or auction house within the 30-day window, the average price is used in the comparison. To isolate the effects of outliers, we also report the results for a subsample in which pairs are excluded if the higher-priced print sold for more than double the price of the other. Because of the reduced number of observations for the Vollard Suite, the exercise is repeated for a 90-day window. In addition, we examine the extent to which the substantial price differences observed in auction outcomes are reduced if we focus on a more homogeneous set of prints (i.e., Picasso) where unobserved variations in quality and condition are less important than for the market as a whole.

In addition to summary statistics on price differences, we also record

[2]Picasso, Chagall, Miro, Matisse, Whistler, Nolde, Heckel, Schmidt-Rottluf, Kirchner, Kandinsky, Klee, Mueller, Bellows, Benton, Hopper, Munch, Renoir, Sloan, Vuillard, Braque, Bonnard, Cassatt, Kollwitz, Laurencin, Leger, Rouault, Toulouse-Lautrec, and Villon.

the difference in sales dates between each pair of sales. This information is necessary to determine how closely aligned are the "contemporaneous" sales. In the comparisons with a 30-day window, for example, the mean difference in sales dates never exceeds 15 days. This mean difference is typically much smaller, and occasionally zero.

3.1 The market for Picasso prints

In Table 2, we report the results pertaining to the law of one price across international markets and across auction houses for a 30-day window. The first row indicates, for example, that there were 188 sales of the same Picasso print in the United States and London that occurred within 30-days of each other during the period 1977 to 1993. Of these, 48 percent were positive, indicating that the prices were higher in the first market (United States) 48 percent of the time. The mean difference between the prices was 7 percent, which is not statistically significant ($t = 0.72$). If the outliers are removed by imposition of the filter, the number of paired sales declines from 188 to 169. The mean difference in prices declines to 2 percent, which again is insignificant.

As in Pesando (1993), we reject the null hypothesis that there is no price difference between identical prints sold in the United States and in Europe (excluding London) at the 5 percent level. Prices are also significantly higher at Sotheby's than at Christie's in New York, and at Kornfeld than in the rest of the world. However, compared with the prior study that used data on 28 artists, the mean and mean absolute price differences for the prints of Picasso are typically smaller.

Consider, for example, Picasso prints sold at Christie's and Sotheby's in New York. As reported by Pesando (1993), the mean price difference is 14 percent for the aggregate sample of 28 artists. This price spread is only 7 percent for the prints of Picasso. The systematic price differences that do exist in the market for Picasso prints are smaller, a result that may be due to the fact that these prints are of more uniform quality and condition. Nonetheless, the fact that systematic price differences *do* exist in the market for Picasso prints merits emphasis.

The mean *absolute* price difference divided by the average price is a natural measure of the "noise" in auction outcomes. Based on the 30-day window for prints sold at Christie's or Sotheby's in New York, this ratio is equal to

Table 2
The Market for Picasso Prints and the Law of One Price:
30-Day Window, 1977-1993

	Markets		Price Difference [(1)-(2)]					
Filter	(1)	(2)	No. Pairs	Percent Positive	Mean Difference ÷ Mean Price	Mean Absolute Difference ÷ Mean Price	Significance of Mean Difference	Mean Difference in Sales Dates
None	U.S.	London	188	48	0.07	0.32	0.72	-12
2x	U.S.	London	169	49	0.02	0.20	0.66	-12
None	U.S.	Europe	146	55	0.12	0.30	2.31	-10
2x	U.S.	Europe	124	55	0.08	0.23	2.18	-10
None	London	Europe	282	49	0.03	0.27	1.06	-1
2x	London	Europe	248	48	0.03	0.22	1.08	-1
None	Chr(NY)	Soth(NY)	96	35	-0.07	0.16	-2.09	0
2x	Chr(NY)	Soth(NY)	94	34	-0.08	0.15	-2.25	0
None	Chr(Lon)	Soth(Lon)	40	42	0.02	0.15	0.42	0
2x	Chr(Lon)	Soth(Lon)	39	43	0.03	0.14	0.64	0
None	Kornfeld	R. of World	121	70	0.14	0.25	3.49	2
2x	Kornfeld	R. of World	114	68	0.10	0.22	2.69	3

The significance of the mean price difference is the t-statistic for the null hypothesis of no price difference. If negative, the mean difference in sales dates indicates that, on average, the sales in market 1 precede those in market 2. Price comparisons are for sales of the identical print (catalogue raisonné, signed or unsigned) that occur in the two markets within 30 days of each other. In the 2x results, pairs are excluded if the higher-priced print sold for more than double the price of the other. Europe refers to Continental Europe, in this and in subsequent tables.

16 percent for the prints of Picasso, compared to 28 percent for the market as a whole (Pesando (1993)). In light of the fact that the mean difference in sales dates for the Picasso prints is *zero*, the 16 percent spread will seem large to many observers. Further, even if the filter is imposed to eliminate extreme price discrepancies, the mean absolute price difference divided by the average price is still 20 percent or more in four of the six comparisons presented in Table 2. Hence, the prior finding by Pesando of substantial "noise" in auction outcomes, although attenuated, is again evident in the market for the prints of Picasso.

3.2 The market for the Vollard Suite

In Table 3, we find that the statistically significant price differences between the United States and Europe, and between Kornfeld and the rest of the world, disappear if the sample is limited to the 100 prints that comprise the Vollard Suite. However, prices are 7 percent higher at Sotheby's than at Christie's in New York, and this spread is statistically significant at the 5 percent level. A puzzling result in Table 3 is the emergence of a significant price discrepancy between identical prints in the Vollard suite sold at Sotheby's and at Christie's in *London*. In particular, prices average 21 percent higher at Sotheby's than at Christie's. Further, there is no time lag between each pair of sales on average, as the mean difference in sales dates is zero. However, there are only 11 observations in the sample. Interestingly, even for this most homogeneous subset of Picasso's prints, the mean absolute price difference divided by the average price – the natural measure of the "noise" in auction outcomes – exceeds 20 percent in four of the six comparisons, prior to the application of the filter.

Because of the relatively modest size of the sample used in Table 3, we also expand the width of the window to 90 days in our examination of the Vollard Suite (Table 4). The mean price difference of 7 percent in favour of Sotheby's versus Christie's in New York is unchanged for this slightly larger sample (35 pairs compared with 28), although the statistical significance of this difference is somewhat higher. Unfortunately, there is only one additional pair of sales in the London market (Sotheby's versus Christie's) within this 90-day window. Since the higher-priced print sold for more than double the price of the other, the results with the filter are the same as those reported in Table 3. In the comparison between Kornfeld and the rest of the world,

Table 3
The Market for Picasso Prints and the Law of One Price:
30-Day Window, 1977-1993

	Markets		Price Difference [(1)-(2)]					
Filter	(1)	(2)	No. Pairs	Percent Positive	Mean Difference ÷ Mean Price	Mean Absolute Difference ÷ Mean Price	Significance of Mean Difference	Mean Difference in Sales Dates
None	U.S.	London	59	55	0.00	0.15	0.09	-14
2x	U.S.	London	58	55	0.00	0.15	0.02	-15
None	U.S.	Europe	30	46	-0.02	0.28	-0.18	-15
2x	U.S.	Europe	28	46	-0.04	0.18	-0.57	-14
None	London	Europe	63	0.04	0.29	0.54	-2	
2x	London	Europe	61	39	0.04	0.27	0.52	-2
None	Chr(NY)	Soth(NY)	28	28	-0.07	0.11	-2.48	1
2x	Chr(NY)	Soth(NY)	28	28	-0.07	0.11	-2.48	1
None	Chr(Lon)	Soth(Lon)	11	36	-0.21	0.22	-2.57	0
2x	Chr(Lon)	Soth(Lon)	10	40	-0.18	0.19	-2.18	0
None	Kornfeld	R. of World	36	77	0.09	0.25	1.30	2
2x	Kornfeld	R. of World	35	77	0.09	0.25	1.23	2

The significance of the mean price difference is the *t*-statistic the null hypothesis of no price difference. If negative, the mean difference in sales dates indicates that, on average, the sales in market 1 precede those in market 2. Price comparisons are for sales of the identical print (catalogue raisonné, signed or unsigned) that occur in the two markets within 30 days of each other. In the 2x results, pairs are excluded if the higher-priced print sold for more than double the price of the other.

Table 4
The Market for Picasso's Vollard Suite and the Law of One Price:
90-Day Window, 1977-1993

Filter	Markets (1)	Markets (2)	Price Difference [(1)-(2)]: No. Pairs	Percent Positive	Mean Difference ÷ Mean Price	Mean Absolute Difference ÷ Mean Price	Significance of Mean Difference	Mean Difference in Sales Dates
None	U.S.	London	100	56	0.00	0.16	-0.14	-14
2x	U.S.	London	97	55	-0.01	0.15	-0.18	-16
None	U.S.	Europe	77	31	-0.08	0.23	-1.48	-24
2x	U.S.	Europe	74	31	-0.08	0.18	-2.29	-24
None	London	Europe	113	32	-0.02	0.27	-0.30	-14
2x	London	Europe	110	32	-0.02	0.24	-0.31	-14
None	Chr(NY)	Soth(NY)	35	31	-0.07	0.11	-2.81	1
2x	Chr(NY)	Soth(NY)	35	31	-0.07	0.11	-2.81	1
None	Chr(Lon)	Soth(Lon)	12	41	-0.19	0.23	-2.29	2
2x	Chr(Lon)	Soth(Lon)	10	40	-0.18	0.19	-2.18	0
None	Kornfeld	R. of World	70	77	0.15	0.24	3.30	23
2x	Kornfeld	R. of World	69	76	0.14	0.24	3.15	22

The significance of the mean price difference is the t-statistic for the null hypothesis of no price difference. If negative, the mean difference in sales dates indicates that, on average, the sales in market 1 precede those in market 2. Price comparisons are for sales of the identical print (catalogue raisonné, signed or unsigned) that occur in the two markets within 90 days of each other. In the 2x results, pairs are excluded if the higher-priced print sold for more than double the price of the other.

there are 70 pairs of sales. This is almost double the number in the 30-day window. The mean difference in sales dates, at 23 days, is also higher. Unlike the results with the 30-day window, the price difference in favour of Kornfeld (15 percent) *is* statistically significant, at the one percent level.

3.3 The market for Picasso prints and the boom period

Logue and Willett (1976), Fischer (1981), Taylor (1981) and others have documented the tendency for the variance of inflation to rise with its level. They observe this relationship across countries, as well as across time in the United States. Fischer (1981) notes that uncertainty about inflation (measured by the variation in expected inflation across individuals) also tends to increase with the rate of inflation.[3] A possible explanation for this empirical relationship is that the acquisition of information becomes more expensive as the rate of inflation rises.

In Figure 1, we observe a boom in the market for Picasso prints between 1983:2 and 1990:1. In fact, this "bubble-like" behaviour in the price index is representative of the entire market for modern prints. For this reason, we wish to determine if the anomalous behaviour of auction prices is confined to periods of rapidly rising prices.

To examine this issue, we divide the data into two sub-periods. The first, which corresponds to flat or falling prices, comprises the period from 1977:1 to 1983:1 and the period from 1990:2 to 1993:2. The second consists of the boom period, from 1983:2 to 1990:1. We repeat the "law of one price" exercises for each sub-period. The results for the 30-day window are presented in Table 5.

In general, there is a tendency for *significant* price dispersion to occur during the period of rapidly rising prices rather than in the period of flat or

[3]Logue and Willett (1976) employ data for 45 countries from 1949 to 1970, and find a positive relationship between the standard deviation and the mean of the rate of inflation in the cross section. Fischer (1981) shows that there is a robust positive association between the variance and the mean of the inflation rate in the United States, both over long and short periods, and for annual as well as quarterly data. Taylor (1981) obtains similar results. Using data from the Michigan and Livingston surveys, Fischer finds that the cross-sectional variance of expected inflation among individual (representing uncertainty about inflation) also has a tendency to increase with the rate of inflation.

Table 5
The Market for Picasso Prints under Different Market Conditions:
30-Day Window

Subsample	Filter	Markets (1)	Markets (2)	No. Pairs	Price Difference [(1)-(2)]: Percent Positive	Mean Difference ÷ Mean Price	Mean Absolute Difference ÷ Mean Price	Significance of Mean Difference	Mean Difference in Sales Dates
Non-boom	None	U.S.	London	102	52	0.18	0.35	0.90	-12
	2x	U.S.	London	95	52	-0.01	0.19	-0.27	-12
Boom	None	U.S.	London	86	43	-0.03	0.29	-0.42	-13
	2x	U.S.	London	74	44	0.05	0.21	0.89	-13
Non-boom	None	U.S.	Europe	73	50	0.13	0.34	1.45	-7
	2x	U.S.	Europe	56	48	0.06	0.24	0.89	-7
Boom	None	U.S.	Europe	73	60	0.10	0.26	2.40	-14
	2x	U.S.	Europe	68	61	0.10	0.23	2.53	-13
Non-boom	None	London	Europe	134	38	-0.05	0.32	-0.88	0
	2x	London	Europe	110	37	-0.05	0.22	-1.42	0
Boom	None	London	Europe	148	58	0.09	0.24	2.60	-2
	2x	London	Europe	138	57	0.07	0.22	2.27	-2
Non-boom	None	Chr(NY)	Soth(NY)	35	40	-0.02	0.15	-0.65	2
	2x	Chr(NY)	Soth(NY)	34	38	-0.03	0.14	-0.93	3
Boom	None	Chr(NY)	Soth(NY)	61	32	-0.09	0.16	-1.99	0
	2x	Chr(NY)	Soth(NY)	60	31	-0.09	0.16	-2.08	0
Non-boom	None	Chr(Lon)	Soth(Lon)	10	50	0.21	0.34	-0.99	3
	2x	Chr(Lon)	Soth(Lon)	9	55	-0.01	0.18	-0.14	3
Boom	None	Chr(Lon)	Soth(Lon)	30	40	0.04	0.14	0.65	0
	2x	Chr(Lon)	Soth(Lon)	30	40	0.04	0.14	0.65	0
Non-boom	None	Kornfeld	R. of World	64	73	0.23	0.31	3.25	2
	2x	Kornfeld	R. of World	59	71	0.17	0.27	2.51	3
Boom	None	Kornfeld	R. of World	57	66	0.06	0.19	1.44	3
	2x	Kornfeld	R. of World	55	65	0.04	0.18	1.07	3

"Non-boom" is the period 1977:1 to 1983:1 and 1990:2 to 1993:2. "Boom" is the period 1983:2 to 1990:1. The significance of the mean price difference is the t-statistic for the null hypothesis of no price difference. If negative, the mean difference in sales dates indicates that, on average, the sales in market 1 precede those in market 2. Price comparisons are for sales of the identical print (catalogue raisonné, signed or unsigned) that occur in the two markets within 30 days of each other. In the 2x results, pairs are excluded if the higher-priced print sold for more than double the price of the other.

declining prices. For example, the higher prices realized for Picasso prints at Sotheby's relative to Christie's in New York are concentrated in the "boom" period of 1983:2 to 1990:1. During the boom period, prices realized at Sotheby's average 9 percent higher than prices at Christie's. Further, there is no mean difference in the sales dates. During the non-boom period, in contrast, prices average only 2 percent higher at Sotheby's. This difference is not statistically significant. A similar pattern is obtained for the comparisons between London and Europe, and between the United States and Europe. The only exception to this finding is the comparison of prices realized at Kornfeld versus the rest-of-the-world, where the price spread in favour of Kornfeld was much greater (23 percent versus 6 percent) in the non-boom period.

4 The declining price anomaly

Ashenfelter (1989) finds that when identical lots of wine are sold in a single auction, the price of the first lot is more likely to exceed than to fall short of the price of a later lot. Although it is common for the price to remain constant, prices of identical lots of wine sold in a single auction in London, Chicago and San Francisco during the period 1985 to 1989 are at least twice as likely to decline as to increase. One explanation is that bidders are risk averse and are willing to pay a premium to avoid the risk of losing out on an item, so that the earlier bid can be viewed as the expected later price plus a risk premium associated with the risky future price. In addition, in the case of wine, many of the bidders are buying to fill orders, and are effectively quantity constrained. For this reason, they tend to bid more aggressively at the beginning of the auction.

Ashenfelter and Genesove (1992) observe a similar price pattern at auctions for real estate. Their data set contains auction prices of condominiums in a single development, the order in which the units are put up for bid, and the resale price of the units in subsequent face-to-face bargaining. Although the units are in the same development, their prices are likely to be affected by unobserved quality differences (for example, floor and view). Ashenfelter and Genesove control for the heterogeneity problem by studying the relationship between the order in which each unit is sold at the auction and the subsequent resale price. If the observed price pattern were a result of the auction mechanism, it should disappear when the condominiums are resold in face-to-face bargaining. However, if the observed price pattern were due to omitted quality differences, then the subsequent resale price of each unit would still be related to the order of sale at the auction. Ashenfelter and Genesove find that prices of condominium units typically declined as the auction progressed, *and* there is no relationship between the resale price and the order in which the unit was sold in the auction held earlier. These results, in juxtaposition, provide evidence of the declining price anomaly in the market for condominiums.

In this section, we use the print market to provide another test of the declining price anomaly. For the full sample of Picasso prints, we compare the prices of each pair of sales of an identical print in the same auction. We do so for the entire data set (i.e., all markets), as well as the geographically distinct markets of the United States, London and Europe. Due to the lack of observations, we do not repeat the exercise for the Vollard Suite. The results are presented in Table 6.

Table 6
Picasso's Prints and the Declining Price Anomaly

Filter	Market	Price Difference [(1)-(2)]					
		No. Pairs	% Posit.	% Negat.	Mean Difference ÷ Mean Price	Mean Absolute Difference ÷ Mean Price	Signif. of Mean Difference
None	World	101	65	23	0.09	0.18	1.97
2x	World	97	64	24	0.10	0.17	2.07
None	U.S.	27	59	22	0.12	0.18	2.48
2x	U.S.	25	56	24	0.12	0.18	2.29
None	London	26	65	27	0.10	0.17	1.29
2x	London	24	66	26	0.12	0.15	1.48
None	Europe	48	68	22	0.07	0.18	0.89
2x	Europe	48	68	22	0.07	0.18	0.89

The significance of the mean price difference is the t-statistic for the null hypothesis of no price difference. Price comparisons are for sales of the identical print (catalogue raisonné, signed or unsigned) that occur in the same auction in the indicated market. Price (1) is the first impression sold, while Price (2) is the second. In the 2x results, pairs are excluded if the higher-priced print sold for more than double the price of the other. Percent positive and negative do not add to 100, since prints are sometimes sold for the same price.

We find that the price of the later sale changes from the earlier one at least 80 percent of the time. (This is the sum of the percentage of positive and negative price changes.) This frequency is much higher than the 35 to 61 percent range documented at auctions for wine (Ashenfelter (1989)). In addition, the price of the later sale is *more than* twice as likely to decline as it is to increase. For our full sample of 101 pairs of sales, the price of the first impression sold was on average 9 percent higher than the price of the second. This mean price difference is significant at the 5 percent level. The results with the filter designed to remove outliers are similar. For the reduced sample of 97 pairs, the mean price spread is 10 percent and is again significant at the 5 percent level. The spread is highest (12 percent) for prints sold in the United States, and lowest (7 percent) for prints sold in Europe.

The above evidence suggests that the declining price anomaly also exists in the market for Picasso prints. Our findings thus imply, as do other studies, the potential importance of risk aversion in auction theory.[4] Given the existing pattern of prices, the optimal strategy for a risk-neutral bidder would be to wait and bid for the later lot. In the presence of risk aversion, the earlier bid can be viewed as the expected later price plus a risk premium.[5]

There is, however, a potentially important caveat to our results. Different impressions of the same print – unlike, for example, different cases of wine – are not likely to be truly identical. One impression may be better, or in better condition, than another.[6] We expect the unobserved variation in the

---

[4]In an independent, private values model with *risk-neutral* bidders, Milgrom and Weber (1982) show that expected prices of identical lots should remain constant as the auction progresses. With affiliated instead of private values, they show that expected prices should rise. Expected prices should rise over time because earlier bids by others release information about the value of the item, thereby reducing concerns about the winner's curse. The latter is the term for the bad news conveyed to the successful bidder that everyone else estimated the value of the item to be less. The evidence presented in this section, as in Ashenfelter (1989) and Ashenfelter and Genesove (1992), is inconsistent with these theoretical predictions.

[5]However, McAfee and Vincent (1993) demonstrate that pure strategy equilibrium bidding functions exist only in the presence of nondecreasing absolute risk aversion. In addition to explaining the theoretical link between risk aversion and the declining price anomaly, McAfee and Vincent use data from Christie's 1987 wine auctions in Chicago to provide supporting evidence for the existence of the declining price anomaly.

[6]We do not explore the possibility that lower-numbered impressions (or artist proofs) command different prices, for two reasons. First, *Gordon Print Price Annuals*, from which our data are drawn, do not include the number of the print in the edition. Second, there

quality and condition of Picasso prints to be less than that in the print market as a whole. Nonetheless, this variation is not zero. Experts at Christie's and Sotheby's in New York have indicated that, as a general rule, they try not to offer more than one impression of a print in an auction.[7] When two impressions are included in the same auction, the better impression – in quality or in condition – is offered first. If this is the practice of most auctioneers, then we would expect the later lot to realize a lower price on average, even in a market characterized by risk-neutral bidders and the absence of quantity constraints.

To provide an additional perspective on this issue, we exploit the fact that the major print auctions at Christie's and Sotheby's in New York, in the spring and the fall, take place in close proximity, often in the same week. If the two auctions occur sufficiently close in time to be viewed as a single auction by dealers and collectors, then the presence of the declining price anomaly can be tested in an indirect manner. In those cases where the auction at Christie's occurs first, the mean price spread in favour of Sotheby's should be less than that in the sample as a whole. The situation should be reversed when the auction at Sotheby's occurs first. In this case, the presence of the declining price anomaly would *reinforce* the observed tendency for realized prices to be higher at Sotheby's.

During the period 1977 to 1993, there are 56 sales of the same Picasso print at Christie's and Sotheby's in New York when the auction at Christie's occurs first. The mean price realized at Christie's is 9 percent less than the mean price realized at Sotheby's. For the 39 sales of the same Picasso print when the auction at Sotheby's occurs first,[8] the mean price spread is less, at

is no a priori reason to believe that lower-numbered impressions are likely to be of higher quality, since the fact that a print has a lower number does not imply that it was pulled first.

[7]Both experts indicate that to place two impressions of the same print in an auction is likely to remove one bidder for the later impression, which tends to lower its price. During the sample period 1977 to 1993, there were only 26 cases (representing 52 lots) in which two impressions of the same Picasso print were offered for sale in the same auction at either Christie's or Sotheby's in New York. This figure represents 1.33 percent of the 3908 lots of Picasso prints sold at these auction houses during the period. At Christie's and Sotheby's in London, this percentage is higher, at 2.22 percent. This percentage is also higher at the remaining auction houses, at 2.64 percent.

[8]There are thus a total of 95 observations, instead of the 96 reported in Table 2. The loss of one observation is due to the fact that one pair of sales took place on the same day,

5 percent. For the sample as a whole, the mean price difference in favour of Sotheby's is 7 percent.

On the surface, these additional results provide no support for the declining price anomaly, under the maintained assumption that the two auctions are in sufficiently close proximity in time to be viewed by dealers and collectors as a single auction. In this context, however, it should be noted that the average number of days that separate the two sales when the auction at Christie's occurs first is one day. When the auction at Sotheby's occurs first, this average spread is five days. To provide an additional perspective, we repeat the above exercise using data from sales that are no more than two days apart. When the Christie's sale occurs first, the number of observations is only slightly reduced, from 56 to 54, and the mean price spread in favour of Sotheby's remains equal to 9 percent. When the Sotheby's sale occurs first, the number of observations drops dramatically, from 39 to 5. The mean price spread in favour of Sotheby's rises sharply, to 28 percent. However, the number of observations is too small for the result to be statistically significant.

5 Conclusion

Pesando (1993) notes the existence of systematic price differences in the contemporaneous sale of identical prints across international markets and across auction houses, and suggests that this violation of the law of one price is an important "stylized fact," at least in the market for modern prints. Since impressions of the prints of Picasso are likely to be of uniform quality and typically in good condition, the extent of the systematic price differences in this sub-market provides a useful perspective on Pesando's result. In addition, we use this more homogeneous segment of the print market to provide another test of the declining price anomaly, observed at auctions for wine and for real estate.

The substantial findings of this paper are as follows. First, the price of Picasso prints (and, presumably, the market for modern prints as a whole) continued to decline in 1993, but at a slower pace than in the preceding years. Second, tests of the "law of one price" suggest attenuated, but still important, variation in the prices of identical prints sold within 30 days of

and we are unable to determine which one occurred first.

each other. In other words, evidence *against* the law of one price persists in the market for Picasso prints. Third, as measured by the ratio of mean absolute price difference to the average price, there is substantial "noise" in auction outcomes. Even if one ignores the systematic price differences that exist across auction houses or across geographic markets, the fact that this ratio is so large – 16 percent for the prints sold at Christie's and Sotheby's in New York – may be disconcerting to those who adhere to the paradigm of market efficiency. Fourth, our results suggest that systematic differences in print prices were typically greater during the boom of the print market, which occurred in the period 1983:2 to 1990:1. Fifth, the comparison between prices of identical prints sold at the same auction provides support for what has been termed the "declining price anomaly." In particular, we find that at auctions in the United States, London and the rest of Europe, the price of the same print sold later in the auction was more than twice as likely to decline as to increase. There is, however, an important caveat to this finding. At least some auction houses consciously offer the stronger impression for sale first if two impressions of the same print are placed in the same auction. To the extent that this is a common practice, the tendency for the print offered later in the sale to command a lower price has a ready explanation.

6 References

Ashenfelter, O. (1989), How auctions work for wine and art, *Journal of Economic Perspectives*, 3, 23-36.

Ashenfelter, O. and D. Genesove (1992), Testing for price anomalies in real estate auctions, *American Economic Review (Papers and Proceedings)*, 82, 501-505.

Bloch, G. (1968), *Picasso, Volume I, Catalogue of the Printed Graphic Work 1904-1967*, Berne: Kornfeld and Klipstein.

Case, K. and R. Shiller (1987), Prices of single-family homes since 1970: new indexes for four cities, *New England Economic Review*, 45-56.

Case, K. and R. Shiller (1989), The efficiency of the market for single-family homes, *American Economic Review*, 79, 125-137.

Fischer, S. (1981), Towards an understanding of the costs of inflation: II, in K. Brunner and A.H. Meltzer, eds., *The Costs and Consequences of Inflation*, Carnegie-Rochester Conference Series on Economic Policy, vol. 15, Amsterdam: North-Holland.

Goetzmann, W.N. (1992), The accuracy of real estate indexes: repeat sales estimates, *Journal of Real Estate Finance and Economics*, 5, 1-51.

Gordon's Print Price Annual, 1978-1994.

Logue, D. and T. Willett (1976), A note on the relation between the rate and variability of inflation, *Economica*, 43, 151-158.

McAfee, R. P. and J. McMillan (1987), Auctions and bidding, *Journal of Economic Literature*, 25, 699-738.

McAfee, R. P. and D. Vincent (1993), The declining price anomaly, *Journal of Economic Theory*, 60, 191-212.

Milgrom, P. and R. Weber (1982), A general theory of auctions and bidding, *Econometrica*, 50, 1089-1122.

Pesando, J. E. (1993), Art as an investment: The market for modern prints, *American Economic Review*, 83, 1075-1089.

Taylor, J. B. (1981), On the relation between the variability of inflation and the average inflation rate, in K. Brunner and A.H. Meltzer, eds., *The Costs and Consequences of Inflation*, Carnegie-Rochester Conference Series on Economic Policy, vol.15, Amsterdam: North-Holland.

Economics of the Arts - Selected Essays
V.A. Ginsburgh and P.-M. Menger (Editors)

6

Auction Theory and Practice: Evidence from the Market for Jewellery*

Olivier Chanel, Louis-André Gérard-Varet and Stéphanie Vincent
GREQAM

1 Introduction

Several recent papers discuss "anomalies" that occur at auctions (Ashenfelter (1989), Salamon (1992), McAfee and Vincent (1993), Bauwens and Ginsburgh (1994); see also McAfee and McMillan (1987) for an extensive review of empirical studies). Among the anomalies we mention: (a) the large price variability for similar objects sold at the same place and time; (b) the so-called "afternoon effect" (or "linkage principle") qualifying the fact that similar objects sold sequentially follow a decreasing (or an increasing) pattern of prices; (c) the inefficiency of estimates of prices provided to the market by experts or auction houses; (d) more generally, possible informational inefficiencies.[1]

As Ashenfelter (1989) has pointed out, auction houses go to considerable effort to estimate the price that a unique item offered will fetch. Predicting individual prices requires a lot of expertise. It is interesting to see how good these estimates are. The theoretical literature on auctions emphasises the idea that it is in the interest of auctioneers to provide truthful information on the items put on the market, and that pre-sale prices should be unbiased estimates of actual prices (Milgrom and Weber (1982)). The main argument is that by revealing information and removing uncertainty, auctioneers make

*We are very grateful to Russell Davidson, Victor Ginsburgh and Peter Lyk-Jensen, for valuable comments and helpful discussions, to two anonymous referees for very interesting suggestions and to Crédit Municipal de Paris, in particular Claire Bois, for allowing us to use their database.

[1]There are also issues on competition among auction houses, on "rings" or on "bought-in" objects, that we do not consider in this paper.

bidders with low estimates more aggressive and thus put pressure on the bidding of others. Ashenfelter (1989) reports on findings about auctions in paintings (at Christie's and Sotheby's) which tend to confirm the prediction that honesty is a profitable policy rule for an auctioneer. In particular, price estimates are close to being unbiased. Salamon (1992) has challenged Ashenfelter's conclusion. Bauwens and Ginsburgh (1994) study a sample of lots of English silver sold by Christie's and Sotheby's, and also reach a slightly different conclusion; they show that there is a significant (although rather small) bias on pre-sale estimates, with different auction houses behaving differently. Another interesting observation by Bauwens and Ginsburgh (1994) is that experts do not seem to take full account of the information given in the catalogues set up before the sale.

It is also often taken as a common belief among auctioneers that when "identical" items are sold in a single auction, prices are more likely to decline than to increase with later lots. Ashenfelter (1989) obtains results on wine auctions which confirm such beliefs. However this afternoon effect (McAfee and Vincent (1993)) is inconsistent with predictions relying on the standard affiliated values (risk neutral) model. According to the received theory, expected prices should follow a martingale, at least with independent private valuations and risk neutrality (Weber (1983)). Actually, if the bidders' valuations are affiliated[2] or, more generally, when there is correlation, expected prices should rise over time. This is the linkage principle (Milgrom and Weber (1982)). In this paper, we test the afternoon effect and the linkage principle for different types of objects included in the database.

Like wines, paintings and many other objects, jewellery has been sold for a long time in auctions, providing material for a better understanding of how auctions really work. This paper reports on empirical findings obtained from a dataset on jewellery auctions at the Crédit Municipal de Paris, (CMP, formerly Mont-de-Piété). The fact that CMP is a French modern "pawnshop" which manages judicial auctions, has important consequences.

As is well known, auctioneers know very well how to get an auction started on an item, without revealing the seller's reservation price. Secret reservation prices and high buy-in rates have important implications on how auctions work. However, this is not the case with judicial auctions, where it is known

[2]Bidders' valuations are said to be affiliated if, roughly speaking, when one bidder perceives the item's value to be high, so will other bidders.

to be in the interest of the saleroom to recover its loan and where the first price quoted is usually informative about the seller's reservation price (here CMP). Furthermore, CMP has a monopoly position in Paris for this type of auction.

The data collected at CMP over almost a full year are rich enough to allow consideration of different phenomena. Section 2 presents the underlying model derived from a "hedonic price equation." We deal with experts' estimates of pre-sale prices in the third section, and with the so-called declining price anomaly in the fourth section. Section 5 concludes the paper.

2 The market

Items of jewellery are heterogeneous goods bought and sold for their characteristics, rather than standard commodities. Such goods are called "hedonic goods." In this section, we consider how a hedonic approach can be used to explain how prices form. We describe first the features of the auction market, emphasising its organisation and the status of the actors.

2.1 Judicial auctions of jewellery in Paris

We focus on jewellery sold in English public auctions between June 1993 and May 1994 at CMP. We concentrate on regular sales (exceptional value items are not included in the data). CMP is a modern pawnshop, which lends some 30 to 50% of the estimated value of items put in deposit by borrowers. In case the owner defaults before the end of a fixed term (up to 18 months), CMP carries out an English auction, i.e. an oral auction where buyers submit ascending bids; the winner pays the price he bids plus a mandatory 14.19% tax. CMP recovers its loan plus a premium (to cover organisation and storage costs as well as risk), and returns the possible surplus to the borrower. This type of auction is special, since we have a captive seller, with no strategic freedom with respect to the sale (in particular without influence through a reservation price. Moreover, casual observation and discussions with auctioneers indicate that two types of buyers coexist on the market: "professionals" who behave rationally on the basis of some objective utility and who look for resale opportunities, and "amateurs" more subject to irrationalities and brief craze.[3]

We have selected five types of objects sold during the period of interest: objects in gold,[4] bracelets, necklaces, rings and watches (sometimes split in three sub-categories: men's wristwatches, women's wristwatches and other watches). For each item, we observe the day and the time at which it was sold, the pre-sale estimate (actually a high and a low estimate), the hammer price and the characteristics of the object sold: weight, main and secondary gem, main and secondary metal (gold, platinum, silver), state of the jewel, the way the gem is cut, etc. The database contains 4,024 observations.

2.2 A hedonic model of the market

When modelling the market, we must take into account the fact that jewellery items are hedonic goods. Previous studies on works of art (Chanel et al. (1994, 1996)), have shown that hedonic price regressions are particularly well adapted to capture the varying nature of the goods which are exchanged.

Roughly speaking, hedonic regressions postulate that the amounts of characteristics embodied in a good reflect its quality and directly influence its price through the utility derived by their consumption. More formally, we estimate a relationship between the observed price of a jewel at date t and its objective characteristics:

$$P_{ht} = a(x_{h1}, ..., x_{hm}, ..., x_{hM}) + b(t) + \epsilon_{ht}, \tag{1}$$

where $t = 1, ..., T$ denotes time (the forty sales over the year), $h = 1, ..., H$ denotes jewel h, P_{ht} represents the hammer price of jewel h at time t, x_{hm}, $m = 1, ..., M$ denotes the objective characteristic m specific to jewel h, $a(.)$ and $b(.)$ are two functions, and ϵ_{ht} is an error term.

Different specifications for $a(.)$ and $b(.)$ can be considered. The best results are obtained with a log-linear form for each type of objects. This leads to:

---

[3]When there are systematic differences among bidders' valuations which are common knowledge, in the absence of a reservation price, an English auction always yields an efficient outcome, the winners being the bidders with the highest valuation. However, in practice, differences among bidders may not be observable.

[4]These are sets of low individual value jewels – usually in gold – which are sold together.

$$p_{ht} = \sum_m \alpha_m x_{hm} + \sum_t \gamma_t d_t + \epsilon_{ht}, \tag{2}$$

where p_{ht} is the log of P_{ht}, d_t is a dummy variable taking the value 1 for a sale at date t and 0 otherwise and α_m is the market valuation of characteristic m (its implicit price).

We do not want to discuss in detail the results obtained for the hedonic regressions. However, it is interesting to note that ranks derived from the implicit prices α_m are consistent with casual observations about the influence on the market price of variables such as the type of metal (platinum first, then gold and silver), or the type of gem (diamond, ruby, emerald, sapphire, and so on). Also, according to our estimates, the weight of a jewel has a positive significant effect on prices, especially for objects in gold, bracelets and necklaces. These results hold for all types of jewels, even in the two worst cases (rings and watches). Note also that the variables included explain 50 to 75% of the price variability (see Table 1 for the main results).

Table 1
Main Results of Hedonic Regressions

Type of jewel	n	k	R^2	St. dev.
Objects in gold	782	63	0.72	0.32
Bracelets	626	87	0.75	0.33
Necklaces	539	87	0.71	0.34
Rings	850	96	0.49	0.57
All watches	367	68	0.55	0.57

n: nb. of observations; k: nb. of regressors.

3 Experts, markets and accurate information

We recall that, for each jewel, our database contains an estimation of the pre-sale valuation (actually an interval), which is known by buyers before the sale. This allows testing the behaviour of experts.

In principle, it is in the interest of an auction house to reveal any information which is correlated with the value of the item. This is so because such information tends to increase the estimates of those bidders who perceive the item value to be low, causing them to bid more aggressively (Milgrom and Weber (1982)). Accordingly, the theory of auctions with affiliated values suggests that pre-sale estimates made public by the auction house should be unbiased predictors of the market.

3.1 Experts do not provide unbiased estimates

We first check if ex-ante valuations can be considered as unbiased predictors of market prices. Let P_{ht} be the market price, P^e_{ht}, the average of the low and the high pre-sale valuations and ϵ_{ht}, a random disturbance with zero mean. For each type of jewel, we run an OLS regression[5] of P_{ht} on P^e_{ht}:

$$P_{ht} = \alpha + \beta P^e_{ht} + \epsilon_{ht}. \tag{3}$$

As can be checked from the results reported in Table 2, the Goldfeld-Quandt test[6] rejects homoscedasticity for objects in gold, bracelets, necklaces and rings. For these cases, we correct for heteroscedasticity by running artificial regressions using instrumental variables estimation which leads to an heteroscedasticity-consistent estimate of the covariance matrix.

Then, we test for unbiasedness ($H_0 : \{\alpha = 0 \text{ and } \beta = 1\}$). The test-statistic follows a χ^2 distribution with 2 degrees of freedom.

---

[5]In our case, there is no room for a possible bias due to objects that are "bought-in." As already mentioned and given the specific nature of the sale (judicial auction), the seller's reservation price is fixed on the basis of the loan to be recovered through the sale. As a matter of fact, more than 97% of the objects presented during the auction are actually sold. The remaining 3% for which there are no bids are generally put up in the sales that follow. Thus, it is not necessary to compute a truncated model (as in Bauwens and Ginsburgh (1994)) to take into account the fact that the price is observed only when the bids reach the reservation price.

[6]This test follows a Fisher statistic F with $(n_1 - k)$ and $(n_2 - k)$ degrees of freedom, where n_1 and n_2 are the numbers of observations of the subsamples obtained after omission of r central observations (here, r is one third of the sample); k is the number of parameters that are estimated.

Table 2
Unbiasedness Tests

Type of jewel	n	k	Homosc. test	p-value	Unbiasedn. test	p-value
Objects in gold	782	2	11.02	0	88.06	0
Bracelets	626	2	17.41	0	137.35	0
Necklaces	539	2	24.81	0	218.18	0
Rings	850	2	33.03	0	114.70	0
Women's wristwatches	179	2	0.30	1	8.53	0.01
Men's wristwatches	117	2	0.22	1	3.07	0.22
Others watches	71	2	0.11	1	1.43	0.49

n: nb. of observations; k: nb. of regressors.

The results, reported in Table 2, show that H_0 is accepted for men's wristwatches and other watches, and is rejected in all other cases. More precisely, we accept ($H_0 : \{\alpha > 0$ and $\beta = 1\}$) for objects in gold, ($H_0 : \{\alpha = 0$ and $\beta > 1\}$) for necklaces, women's wristwatches and rings and ($H_0 : \{\alpha > 0$ and $\beta > 1\}$) for bracelets. The results show that, on average, experts have an ex-ante valuation that is lower than the hammer price for all types of jewels, except for men's wristwatches and other watches.

There is probably some strategic undervaluation going on. One possible rationale is to attract more buyers with appealing estimates, raising the probability to sell the object and to obtain higher prices through greater competition.

3.2 Experts have superior information

We now check whether experts and the market (in fact, buyers) construct their valuations on the same basis. Since an implicit price represents the influence that a characteristic may have on the pre-sale estimate or on the hammer price, one can verify if there is some consistency between the two types of valuations by testing whether there is a "difference" between the corresponding implicit prices.

We consider two hedonic regressions for each type of jewel, using the same characteristics as regressors. The dependent variable is either the (log of the) hammer price (p_{ht}) or the (log of the) mid-point of the pre-sale price estimate (p^e_{ht}):

$$p_{ht} = \sum_m \alpha_m x_{hm} + \epsilon_{ht}, \tag{4}$$

$$p^e_{ht} = \sum_m \alpha^e_m x_{hm} + \epsilon^e_{ht}, \tag{5}$$

where ϵ_{ht} and ϵ^e_{ht} are error terms with variances $\mathrm{var}(\epsilon)$ and $\mathrm{var}(\epsilon^e)$ respectively.

We first compare the variances of equations (4) and (5) using an equality test $H_0 : \{\mathrm{var}(\epsilon)/\mathrm{var}(\epsilon^e) = 1\}$. Under the null hypothesis the ratio $\mathrm{var}(\epsilon)/\mathrm{var}(\epsilon^e)$ is an F-variable, where $\mathrm{var}(\epsilon)$ (resp. $\mathrm{var}(\epsilon^e)$) is the usual (OLS) estimate of the variance of ϵ (resp. ϵ^e). As expected, we find that $\mathrm{var}(\epsilon^e)$ is always smaller than $\mathrm{var}(\epsilon)$, but significantly smaller only for objects in gold, bracelets and necklaces. This higher variability in hammer prices is certainly due to the fact that buyers are more heterogeneous than experts and may behave irrationally.

Table 3
Comparing the behaviour of markets and experts

Type of jewel	n	k	Wald-test	p-value	ρ
Objects in gold	782	24	0.15	1.00	0.66
Bracelets	626	48	18.25	1.00	0.75
Necklaces	539	48	8.62	1.00	0.74
Rings	850	57	2.54	1.00	0.85
Women's wristw.	179	27	10.99	0.99	0.54
Men's wristw.	117	24	4.32	1.00	0.81
Others watches	71	19	11.06	0.92	0.86

n: nb. of observations; k: nb. of regressors.

Secondly, we test whether implicit prices in both equations are equal. In order to avoid problems due to unequal variances, we construct a test-statistic which takes into account heteroscedasticity. Let X be the matrix of regressors x_{hm} and let D be the vector of differences between the α_m and the α^e_m estimates in (4) and (5). The variance-covariance matrix V of D is:

$$V = X'X(var(\epsilon) + var(\epsilon^e) - 2cov(\epsilon\epsilon^e)),$$

where the last term is an estimate of the covariance between the OLS residuals of the two equations. Equality of the coefficients α_m and α_m^e is tested through the (Wald) statistic $D'V^{-1}D$, which, under the null hypothesis of no differences, follows a χ^2 distribution with k degrees of freedom. The main results are displayed in Table 3.

We accept that the parameters of both models are equal in all cases. This suggests that experts and buyers use the same information on characteristics. The relatively high variances in equations (4) and (5), especially for rings and watches, may be due to missing characteristics in the hedonic equations. This is confirmed by the high and positive correlation coefficients ρ between the disturbances of equations (4) and (5) (see the last column of Table 3). The fact that equality of the coefficients is accepted indicates that experts and buyers do observe these missing characteristics (information about the quality of the gem, minors defects, purely aesthetic characteristics, market trends, etc.), while our models do not include them.

4 Price patterns

We now turn to the study of price patterns during an auction (to check for the afternoon effect or the linkage principle) and over the year (to check for possible seasonal effects).

4.1 On the declining price anomaly

Ashenfelter (1989) reports on empirical regularities that he and others have observed in wine auctions. Comparing the price of every pair of similar wines sold in the same auction, Ashenfelter finds that, although prices usually remain constant, they are at least twice as likely to decline than to increase. Going one step further in the analysis, he computes the ratio of the second to the first prices and notes that all ratios are significantly smaller than one for each sale: this is the afternoon effect.

As already mentioned, the standard model with independent private values and risk neutrality predicts that, in sequential English auctions, expected prices should follow a martingale. Otherwise, agents bidding in the high price period and the presence of a declining price pattern would signal unexploited opportunities. However, when there are risk-averse bidders with non-decreasing absolute risk aversion, the equilibrium time path of expected prices is consistent with the afternoon effect. Expected first-period prices are higher than in any other period because of risk premia related to future uncertainty (McAfee and Vincent (1993)).[7] On the other hand, with risk neutral bidders but affiliated valuations, under possible winner's curse[8] effects, the theory predicts a linkage principle (Milgrom and Weber (1982)). The rise of expected prices over time when there is correlation among valuations is due to the fact that early auctions release information about the underlying value of a good. To determine which kind of phenomenon is present in auctions for jewellery, we run two types of tests.

However, before exploring how prices vary during an auction, we need to define what we mean by "similar objects," since jewels are heterogeneous. We take as being similar, two jewels of the same type (rings, necklaces, etc.) for which the ranges of pre-sale price estimates are identical, and that are sold during the same sale (the same day at the same place). This definition allows us to record the number of rising and falling price sequences. As can be seen from Table 4, the number of increases and decreases is roughly the same.

We now turn to testing whether there are difference in the number of increases and decreases. The first test is rather classical. It consists in computing the mean of ratios of the second auction over the first for the 351 "similar objects," and running a t-test for equality. The results are given in Table 5. All the ratios are larger than one, but the differences are significant for men's wristwatches only. The standard deviations are large, due to the wide range of prices, and the t-values are accordingly low.

The second type of test – which is less traditional – has been introduced by Di Vittorio and Ginsburgh (1994). It consists in using hedonic regressions to "standardise" goods, and then to test for the influence of the order in the sale, by including in the hedonic equation (2) the lot number (i.e., the order

---

[7] Quantity constraints provide an alternative explanation for declining prices. Some bidders buy to fill orders. This would require a model with specific asymmetries among bidders.

[8] In the common value model, the fact that the winner obtains the object because his estimate of the common value is higher than that of all the other bidders is often called the winner's curse.

Table 4
Price Changes for Similar Objects

Type of jewel	Increases	Decreases	No changes	Nb of cases
Objects in gold	20	18	8	46
Bracelets	40	39	10	89
Necklaces	45	43	9	97
Rings	49	49	9	107
Women's wristw.	5	2	0	7
Men's wristw.	2	0	0	2
Other watches	2	1	0	3
Total	163	152	36	351

in the sale). In our case, the coefficient picked by this variable is significantly negative for objects in gold, significantly positive for rings and watches, and not significantly different from zero for other type of jewels.

The fact that parameter estimates for rings and watches are positive and significantly different from zero[9] provides some evidence of a linkage principle, assuming that the auction is consistent with an affiliated values risk neutral model. However, for objects in gold, there is also evidence of an afternoon effect, which is inconsistent with the prediction of the affiliated values model and is often attributed, under independent values, to risk averse bidders having nondecreasing absolute risk aversion. However, empirical observations also show that objects in gold are mainly bought by professionals, suggesting a possible common value phenomenon. In any case, the behaviour of bidders differs with the type of jewel auctioned.

Actually, the results could well be due to the specification of the model. A convenient way to check for this is to use the same methodology but with the experts' valuation as dependent variable, rather than the hammer price. Clearly, prices for objects sold during the same auction should not vary, since experts provide their estimation long before the sale, and without information on the order of the item in the auction. Running equation (2)

[9] At the 10% probability level.

Table 5
Statistics on Mean Ratios

Type of jewel	Mean value of 1st object	Mean value of 2nd object	Ratio 2nd to 1st	St.dev. 2nd to 1st	t-test	p-value
Objects in gold	1814	1755	1.03	0.29	0.11	0.46
Bracelets	2544	2622	1.22	0.64	0.34	0.37
Necklaces	2001	1986	1.07	0.45	0.16	0.47
Rings	2015	2017	1.10	0.47	0.21	0.47
Women's wristw.	1785	2057	1.26	0.31	0.84	0.24
Men's wristw.	2200	2850	1.27	0.05	5.40	0.06
Other watches	833	1166	1.47	0.66	0.71	0.24

with experts' valuations as dependent variable and the lot number added among the independent variables, leads to a significant positive influence of the "order in sale" variable for rings only.

Since for that category of items, there is a positive effect of the lot number both on the hammer price and on the pre-sale valuation, we are led to reject the assumption that the observed price behaviour (a linkage effect) can be attributed to market dynamics only. Some alternative model of price dynamics is called for in that case. On the contrary, for objects in gold and for watches, the lot number has no significant effect on the pre-sale valuation, which leads to consider that the data involve only a market phenomenon. Hence, the results observed from hammer prices are confirmed by pre-sale valuations: the linkage principle holds for watches and the afternoon effect for objects in gold.

4.2 Seasonal behaviour

The fact that the database covers a whole year[10] makes it possible to study the dynamics of prices over time. We first check for temporal effects, using an equation of type (2) and test, using and F-test, whether "time" coefficients are equal. The results obtained for hammer prices and pre-sale estimates are reproduced in Table 6 and show that valuations vary significantly over

[10]There are no sales in August and September, and October sales are not included in our database.

Table 6
Tests for Seasonal Differences

Type of jewel	n	k	Hammer price		Pre-sale valuation	
			F-test	p-value	F-test	p-value
Objects in gold	782	63	3.69	0	2.38	0
Bracelets	626	87	1.64	0.01	1.41	0.05
Necklaces	539	87	1.63	0.01	1.62	0.01
Rings	850	96	2.82	0	2.71	0
Watches	367	68	1.82	0	1.66	0.01

n: nb. of observations; k: nb. of regressors.

the year. This implies that dates are relevant variables in explaining price volatility.

The lowest prices are obtained during the winter season, the highest, in June. According to CMP specialists, this is a normal pattern: autumn and spring sales are traditionally the most important.

5 Conclusions

Data on auctions are a rich source for analysing economic behaviour. Auctions on works of art raise interesting questions, and the use of the CMP database made it possible to single out some empirical facts, though many features of the environment are not observed.

We first find that pre-sale prices are strategically undervalued, except for men's wristwatches and others watches. Nevertheless, according to hedonic models, experts and bidders use in the same way the information that is available. Note however, that pre-sale valuations have lower variances than market prices.

Focusing on price dynamics during an auction, we show that prices for watches increase, while they decline for objects in gold. The fact that two types of bidders (amateurs and professionals) coexist on this market could explain the patterns, though this has to be confirmed by further studies.

Auctions for jewellery at CMP lead to questions with respect to the standard model with independent valuations, symmetric bidders and risk neutrality. The assumption of independent private valuations, which requires no resale opportunities, does not easily fit with a market where there is evidence that one third of the buyers are professionals. It may also be the case that there are risk-averse buyers entering the market. However, theory shows that risk aversion and correlated valuations move the conclusions in opposite directions. English auctions, for instance, will on average yield the highest price with risk neutral correlated bidders; if bidders are risk-averse and have independent private valuations, first-price auctions yield higher prices.

Risk aversion is likely to be important in English auctions only when the items sold are valuable, so that bids may be large relative to bidders' assets. Presumably, this is not the case for jewellery sold in regular sales, which exclude exceptional value items. It may actually be that correlations among bidders' valuations outweigh the effects of risk aversion.

A drawback of our analysis is that it uses a reduced form. To reach a precise conclusion, we should rely on a structural model of the market. Some preliminary questions are also relevant: (1) How appropriate is an affiliated model with asymmetric bidders? (2) What determines the number of bidders? Standard approaches take this number as exogenous; actually, bidders collect information and make a decision to enter an auction, so that their number may partly be determined by pre-sale estimates. How does this affect the performance of the auction?

6 References

Ashenfelter, O. (1989), How auctions work for wine and art, *Journal of Economic Perspectives*, 3, 3-26.

Bauwens, L. and V. Ginsburgh (1994), Do experts make rational estimates of pre-sale prices?, CORE Discussion Paper 9438, Université Catholique de Louvain.

Chanel, O., L.-A. Gérard-Varet and V. Ginsburgh (1994), Prices and returns on painting : an exercise on how to price the priceless, *The Geneva Papers on Risk and Insurance Theory*, 19, 7-21.

Chanel, O., L.-A. Gérard-Varet and V. Ginsburgh (1996), The relevance of hedonic price indices. The case of paintings, *Journal of Cultural Economics*, forthcoming.

Di Vittorio, A. and V. Ginsburgh (1994), Pricing red wines of Médoc vintages from 1949 to 1989 at Christie's auctions, CEME Working Paper, Université Libre de Bruxelles.

McAfee, R. P. and J. McMillan (1987), Auctions and bidding, *Journal of Economic Literature*, XXV, 699-738.

McAfee, R. P. and D. Vincent, (1993), The declining price anomaly, *Journal of Economic Theory*, 60, 191-212.

Milgrom, P. and J. Weber, (1982), A theory of auctions and competitive bidding, *Econometrica*, 50, 1089-1122.

Salamon, M. (1992), Auction of works of art, in R.A. Towse and Khakee, eds., *Cultural Economics*, Berlin: Springer Verlag.

Weber, R. (1983), Multiple-object auctions, in R. Engelbrecht-Wiggans, M. Shubik and R.M. Stark, eds., *Auction, Bidding, and Contracting: Uses and Theory*, New York: New York University Press.

Economics of the Arts - Selected Essays
V.A. Ginsburgh and P.-M. Menger (Editors)

7

Experimental Examination of the Declining-price Anomaly*

Claudia Keser
University of Karlsruhe

Mark Olson
University of Amsterdam

1 Introduction

Many different types of goods, both homogeneous and heterogeneous, are sold by sequential auction. For example, flowers, cattle, and wine are auctioned sequentially. With the increased speed and lower cost of computers, simultaneous auctions could reasonably replace sequential auctions at a substantial time savings. However, it is not clear what other consequences this might have. While there is an abundance of information about single unit auctions, little is known about multi-object auctions and, in particular, the sequential sale of multiple units of an object.

One particularly interesting observation made in sequential auctions is the so-called "declining-price anomaly" (Ashenfelter (1989), Ashenfelter and Genesove (1992) and McAfee and Vincent (1993)). The declining-price anomaly describes the phenomenon that the prices of homogeneous goods are observed to decline during a sequential sale more frequently than expected. It is a well known phenomenon; Ashenfelter (1989) mentions that in the wine auctions he observed, it is known as the "afternoon effect" to auctioneers and experienced participants. Some auctioneers attempt to disguise the existence

* Both authors are grateful to the Center for Research in Experimental Economics and Political Decisionmaking (CREED) for financial support and the use of its facilities. We would also like to thank Victor Ginsburgh and an anonymous referee for comments that significantly improved the paper. Of course, all errors are the responsibility of the authors.

of the declining-price effect by selling like goods out of sequence. Sometimes, the lot sizes are varied in order to mask the effect by quantity discounts. Declining prices are described as an anomaly because economic intuition suggests that there should be little variability in prices for identical items sold in a sequence at the same time and place. Weber (1983) has shown that, with risk neutral bidders who have independent private values, expected equilibrium prices are the same for each unit sold in a sequence. If bidders' values are affiliated[1] then prices should even increase as with any purchase information is released about the value of the object and, thus, uncertainty decreases.

Ashenfelter (1989) has suggested that risk aversion may be the culprit for the observed price decline but McAfee and Vincent (1993) argue that risk aversion is not sufficient as an explanation. Burns (1985b) suggests that bidders act as agents for others and place high value on obtaining items, which might outweigh the possible gain from obtaining items below their reservation value. Black and de Meza (1993) and Burguet and Sákovics (1994) show that equilibrium prices may decrease even without appealing to risk aversion. Black and de Meza (1993) argue that in the wine auctions observed by Ashenfelter there is a buyers' option according to which the winner of the first auction in the sequence has the opportunity to buy further items at the same price. Burguet and Sákovics (1994) demonstrate that the existence of uncertainty about future opportunities to buy, leads to decreasing equilibrium prices. Bernhardt and Scoones (1993) derive declining prices in the case of two goods when valuations are drawn from independent, identical distributions, but bidders do not know their value for the second good until after the first good is sold.

Understanding the declining-price phenomenon is important because its presence may influence the choice of auction mechanism, for example, the choice between a simultaneous and sequential auction. The declining-price phenomenon could affect the profits of the seller or buyers by the order in which goods are sold. For example, if there are multiple sellers of a homogeneous good, the question of which seller is allowed to sell first could become contentious.

Evaluating new or comparing different auction mechanisms using field

[1]Bidders' values are called affiliated when each bidder's value of an object is correlated to how the other bidders value this object.

tests can be very costly and risky. However, experimental methods have been used by economists to study the behavioral characteristics of different auction procedures (see Kagel (1995) for a survey). Most experimental studies consider the behavior of auctions when there is a single unit to be sold.

In this paper, we present a series of experiments designed to analyze the declining-price phenomenon in sequential auctions of multiple homogeneous goods. We construct a simple environment, with only a single-unit demanded by bidders. This simple environment is constructed to eliminate explanations of the declining-price anomaly such as uncertainty of supply or value, the buyers option, the institutional structure of the English auction, or the presence of buyers' agents in the bidding pool, that have been suggested by the authors discussed above.

Because risk aversion is an attribute of the experimental subjects, it is one possible explanation that we cannot eliminate with our experimental environment. We do however attempt to measure its presence to see if it can be eliminated as a possible cause. We also investigate, in a separate treatment, the effect of bidders acting as agents (such as those described by Burns (1985b) and discussed below) as a possible contributing factor. In addition, the presence of agents may change the behavior of some auction formats and little is known of their effect.[2] However, we do not attempt to represent a particular field situation here. Instead, since our interest is in contributing to the understanding of the basic properties of the auctions, the choice of experimental design is made to enable simple comparisons across treatments and with previous (and possibly future) studies. The design enables simple testing of game-theoretic models in some of the treatments.

As we discuss in Section 2, the revenue generating properties of sequential auctions are not theoretically different from the revenue generated from the simultaneous auction of the same homogeneous goods (under the usual auction forms). However, previous experimental research and practical experience indicate that this may not always be true in practice. In section 2 we discuss the revenue equivalence results and describe a risk-neutral bidding model that we will use as a reference point. In section 2 we also explain that we should not expect to see the same number of price declines as price

[2]See McDaniel, Olson, Schram and van Winden (1996) for an example of an environment where the presence of agents may have an important effect.

increases, even though we may expect average prices to be the same. It has been assumed, at least implicitly, in every study of the declining-price anomaly that the equivalence of prices results in an equal number of price decreases as price increases. However, as we show, this is not the case and the observations of declining prices may be understated (or perhaps overstated).

We find strong evidence for the declining-price phenomenon in our experiments and are able to eliminate many of the explanations that have been postulated in the literature. However, we are not able, at this stage of the research to give clear explanations of why it is so prevalent. Risk aversion can not be totally ruled out but it does not give a satisfactory explanation by itself. In Section 3 we describe some related experiments; in Section 4 we describe the experimental design. Section 5 provides the results of the experiments and Section 6 concludes with a discussion.

2 Theoretical considerations

Theoretical literature on sequential auctions is sparse. A basic result presented by Weber (1983) and Engelbrecht-Wiggans (1988) is a revenue equivalence theorem. This theorem states that under risk neutrality, independent private values, single-unit demand, and some reasonable border conditions, any auction mechanism, with an efficient Nash equilibrium has the same expected revenue to the seller in the Nash equilibrium. Weber (1983) derives, by backward induction, equilibrium bid functions for risk neutral bidders who desire only one unit each. He also shows that, under these conditions, the expected prices of all units in a sequence are the same.

2.1 Risk-neutral bid functions and expected prices

Weber derives equilibrium bid functions under the assumption of independent private values[3] in the sequential first-price auction when bidders are allowed to purchase at most one unit. Each subject is permitted to submit one sealed bid for each unit auctioned. The bids are collected by the auctioneer, who accepts the highest bid. The items are awarded to the subjects who placed

[3]The independent private values model assumes that each bidder knows the values of the items to himself, but not of the other bidders, and that the values of the other bidders are drawn independently from a known distribution.

the accepted bids. Ties for the highest bid are broken by randomly allocating the unit to the tied bidders with equal probability.

Each subject's profit equals the difference between her valuations and the price she pays for the units she receives. In an independent private values environment with $n \geq 2$ bidders and $k < n$ units to be sold, if each demander is risk-neutral and draws one valuation from a common uniform distribution in which the lowest possible valuation is 1 (the conditions present in our experiment), a symmetric Bayes-Nash equilibrium for the auction is:

$$b^l(v) = \frac{n-k}{n-l+1} \cdot (v-1) + 1, \tag{1}$$

where $b^l(v)$ is the common equilibrium strategy of all bidders, v is the bidder valuation, and l is the unit currently being auctioned, where $l \leq k$. $b^l(v)$ is the bid made by a bidder in round l if she has not yet received an item.

Since $b^l(v)$ is monotone increasing in v, the outcome is Pareto-optimal. In the special case where $k = 1$ and $l = 1$, we obtain the equilibrium bidding function for the first price auction (in which the highest bidder gets the one item sold and pays the amount of her bid) first derived by Vickrey (1961). This auction has not been modeled to date in an independent private values environment in which demanders may wish to buy more than one unit.

The Weber model and its equilibrium bid functions yield some strong predictions. An individual bidder should increase her bid for each subsequent unit. However, on average, prices should not differ over the sequence of units auctioned. The expected price P_k for each unit is:

$$P_k = E[V_{k+1}] = \frac{n-k}{n+1} \cdot (\bar{v} - 1) + 1, \tag{2}$$

In (2), k units are sold sequentially; $E[V_{k+1}]$ denotes the expectation of the $(k+1)$-highest value, and $\bar{v}$ is the highest possible value. The Weber model and the revenue equivalence theorem predict that the a seller will make the same amount of profit in a sequential auction as she would make in a simultaneous auction where the top bidders receive the units.

If a bidder knew all the valuations of the other bidders, then she would know that any bid above the $k+1$ highest value would win an item with certainty as long as no bidder bid above their value. A bidder's bid function then depends on her estimate of the $k+1$ highest value, and under risk neutrality she bids her expectation of the $k+1$ highest value. To determine this expectation, the only information that a bidder has, in the independent private values model, is her own value and her knowledge of the distribution of values. For the first unit auctioned each bidder computes her expectation of the $k+1$ highest value given the assumption that her own value is the highest value. If she does not win the item, she computes the expectation given the assumption that her own value is the second highest value since in equilibrium the bidder with the highest value wins the first item. This continues until the last item is auctioned. The auction for the last item is essentially a single unit auction with $n-k+1$ bidders. For each unit, this expectation increases so the bid for each unit increases. The expected price is the same for each unit because the distribution of the remaining values shifts downward at each unit and, in equilibrium, the bid function and the distribution of values compensate each other.

2.2 Expected price increases and decreases

The above mentioned empirical studies on the declining-price anomaly (Ashenfelter (1989), McAfee and Vincent (1993)) are all based on the assumption that "on average" the number of price decreases should be equal to the number of price increases. This assumption is based on the risk neutral equilibrium prediction that the expected prices should be the same for each unit sold in a sequence. However, this assumption is only true if the price distributions of all units in the sequence are symmetric. Since the distribution of prices is based on the order statistics of the distribution of values, the price distributions of all units are generally not symmetric. In the case of uniformly distributed values, the price distribution is a beta distribution. It can be shown that, when values are distributed uniformly on $[0,1]$, and bidders use the Weber risk neutral bid functions, the price of the second good auctioned is below the price of the first good auctioned about 40 percent of the time. This asymmetric price decline occurs even though the average prices are the same. The percentage varies according to the distribution, the number of bidders, and the number of objects. For the uniform distribution of values, risk neutral bidding implies that the probability of a price decline from unit l to unit $l+1$ is:

$$\left(\frac{n-l}{n-l+1}\right)^{n-l} \quad \text{for } l < k. \tag{3}$$

This probability is at most $(\frac{2}{3})^2 = 0.444$ and at least 0.367. Thus, for the uniform distribution the probability of a price decline is always less than $\frac{1}{2}$.[4]

While this analysis does not help explain the occurrence of price declines, particularly in the case of uniform distributions, it does indicate that number of price declines may be dependent on the place in the sequence in which an item is sold. It also implies that the observation of price declines may be understated in empirical observations; and, that the basis for comparison should not be the equality of increases and decreases of price used in most studies.

2.3 Risk aversion

As noted by McAfee and Vincent (1993), Ashenfelter (1989) suggested that declining prices are consistent with risk averse bidders, because then the expected first unit price will equal the expected price of the next unit plus a risk premium for the randomness in the price of the next unit. However, McAfee and Vincent show that this requires an assumption not likely to be satisfied in practice. For the case when there are two objects and bidders have identical utility functions $u(v-p)$, where v is the bidder's value for the item and p is the price paid, McAfee and Vincent find that equilibrium bidding functions exist only if u displays nondecreasing absolute risk aversion. Under these conditions the expected prices will decline for all value distributions with continuous densities. However, as McAfee and Vincent claim, increasing absolute risk aversion is an unsatisfactory characterization of attitudes to risk (See Stiglitz (1991)). If utility does not display nondecreasing absolute risk aversion then there does not exists a pure strategy bid function but there are non-trivial mixed strategy bid functions. Nothing is known about the structure of these mixed strategy bid functions.

While not a complete solution, these results may provide a hint about the direction to search. There are two predominant models of competitive bidding in single-unit auctions that include risk aversion. They are the constant relative risk aversion and log-concave models of Cox et al. (1982, 1983, and 1988). At present these have not been incorporated into the model of

[4]For nonuniform distributions, the probability of a price decline is difficult to calculate. We do not know whether there are distributions where the probability of a price decline is greater than $\frac{1}{2}$. It may be the case that for some value distributions, the expected number of price decreases is greater than the expected number of price increases.

sequential bidding. So at present there is little theoretical background to rely on, in examining risk aversion in sequential auctions. For the purposes of this study, we rely on the intuitive result that risk averse bids should be higher than risk neutral bids, under the same conditions.

3 Previous experiments

The price-decline phenomenon in sequential auctions is not restricted to field observations. It has also been observed in auctions conducted in economic laboratories. Both Burns (1985a, 1985b) and Dorsey (1989) describe sequential auctions experiments where declining prices were observed. In the experiments by Burns (1985b), both experienced wool bidders and students participated in a series of sequential auctions. Price declines were observed in both subject pools but they disappeared in the student subject pool with repetition while they did not disappear in the sessions with experienced wool bidders. Interestingly, seven out of the nine experienced bidders did not even see the price declines when questioned after the experimental session. Burns provides some conjectures for this difference in observed behavior. These conjectures are mostly based on the observation that the professional buyers brought behavior into the laboratory which was learned in the wool auctions and that the students, having no previous experience, adapted to the new situation faster. This implies that the auction environment in the laboratory was significantly different from the auction environment that the wool buyers were familiar with. Probably the most important difference was related to the fact that, in the wool auctions, bidders act as agents for others and place high value on obtaining items, which might outweigh the possible gain from obtaining items below their reservation value. Another conjecture relates to the fast speed of the wool auctions which makes strategic planning difficult. In a fast moving auction, price differences may be clouded by quality and quantity differences, and buyers have little time to separate the effects. Furthermore, in the wool auctions, it is a common practice to bid up prices for one's competitors.

When Burns interviewed the wool buyers after the experiment, it became clear that they were very much concerned about not being able to make a purchase in the experiment. Previous experimental work has shown that, generally, losing and winning are not treated symmetrically by decision makers. Therefore, we will compare, in this study, the results from auctions with a penalty for unmet demand and the results from auctions without a penalty. If the aversion to loss has an impact on the declining prices then we should see a smaller number of declining prices in the auctions without a penalty. Burn's experimental results and the field observations of the declining-price anomaly are from English auctions. However, Dorsey (1989) reports experimental evidence of declining prices also in first-price and second-price sealed-bid auctions.

The welfare measure used in this study to compare the allocations in our various treatments, is the percentage of the maximum possible gains from trade which is realized by the allocation process. This fraction is called the *efficiency* of the allocation. It is computed as the sum of the producer and consumer surplus (producer surplus is the revenue to the auctioneer) resulting from the allocation process, divided by the sum of the producer and consumer surplus occurring in the competitive equilibrium. The efficiency attained is 100 percent in the competitive equilibrium, in which the demanders with the k highest valuations receive the k units. This measure has been used extensively in previous studies, including many of those mentioned in this section.

McCabe et al. (1991) report a very high mean efficiency of 99.98 percent for the English clock in single-unit demand, multiple-unit auctions. Burns (1985a), however, reports some inefficiency in sequential English auctions, particularly when there is a larger number of bidders and, perhaps surprisingly, more efficient outcomes under multi-unit demand than under single-unit demand. Simultaneous sealed-bid auctions have not generated high efficiency as consistently under single-unit demand as the English clock. Cox et al. (1985) report an average efficiency of approximately 97.2 percent for the uniform-price sealed-bid auction with highest-rejected-bid pricing and 97.7 percent for the discriminative auction.

4 Experimental design

The major question we want to address in our experiments is: Do we observe declining prices? This would be true if we observe more price declines than would be expected with risk-neutral bidding under the realized valuations. A related question asks whether average prices increase or decrease. Other important questions address the efficiency and the predictive power of Weber's bidding model and individual bidding behavior, including the observation of risk aversion and non-linear bid functions.

Since one explanation to the declining-price anomaly is the incentives that agents have in a sequential auction, we shall also examine the effect of a penalty for not purchasing a unit when overbidding is prohibited. We wish to observe if the incentives of agents increase the occurrence of the declining-price anomaly or effect the efficiencies and prices of the sequential auction. In case of a penalty, we shall also analyze what happens when overbidding is allowed; this treatment is designed to remove the confounding effects of a penalty and the prohibition of overbidding. That is, if we observe a difference in behavior in the *agent* treatment, we cannot be sure if it is due to the penalty or the prohibition of overbidding.[5]

We investigate the first-price sealed bid auction under single-unit demand. While most observations of the declining-price anomaly occur for the English auction, we investigate the sealed-bid auction for a number of reasons, one, it was the easiest to implement in the laboratory, and two, in a sealed bid auction we receive information on losing as well as winning bids. In addition, investigating the sealed-bid auction allows us to see if declining prices are a result of the institutional[6] details of the English auction.

In the following, we present the *no-penalty baseline* treatment which is also the basis of the *penalty* treatment variations.

4.1 Treatments

In each experimental session we conducted a computerized twenty-period auction with 8 bidders. In each period, 4 homogeneous units of a fictitious good were sold sequentially by a first price sealed bid auction. At the beginning of each period, each player was communicated his private valuation (in tokens) for a unit of the good auctioned in the period. Bidder's valuations were independently drawn from the discrete uniform distribution on the interval $[1, 1000]$, and are listed in the Appendix. This same set was used for each experimental session. Using a fixed set of valuations in each session

[5] As overbidding is hardly observed in the no-penalty case, we do not examine the effect of prohibiting overbidding in the no-penalty case.

[6] In a related study the effect of the auction institution (e.g. English and Dutch) will be examined.

allows for better treatment and session comparisons. In each experiment, the same eight values (one for each bidder) are used in the period possessing the same period number, yielding identical market demand, allowing us to use data with a common period number as paired observations from different treatments. For example, period 17 in all 12 sessions had the same market demand so any differences across treatments and sessions in period 17 could not be attributed to a difference in market demand.

Each bidder had to make a bid for the first unit sold in the sequence and the bidder with the highest bid received this unit for the price of his bid. Then bids were asked for the second unit, and this unit was sold to the highest bidder. The same procedure was used for the third, and the fourth unit. Any bidder who had purchased a unit was not allowed to make a positive bid for any following unit auctioned in the sequence. If no bidder made a positive bid for a unit, this unit was not sold to anybody.

An additional restriction prohibiting overbidding (not allowing subjects to bid above their value) was implemented to induce incentives similar to those which an agent, as we described above, might face. This is a limited form of an agent; in the extreme case, an agent would receive no profit from the difference between value and price, and only receive a fixed profit upon the purchase of an item (or a fixed penalty for not purchasing an item). The *agent* treatment is the same as the *baseline* treatment but, in each period, a penalty of 100 tokens had to be paid if a bidder did not buy a unit. As there were eight bidders and only four units sold, at least four bidders were subject to the penalty in each period. Thus, to avoid the possibility of bidders' bankruptcy, each subject began with an endowment of 2,000 tokens. As an example of the restriction of overbidding, suppose a bidder has a valuation of 400; if he makes a bid of 400 and does not win a unit, he sustains a loss of 100 tokens. On the other hand, if overbidding is allowed and he bids 450 and wins a unit, he sustains a loss of 50 (his value 400 less his price of 450); he therefore, may have an incentive to bid over his value. The restriction of no-overbidding does not allow him to bid above 400.

The *penalty with overbidding* treatment was implemented to control any confounding effects of restricting the bidding and introducing a penalty. In this treatment, the subject in the above example would be allowed to bid above his valuation of 400. We would expect that bids *without* the prohibition of overbidding will be higher than bids *with* the prohibition of overbidding. In the risk neutral model of bidding, a penalty has the effect of increasing the bid by the amount of the penalty.

4.2 Organization

The experiments were organized at the Center for Research in Experimental Economics and Political Decision making (CREED) at the University of Amsterdam. We conducted twelve sessions of direct interactive play in the laboratory. Four of these sessions were under the *baseline* treatment, four sessions under the *agent* treatment and four sessions under the *penalty with overbidding* treatment. Subjects were recruited voluntarily from the student body of University of Amsterdam, and were not allowed to participate in more than one of the sessions in this series. All subjects were undergraduate students, and most were economics or business students. Subjects were paid immediately after at the conclusion of the experiment. Subjects received profits during each period equal to the sum of their valuations for the units they purchased minus the total amount they spent to acquire the units.[7] Sessions lasted about 90 minutes including computerized instructions, one unpaid period of practice, and 20 auction periods for which the subjects were paid. The subject instructions are available from the authors.

4.3 Theoretical considerations

For our experimental parameters the risk neutral bidding functions of the *baseline* treatment are:

$$
\begin{aligned}
b^1(v) &= \frac{1}{2}(v-1)+1 \\
b^2(v) &= \frac{4}{7}(v-1)+1 \\
b^3(v) &= \frac{4}{6}(v-1)+1 \\
b^4(v) &= \frac{4}{5}(v-1)+1.
\end{aligned}
\tag{4}
$$

These bidding functions are based on equation (1). With the penalty of 100 tokens if no unit is bought in a period, the risk neutral bidding functions

[7] The conversion rate from tokens to Dutch guilders is 50 tokens to 1 guilder (1 guilder = US$0.60).

become:

$$
\begin{aligned}
b^1(v) &= \frac{1}{2}(v-1)+101, \\
b^2(v) &= \frac{4}{7}(v-1)+101, \\
b^3(v) &= \frac{4}{6}(v-1)+101, \\
b^4(v) &= \frac{4}{5}(v-1)+101.
\end{aligned} \tag{5}
$$

Thus, the introduction of the penalty simply shifts the risk neutral bidding functions upward by the amount of the penalty. We do not have clear theoretical results when the restriction of no overbidding is imposed.

The expected equilibrium price and the realized[8] equilibrium prices for each unit sold in the sequence (average over the 20 periods) in the *no-penalty baseline* treatment are presented in Table 1, together with the respective standard deviations. Given our parameters, the expected equilibrium price for each unit and in each period is 445 tokens (see equation (2)) in the *baseline* treatment and 545 tokens in the *penalty with overbidding* treatment (equivalent to an upward shift of 100 tokens). As with the bidding functions, we do not have clear theoretical results when the restriction of no overbidding is imposed. We see that, although the expected equilibrium price is the same for each unit, the standard deviation increases from the first to the last unit. The realized equilibrium prices are calculated from the Nash equilibrium bid functions, that is, $b^4(4^{th}$highest value) from equation (1). The realized equilibrium prices are slightly different for each of the four units and are different from the expected price. When a penalty is imposed, the realized prices are 100 tokens higher than in the *no-penalty* treatment. If the prohibition of overbidding is imposed, we have no theoretical results to compute expected or realized prices.

Table 2 presents the expected percentage of price declines in equilibrium calculated from equation (3). These numbers are independent of whether there is a penalty imposed or not. Table 2 also gives, for the realization of values, the actual number of price declines (from unit 1 to 2, unit 2 to 3, and unit 3 to 4) that are predicted by the Weber risk neutral theory. For the parameters of our experiments the expected probability of a price decline

[8]The realized prices are the prices computed from the valuations used in the experiment.

Table 1
Expected and Realized Equilibrium Prices (No Penalty)

	Unit 1	Unit 2	Unit 3	Unit 4
Expected	445	445	445	445
St. dev.	(47)	(70)	(96)	(125)
Realized	444	446	449	426
St. dev.	(41)	(80)	(100)	(133)

Table 2
Expected and Realized Price Change Statistics

	Units 1-2	Units 2-3	Units 3-4
Probability	0.393	0.396	0.402
Decreases	8	5	10
Increases	12	15	10
Eqalities	0	0	0

is about 40% for a random realization of values. Again, if overbidding is prohibited, we have no theoretical results.

5 Results

5.1 Aggregate results

Table 3 gives an overview of the mean, median, and standard deviations of the observed prices for each unit sold, for each sequence over all sessions, for each main treatment. We see that average prices decrease under each experimental treatment. At the individual session level[9] in seven of the

[9]The detailed data are available from the authors.

Table 3
Observed Average Prices and Standard Deviations
All Periods and Sessions

		Unit 1	Unit 2	Unit 3	Unit 4
No	Mean	500	474	463	454
penalty	St.dev.	(104)	(76)	(70)	(121)
	Median	492	470	461	456
Penalty	Mean	615	570	561	559
with	St.dev.	(101)	(100)	(133)	(136)
overbid	Median	600	567	600	600
	Mean	554	523	496	494
Agent	St.dev.	(109)	(84)	(94)	(139)
	Median	512	504	500	495

twelve sessions, average prices for each unit decline persistently; each of the remaining 5 sessions have a single instance where the price increases between units, but there is no consistency of which units these are. In all but one session, the average price of the first unit is higher than the average price for the last unit, and the average of the prices for unit 1 and 2 are higher than the average of the prices for unit 3 and 4. In our experiments declining prices appears to be consistent.

The average prices in the *no-penalty* and the *penalty with overbidding* cases are always above the respective equilibrium prices (see Table 1). Using a repeated measures ANOVA model, a Fisher LSD Multiple-Comparison test[10] shows that, at the 5% level, there is no significant difference between the prices (adjusted for the penalty in a treatment) in each treatment for units 1 and 2. The *agent* treatment shows a significant difference from the other two treatments for unit 3 and 4. Hence, the use of buyers' agents as bidders does not yield the same outcomes as the non-agent bidders, but a complete examination of this point is beyond the scope of this paper.

[10]See Winer (1971).

Table 4
Average Number of Observed Price Decreases and Increases
All Periods and Sessions

		Units 1-2	Units 2-3	Units 3-4
No penalty	Decreases	10.75	9.00	7.75
	Increases	8.50	10.50	11.50
	Equalities	0.75	0.50	0.75
Penalty with overbid	Decreases	11.50	8.75	6.50
	Increases	7.75	10.75	12.50
	Equalities	0.75	0.50	1.00
Agent	Decreases	9.75	10.75	7.25
	Increases	9.25	8.00	12.50
	Equalities	1.00	1.25	0.25

Table 4 presents the average number of observed price decreases for each treatment. For the sequence of unit 1 to 2 and unit 2 to 3, there are more declines than predicted by the risk neutral model (see Table 2) for each treatment. But there are fewer price declines than predicted in the sequence of unit 3 to 4. However, the difference between the treatments is small. Using a repeated measures ANOVA model, there is no significant difference between the treatments (at the 5% level). Using a $t-$test we find that there are significantly more observed price decreases compared to the number of realized equilibrium price decreases from unit 1 to 2 (at the 10% level), and from unit 2 to 3 (at the 5% level), and significantly less from unit 3 to 4 (at the 5% level), than would be expected under the Weber risk-neutral model. So, we find in our experiments in 2 of the 3 price sequences, more than the expected number of price declines.

In Table 5, we present the average efficiencies by treatment. There is no apparent difference between treatments, and the general efficiency is high, with over half of the periods having efficiencies of 100%. The overall average efficiency of 98% is slightly higher than the 97% efficiency reported in Cox et al. (1985) in simultaneous auctions. As a guard against vacuous efficiency

Table 5
Observed Average Efficiencies and Standard Deviations
All Periods and Sessions

	Observed efficiency	Periods with 100% efficiency
No penalty	0.98 (0.04)	56%
Penalty with overbidding	0.98 (0.05)	61%
Agent	0.98 (0.04)	64%

measurements due to the experimental design, we compare the observed efficiency to the average efficiency generated by a random allocation of the units to the bidders with the six highest valuations. A vacuous efficiency measurement could occur if all bidders had the same value since then, any allocation would yield a 100% efficiency. The top 6 randomization scheme yields an efficiency which is about 13 percentage points below the efficiency observed in the experiment, so the sequential auction reports an improvement over a random allocation. In our experimental environment of homogeneous goods, the sequential auction appears to have efficiency comparable to other auction forms.

To test some of the predictions of the Weber risk neutral model we estimate aggregate bid functions for each unit. Table 6 gives the OLS regression estimates linear (i.e. $b^l = \beta v$, where b^l is the bid for unit l adjusted for the penalty if applicable, v is the value, and β is the regression coefficient) and quadratic bid functions (i.e. $b^l = \beta v + \gamma v^2$, where γ is the coefficient of the squared redemption value). Note that the Weber model prescribes equilibrium bid functions which are linear in the redemption value. Therefore, we start out with an estimation of linear bid functions. However, from previous experiments (Dorsey (1989)), we know that higher redemption values may be discounted more. This would suggest higher order bid functions. Indeed, the quadratic bid functions describe our data better, when there is no penalty. The adjusted R^2 of 3rd degree bid functions show no increase over the 2nd

Table 6
Regression Results
Linear and Quadratic Bid Functions

	Linear bid f.			Quadratic bid f.		
	Unit	β	adj. R^2	β	γ	adj. R^2
No penalty	1	0.57*	0.64	0.86*	-0.00039*	0.72
	2	0.61*	0.71	0.96*	-0.00048*	0.82
	3	0.66*	0.75	1.01*	-0.00052*	0.87
	4	0.75*	0.87	1.00*	-0.00039*	0.91
Penalty with over-bidding	1	0.52*	0.73	0.56*	-0.00005	0.73
	2	0.56*	0.70	0.70*	-0.00019*	0.72
	3	0.63*	0.77	0.76*	-0.00020*	0.78
	4	0.73*	0.85	0.87*	-0.00023*	0.85
Agent	1	0.46*	0.64	0.61*	-0.00020*	0.65
	2	0.50*	0.73	0.64*	-0.00021*	0.75
	3	0.54*	0.80	0.70*	-0.00023*	0.82
	4	0.65*	0.89	0.68*	-0.00005*	0.88

*Coefficient significantly different from zero at the 1% level.

degree bid functions. Therefore, we do not present the regression results of any higher order bid function here. As the Weber model predicts, the linear estimated bid function for any unit has a larger coefficient than the bid function for the previous units sold in the sequence.

5.2 Individual bidding behavior

In this section we look at individual bidding behavior. We will use Weber's risk-neutral bidding as a reference point. In many experimental studies of the single unit first price sealed bid auctions, bidding behavior is generally interpreted as risk averse.[11] Table 7 shows for each unit, the percentage of bidders that can be classified as risk averse in the *penalty with overbidding*

[11]This interpretation has been questioned. See Kagel (1995).

Table 7
Risk Averse Bidders (in %)

	Unit 1	Unit 2	Unit 3	Unit 4
No Penalty	84	81	72	53
Penalty with overbidding	41	31	31	34
Agent	31	16	06	0

and the *no-penalty baseline* treatments (we have no basis to classify behavior in the *agent* treatment). A bidder is classified as risk averse if his number of bids above the risk neutral bid is greater than his number of bids below the risk neutral bid. The low percentage of bidding behavior that can be classified as risk averse as opposed to risk taking is in sharp contrast to results of single-unit first price auctions where up to 94% of the subjects exhibit risk averse behavior (Cox, Smith and Walker (1988)). The interesting observation is that the measure of risk aversion is different for each unit auctioned and for the two treatments. Thus, this measure of risk averse behavior is not the universal phenomenon that is indicated in first price auctions.

Figures 1 and 2 show all individual bids made for each of the four units for the *no-penalty* treatment and for the *penalty with overbidding* treatment, respectively. The solid line which appears to be an upper bound for bids is the value line in the *no-penalty* treatment and the value + 100 line, in the *penalty with overbidding* treatment. The noticeable point about these figures is that starting at about the 700 value, bidders appear to discount their bids for high values by a higher percentage than for low values. Also in the penalty with overbidding, many subjects do not appear to take full account of the penalty in their bidding. Many subjects bid their value or below when the risk neutral strategy was to bid above their value; this would tend to indicate a risk taking attitude and would account for the lower measure of risk aversion in the *penalty with overbidding* treatment. This risk taking attitude calls into question any risk averse explanation for bidding in these experiments.

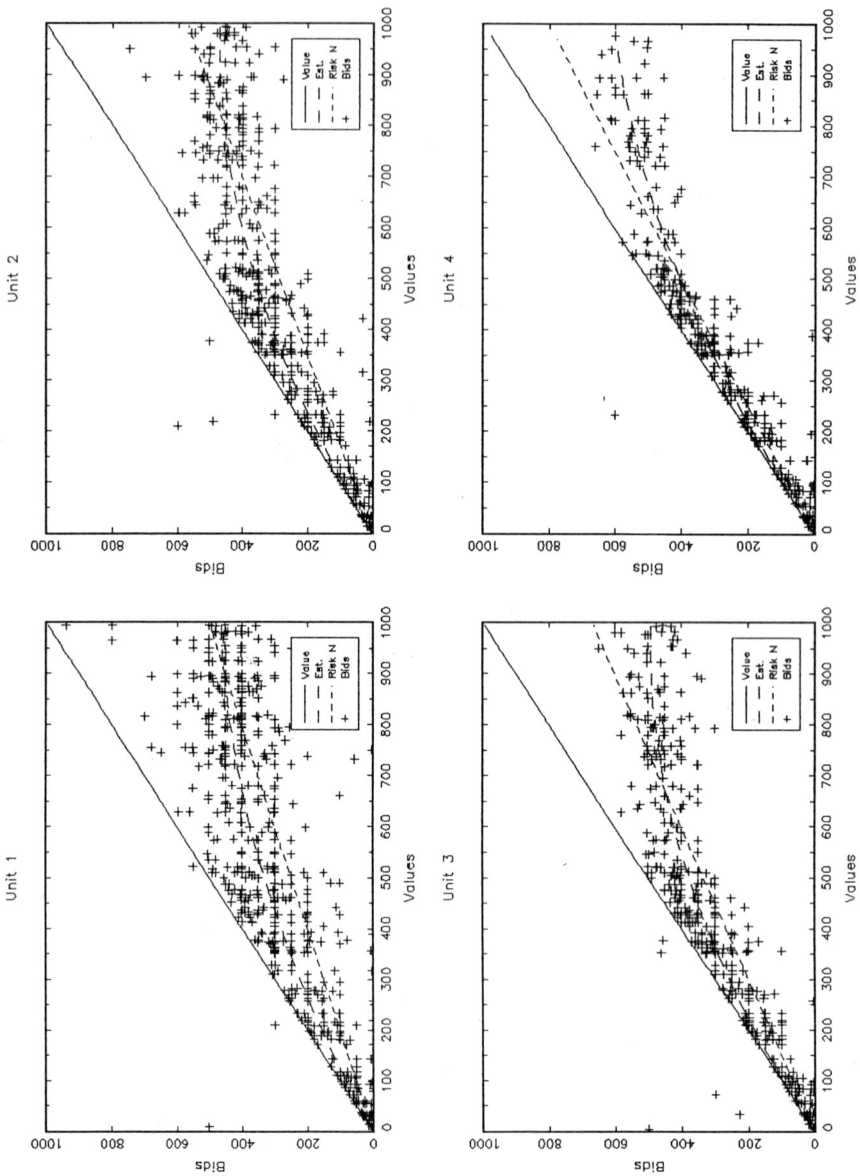

Figure1: Bids. No penalty

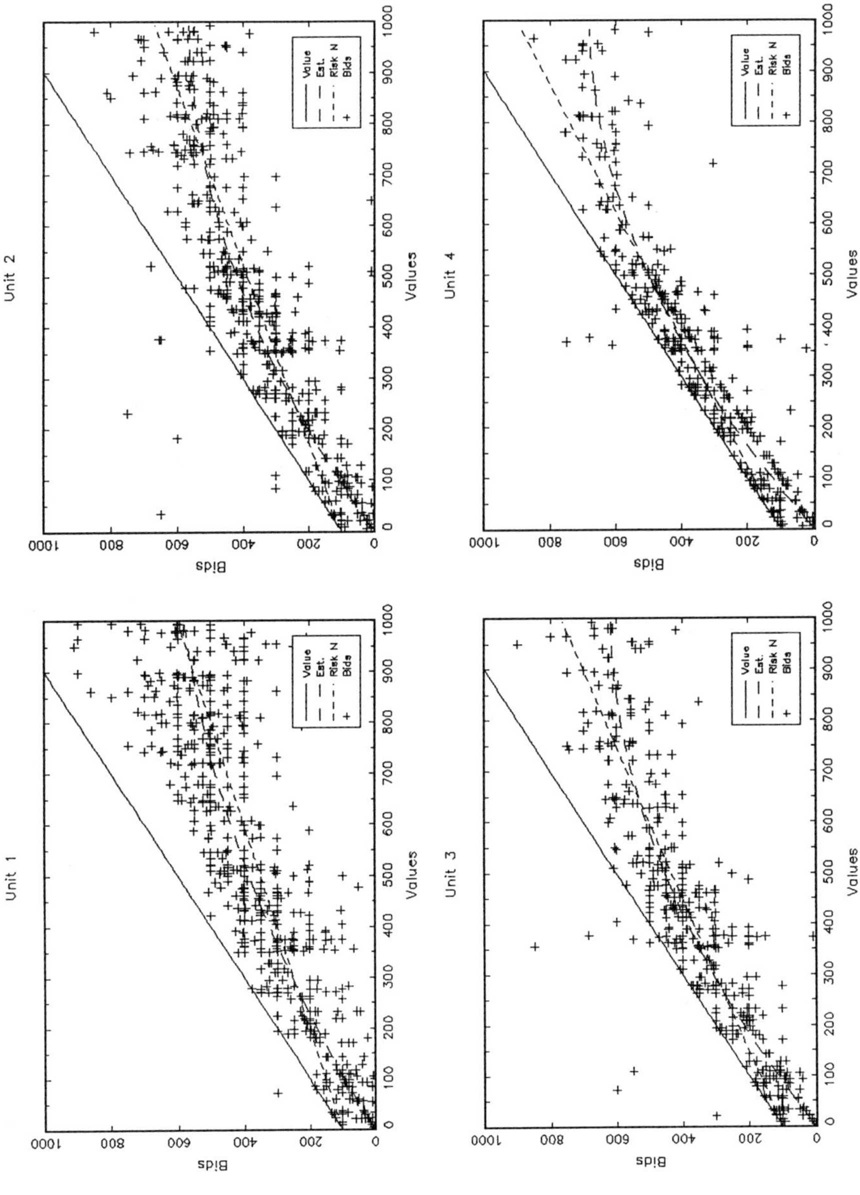

Figure 2: Bids. Penalty with overbidding

We would not predict the Weber bid function to perform well in our experiments if subjects made less money following this strategy. We compare each bidder's actual earnings for each unit with the earnings a subject would have made if he had bid according to the Weber risk-neutral bid function. We find that almost two-thirds of the subjects would have made more money following the Weber model. At the conversion rate of 50 tokens per guilder (a guilder is about 60 cents), subject 8 in session 2 would have made 25 more guilders by playing the risk neutral bidding strategy. Subject 7 in session 4 would have made 44 guilders more, but this is mainly due to an unfortunate typo (he made an entry mistake in his bid). Subject 4 in session 2 would have lost 7 guilders by playing the risk neutral strategy. Almost two-thirds of the subjects would have earned an average 8.5 guilders more, by using the risk neutral bidding strategy. The remaining subjects would have earned an average of 3 guilders less, by using the risk neutral bidding strategy.

6 Closing remarks

While we are still at the beginning of an investigation in bidding behavior in sequential auctions, there are a few results that tend to stand out which allow us to make a few conjectures. In our environment of a uniform distribution of values, we find evidence for the declining-price anomaly. We observe declining prices more often than would be expected under risk neutral bidding. Note that for the evaluation of the declining-price anomaly phenomenon, the distribution of prices (and hence bids) and not the expected price matters. For the last unit, we find fewer than expected price declines. It seems that the extent of price declines may depend upon the place in the sequence where the units are sold.

Since the declining-price phenomenon appears in our restricted environment, we feel that its previous observation cannot solely be attributed to the uncertainty of supply or value, the buyers option, the institutional structure of the English auction, or the presence of buyers' agents in the bidding pool, although these may be contributing factors. In fact, when we induce incentives to more closely replicate agent behavior, we do not find any significant increase in the number of declining prices. The declining-price phenomenon is an attribute of the sequential nature of the auctioning process. It is widespread and cannot be dismissed as being attributable to a specific environment.

In both the experiments with and without a penalty for unmet demand, there are a number of subjects who display behaviour that is consistent with risk aversion. But the amount of risk aversion present seems to be dependent on the unit sold and the existence of a penalty, which is not consistent with risk aversion being an attribute of the individual subject. Together with the observation that subjects tend to discount their bids more when the value of the item is higher, this leads us to conjecture that there are behavioural aspects that are missing in the bidding models. Two possible explanations come to mind, one is that the risk averse subjects are more likely to win units earlier in the sequence and are underrepresented in the bidding for later units. This explanation of our observations would lead us to postulate that heterogeneity of the bidders is an important attribute. This was a component missing from the McAfee and Vincent model of bidding: they assume that every bidder had the same utility function.

Second, is that subjects may focus on a price that they expect in the market, and may bias their bids toward that price. For low valuations, this has the effect of raising the bid, making it appear to be risk averse behavior; for higher valuations, this has the effect of lowering the bid below the risk neutral bid. This type of behaviour would be consistent with our observations but requires further investigation.

In conclusion, we have been partly successful in what we have set out to do. We have eliminated some direct causes of the price decline phenomenon; those causes that are directly related to the description of the environment, uncertainty of value, a buyers option, and institutional details of the English auction. We have not been entirely successful in eliminating those causes which are behaviourally motivated such as risk aversion, nor have we been successful in explaining the causes of the phenomenon. However, we feel that we have come a step closer to an explanation.

7 References

Ashenfelter, O. (1989), How auctions work for wine and art, *Journal of Economic Perspectives*, 3, 23-36.

Ashenfelter, O. and D. Genesove (1992), Testing for price anomalies in real-estate auctions, *American Economic Review, (Papers and Proceedings)*, 80, 501-505.

Bernhardt, D. and D. Scoones (1994), A note on sequential auctions, *American Economic Review*, 84, 653-657.

Black, J. and D. de Meza (1993), Systematic price differences between successive auctions are no anomaly, *Journal of Economics and Management Strategy*, 1, 607-628.

Burguet and J. Sákovics (1994), Sequential auctions with supply or demand uncertainty, Working Paper, Instituto de Análisis Económico, Barcelona.

Burns, P. (1985a), Market structure and buyer behavior: Price adjustment in a multi-object progressive oral auction, *Journal of Economic and Business Organization*, 6, 275-300.

Burns, P. (1985b), Experience and decision making: A comparison of students and businessmen in a simulated progressive auction, *Research in Experimental Economics*, 3, 139-157.

Cox, J.C., V.L. Smith and J.M. Walker (1982), Auction market theory of heterogeneous bidders, *Economics Letters*, 9, 319-325.

Cox, J.C., V.L. Smith and J.M. Walker (1983), Test of heterogeneous bidders theory of first price auctions, *Economics Letters*, 12, 207-212.

Cox, J.C., V.L. Smith, and J.M. Walker (1985), Expected revenue in discriminative and uniform price sealed bid auctions, in V. L. Smith, ed., *Research in Experimental Economics*, 3, Greenwich, CT: JAI Press.

Cox, J.C., V.L. Smith and J.M. Walker (1988), Theory and individual behavior of first-price auctions, *Journal of Risk and Uncertainty*, 1, 61-99.

Dorsey, R.E. (1989), Sequential sealed bid auctions, Ph.D. Dissertation, University of Arizona.

Engelbrecht-Wiggans, R. (1988), Revenue equivalence in multi-object auctions, *Economics Letters*, 26, 15-19.

Kagel, J. (1995), Auctions: a survey of experimental research, in J. Kagel and A. Roth, eds., *Handbook of Experimental Economics*, Amsterdam: Elsevier Science Publishers.

McAfee, R.P. and D. Vincent (1993), The declining price anomaly, *Journal Economic Theory*, 60, 191-212.

McCabe, K., S. Rassenti and V. Smith (1991), Testing Vickrey's and other simultaneous multiple-unit versions of the English auction, in V. L. Smith, ed., *Research in Experimental Economics*, 4, Greenwich, CT: JAI Press.

McDaniel, T., M. Olson, A. Schram, and F. van Winden (1996), An experimental environment for investigation of the Dutch flower auctions, Working Paper, CREED, University of Amsterdam.

Stiglitz, J. (1991), Symposium on organizations and economics, *Journal of Economic Perspectives*, 5, 15-24.

Vickrey, W. (1961), Counterspeculation, auctions, and competitive sealed tenders, *Journal of Finance*, 16, 8-37.

Weber, R.J. (1983), Multiple-object auctions, in R.E. Engelbrecht-Wiggans, M. Shubik and R. Stark, eds, *Auctions, Bidding and Contracting: Uses and Theory*, New York: New York University Press.

Winer B. (1971), *Statistical Principles in Experimental Design*, New York: McGraw-Hill.

Appendix: List of subject valuations.

	Subject							
Period	1	2	3	4	5	6	7	8
1	210	862	546	965	629	373	950	232
2	521	233	898	375	413	745	356	377
3	219	72	588	675	432	822	34	661
4	257	743	851	171	756	431	404	143
5	510	466	487	84	836	882	550	509
6	97	361	718	8	128	86	884	93
7	316	627	653	489	354	793	427	20
8	216	842	392	738	374	954	722	477
9	786	388	743	456	696	208	369	109
10	769	4	573	795	599	499	183	535
11	110	460	780	442	894	810	981	995
12	14	357	890	819	295	30	993	117
13	644	54	283	422	428	941	895	816
14	436	722	33	277	461	328	468	309
15	37	512	389	516	351	225	890	262
16	875	863	869	93	732	270	636	59
17	350	924	982	608	412	197	22	195
18	649	106	575	271	504	451	362	800
19	189	758	811	977	181	923	750	278
20	680	967	759	520	55	814	475	79

Essays in the Economics of the Arts
V.A. Ginsburgh and P.-M. Menger (Editors)

8

The Economics of Legal Disputes Over the Ownership of Works of Art and Other Collectibles*

William M. Landes and Richard A. Posner
University of Chicago

1 Introduction

Economic analysts of law have paid a great deal of attention to the creation, definition, protection, and voluntary and involuntary transfer of property rights both tangible and intangible, but relatively little attention to the issues that arise when a dispute over the ownership of property is rooted in genuine uncertainty about who owns a particular piece of property. The legal doctrines that bear on this question include the doctrines of adverse possession, good faith purchasers, abandonment, finders, and laches, among others. There has been some economic analysis of the question[1] and there is a vast legal literature, but there is surely room for additional economic analysis.

1.1 Why art?

We limit our consideration to disputes over the ownership of works of art, broadly defined to include paintings, sculptures, rare books and manuscripts,

* We thank Richard Craswell, Victor Ginsburgh, Martha Nussbaum, participants in the law and economics workshops of Harvard Law School and the University of Chicago Law School for helpful comments on a previous draft and Kevin Cremin for his helpful research assistance. We also thank the John M. Olin Foundation and the Lynde and Harry Bradley Foundation for their generous support.

[1]See Landes and Posner (1978, pp. 105-106); Weinberg (1980); Schwartz and Scott (1982, pp. 476-479); Epstein (1986, pp. 674-693); Ellickson (1986, pp. 725-734); Levmore (1987); Posner (1992, pp. 79-81); Shavell (1996).

archaeological artifacts, early musical instruments, other antiques (silverware, jewelry, etc.), and similar collectibles. The reason for limiting our analysis to such works is that they share several characteristics that make ownership disputes both more likely to arise than in the case of other goods and more difficult to resolve when they do arise. If the law can deal with these disputes efficiently, the chances are that it can deal efficiently with more routine types of dispute over ownership.

Most works of art are durable, highly portable, and limited in number (often one of a kind). And often a work of art is of such questionable identity and authenticity that its value depends on its provenance (history), including information about prior owners,[2] yet there is no system of recorded titles, as in real estate, that would make it possible to trace the history of ownership of a work of art with total confidence. Works of art have characteristics that make it both possible to trace the chain of title over a long period of time, which increases the chance that a dispute will arise between an earlier owner and the current owner, and difficult to trace the chain of title with certainty, which increases the potential for dispute between the current owner and persons who claim to be in the chain before him. A person claiming to be the real owner may have incomplete documentation to prove that his grandfather, say, of whom he is the heir, was the lawful owner of a work of art that disappeared fifty years ago. Even if he can establish original ownership, he may not be able to prove how the work disappeared from his grandfather's possesion. A purchaser of a work of art may have a bill of sale

[2] *Why* value depends on provenance is an interesting question but one beyond the scope of this paper. Likely reasons include the protection that a reliable pedigree offers against the risk of forgery (it is particularly good protection, of course, if the work can be convincingly traced back to the artist); the value of an association of the work with prestigious previous owners (as dramatically shown by the recent auction of Kennedy memorabilia, James Barron, "What to Do with Souvenirs of Camelot? Use Them, If You Dare," *N.Y. Times* (national ed.), April 27, 1996, p. 16); and the information that the pedigree conveys about how the work has been valued by others. The fact that the work was part of the collection of a well-known connoisseur is evidence that the work is truly outstanding. But perhaps the most important reason is the lack of agreed-upon standards of artistic excellence, as a result of which the reputation of the artist is more important to the value of a work than the work's intrinsic qualities are. This is why correct identification of the artist is so important to the value of the work, and explains why, when a work is discovered to have been incorrectly attributed to a famous artist, its value plunges, even though it is the same work it was before the discovery. See Bonus and Ronte (1995).

from a reputable gallery, but the bill may provide only sketchy information on previous "owners." The previous owners may be dead, and if living may have imperfect recollection and in any event be unable to provide witnesses to or documentation of their recollections. The work may have been resold a number of times, and in different geographic areas. Multiple transfers without a public registry that conditions a lawful transfer of title on a search of the registry increase uncertainty about ownership and hence the likelihood of a dispute.

Disputes over title are more likely if a work is valuable, mobile, relatively easy to hide, but still traceable – conditions frequently satisfied in the case of works of art. Because a valuable work of art is likely to appreciate rather than depreciate over time, a search even for a work that has been missing for many years may be profitable. Such characteristics of works of art as value, appreciation, durability, and concealment also create the possibility that works of art will resurface, often by chance, after many years of being thought destroyed or otherwise gone for good.

Uniqueness facilitates recollection of a particular work, so that, even with limited access, tracing may be possible because the few people who have seen the work will remember having seen it and can provide valuable information to the searcher. (It would be much more difficult to track down a stolen diamond after many years, because to the untrained eye it will look just like many other diamonds.) Even in the case of a unique work, the artist may have created similar works of which only some have survived, and if there is uncertainty over which survived several people may claim ownership of the same surviving works.

A related characteristic of art that facilitates tracing a work of art over generations of owners is that the work must be preserved in its original form if its value is to be maximized. Some conservation or repair of a work will increase its value, but only to the extent that the reparative effort restores the work to something like its original, or at least an earlier, state. Overpainting a Picasso or cutting it into fifty pieces and selling each piece separately would make tracing more difficult, but it also would greatly reduce the value of the original painting.[3] In contrast, a large diamond can be cut into smaller stones. This may reduce its value, but to a far lesser degree than in the case

[3]See, for example, de Balkany v. Christie, Manson & Woods Ltd., *The Independent*, Jan. 19, 1995, p. 8 (Q.B. 1995), discussed in Posner (forthcoming, lect. 2).

of a work of art.

Although a registry for art similar to a land registry would eliminate many ownership disputes, it is probably not feasible, because of the huge number of works that the registry would have to contain. Land registries work well because land doesn't move around, so a local registry can contain a complete inventory of the land in its area. A registry of works of art would, because of their mobility, have to be worldwide, and would have millions of works in it. Many of the works would be so similar that even photographs would not enable them to be distinguished.[4] It is true that there are recording systems not only for land but also for security interests in personal property, but these UCC registries mainly record classes of personal property (for example, an automobile dealer's ever-changing inventory of cars) rather than individual items.

The feasible alternative to a comprehensive registry of works of art[5] is a registry limited to missing works of art. Works that are both missing and sufficiently valuable for owners to search for them are of course a tiny subset of all works of art. And there will usually be enough time between the theft or loss of a work (assuming the owner is aware of that the work is missing), and its resale by reputable auction houses, galleries taking works on consignment, or buyers, to enable the registry to be checked to determine whether the work has been stolen from or mislaid by the rightful owner. In 1976 the International Foundation for Art Research, a private nonprofit organization, created (in cooperation with unnamed "partners in London"[6]), the Art Loss Register, which now lists 60,000 stolen or otherwise lost works

---

[4]It might seem that another reason why land registries are much more common than art registries is that most owners of art are in possession of the art, whereas possession and ownership of land are often divided. But the principal function of a land registry is not to enable a prospective purchaser to identify the owner (as distinct from a tenant who may be in possession of the owner's property), but to enable him to determine whether the owner has good title.

[5]We include the qualification "comprehensive" in recognition of the fact that there are some specialized registries for classes of collectibles (such as Stradivarius violins) and works of particular artists. These registries are feasible because they list only a modest number of items.

[6]*IFAR Reports*, Oct. 1995, back cover. The reason may be that, as noted by Levmore (1987, p. 61), the English doctrine of "market overt" makes it easy for persons buying stolen art from London art dealers to obtain good title to the art. Parliament, however, has recently abolished the doctrine. See Sale of Goods (Amendment) Act of 1994, §1.

of art. The Register will list a work only after the owner has reported the theft or loss to the police. The purpose of this restriction is to discourage practical jokers, extortionists, and lunatics from listing themselves as owners of lost works of art, thereby creating a cloud on title that would impede the recovery and transfer of the works by the rightful owners. It has been argued that no buyer of a work listed in the Register should be deemed a good faith purchaser and that no statute of limitations should be enforced against an owner who sues for the return of a work that he has listed in the Register.[7]

A final explanation for why the chain of ownership of a long-lost work of art can often be traced has to do with why people own art. Economists since Veblen have described art as a prestige good that enables the collector to signal to others that he is a person of both wealth and good taste. The collector gets utility not only from admiring the work hanging in his living room but also from believing that other people envy or admire him because he owns it. To obtain this additional utility, people who buy art don't want to keep it hidden away. They brag about owning it, show it to friends, lend it to museums and galleries for exhibitions.[8] Rarely (in the United States anyway) will a collector refuse to lend a piece to a museum for a show or provide a transparency of the work for publication in a book. On the contrary, most collectors go out of their way to get their paintings included in shows and books. They do this partly to confirm and enhance the value of the works but also to obtain utility from having one's name ("lent by" or "in the collection of") publicly associated with the work. If a lender's sole concern were the increase in the work's value, museums would not identify the lenders of works for exhibition. Art's signaling value makes it more likely that the rightful owner will eventually find his long-lost work.[9]

---

[7]Bibas (1994).

[8]An offset is that letting the world know that you own valuable art provides information to potential thieves that will increase the likelihood that the art will be stolen. Offsetting the offset, however, is the fact that publicizing a work of art may make it more difficult for a thief to "fence" it, thus reducing the expected gains of theft.

[9]This suggests that the high bidders for known stolen art will be art lovers rather than status seekers.

1.2 The disputes

We are interested in ownership disputes involving "innocent" persons. But we use the term in a very broad sense, excluding only – besides of course thieves – persons who know they are buying a stolen work of art as opposed to buyers who fail to take proper precautions against the possibility that the work is stolen. The "good faith" purchaser, roughly the purchaser who both believes that the work he is buying is not stolen *and* takes optimal precautions against a mistake about title which fail however to reveal the fact that the work *is* stolen, is thus a subset of the innocent purchaser. We try to make these distinctions more perspicuous a little later in the paper.

We are less interested in the original or previous owner's remedies against the thief himself, but will discuss them briefly. It is reasonably clear as a matter of economics that the owner should be able to get his work of art back from a thief even if the owner was careless in protecting the work against theft; hence the law's rejection of a defense of contributory negligence to theft or its tort counterpart, conversion, makes economic sense. Since a thief incurs costs to bring about a transfer that is not (on average) socially wealth-maximizing, while an owner incurs costs to prevent such a transfer, the most efficient method of avoiding this inefficient transaction is for the thief to be deterred rather than for the owner to incur costs of self-protection.[10] This result is achieved by punishing the thief and restoring the work to its rightful owner. Unless stolen property is recoverable by the owner, owners will have an incentive to incur increased costs of self-protection against theft, costs that may exceed the costs of deterring theft through punishment alone. The higher the costs of self-protection, moreover, the smaller will be the demand for art (because it will cost more to own); so the smaller will be the amount of art created, preserved, and found than under a legal regime that entitles the owner to the return of his property from the thief. Giving the owner a right to get his property back also reduces the costs of public enforcement. It does this both by allowing the same level of deterrence to be achieved with less severe public sanctions (the right of return operates as a fine equal to the value of the work of art to the thief) and by giving victims of theft an incentive to cooperate with the law enforcement authorities.

Were the costs of apprehending and convicting a thief very high relative to the costs of preventing theft by owner self-protection, it might make sense

[10] Landes and Posner (1987, ch. 6).

to "privatize" the enforcement of the law of larceny by leaving the prevention of theft entirely to the potential victims, the owners. But this is unlikely to be the optimum solution. It would give thieves an incentive to invest more in penetrating the defenses of the potential victims, which in turn would lead the latter to invest more in self-protection, leading to a kind of arms race. And since both the private and the social value of art depends to a significant extent on public display, the prevention of theft by owners involves heavy nonpecuniary as well as pecuniary costs, such as the owner's losses in status and prestige from suppressing information on his ownership and the location of the work by refusing to lend the work for public exhibition and denying access to publishers and others who may want to reproduce or examine the work.[11] The prevention of theft of art must already be very costly, notwithstanding the criminal penalties and the owner's right of recovery, judging by the large amount of such theft, including audacious thefts from famous museums, such as the Gardner in Boston. Recall that the Art Loss Register lists some 60,000 works (not all stolen, however – some are lost without being stolen), probably only a fraction of the total number of stolen works of art.

Of course, in saying that there is a large amount of art theft, we are speaking very loosely. For there is also a very large amount of art (as we emphasized in discussing the infeasibility of a comprehensive register of art objects), and no one has tried to measure the prevalence of art theft relative to other forms of theft. Our basic point is not affected. An object that is at once very valuable and very small is a natural target for thieves, and this implies that a low prevalence of theft of such objects would have to be purchased at a high cost in expenditures on preventing and punishing such theft, so that the social costs of art theft would still be high.

The idea that secrecy is a socially costly method of protecting property rights is not limited to the art market. The idea is a cornerstone of patent law, which invites the inventor to disclose his invention (rather than keeping it a trade secret) in exchange for a right to prevent copying for a period of years. The more secure that property rights in works of art, the more likely those works are to circulate, conferring value on art lovers, scholars,

[11] An offsetting factor, noted earlier, is that the more widely displayed a work of art is, the more difficult it is to "fence" it. Everyone will know that it is a stolen work, so it will be difficult for a thief or buyer of such a work to display it publicly.

and artists. An analogy from the domain of copyright is the refusal of Elizabethan playwrights, such as Shakespeare, to publish their plays, which (in an era before there was a copyright law) would have facilitated plagiarism. Indeed, actors were not given complete scripts of the play in which they were appearing, but just their own parts, to prevent pirates from obtaining the complete text of the play without negotiating with all the actors. This is a good example of the paradox of protecting a form of property that is valuable in virtue of being displayed by suppressing its display.

Although the proper legal status of the art thief is straightforward, theft remains an important factor in the analysis of disputes between original owners and subsequent purchasers of works of art because the rules for resolving those disputes may affect the amount and the social costs of theft. As we are about to see, the more rights that the original owner has against a purchaser of a stolen work (even though many transactions may separate the purchaser from the thief), the lower will be the price at which a thief can sell a work of art, thus reducing the incentive for art theft. But the less will be the incentive of the owner to protect his property against theft, which will reduce the cost of stealing to the thief. Analysis of the optimal legal regime is complicated not only by this tradeoff but also by the fact that the interests of other persons besides owners, thieves, and the beneficiaries of wide public display of works of art – namely purchasers – must be considered once an innocent purchaser enters the picture. Loss as well as theft of property must also be considered.

Thieves (and their fences, principals, and knowing purchasers) are not the only criminals in the art market. An important class of art criminals that we do not discuss is forgers. The analytical difference between art forgery and art theft is that the optimal rule for deterring forgery requires consideration only of the forger and the purchasers of the forged work, whereas the corresponding rule for theft requires consideration of the thief, the purchasers, *and* the owner of the work stolen.

2 The model

2.1 Behavior of owners and purchasers of stolen art

Let A denote the original owner of a work of art. By "original" we mean simply and inaccurately the person who had valid legal title to the work when it was lost or stolen, rather than the person who first acquired the work from the artist, or the artist himself – the true original owner, unless it was a work for hire.

A knows there is some probability that the work will be stolen, lost, or (a subset of lost) entrusted by him to a dealer who will sell it without A's permission and later disappear with the proceeds. We can write

$$p = p(x, \phi), \tag{1}$$

where p denotes the probability (> 0) of such an eventuality. We assume that p is negatively related both to A's expenditures (x) on self-protection and to the probability (ϕ) that the law will revest title in the original owner after it has been found; equivalently it denotes the degree to which the law favors an original owner over someone who currently possesses the work (call him B).[12] Expenditures on self-protection include both monetary costs (alarm systems, guards, and so forth) and the loss of prestige from not publicizing one's ownership of the work in the hope of reducing the likelihood of its being stolen. We assume diminishing marginal products throughout, so that x lowers p but at a decreasing rate – so $p_x < 0$ and $p_{xx} > 0$.[13] ϕ lowers p because the more the law favors original owners, the lower will be the expected value to subsequent purchasers of acquiring works some of which may ultimately have to be returned to original owners. This prospect will in turn lower the price for such works and hence the incentive of thieves to steal them in the first place. Lower prices may also reduce p by increasing the likelihood that someone who finds a missing work will immediately return it to the original owner rather than sell it to a third party. Initially we take ϕ as given and assume that $p_\phi < 0$ and $p_{\phi\phi} > 0$. Although ϕ can range from 0 to 1, we focus primarily on the values 0 and 1. Once A sues to recover

[12] The variable p depends on other factors as well, including the returns and expected sanctions from theft and the possibility of permanent loss from war, fire, flood, bombing, an earthquake. We take these factors as given and outside our analysis.

[13] We use subscripts throughout the paper to denote derivatives.

the work a court will either award the work to A ($\phi = 1$) or let B keep it ($\phi = 0$). Ex ante, ϕ can of course take intermediate values.

We assume that if the work is stolen or lost, A will eventually discover its whereabouts. But this will take time and A will suffer a loss from not possessing the work in the interim. Let q be the fraction of the value of the work that A recovers (assuming the law returns the work to A), where q is positively related to the time that it takes A to locate the work and to A's discount rate.[14] So $1 - q$ is the fraction of the work that A loses from delay in finding it or, equivalently, that the person who possesses the work before A finds it gains from the delay by retaining possession longer.

We can write

$$q = q(y, z), \tag{2}$$

where y denotes A's search expenditures, which reduce the time it takes to recover the work, and z denotes expenditures by B, which increases that time. A's search can include checking catalogues and exhibitions of the artist's work, inquiring of enforcement agencies, inspecting registries of lost art, hiring investigators, consulting art historians, and – perhaps – advertising the loss in art periodicals. We say "perhaps" because it has been argued that publicity will drive a stolen, as distinct from an inadvertently taken, work of art underground and out of ordinary commercial channels, reducing the likelihood of its discovery. This argument was made by the Guggenheim Museum in its successful suit to recover a Chagall gouache that had been stolen from a storage area in the museum more than twenty years earlier.[15]

B's counterefforts might include concealing his acquisition of the work, refusing to display or lend it out for public exhibition, or, in the extreme, building a secret room in which to store it. Like A's expenditures on preventing theft, B's on preventing the discovery of defective title reduce the public display of art. Another cost of B's efforts may be a nonmonetary loss of prestige from being unable to disclose his ownership of the work.

B will make counterefforts even if he is an innocent purchaser, because there is always a chance that an ownership dispute will arise and the work will be returned to a previous owner. We assume that A's efforts increase q

[14] We could instead define q as the probability that the work will be found by A conditional on its having disappeared. We use the definition in the text because it is more convenient for analyzing statute of limitation questions.

[15] See Guggenheim Foundation v. Lubell, 569 N.E.2d 426 (N.Y. 1991).

at a decreasing rate ($q_y > 0$ and $q_{yy} < 0$) and that B's efforts lower q at a decreasing rate ($q_z < 0$ and $q_{zz} > 0$). For simplicity we assume that B incurs his costs after buying the work, but part of his search costs before he buys the work will be costs of verifying A's title, and will thus be higher the more the law favors original owners.

Another assumption is that B does not shift the risk of defective title back to the dealer or other seller from whom he bought the work, via warranty, or to the pool of art buyers, via title insurance. Interestingly, auction houses and art dealers generally disclaim any warranty of the provenance, as opposed to the authenticity, of the works of art that they sell.[16] A dealer that issued such a warranty would have to increase his sales commission. His customers, most of them wealthy people advised by their own experts, might not want to pay the extra price, being able to protect themselves against the risk and cost of a defective title as cheaply as the dealer. The absence of title insurance for works of art to emerge may be due to adverse selection and to the difficulty of calculating the risk of defective title to art with actuarial precision. The first point is especially important. Insurance companies normally insure against the risk of something happening in the future rather than against the consequences of something that has already happened.[17] The insured is more likely to know the past than the future and so more likely, in the case of insurance against the consequences of something that has already happened (such as a thief in the chain of title), to be exploiting information known to him but not to the insurer. Title insurance in real estate is only an apparent exception, since all the title insurer insures against is the risk of its having failed to conduct a thorough search of the public registry of real estate titles.

The net expected value (W^a) or utility that A receives from the work of

---

[16] For example, the auction agreements reproduced in the Christie's and Sotheby's catalogues disclaim any warranty of the provenance or merchantability (title) of the works auctioned. In view of the importance of the art dealers and auction houses of New York City in the art trade, it should be noted that the New York City Administrative Code, tit. 20, ch. 2, subch. 13, reg. 24, forbids auction houses to disclaim warranty of title. The reluctance of the auction houses to warrant title, but not authenticity, makes economic sense, although we cannot explore the issue fully within the scope of this paper. The auction houses have expertise in connoisseurship, but not in reconstructing the history of the ownership of a work.

[17] For example, medical insurers usually disclaim insuring against the consequences of preexisting conditions.

art will be affected by the risk of loss, the time it takes to find a lost work, and the likelihood that the law will return it to A, as in

$$W^a = [1 - p(x, \phi)]V^a + p(x, \phi)[q(y, z)\phi V^a - y] - x, \tag{3}$$

where V^a is the value of the work to A at present, that is, before any loss. Maximizing (3) with respect to x and y (and assuming that A is risk neutral and takes z and ϕ as given) yields the first-order conditions for a maximum for these variables:

$$- p_x[V^a - (q(y, z)\phi V^a - y)] - 1 = 0 \tag{4}$$

$$q_y \phi V^a - 1 = 0. \tag{5}$$

Equation (4) shows that A will expend resources on protecting himself from a possible theft until the marginal return (the reduction in p multiplied by the value of the work net of the expected recovery if it is stolen or lost) equals the cost of spending one more dollar on x. The larger V^a is, the more responsive p is to x (that is, the greater $-p_x$ is), and the lower A's expected recovery is (that is, the lower $q(y, z)\phi V^a - y$ is), the greater will be the return from self-protection and hence the greater will x^* be. (We use x^* and y^* to denote the values of x and y that satisfy equations (4) and (5).) Thus, if a particular type of missing work is very difficult to find, $q(y^*, z)$ and hence A's expectation of recovering the work will tend to be low, with the result that x^* will be high even if the law strongly favors original owners. Alternatively, the sooner A expects to recover his missing work, the lower x^* will be. Thus, self-protection and the prospect of quickly recovering the missing work of art are substitutes.

We can see from equation (5) that y^*, A's optimal[18] expenditure on searching for a missing work of art, depends positively on ϕ, on V^a, and on the responsiveness of q to y.[19] A's expenditures on search take place only after the work is missing. So although efforts at self-protection reduce the likelihood that the work will be stolen or lost and hence that A will spend anything at all on y, once the work is missing y^* will be independent of x^*.

We must consider how the law's decision whether to return stolen or lost property to original owners or leave it with the purchasers will affect

[18]Privately, not necessarily socially.

[19]To simplify, we assume that $q_{yz} = 0$, so that A's search effort does not depend on B's behavior.

the original owner's behavior. Suppose the law always favors purchasers, provided they do not have actual knowledge that the work they are buying is stolen property, over original owners ($\phi = 0$). From (3) and (5) we see that $y^* = 0$, since even if A finds the missing work quickly he will not get it back. This implies that the benefits from self-protection are greatest when $\phi = 0$. That is, x^* will take its highest value then because $q(y,z)\phi V^a - y$ in equation (4) will be zero. In contrast, if the law always favors original owners ($\phi = 1$), A's search effort (y^*) will be at its greatest. And since $q(y^*, z)\phi V^a - y^*$ must be positive (otherwise A would spend nothing on y), x^* will fall as ϕ increases from 0 to 1.

In words, the more the law favors original owners over purchasers, the less will original owners spend on self-protection and the more they will spend on searching for their missing works. That is, x^* and ϕ are substitutes, since $dx/d\phi < 0$, while y^* and ϕ are complements ($dy/d\phi > 0$).[20] The effect on search is likely to be greater than the effect on self-protection, however. The owner has strong incentives to prevent the theft of his art even if the law will restore the art to him should it be stolen and later resurface; the incremental effect of the legal position on those incentives is likely to be small, because it will alter the (already small) probability of his recovering a stolen work only slightly. Once the art is stolen, however, the owner has a strong incentive to

[20] Assuming that ϕ can take intermediate values between 0 and 1, we can solve for $dx/d\phi$ and $dy/d\phi$ by taking the total differentials of equations (4) and (5) with respect to x, y, z, and ϕ. This yields (assuming the relevant cross-partial derivatives are 0):

(i) $dx/d\phi = p_x V^a(q(y,z) + \phi q_z dz/d\phi)/[p_{xx}[V^a - (q(y,z)\phi V^a - y)] < \mathit{or} > 0$

(ii) $dy/d\phi = -q_y/q_{yy}\phi > 0$.

The sign of $dx/d\phi$ is indeterminate because $dz/d\phi$ is positive. But as we show later, its value is likely to be small. An innocent or good faith purchaser, by definition, believes that he receives good title to the work, and so an increase in ϕ should have only a minor effect on his expenditures on z. The indeterminacy of the sign of $dx/d\phi$ implies that $\phi q_z dz/d\phi$, although negative, is probably close to zero. But it is possible that for some values of ϕ (those closest to 1, since if ϕ is close to 0 this will not hold), the numerator in (i) could be positive (since $p_x < 0$) and hence $dx/d\phi$ would be positive. This possibility, however, is not of great interest to us. We focus on cases where ϕ is either 0 or 1, and we have shown that x^* takes its maximum value when $\phi = 0$. Hence, $dx/d\phi < 0$ when ϕ increases from 0 to 1 and it is probably negative as well for all intermediate values of ϕ. The assumption of zero cross-partial derivatives seems reasonable because there is no clear reason why, for example, the marginal productivity of self-protection or search will depend on the legal rule. Finally, notice that the partial derivative of (4) with respect to y is zero, so that the effect of changing y and ϕ together appears only in (5) and not in (4).

find it – but only if he is entitled to its return.

2.2 Good faith purchasers and the stock of art works

The case for giving the purchaser from a thief a superior title to that of the original owner, the thief's victim, is strongest in the case of those purchasers whom the law calls "good faith purchasers." We define a good faith purchaser, in economic terms that are broadly consistent (as we shall argue) with the legal concept, as one who, having made the optimal investment in obtaining information about the title of the work prior to purchase, believes that there is a very high probability that the seller can transfer good title to him.[21] That is, not only is his belief that the seller can transfer good title to him sincere; it is also reasonable because the cost of additional investigation would exceed the savings from rejecting the work should its title prove defective discounted by the very low probability that the additional investigation would reveal that the seller's title was indeed defective. Suppose there is a .05 probability that the seller can't transfer good title to B, the price of the work is $1,000, and the cost of additional information that would eliminate any uncertainty about title is $500. B is a good faith purchaser because the probability is very high that the seller can transfer good title to him and because B's refusal to spend $500 is reasonable since such an expenditure would yield only a $50 expected benefit (.05 times the $1,000 purchase price he would save upon learning that the seller could not convey good title to him).[22] But suppose B refused to acquire this information when it cost only $10. He would not be a good faith purchaser; his belief that he was acquiring good title, though honest, would

[21]We are not claiming that the good faith purchaser's expenditure on obtaining information is *socially* optimal. To the extent that the expenditure reduces the probability of theft by lowering the prices at which thieves can sell stolen works of art, it has social value. To the extent that it merely shifts a loss to someone else (for example, to the true owner, if the effect of the expenditure is not to discover the theft but to secure the purchaser's title), it has a purely private value.

[22]The example assumes that B would not purchase the work if he knew it was stolen or its title otherwise defective and he would lose the purchase price if and when the work was eventually returned to A. It is immaterial to the analysis if, through warranty, B is able to shift the loss of the purchase price to the dealer from whom he purchased. And we have already noted that warranty is often disclaimed. Moreover, the interval between B's purchase and A's claim may be so great that the dealer is no longer in existence and its warranty is therefore worthless.

not be reasonable, because he could have eliminated uncertainty about the title at slight cost.[23]

In ascribing a burden of investigation to the good faith purchaser, we depart from the formal legal concept, which is sometimes paraphrased as "a pure heart and an empty head." There is no real inconsistency. For a consumer dealing in the ordinary course of business with a reputable-appearing merchant, the optimal expenditures on investigating the merchant's ability to convey a good title to the goods he sells is close to zero; imagine the aggregate costs if all such consumers were expected to conduct a form of title search. If suspicious circumstances make the optimal expenditure positive yet the consumer goes ahead and buys without any investigation, we assume that he will be denied the status of good faith purchaser.

A related point is that because the purchaser's belief that he is getting good title must be sincere as well as reasonable for him to be given the status of a good faith purchaser, he may lose that status even if the cost of acquiring additional information about title would be prohibitively high, simply because the known probability that the seller could not convey valid title was also high. This will often be the case with recently discovered antiquities, a class of works in which the documenting of previous ownership can be highly uncertain. Suppose that the probability is .7 that the seller cannot convey good title, the price of the work is \$1,000, and the cost of additional information that would eliminate any uncertainty over title is \$5,000. It would be wasteful for B to spend \$5,000 for an expected return of \$700. Although B would be an innocent purchaser rather than a receiver of stolen goods, he would not be a good faith purchaser because he would think it likely that his seller did not have good title. The point is related to the previous one because, since the good faith purchaser by definition does not think there is any problem with his seller's title, he has little incentive to conduct an investigation.

Table 1 expands on these points. For simplicity we treat as discontinuous what is actually a continuum. The first row illustrates the good faith purchaser. The next two rows illustrate two types of innocent but not (in the contemplation of the law) good faith purchasers. One faces a low probability

[23] Although a reasonable B would have acquired this information, a particular B might not have because, in effect, his costs of information were much higher than those of a reasonable person. For example, this B may be too stupid to acquire or process relevant information about the work's title. We ignore this detail.

Table 1
Examples of purchasers

Type	Probabiliy	Price ($)	Cost ($)	Acquire Information?
Good Faith	.05	1,000	500	yes
Innocent	.05	1,000	10	no
Innocent	.70	1,000	5,000	no
Bad Faith	.55	1,000	1	no
Bad Faith	.95	1,000	1	no
Willfully Ignorant	.70	1,000	-10	no

Definitions: Probability = probability that seller cannot convey good title. Price = price of product. Cost = cost of additional information that would eliminate all remaining uncertainty about title.

that the title is defective but fails to spend the optimal amount on information; the other faces a high probability that the title is defective but spends reasonably on information.

The last three rows depict three types of the *really* bad faith purchaser.[24] The first believes it more likely than not that the title is defective and refuses to spend the trivial amount on information that would eliminate that uncertainty. The second is highly confident that the title is defective and also refuses to spend even a dollar to verify his expectation. The third, the "willfully ignorant" purchaser, has a negative cost of information because he goes out of his way – that is, incurs added costs – to avoid discovering whether the work is stolen, even though he strongly suspects that it is. He behaves this way because he hopes that the law will treat him more favorably than the *really* bad faith purchaser. An "ostrich" instruction, often given in criminal cases, tells the jury to treat as an intentional wrongdoer one who takes steps to avoid the acquisition of knowledge that would convert a suspicion – for example, that he is buying stolen property – into a certainty. As

[24] All purchasers who are not good faith purchasers are, in the eyes of the law, bad faith purchasers. But we are trying to distinguish between the good faith purchaser and other innocent purchasers, and between innocent purchasers and purchasers who are acting in such bad faith that their conduct invites criminal sanctions.

a practical matter, however, the willfully ignorant may be somewhat more likely to escape the law's clutches than the fully deliberate wrongdoer.

A bad faith purchaser chooses not to acquire information because it has no value to him; he would purchase the work even if he knew for certain that it was stolen or that its title was otherwise defective. "No value" is a bit of an exaggeration, however. Our bad faith purchaser would alter his expenditures on suppressing information about the acquisition if he knew for certain that the work was or was not a stolen work, rather than merely strongly suspecting that it was the latter; he would spend more on suppression if he learned the work was stolen and zero if he learned it was not. And the willfully ignorant purchaser believes that the law will be less successful in prosecuting him criminally for selling or possessing stolen goods if he can claim lack of knowledge, even though his information costs are zero or even negative.

The distinction that we (and the law!) draw between an innocent and a good faith purchaser makes economic sense in light of our earlier discussion of theft. If purchasers who actually suspect that they are buying stolen or lost art are able to obtain good title notwithstanding the high cost of information, the market for such art will be greatly enlarged, which in turn will greatly increase the expected return from art theft.

One who buys a work of art from a reputable art dealer or an established auction house, and knows the provenance of the work, including the history of its prior ownership and also knows that there is nothing fishy in the chain of title, and pays a price that he has no reason to believe has been discounted to reflect a substantial probability that the title is not good, will ordinarily be a good faith purchaser. He will have no reason to suspect that the seller can't convey good title; and it would not pay for him to make additional inquiries about the seller or the work. While we have explained why other innocent purchasers should not be allowed to obtain good title from a thief, we have yet to consider whether the good faith purchaser should.

We begin our exploration of this issue by noting that if the good faith purchaser has no feasible means of dispelling the slight uncertainty that he is buying stolen art, it does not follow that his post-purchase behavior will be totally unaffected by the chance than an original owner will some day pop out of the woodwork and seek to recover the work from him. The seller, to maximize the sale price, will represent that he owns or is the consignee of the work of art and can lawfully transfer title to the buyer for a price of, say, π. But because the seller may be dishonest or uninformed, the buyer,

B, who in this section of the paper is a good faith purchaser, will assign a probability, r, to the risk that the work may have been stolen or lost. Although r depends on p, it also depends on the number of comparable works for sale. Suppose that the total number of works of some particular type is 1,000, that 10 percent are sold each year by or with the authorization of the original owners, and that each original owner faces a .01 probability of loss ($= p$) this year. Assume that all lost or stolen paintings are offered for sale but that prospective buyers cannot distinguish between works with good title and those with defective title. The annual number of paintings sold will be 109 ($.01 \times 1{,}000 + .1 \times .99 \times 1{,}000$), all at the same price, π. Of these 109 paintings, 10 paintings – .092 ($= r$) of those sold – will lack good title. More generally, if the buyer cannot determine which works are stolen or lost and which are not, then

$$r = p/(p + \alpha(1-p)), \tag{6}$$

where $r > p$, provided that $\alpha < 1$, where α is the fraction of the stock of paintings that is sold each year.[25] The smaller that fraction, the greater r will be relative to p (because $\partial(r/p)/\partial\alpha = -(1-p)/(p+\alpha(1-p))^2 < 0$). If the entire stock turns over each year ($\alpha = 1$), then $r = p$; and if no works are sold from the stock ($\alpha = 0$), then $r = 1$ – but then one could not maintain the assumption that B was a good faith purchaser.

B faces uncertainty not only with respect to whether the work's title is defective (r) but also with respect to whether, if it is defective, how soon this will be discovered (q) and whether, when it is discovered, the work will be returned to the original owner (ϕ). Assuming that if the law returns the work to the original owner the buyer will forfeit π, we can write B's expected value from the purchase of the work as

$$W^b = (1 - rq(y,z)\phi)V^b - z. \tag{7}$$

[25] Obviously the example is drastically simplified. Not all lost or stolen works or art will show up for sale this year; some may be destroyed, or lost for many years. Works missing in year t may not be offered for sale until $t+n$. The stock may be growing, so that the number lost in any year may overstate the number of lost or stolen works of art that are for sale. Many of the missing works may be bought by people who know they have been reported stolen or missing. With all these factors taken into account, the number of lost or stolen works that are for sale will be βpK, where K equals the stock and $\beta < 1$. Provided $\beta/\alpha > (1-\beta p)/(1-p)$, r will be greater than p when $\beta > \alpha$ (that is, when the probability of selling a stolen or lost work of art is greater than the probability of selling a work from the stock in a given year) and p is relatively low.

V^b is the value of the work if there is no chance of a prior claim, and $rq(y,z)\phi V^b$ is the expected loss to B if there is such a chance. Maximizing (7) with respect to z (and taking r, y, and ϕ as given) yields

$$- rq_z\phi V^b - 1 = 0. \tag{8}$$

B will increase his expenditures on z until the marginal benefit of those expenditures in lowering q equals the marginal cost. Call that optimal value z^*. It will be positive only if B purchases the work, which he will do only if $W^b - \pi \geq 0$.[26]

We now investigate B's purchasing decision and how the market will determine the price and quantity of works of art that are sold. Since the stock is fixed and, for convenience, normalized at 1, we can write the quantity sold as $p + \alpha(1 - p)$. The supply curve of works for sale will be upward sloping because both α and p are increasing functions of π – more owners will prefer to sell than to retain their works as π increases, and the gains from stealing and selling works with defective titles will also increase with π, provided that the greater effort devoted to stealing works of art is not completely offset by increases in self-protection by original owners.[27] To simplify, we shall let α and p increase proportionately as π increases, so that r in (6) remains constant.[28] The demand curve for the works will be downward sloping, provided there are differences in valuations among B's. If there are, then as π decreases more B's will buy.

Suppose ϕ increases; that is, the law shifts in favor of original owners. W^b will fall because there will be a greater risk that B will have to give up the work should his title prove defective. This is another oversimplification. For

[26]Even if B purchases the work, $z^* = 0$ if $-pq_z\phi V^b < 1$ for all values of z. We also adopt the convention that if $W^b - \pi = 0$, B will purchase the work. And recall our assumption that B does not expend any resources investigating his seller's title, in advance of buying the work. This is plausible because, by definition of a good faith purchaser (one who has already made the optimal investigation, normally zero or slight because he is dealing in the ordinary course with an apparently reputable dealer), additional expenditures by him on investigating his seller's title are unlikely to be productive.

[27]Notice that x does not depend on π in equation (4) but on V^a. If, however, $\pi > V^a$, A will sell it – the market sets a higher value on the work than he does. Only among those A's will an increase in π induce greater self-protection.

[28]This is not quite correct, because if both α and p increase by the same proportion, say λ (> 1), the increase in r will be slightly greater since it now equals $p/(p + \alpha(1 - \lambda p))$. We ignore this difference.

B may one day find himself in the position of an original owner, trying to get his work back from a purchaser of the work from a thief.[29] By definition, good faith purchasers believe they're acquiring good title, which if so will make them "original owners" (as we are using this term) should the works ever be lost or stolen. The converse of this point[30] is that original owners may benefit from rules protecting good faith purchasers. For unless the original owner is the artist himself, the original owner is always subject to a claim by some previous owner in the chain of title. We ignore the point, interesting and important as it is, since it seems to cut in both directions.

So assuming that W^b will fall as ϕ increases, the demand curve will shift downward, leading to a reduction in π and a decline in both p and α. In words, increasing the protection of original owners lowers the price that buyers will pay for paintings and reduces the quantity sold both of stolen works and of works with good title. This point assumes that all paintings sell at identical prices because buyers cannot distinguish between works with good and defective titles. If they can distinguish, but not perfectly, works with a higher probability of having a good title will command higher prices. The quality premium will increase as ϕ increases, because the adverse consequences to B of buying a work that turns out to have bad title increase with ϕ.

What are the consequences of the legal position for B's behavior? If B knows for certain that the seller can convey good title to the painting, then $r = 0$ (since $p = 0$) and, of course, $z^* = 0$. B will have no incentive to incur any cost, including any loss of prestige from keeping his ownership of the work secret, to prevent the original owner from recovering the work. At the other extreme, if B knows for certain that the work is stolen and the seller cannot convey good title, $r = 1$ (for now the number of similar but lawful works offered for sale is not relevant to B's behavior), and z^*, which must satisfy $q_z \phi V^b - 1$, takes its highest value. Thus, $dz^*/d\phi > 0$ as ϕ increases from 0 to 1.[31] In this part of the paper, however, we are interested only in

[29] Compare the analysis in Landes and Posner (1989), of the mirror-image case in which creators of copyrighted works may be hurt by too-strict rules on copyright infringement. While wanting to protect their own work from being copied, the creators also want to make use of previous work in their creative process.

[30] To which the analysis in Landes and Posner (1989) is even more directly applicable.

[31] For intermediate values of ϕ, and assuming that $dr/d\phi = 0$ (see the earlier discussion of the determinants of π), we have $dz/d\phi = -q_z/q_{zz}\phi > 0$.

the very low values of r, since at any higher values B would no longer be a good faith purchaser.

A comparison of equations (8) and (5) reveals that A's search efforts will be more intensive than B's offsetting efforts at suppressing information. The reason is that A undertakes these efforts knowing that his work is missing, while B knows only that there is a small risk (since B is assumed to be a good faith purchaser) that the work has a defective title. Yet the aggregate expenditures of all B's could well exceed those of all A's. Every B makes a small expenditure on lowering q while only a subset of A's – those who are missing a work of art – will undertake expenditures to raise q.

The more B cares about the prestige of owning art, the greater will be his nonpecuniary cost of suppressing information on his acquisition. Thus, other things being equal, $1-q$ in its sense of the fractional share of the value of the work enjoyed by the purchaser will be greater for buyers who are art lovers rather than status seekers.[32]

We have assumed that the stock of art works is invariant to the choice of the legal rule, and this assumption has now to be defended. Recall that if good faith purchasers do not have secure rights (as ϕ goes from 0 to 1), we assume that the price of works of art will be depressed and fewer existing works will be sold and stolen. It might also be argued that fewer works will be created. But because of the durability of works of art and the tendency of art to appreciate over time, the existing stock, especially when weighted by value, is very large relative to the annual production of new works. Hence the effect of a change in legal rules on the total amount of art is likely to be small, at least for a very long time. True, the existing stock is not *really* fixed, because some works are missing and hence not part of the stock in an economic sense, and the legal rules may affect the incentive to discover them. But this margin depends mainly on a separate set of rules, the rules rewarding finders of lost art, which we discuss later.[33]

[32] To show this, we can rewrite B's expenditures on z as bz where b (>0) is the cost of a unit of z and hence is greater for status seekers than for art lovers. In equilibrium we have $-rq_z\phi V^b - b = 0$. Thus, the larger b is, the larger will q_z be in equilibrium, which implies fewer z's and hence a higher q or lower $1-q$ (from the assumptions that $q_z < 0$ and $q_{zz} > 0$).

[33] Another consideration that bears on the stock of art is that the price of new as opposed to old art may rise if the law gives greater protection to original owners. Imagine that the initial purchaser from the artist can determine with certainty that he has acquired valid

2.3 The optimal legal position

Having considered how owners and buyers respond to different values of ϕ, we are now in a position to analyze the optimal ϕ. Let W equal the net social welfare from the stock of works of art:

$$\begin{aligned} W = {} & [(1 - p(x^*, \phi))(1 - \alpha)V^a] \\ & + p(x^*, \phi)[q(y^*, z^*)\phi V^a + (1 - q(y^*, z^*)\phi)V^b - y^* - z^*] \\ & + [(1 - p(x^*, \phi))\alpha(V^b - z^*)] - [x^* + C(p(x^*, \phi))] \end{aligned} \tag{9}$$

title in the work. This should be relatively easy to do because he only has to trace his purchase back to one previous owner (the artist himself) not numerous parties as would be the case for old art with many previous owners. Thus, the purchaser of a new work should be willing to pay more if the law favors original owners since this gives him greater protection against subsequent good faith purchasers if the work is stolen or lost and he has little concern about prior owners. Contrary to our assumption that the stock of art is fixed, this factor suggests that the more the law favors original owners, the more new art that will be created and, therefore, the greater the growth in the stock of art. But there are added complications that make this conclusion uncertain. Original owners and good faith purchasers are, as we pointed out earlier, really the same people viewed at different times. Hence a shift in the balance of legal protection in favor of original owners may have offsetting effects on the prices of both new and old art. On the one hand, it decreases the resale price because good faith purchasers may be compelled by the law to restore the work of art to an owner original to them. And a decline in the expected resale price will reduce the price one is willing to pay at the outset for both new and old art. On the other, it may increase price because purchasers will know that they will have greater legal protection should their art ever be stolen from them and show up later in the hands of some other good faith purchaser, to whom they will stand in the relation of original owner. Finally, purchasers of art may substitute new for old art as the balance of protection shifts in favor of original owners. This occurs because buyers of new art are mainly concerned about their rights as original owners against subsequent good faith purchasers while buyers of old art are concerned with both their rights against previous owners and subsequent purchasers. How this factor affects the stock is unclear because it both reduces the incentive to maintain old art and increases the incentive to create new art.

In the text we have assumed that the price of old art will decline as ϕ increases from 0 to 1 because we have treated the original owner and good faith purchaser as separate parties in which the latter is only concerned with the possibility that he will have to restore the work to an original owner if the work turns out to have been previously stolen or lost. To this, we should add another factor – the substitution between new and old art as the balance of legal protection shifts to original owners – which tends to reduce the price of old art.

where x^*, y^*, and z^* satisfy the first-order conditions in equations (4), (5), and (8), respectively. We have simplified (9) by setting the stock equal to 1 and by assuming that all A's and all B's are identical in their valuations of the works of art, although A's as a group and B's as a group are permitted to have different valuations. The assumption that all A's and all B's are identical in their valuations of given works of art is obviously false, since there would be no voluntary sales of works of art by some but not all A's unless there were differences in valuation among the A's. The market price would be either greater or lower than the valuation placed on the works by all the owners, and in the first case all would sell and in the second case none would sell. But the assumption creates only minor difficulties with equation (9).[34]

The first set of terms (bracketed) on the right-hand side of equation (9) represents the expected value of works neither missing nor sold. The second set represents the expected value of works that are stolen, or lost, and then sold to the various B's, but are later found. That value is divided between the A's and B's depending on the values for $q(y^*, z^*)$ and ϕ. Notice that the second set of terms also nets out the expenditures that A and B make on y and z in hopes of influencing q.

The third set of terms (bracketed) gives the value of works with good title that are purchased by various B's. Since these purchasers know only that there is a probability of $(1-p)\alpha/(p+(1-p)\alpha)$ that these works are free of prior claims, they still incur expenditures on z. Last come A's expenditures on self-protection (x) and the total costs (C) incurred by persons who steal works or find missing works and sell them without the original owner's authorization. Those costs increase with the number of works stolen or lost. But since the stock of works is set equal to the numeraire 1, the number of works stolen or lost equals p and hence $C_p > 0$.

[34] The variable x^* is the weighted average of the self-protective efforts of those A's who would sell and those who would not. Those efforts will be less in the former group because, by definition, they receive less utility from owning their works of art. Some A's, moreover, who would have sold their work lost this opportunity when their work was stolen or lost. The second term in brackets in equation (9) includes the value for all A's whose works are taken. Since some would have sold and others would not have, the relevant V^a in the second term is a weighted average of the V^a's of the two groups. To allow for these differences would have complicated the notation while leading only to negligible changes in the outcomes, and so we ignore them in the formal model.

As a further simplification, we assume that original owners and good faith purchasers attach identical values to paintings with good title – $V^a = V^b$. This assumption is not as limiting as it may seem. If B is a good faith purchaser the value he receives from the work should not differ much from the value received by the typical A who chooses not to sell his work. Indeed, as noted earlier, original owners and good faith purchasers are largely interchangeable – most original owners were once good faith purchasers and most good faith purchasers become (from the standpoint of subsequent purchasers) original owners. In some cases $V^a \neq V^b$, for example when the painting has an idiosyncratic value to A or when B is not a good faith purchaser. We consider later how distributive considerations affect the determination of the optimal ϕ.

With $V = V^a = V^b$, equation (9) simplifies to

$$W = V - x^* - p(x^*, \phi)y^* - [p(x^*, \phi) + (1 - p(x^*, \phi))\alpha]z^* - C(p(x^*, \phi)). \quad (10)$$

Maximizing (10) with respect to ϕ and assuming that the first-order conditions in equations (4), (5), and (8) continue to hold, we have

$$\begin{aligned} -dx^*/d\phi - (dp/d\phi)y^* - [(dp/d\phi)(1 - \alpha) + (d\alpha/d\phi)(1 - p)]z^* \quad (11) \\ -(dC/dp)dp/d\phi = pdy^*/d\phi + [p + (1 - p)\alpha]dz^*/d\phi. \end{aligned}$$

The left-hand side of this equation summarizes the marginal benefits from increasing ϕ and the right-hand side the marginal costs. We assume that the second-order conditions for a maximum hold at the point of equality of marginal benefits and costs. On the benefits side notice that $dp/d\phi = p_x dx/d\phi + \partial p/\partial\phi$. The first term is the increase in p caused by a decline in self-protection in response to an increase in ϕ (the substitution effect noted earlier). The second term is the decline in p (the probability of theft or loss) as the price of the work of art (π) falls in response to a higher ϕ. Because the substitution effect is, in part, a response to the lower p, it is unlikely to swamp the direct effect of ϕ on p. So we assume initially that the net effect ($dp/d\phi$) of a higher ϕ is a lower p. That is, giving more legal protection to original owners reduces the likelihood that art will be stolen or lost.

Stepping outside our formal model for a moment, we add that a high level of legal protection of original owners will give art dealers, with whom most good faith purchasers deal, a greater incentive to investigate the provenance of the works they acquire, in order to be able to sell them at a high price to purchasers who face an enhanced risk of having one day to restore them to the original owners. Such investigation may reduce the amount of art theft at lower cost than increased self-protection by owners.[35] Investigation is not costless, but the only point we are making at the moment is that favoring original owners over good faith purchaser is likely to reduce the amount of stolen and lost art. Later we consider the implications of relaxing the assumptions of the model that lead to this conclusion.

The marginal benefits in equation (11) of increasing ϕ consist of the savings in expenditures on self-protection by original owners of works of art; the reduction in those owners' search costs for missing art (y) that is brought about by the decline in the probability that works with defective titles will be sold; the reduction in purchasers' expenditures on suppressing information (z) that is brought about by the overall decline in demand in the art market; and the savings in the costs of stealing and selling missing works as p declines. The marginal costs of increasing ϕ result from the greater incentive of both A and B to increase their expenditures on y and z in the hope of influencing q (the fraction of the value of the work that A recovers) holding constant the number of works being sold with defective titles and, in B's case, the number of all works sold. Recall that at $\phi = 0$, these expenditures by B are zero – his title is secure – but they become positive, and increase, the more likely it is that the law will restore the work to its original owner.

Suppose that p remains constant as ϕ increases because the effect of higher ϕ in reducing A's incentive to self-protect fully offsets the effect of higher ϕ in reducing p by reducing the incentive to steal. Then equation (11) simplifies to $-dx^*/d\phi + (d\alpha/d\phi)(1-p)z^* = pdy^*/d\phi + [p + (1-p)\alpha]dz^*/d\phi$. Now the marginal benefits of increasing ϕ consist only of the savings in A's expenditures on self-protection and in B's expenditures on reducing q. The latter savings come about because the B's purchase fewer works and cannot distinguish works with good title from those with defective title. The decline in the number of works purchased, however, is limited to works with good title because the number of stolen works remains constant (from the assumption that the decline in self-protection fully offsets the increase in ϕ).

If ϕ can be only either 0 or 1 (that is, either no legal protection or complete legal protection for original owners), then the original owner should be

[35] As emphasized in Bibas (1994, p. 2454).

protected if

$$(x^0 - x^1) + (C(p^0) - C(p^1)) \geq p^1 y^1 + [p^1 + (1 - p^1)\alpha] z^1, \qquad (12)$$

where the superscripts "1" and "0" correspond to optimal values of the superscripted variables when $\phi = 1$ or 0. The left-hand side of the equation denotes the benefits in reduced costs of self-protection and of stealing and selling works without the original owner's permission when ϕ goes from 0 to 1.[36] The right-hand side denotes the costs of searching for missing works and of suppressing information on their location when $\phi = 1$, or equivalently the increase in these costs, since they are zero when $\phi = 0$. When the benefits exceed the costs, the law should favor the original owner ($\phi = 1$).

2.4 Statutes of limitations

Recall that q is the fraction of the value of the work that is restored to the original owner (assuming $\phi = 1$) and $1 - q$ is the fraction received by the good faith purchaser (assuming $\phi = 1$). Suppose q is directly proportional to the time it takes to locate the work, so that the less time it takes the greater q will be. The period allowed for suit by a statute of limitations we denote by q^s and define as follows: if A discovers (or makes a demand on B) before $q \leq q^s$, then $\phi = 1$ (the original owner gets the work back – his suit is timely); and if $q > q^s$, then $\phi = 0$ and B gets to keep the work – A's suit is untimely.

The longer the statute of limitations is, the greater the rights of the original owner are. Put differently, *any* statute of limitations, which is to say any finite period within which suit must be brought, makes $\phi < 1$, so that if we wanted to make $\phi = 1$ this would argue for setting *no* deadline for suing a purchaser of art from a thief. In substance though not in form, this is the tendency of the case law. In some states, the statute of limitations begins to run only when the original owner makes a demand on the purchaser. In others a combination of the discovery rule and the doctrines of equitable tolling and equitable estoppel allows the owner to delay suing until he knows that his work has been stolen and who now possesses it and he can obtain service of

[36] The term $(dp/d\phi)y^* - [(dp/d\phi)(1-\alpha) + (d\alpha/d\phi)(1-p)]z^*$ in (11) equals 0 when ϕ increases from 0 to 1, because it is evaluated at $\phi = 0$, where both y^* and z^* equal 0.

process on the possessor.[37] In other words, the owner can delay suit until it is feasible for him to do so.[38] This may be decades or, in principle, centuries after the work was stolen, although the doctrine of laches[39] is available as a backstop against suits that the defendant can show were unreasonably delayed by the plaintiff, to the defendant's prejudice.

Since long delays in suing increase the risk of legal error by making it difficult to unmask spurious claims,[40] there is an argument for having *some* fixed deadline for suit. At some point, the incremental effect of a very long statute of limitations in discouraging theft by reducing the price of stolen art will be offset by the effect on legal error costs. Moreover, these error costs are borne ex ante by original owners as well as by bona fide purchasers, since most original owners were once bona fide purchasers and they don't want to be harassed by persons claiming to be previous owners. Hence, even original owners would favor the law's imposing some period of limitations on suits for the recovery of stolen or lost art.[41]

Concern with the legal error costs that are produced or exacerbated by long delay in bringing suit is the principal concern that lies behind statutes of limitations as well as the concern based most firmly on the economics of legal procedure. For example, much more time is allowed for suing for breach of a written contract than for suing for breach of an oral contract. Courts usually

---

[37]The discovery rule starts the statute of limitations running when the potential plaintiff discovers his loss. Equitable estoppel stops the statute of limitations from running when the potential defendant takes active measures to prevent the plaintiff from suing (for example, by concealing his identity from the plaintiff). Equitable tolling stops the statute of limitations from running when, even though the potential defendant has not done anything to delay suit by the plaintiff, the plaintiff, despite the exercise of due diligence, does not yet have enough information to be able to bring a suit. See Cada v. Baxter Healthcare Corp., 920 F.2d 446 (7th Cir. 1990).

[38]Once it is feasible, he must sue promptly. This makes sense in terms of costs of legal error, discussed below.

[39]Discussed in the Guggenheim case cited earlier.

[40]Not spurious defenses. A plaintiff will not delay suit if the effect is to increase the probability that the defendant will be able to "fake" a defense to the suit. Only in the minority of cases in which the defendant can accelerate the plaintiff's suing, for example by bringing a suit for declaratory relief, can the defendant prevent the plaintiff from using the delay permitted by the statute of limitations to bolster a weak claim.

[41]There is an analogy to the point that we make in our copyright article, that even copyright owners would, ex ante, prefer a finite to an infinite period of copyright protection. See Landes and Posner (1989).

resolve disputes over written contracts without recourse to evidence outside the contract itself, and that evidence does not fade significantly with time (it fades a little, because the meanings of words and the various contextual clues to interpretation change with time). Statutes of limitations tend also to be longer in criminal than in civil cases, perhaps because the higher standard of proof in the former type of case makes it more difficult for the plaintiff (the prosecutor) to fake a charge. For remember that a long statute of limitations encourages spurious claims but not spurious defenses.

Statutes of limitations that impose definite limitations on the time within which suit can be brought (as distinct from statutes of limitations that are rendered porous by the combined effect of the discovery rule and the doctrines of equitable tolling and equitable estoppel) are also said to be supported by the interest in "repose," that is, the interest in knowing for certain what one's rights are. Without statutes of limitations, property and other rights would be subject to additional contingencies besides changes in tax law, eminent domain, trespass, theft, and so on. If, however, there were no net positive effect of time on the costs of legal error, it would be difficult to see why these additional contingencies would be bad from a social standpoint. Owners of property would overinvest from that standpoint if they failed to discount the expected value of the investment by a probability less than one that the property was really theirs. In effect, the statute of limitations induces excessive reliance.[42] The analysis is parallel to that of "coming to the nuisance," a rightly rejected doctrine that if accepted would induce overinvestment in real property by causing owners to ignore changing values.[43] In contrast, the interest in repose is very great in labor cases, where an employer faces an accumulating and thoroughly uncertain obligation to pay a terminated worker backpay between the date of termination and the date of judgment in any suit brought by the worker (and there may be many workers similarly affected).[44] So statutes of limitations in labor cases tend to be short.

In the case of art, the interest in repose is likely to be offset by art's

[42]In just the same way that always giving the victim of a breach of contract his full reliance damages may induce excessive reliance, given that there is some positive probability that the promisor will break the contract without fault. See Shavell (1980).

[43]Landes and Posner (1987, pp. 50–51).

[44]The uncertainty is due in part to the fact that the amount of backpay will be affected by whether the employee has obtained, or in the exercise of due diligence (to mitigate his damages) could have obtained, another job.

durability and consumption value. Recall q, which relates the loss to the original owner and the gain to the purchaser forced eventually to return the work to the original owner to the amount of time that the work is missing. The longer the delay in bringing suit, the longer the period in which the purchaser (or his predecessor, if the work has changed hands more than once since its theft or loss) will have derived consumption benefits from the work by having it in his possession. These benefits, being themselves time-dependent, truncate the harm to him from being exposed to a long statute of limitations, which may place his possession at risk indefinitely.

A short statute of limitations would increase B's expenditures on z, expenditures, that is, on concealing a purchased work of art from a possible claimant to be the original owner. If the statute of limitations, unqualified by the discovery rule or any tolling doctrine, expired automatically after the good faith purchaser had owned the work of art for, say, five years, he would have an enhanced incentive to conceal the work for that period, since successful concealment would confer the benefit of a completely secure title beginning in the sixth year. This incentive is smaller the longer the effective statute of limitations.

Our analysis suggests that the only certain cost of a long statute of limitations for suits to recover lost or stolen art is the cost of legal error resulting from the increased likelihood of spurious claims by so-called original owners who aren't really. The function that relates that cost to the length of the statute of limitations presents a difficult empirical question (one that depends in part on the capacity of particular legal systems to reconstruct past events accurately) that we have not attempted to explore or to trade off against the benefits of a long statute of limitations that we have been emphasizing.

3 Considerations bearing on the choice of the legal rule

We have now to consider what "real world" factors determine whether social welfare is more likely to be maximized by returning works to original owners or by letting current possessors retain them. Our model suggests a number of considerations, and by examining them we can offer a tentative conclusion regarding the economic rationality of the current legal rules applicable to disputes over the ownership of art works.

3.1 The costs of search and of suppressing information

Equations (11) and (12) show that the principal social costs of favoring original owners (either by increasing ϕ or setting it equal to 1) are the costs that both owners and buyers incur in influencing q: the former in searching for missing works, the latter in trying to reduce the probability that the works will be found or to delay their discovery. The equilibrium levels of these expenditures by both original owners and good faith purchasers are likely to be low, however. If so, this creates a presumption in favor of a legal rule that restores the work of art to its original owner.

On the owner's side, an inexpensive and relatively productive form of search is simply to report the theft or lost work to one of the central registries of stolen works, of which the best known is the Art Loss Register. For a fee of only $65 the Register will publish a photograph and brief description of the work in the magazine *IFAR Reports*. This alerts auction houses, art dealers, private collectors, museums, and other subscribers, making it unlikely that any reputable seller will offer the listed work for sale. If a subscriber discovers the whereabouts of a listed work, moreover, he has a financial incentive to report it, because normally a reward of 10 percent of the value of the work is offered for information leading to its return.

There is little else the owner can do to accelerate the recovery of the missing work. He can visit galleries, check catalogues, and make inquiry of other collectors of the artist's work, but these are the sorts of activity that collectors engage in anyway, so that the incremental cost attributable to searching for a missing work is likely to be trivial. In sum, the optimal search expenditures of owners are likely to be small even when $\phi = 1$, because beyond the small cost of registering the lost work the marginal productivity of search is likely to diminish very rapidly. Indeed, owners may incur zero search costs simply because they are unaware that their work is missing. For example, after Chagall died his widow stashed more than 3,000 of his works in his studio. Some were stolen by a housekeeper, subsequently authenticated, and later sold by dealers involved in the scheme. Although the scheme was eventually discovered by a police informant and the parties prosecuted, the widow had been unaware of the thefts and had therefore incurred no costs to recover the stolen art. In the case mentioned earlier of a valuable Chagall gouache stolen by an employee from the Guggenheim, the museum was unaware of the theft for several years and did nothing about if even after learning of it. The record-keeping and inventory practices of many museums are out of date, and as a result a work can be missing for many years without the loss being discovered.

Some owners of missing works are reluctant to list them in a register of missing art. They prefer to take a wait-and-see approach, thinking the work more likely to resurface than if the loss is publicized and as a result the thief or his purchaser makes greater efforts to secrete it. In such a case, search expenditures will be close to zero. This was the Guggenheim's view, and it turned out to be right. The gouache was purchased from a reputable dealer and then openly displayed in a Manhattan apartment for more than twenty years. This enabled the Guggenheim to discover the location of the work, and once it did so it sued the current owners and won.[45] So we may not have been completely accurate when we said that listing a stolen work on a register of lost art is a cheap and effective method of owner self-protection. But the implication of this qualification is that the optimal expenditures on search by owners of lost art may be even slighter than we have suggested.

For some categories of work (antiques, for example), as yet no registry of lost works exists.[46] Here the benefits to an owner from even a slight amount of search may not exceed the cost when the works are small and portable, such as antique pocket watches or walking sticks, making them virtually impossible to find without the aid of a register. Then there will be no search and so the search costs actually incurred will approach zero despite a legal rule favoring original owners.

In sum, search expenditures by original owners appear to be low because additional expenditures beyond a minimal level are unlikely to be effective

---

[45]The approach taken by the Guggenheim, while privately optimal in the sense of maximizing its chance of getting the work back, may be socially suboptimal. If all art thefts were publicized, the price of stolen works would plunge, discouraging theft, just as prohibiting ransom reduces the amount of kidnapping even though to the family of a kidnapped victim paying ransom may be value maximizing. This point is emphasized in Bibas (1994).

[46]Substitutes, however, are emerging. Firms now exist that do computerized searches of catalogues for categories of antiques and notify dealers in these works about recent thefts. See Checkland (1995, p. 92).

in terms of locating missing works more rapidly. This implies that a rule designed to encourage original owners to search more, as by conditioning their legal rights on continuing and extensive search efforts or by truncating the statute of limitations for suits to recover lost art from good faith purchasers, is unlikely to be socially cost-justified. As for the good faith purchaser, his expenditures on suppressing information are in many instances likely to be negligible.[47] As we saw earlier, the benefits of such spending would have to be discounted by the very low probability that the title is defective (very low because otherwise the buyer would not be a good faith purchaser). Of course when these expenditures are summed up over all good faith purchasers – for we saw that all will incur them even though only a small fraction will actually have purchased a work with a defective title – they may not be so negligible. But they are still likely to be slight. Most collectors and museums value the prestige and publicity that come from public display of their collection highly, making it very costly to keep major acquisitions secret. It is true that most museums do not display their entire collection, but they would be unlikely to pay a high price for a work that they did not intend to display. We conclude that expenditures on z by good faith purchasers are likely to be small even if original owners have superior rights.[48]

If our analysis is correct, the costs of favoring original owners (represented by the variables on the right-hand sides of equations (11) and (12)) are probably small, implying that the benefits, which we have no reason to believe are small, outweigh them. This implies in turn that the rule that maximizes social welfare is likely to entail ϕ equal or very close to 1: complete legal protection of the original owner vis-à-vis the good faith purchaser. This is the standard legal position in this as in most countries.[49] A purchaser, even though he honestly and reasonably believes that he has acquired a good title, does not acquire a good title from a thief; and there is no exception for art. In a legal contest between the original owner and the good faith purchaser, the former, with qualifications (which turn out to be rather minor as a practical matter) having mainly to do with the statute of limitations,

[47] Unless the purchaser is very concerned about the danger of the theft of the work from himself and therefore conceals it. This is an unusual case, which we can ignore.

[48] We acknowledge, however, that these expenditures would be greater if pre-purchase investigative expenditures to determine good title, expenditures excluded from our formal model, were included.

[49] See Levmore (1987).

which we examine in the last part of the paper, prevails.

3.2 A high probability that the title to the work is defective

We said that if r (the risk known to the purchaser that his seller does not have good title) is high, B will not be a good faith purchaser, and we suggested that this was probably the efficient result. Let us examine the issue a little more closely, in light of our model. Suppose an Indian headdress or wooden effigy has been privately held and is now being offered for sale. The work may have been acquired many years ago from someone who believed that he could lawfully transfer the work. But now it appears that the item may be deemed the property of a tribe that is demanding its return. Similar problems can arise with regard to artifacts and antiquities imported from foreign countries that may be demanding their return on the ground that they are part of the national patrimony.

Here there may be higher costs to a legal rule that favors the original owner. If B does buy the work, he may decide not to disclose his purchase or exhibit the work (implying a high z^*), lest by doing so he reveal it to a potential claimant. The costs of suppressing information may be particularly high because the potential claimants for these works are "original" not only to recent purchasers but also to most current possessors who have no desire to sell the works. *All* parties who currently possess works of this character – both buyers and owners, B's and A's in our model – will have an incentive to spend resources to suppress information about the works in the hope of reducing the likelihood that some third party will claim them. Since the number of persons who incur these expenditures will thus greatly exceed the number of current buyers, the potential savings from setting $\phi = 0$ are likely to be substantial.

But there is a considerable paradox here. We seem to be suggesting that a purchaser who is *not* a purchaser in good faith (though he is an "innocent" purchaser, in our terminology, because he does not know that his seller cannot convey good title, although he suspects this may be the case) should get more legal protection than a good faith purchaser *because* he realizes that his title is contestable. The paradox arises from our having ignored the incentive to commit theft that the protection of the hypothetical innocent purchaser would create. A blanket rule setting $\phi = 0$ for doubtful purchases would incite considerable additional expenditures on taking and on preventing the taking of works embraced by the rule. The rule makes more sense confined to works acquired at a time when society deemed the transaction lawful and the title acquired by it free of claims by any third parties. Such a rule would be supported by the thinking that underlies statutes of limitations.

Many dealers in artifacts and antiquities claim that returning disputed objects to religious or ethnic groups or to foreign nations would destroy the legitimate market in these works. The combination of a high p with an inability to distinguish between objects with and those without clouds on their title implies that the demand for and hence price (π) of these works would fall sharply if ϕ rose to 1. Prices would decline even further because the quantity offered for sale would increase in response to the greater cost of holding these works – since the owners would now incur costs of suppressing information – and because of the greater risk that a court would divest the owner of the work. And greater efforts would be made to suppress information about the location of such works. Fewer works would be sold at public auctions and by reputable galleries and more would be sold privately, while the prices of those works that had impeccable provenance would rise as collectors shifted their demand to them.

These dire effects would only be temporary, however. Eventually, title would be securely vested in the religious, ethnic, or national entities that recovered them. Of course, this would also happen if title were securely vested in the current owners, who could then sell the works to religious, ethnic, or national entities if the latter valued them more. This result might be impeded, however, by the public good aspects of works claimed by large collectives. Each member has an incentive to underreveal the value that he attaches to the return of the works. This is an argument for adhering to the rule that the original owner prevails over the bona fide purchaser even in the case of antiquities.

3.3 The buyer knows that the work is stolen

If $r = 1$, we again have the paradox that the purchaser seems to have a stronger case than the bona fide purchaser for not returning the work of art to the original owner, because a purchaser's incentive to suppress information about the work is at its maximum when $p = 1$ and $\phi = 1$. Consider the speculation that there is a "Mr. Big" – a sinister "Dr. No" type character – who is responsible for the unsolved thefts of Old Masters paintings, including the $300 million worth of paintings taken from the Gardner Museum in 1990. He is "reputed to have art stolen to order and gloat over it in some secret palace hideaway."[50] So if the law's only concern were with minimizing expenditures by "Mr. Big" and other buyers of stolen art on suppressing information about their recent "acquisitions," courts would never order the return of stolen works to the original owners. But we know from our earlier analysis of the economics of art theft that the social costs of such theft would be increased by such a rule, and those higher costs are unlikely to be offset by the reduction in concealment expenditures by thieves and "fences."[51] This is particularly so because the rule would greatly increase the costs of self-protection of all works of art, whereas the savings would be limited to the works that are stolen under the existing legal regime, which presumably deters most thefts. The rule entitling the original owner to the return of his property if it is found is a part of that deterrent regime, as we saw. We add that there are other benefits from deterring theft once we relax the assumption in our model that the number of works is fixed. In particular, the incentive to create new works and to preserve valuable existing works would be increased.

3.4 The work was lost or misplaced rather than stolen

Suppose a good faith purchaser obtains a work that was lost or misplaced by the original owner rather than stolen. Maybe the original owner mistakenly discarded the work and it was eventually found by another party and sold to B. Or maybe the owner made feeble and sporadic efforts to get back a work that he had consigned to a gallery which later closed, disposed of the work to another merchant, and pocketed the proceeds, and years later B purchases it. If the heirs of the original owner seek the return of the work, should the law treat this case the same as a case of theft and thus order the work returned?

By assuming that the work was lost rather than stolen, we eliminate the costs of theft from equations (11) and (12) and therefore reduce the marginal

[50] See Checkland (1995, p. 93).

[51] This would be like arguing that the way to minimize the social costs of theft is to repeal the larceny laws so that stolen goods can circulate freely in the marketplace.

benefits of raising ϕ or setting it equal to 1. Moreover, returning these works to original owners will discourage efforts both to find and to restore them. Lost works are often in terrible condition when found, and immediate restoration may be necessary to prevent irrevocable further deterioration.

Suppose an expenditure (x) by A of \$100 would prevent the loss of his work, which has a value of \$1,000. And suppose that if the work is lost and B finds and restores it, there will be a \$50 loss because the work will yield no benefits while it is missing. (There is no thief gloating over it in his hideaway.) And, finally, suppose that B's cost of finding and restoring the work is \$200. Clearly it would be more efficient for A to spend \$100 to prevent the loss than for B to spend \$200 to find and restore the work. If the law won't order the work returned to A ($\phi = 0$), he will spend the \$100 to avoid the \$1,000 loss. But if the law will order the return of his work ($\phi = 1$), and A is confident that some B will find and restore it, A will not spend \$100 on x. He would prefer to incur the temporary loss of \$50. Although privately optimal, A's decision is socially suboptimal because it reduces aggregate value by \$150 – the \$200 cost of finding and restoration to B plus the \$50 temporary loss to A minus the \$100 savings in A's expenditures on self-protection.

Why would B spend \$200 if the law entitled A to the return of the work? Because we are assuming that B is a good faith purchaser who therefore believes there is only a small probability that any work he purchases will have a defective title. If that probability is .1, B will spend \$200 to find and restore the work, because it is less than his expected benefit of \$855 (.9 × \$950). Actually his expected benefit is a bit less – revealing a further social cost of A's indolence. B anticipates that works with defective titles will be returned to their original owners and so he will have an incentive to suppress (at a cost – z in our analysis – of, let us say, \$10) information about his acquisition, for example by refusing to display it publicly.

Not too much weight can be put on our numerical example, however. If the cost of owner self-protection were \$300 rather than \$100, the efficient solution would be for B to find and restore the work, for this would raise social welfare by \$40 (\$950 - \$200 - \$10 versus \$1,000 - \$300). If the law let B keep the work ($\phi = 0$), A would have an incentive to spend \$300 to prevent the loss in the first place, which would be wasteful.

These examples suggest that the law should impose liability on the party best able to avoid the loss in the particular situation. That would be a negligence-type approach – and it might involve a great deal of uncertainty.

The sequential nature of the parties' expenditures suggests the feasibility of a less uncertain approach. If the law returns the work to the original owner but gives the buyer a right to recover his expenditures on finding and restoring it, A will choose self-protection when it is the less costly alternative and rely on B's rescue efforts when that reliance would be the less costly alternative. For example, if self-protection costs \$100, A will rather self-protect than lose \$50 in services from the work plus a \$200 judgment in a suit brought by B to recover his costs. But if it costs \$300, then A will prefer to lose \$50 in services from the work and pay a \$200 judgment than to self-protect. B will be willing to incur the costs of finding and restoring a valuable work knowing that he will be compensated for his costs (including a reasonable profit, in order to motivate him to incur the costs of finding and restoration) even if a prior owner is successful in reclaiming it. Although the law of restitution, which would govern such a claim by B, is murky, we believe it likely that, provided B's good faith were established along with the reasonableness of his expenditures, a court would allow him to recover his expenditures as an "agent of necessity."[52] It might seem that merely being reimbursed for his expenditures would not be compensation enough to induce B to find and restore valuable works if B were a professional "rescuer" of lost art who encountered a number of "dry holes" before finding a valuable work, as opposed to an amateur who happens to stumble on a lost painting, having incurred no search costs. But we shall see in a moment that even in the case of the professional art "rescuer," reimbursement of his costs of finding and restoring the particular painting may be adequate to create the proper incentives.

Consider the fascinating case of *Mucha v. King*.[53] In 1920 the Czech Art Nouveau painter Alphonse Mucha consigned his large painting *Quo Vadis* to a gallery in Chicago. Before the painting could be sold, the market for Mucha's paintings collapsed. Mucha and later on his son Jiri made some efforts to get the painting back from the dealer, but the efforts were unsuccessful because of problems of communication (including language difficulties), lack of physical proximity, uncertainties about customs levies, and the disruption caused by World War II. Fifty years after receiving the consignment the gallery closed

[52]See Landes and Posner (1978, pp. 108-109).

[53]792 F.2d 602 (7th Cir. 1986). Candor requires disclosure that the judicial coauthor of this paper wrote the opinion.

and liquidated its contents. The owner gave away some rolled-up paintings, one of which was *Quo Vadis*, to a hot-tubs merchant who had bought a $5 fan at the liquidation sale. The merchant resold the painting (whose value he did not appreciate) to an art dealer for $150. King, the defendant in the suit later brought by Jiri Mucha to get the painting back, bought it from the dealer for $35,000 in 1981 and hired an expert to restore it at a cost of $16,000. When a friend of King wrote Mucha for information about the painting, Mucha learned of its whereabouts and sued. The court ordered the painting returned to Jiri Mucha but permitted King to recover the costs he had incurred to restore the work. King did not seek a finder's fee.

The result in *Mucha* is consistent with our economic model. Distance, a language barrier, customs uncertainties, and a world war made the cost of owner self-protection very high. By permitting King to recover his expenses the law gave him an incentive to restore a work valued at $500,000. True, he did not get back the $35,000 that he had paid to buy the work. But assuming (a little doubtfully, in part because of the very low price) that he was a good faith purchaser, the *expected* benefit to him of finding and restoring the painting was strongly positive. For example, if he thought there was a 90 percent probability that the dealer who sold it to him had good title, the expected *net* profit of his purchase was $399,000 (.9 $\times$ $500,000 - $35,000 - $16,000). Had the court forfeited the painting to King, on the theory that the Muchas should have done more to prevent the painting's being mislaid for so long, the effect would have been to encourage owners to incur large costs to prevent such mishaps. Entitling the owner to the return of the painting but entitling the finder-restorer to suitable compensation produces the optimal expenditure on preventing-restoring lost works. As we have emphasized, the owner will automatically incur the costs of preventing the loss when they are lower than "allowing" the work to be lost and then "rescued" for a fee. And because, as the facts of the *Mucha* case illustrate, the *expected* benefit to the bona fide purchaser of a lost painting is very high (since by definition of a good faith purchaser the probability that the seller did not have good title to the painting is small), there will be substantial incentives to search for lost paintings even if the finder's fee does not attempt to compensate for the unsuccessful searches ("dry holes").

If the original owner of a work of art abandons it, then he cannot later claim it back, when it unexpectedly increases in value. This is the general rule of property law, and it is as applicable to art as to anything else. The case can be analyzed as a sale by the owner at a price of zero to a finder who values the work at a much higher price. There is no economic reason to undo the deal by returning the work to the former owner. The former owner can always buy it back from the finder if he values it more highly.

In *Erisoty v. Rizik*,[54] to take just one more example, a badly damaged eighteenth-century painting by Giaquinto was found in a trash bag by a cleaning service hired to remove furniture from a home. The painting was acquired by Erisoty, a professional conservator of paintings, at auction. He then spent four years restoring the painting before it was discovered by the FBI and returned to its original owner, from whom it had been stolen more than thirty years earlier. Unlike *Quo Vadis*, the Giaquinto painting had been stolen, so that the social benefits of deterring theft strengthen the economic argument for returning the work to its owner. The original owner, moreover, appears to have taken reasonable precautions both to prevent the theft in the first place and to search for the missing work afterward. Consistent with our analysis, the court ruled that Erisoty could pursue a claim to recover for his services and expenses in restoring the work.

We speculate that cases involving disputes between original owners of *lost* art and good faith purchasers are less common than cases involving disputes between original owners of *stolen* art and good faith purchasers. The reason is that valuable art is less likely to be lost, but not less likely to be stolen, than art of little value. Moreover, the lower the value of the property in dispute, the less likely the dispute is to repay the expenses of litigation and so become a case. *Mucha* was the relatively unusual case in which art that was of little value when it was initially mislaid later became highly valuable.

3.5 The entrustment exception

Under the doctrine of entrustment, a good faith purchaser can prevail against the original owner in some circumstances. For example, if A entrusts C, a dealer, with a work of art, authorizing him to sell it, and B then buys the work, in the ordinary course of business, from C, who absconds with the proceeds of the sale, B acquires a good title even as against A.[55] Had the

[54] 1995 WL 91406 (E.D.Pa. 1995).

[55] Uniform Commercial Code §§2–403(2), (3). See Gerstenblith (1988, pp. 546–553). There are some closely related exceptions, both in the Code and at common law, to the general principle that the original owner prevails over the good faith purchaser, but we

gallery to which Mucha consigned *Quo Vadis* sold it to King but kept the proceeds, King (provided of course that he was a purchaser in good faith) would have gotten good title. Mucha could proceed against the gallery for the amount he was due but if the gallery were broke he would be out of luck. And in *Erisoty*, had the Riziks consigned the painting to an auction house that kept the proceeds from the sale, Erisoty would have been the lawful owner. The key elements of the entrustment doctrine are that the original owner have entrusted the work to someone whom he authorized to sell it and that the subsequent transaction between that person and the buyer can be described as occurring in the ordinary course of business.

The doctrine can be defended on economic grounds even if there is no question of A's having been careless in his choice of dealers. By definition, A wanted to sell the work, and so presumably fixed a price that exceeded the value of the work to him. B paid that price, implying that he values the work more than A. Hence the work ends up where it would have ended up in a completely voluntary market transaction. In this instance, paradoxically, the argument that the legal system is a poor adjudicator of competing values compared to the market – an argument made by law and economics scholars to explain why the common law protects entitlements by property rights, rather than by liability rules, when transaction costs are low – favors divesting the original owner of his entitlement. For if the law returned the work to A it would be making a judgment about competing values that is inconsistent with that of the market. It would be moving the work of art from a lower-valued to a higher-valued use.

Of course, the move would only be temporary. By hypothesis, there is a price – the price B paid – at which both A and B would be made better off by a sale from A to B. So if the law returned the work to A, he would promptly sell it back to B, unless the loss of the painting so impoverished B as to alter his demand. Setting that possibility to one side, we see that the law prevents unnecessary transaction costs by leaving the work with B.

This conclusion depends, however, on three assumptions. The first, which is innocuous although it reverses one of the simplifying assumptions in our model, is that A and B do not value the work of art in question equally. Our original, simplifying assumption was justified because most owners of works of art keep their works; only a few (the fraction denoted by α) voluntarily sell

---

shall not explore them.

them. But here we are dealing with the set of cases in which the owner has decided to sell his painting at the market price rather than to retain it. In this case $V^b > V^a$, whereas in the case of theft $V^a > V^b$. "Mr. Big" doesn't value the works he has stolen as much as the owners do, if only because value in economic analysis depends (with irrelevant exceptions) on willingness to pay. It is unlikely that he has enough money to buy the art he is thought to have stolen from the Gardner Museum, let alone to buy all the other art that he is thought to have stolen.

A second and more troublesome assumption of our analysis of the entrustment doctrine is that the dealer sold the work at the price fixed by the consignor. If the dealer is dishonest or tottering on the brink of insolvency – neither an unlikely contingency, since by assumption he is going to abscond with the proceeds of the sale – he may have sold it a lower price, and the presumption that B valued the work more highly than A fails. If, however, the dealer offers the work for a price substantially and inexplicably below the market price (which presumably was the price at which A authorized him to sell it), the purchaser's bona fides may be called into question.

Third, the doctrine permits the good faith purchaser to acquire good title even if the work of art was entrusted to the seller for a purpose other than sale, for example restoration. Here there can be no presumption that the buyer values the work more than the original owner does. The economic rationale for allowing the good faith purchaser to keep the work is that as between him the original owner, the latter had the superior ability to avoid the mishap by more careful selection of the person or firm to which to entrust his work of art for repair, restoration, storage, transportation, appraisal, exhibition, etc.

The entrustment doctrine is a categorical exception to a categorical rule (original owner prevails over all purchasers). An alternative approach, which we hinted at in our reference to negligence, would be to substitute a *standard*, whereby the dispute between the original owner and the subsequent purchaser would be decided in accordance with which of the two was, in the particular circumstances of the case, the cheaper cost avoider. Then the owner who had been careless in preventing the theft of his work of art might lose out to a careful purchaser, even if the purchaser was not a good faith purchaser within the meaning of the law because he suspected that his seller's title might be bad; yet he expended the optimal amount of resources on investigating the seller's title without discovering that it was bad. This approach would involve greater cost, in legal and judicial resources and in uncertainty, than the categorical approach. So the question, which we have not attempted to investigate, is whether the categories make a sufficiently close fit with the distribution of cases that the benefits of greater individuation would fall short of the increment in cost.

4 References

Bibas, S.A. (1994), Note, The case against statutes of limitations for stolen art, *Yale Law Journal*, 103, 2437-2469.

Bonus, H. and D. Ronte (1995), Credibility and economic value in the visual arts, Westfälische Wilhelms-Universität Münster, Volkswirtschaftliche Diskussionsbetrag Nr. 219.

Checkland, S.J. (1995), To catch a thief, *Art & Auction*, April, 92-95.

Ellickson, R.C. (1986), Adverse possession and perpetuities law: two dents in the libertarian model of property rights, *Washington University Law Quarterly*, 64, 723-737.

Epstein, R.A. (1986), Past and future: the temporal dimension in the law of property, *Washington University Law Quarterly*, 64, 667-722.

Gerstenblith, P. (1988), Picture imperfect: attempted regulation of the art market, *William and Mary Law Review*, 29, 501-566.

Landes, W.M. and R.A. Posner (1978), Salvors, finders, good Samaritans, and other rescuers: an economic study of law and altruism, *Journal of Legal Studies*, 7, 83-128.

Landes, W.M. and R.A. Posner (1987), *The Economic Structure of Tort Law*, Cambridge: Harvard University Press.

Landes, W.M. and R.A. Posner (1989), An economic analysis of copyright law, *Journal of Legal Studies*, 18, 325-363.

Levmore, S. (1987), Variety and uniformity in the treatment of the good-faith purchaser, *Journal of Legal Studies*, 16, 43-65.

Posner, R.A. (1992), *Economic Analysis of Law*, 4th ed., Boston: Little, Brown and Company.

Posner, R.A. (forthcoming), *Law and Legal Theory in England and America*, Oxford: Oxford University Press.

Schwartz, A. and R.E. Scott (1982), *Commercial Transactions: Principles and Policies*, Mineola: Foundation Press.

Shavell, S. (1980), Damage measures for breach of contract, *Bell Journal of Economics*, 11, 466-490.

Shavell, S. (1996), The acquisition and transfer of property, unpublished, Harvard Law School.

Weinberg, H. R. (1980), Sales law, economics, and the negotiability of goods, *Journal of Legal Studies*, 9, 569-592.

Economics of the Arts - Selected Essays
V.A. Ginsburgh and P.-M. Menger (Editors)

9

A Colloquy about Art Museums: Economics engages Museology

William D. Grampp
University of Illinois, Chicago

This paper argues that art museums are inefficient by the standards a for-profit organization must respect and a non-profit organization is supposed to respect. Nevertheless the conduct of art museums is understandable. It is consistent with the interests of museum professionals and supports the hypothesis that they are engaged in rent seeking. The exposition is in the form of a colloquy between an economist and a museologist, the impartial and the partial spectator, respectively, the former a liberty taken with the moral arbiter invented by Adam Smith and the latter a construct made from what one hears and over-hears in the museum world. Both speak the language of the general reader, but now and then there is a parenthetical expression in words more familiar to economists.

If a business firm, a commercial art gallery for example, managed its affairs as an art museum does, it would be the wonder of the western world. But its time of wonder would be brief and come to an end in a bankruptcy court. Yet art museums, although the very picture of improvidence to the impartial spectator, actually grow in size, numbers, audience, in the extent of their collections, and in their total expenditure, this while their deficits may also increase. How can this be?

It can be, the partial spectator or man from the art world would tell the impartial spectator or man from economics, because museums are non-profit organizations. But that is a poor answer. Non-profit does not in principle signify inefficiency even if it does in practice. A prudent use of resources, which is what efficiency means, should be as important to an art museum as to a commercial gallery. And the common argument made on behalf of non-profit organizations is that they can take into account the costs and benefits which the market does not, hence can use resources more efficiently than a for-profit organization can.

Consider what can be observed about art museums. The information comes from museum handbooks, guides, brochures, reports and other of their publications, from their letters asking for money, from what museum people say in conferences and other public appearances, what they report to the press and what the press reports about them, from what a visitor who takes museums seriously can see and cannot, and from what I have been told in conversation and interviews. The information is, to the best of my knowledge, accurate and describes many museums, probably most of them, certainly enough of them of consequence to give one pause. It is not, admittedly, the kind of information an empirical economist would choose if he had the world to choose from and a battery of econometricians to sort it out. But this he does not have and so must make the best of what he does have as long as it is, to the best of his knowledge, accurate. It is anecdotal, to be sure. But then most economics throughout its history has rested on anecdotal evidence to the extent that it has rested on evidence of any kind. So too has history, and art history, with a few notable exceptions, still does. There may be counter-evidence of the same or of a different kind that contradicts the generalizations of this paper. That is conceivable, just as anything is. But until it materializes I must do with what I have, and although it is anecdotal it is not trivial. It presents itself in more museums than not and does so more often than not.

1 The impartial spectator observes

(a) About acquisitioning. When museums acquire capital, for example a painting, they do not attend it whether it will pay for itself in the sense that its cost will be borne by the people who benefit (receive utility) from it in proportion to the benefit they receive. A commercial gallery would not do what a museum does or would a collector. A gallery before adding a painting to its stock would consider how much it could be sold for and when. A collector before buying it would consider whether it would give him as much satisfaction as something else with the same price.

If price and utility are not attended to, the result is an inefficient use of resources. Too much is produced of some things, too little of others. (The ratio of the price to the marginal utility of the former is below that of the latter instead of being, as they should be, equal for all goods.) An art museum produces cultural services and provides utility to people who have a demand for them. Not everyone does. Those who do pay less than the (marginal) cost of producing them, the remainder being borne by people who have no interest in museums but must pay taxes to support them. This is the state of affairs in a museum that receives no gifts and must look to the government to subsidize it in an amount equal to the difference between its operating expenses and its income from admission charges. In museums that do receive gifts, the givers can be assumed to receive satisfaction from their giving. If a museum's entire income was from gifts and admission charges and its income equaled its expenses it could not be said to be operating inefficiently. There are few in the world about which this can be said and many, many about which it cannot. The inefficiency of the many has been said to be only apparent, because they provide benefits not only to visitors and donors but to the public at large including that part of it which has no interest in art museums and is not aware of how it benefits from them. This claim is made in various quarters (in economics that museums produce a public good or a good that has positive externalities) but it never has been demonstrated.

(b) Capital costs. Museums deny that their collection, which is the art in their possession, is capital although in fact it is and is the largest part of their capital. This makes them ignore or deny that one of their expenses is the implicit interest cost of their art. The cost would be explicit if they borrowed in order to add to their collections (as a museum in fact does when it draws from its endowment to pay for an acquisition and later repays the amount with interest). Ignoring the cost of capital causes the operating expenses of a museum to be understated, quite apart from who bears the expenses and in what amount, and causes a museum to "produce" too much, that is, to have too large a collection, too much space, too many employees, too many visitors, or some combination of these things.

(c) Financial reporting. American museums on their balance sheets do not report the money value of their collections. The omission is of course consistent with their claiming that art is not capital. They do acknowledge it has a money value but deny the money value of art has anything to do with its true or essential value.

The money value (the untrue or inessential value?) is disclosed on occasion, not directly by the museums but by the Association of Art Museum Directors in the U.S. The AAMD asks each of them to report the amount of insurance it has on its collection and what percentage of the collection is insured. Some museums answer both questions, some only one, some neither. From the reports of those that answer both, the AAMD estimates the value of their collections. The numbers signify little and would interest only the idly curious. Just what do we know that we did not know when we learn the collection of the Cincinnati Art Museum is valued at $1,111,111,111 ($100 million divided by nine percent). We would like also to know the value of the other assets. It is not reported by the AAMD but is in the highly informative study Richard Rosett made of the finances of American art museums for a conference of the National Bureau of Economic Research. The value of museum collections, he states, is "in the neighborhood of 90 percent" of the value of all museum assets, reported and unreported. Now we know a little more which is that the value of all of the assets of the Cincinnati Museum is in the neighborhood of $1.23 billion.[1] Perhaps. The reliability of the collection figures is a great unknown. Professor Rosett estimated the value of the collections of the 127 museums which he studied and which are the principal museums in the U.S. The estimate was $32.2 billion, and he immediately added that the actual value might be half of that or three times as much.[2]

That however is not the point at issue. It is that a museum by omitting the value of its collection from its balance sheet understates the value of its capital by a substantial amount. The omission deprives the balance sheet of one of its functions which is to make comparisons possible – comparisons among art museums, between them and other museums, and between them and other organizations, both for- and non-profit. How one would like to see a comparison between the rate of return on the capital of the Metropolitan Museum and that on the capital of the New York Philharmonic Orchestra and to see both returns compared with those of for-profit organizations! A minister of culture could use that information if he would. So could the trustees of non-profit organizations and the legislators who exempt them from taxes that self-supporting organizations must pay.

---

[1] Association of Art Museum Directors (1995a, p. 184).
[2] Rosett (1991, p. 160).

(d) Exhibition/collection ratio. Museums exhibit only a small portion of their collection, many 10 percent or less of the number of objects in it.

The Art Institute of Chicago exhibits 10,000, or three percent, of the 300,000 objects in its permanent collection. That is also the proportion which until 1994 was exhibited by the Whitney Museum of New York and by the Musée National d'Art Moderne of Paris. The Guggenheim Museum of New York, before its recent expansion, exhibited four percent and when the expansion is completed will exhibit eight percent which is also the proportion of the Freer Collection in Washington that is exhibited. The Hermitage in St. Petersburg is said to exhibit seven percent; the Alte Pinakothek in Munich, 10 percent. That is also the proportion which the British Museum exhibits or did in 1991, Sir David Wilson, then director, said at that time. In his book about the museum, published in 1989, he said the collection contains six million objects which implies the visitor had 600,000 things of one kind or another to look at. That may or may not be the fact since the size of the collection – Sir David has stated – is not known with certainty. The museums of Britain together exhibit 20 percent of their "fine art." American museums, according to a newspaper report in 1995 about the use of their collections, generally display five percent of their holdings. The Metropolitan of New York exhibits one third of its collection of European sculpture and decorative arts and in the future will exhibit two thirds, an unusually high proportion. So too is the proportion of its paintings which the Louvre will exhibit when it is completely done over – 60 percent by the report of its conservator, almost 100 percent according to its director. Before the remodeling began it exhibited 33 percent, itself unusually high. The Prado in Madrid exhibits nine percent of its collection. The municipal museums of Venice exhibit half of their paintings. The Uffizi (Florence) exhibited 650 works in 1990 which is about one fourth as many as it exhibited in 1900, and in the intervening years the size of the collection did not decrease.[3]

[3]Art Institute: *Chicago Sun Times*, August 14, 1990 and *Art Newspaper*, October 1990; Whitney: *New York Times*, October 18, 1987; Guggenheim: *New York Times*, October 18, 1987; Musée National d'Art Moderne: *Art Newspaper*, June 1992; Freer: *Art Newspaper*, May 1993; Hermitage: *New York Times*, February 22, 1991; Alte Pinakothek: *Art Newspaper*, April 1993; British Museum: Sir D. Wilson, director, in conversation with writer, April 1991; all UK museums: Lord et al. (1989, p. 19); Metropolitan: *New York Times*, October 18, 1987; all US museums: *New York Times*, December 7, 1995; Louvre: Mme A. Vila, director, reserve facility, interview, May 1990; Prado: *New York Times*,

One would like to know more. What is the ratio of the money value of the art on exhibit to that of the entire collection? That would tell one how much of the capital value of its art a museum utilizes. One then would know (a little) more about how efficiently the capital is used. If a museum exhibited 10 percent of the number of objects in its collection and their average price was nine times the price of that which was not exhibited, the museum would be utilizing about 90 percent of its art capital (and 81 percent of all of its capital). That in itself does not denote efficiency or would it be denoted if the 90 percent in storage was worthless. But the value ratio is more informative than the quantity ratio and directs one to the proper measure of efficiency. That is the rate of return on the art as well as on the other assets of a museum. To ask for the information that is needed in order to compute this measure is, in the present state of museum accounting, like asking for the moon. Not even the denominator of the rate (the value of the collections) is reported and may not be known to the museums themselves since they do not want to value their art in money or could they if they would since they may not know just what they have. What the impartial spectator would encounter if he asked for information about the numerator, which is the money value of the services museums provide (net of cost), is best not thought of.

These matters, as important as they are to economists and as they should also be to museologists, are not as interesting to museum visitors as something else is. That is the contents of what is in storage, the "reserves." To call them that suggests they are drawn on from time to time and exhibited or suggests they may be seen in the storage area. The suggestion is misleading. The Louvre found that rotating the works on exhibit was unduly expensive. Labels had to be changed, catalogues revised, insurance modified, the docents retrained, and the workmen who moved things had to be paid union wages. However, one must report that some museums say they do rotate their holdings. The Tate of London says that 70 percent of what is on exhibit is changed once each year. This need not mean that 70 percent of the collection is exhibited once a year but could mean the Tate shows more of its collection than most museums do. In a few museums a portion of the storage area is open to visitors. Objects are displayed simply, even

August 1, 1990 and *Economist*, May 1, 1993; Venice: Dr. A. Dorigato, director, municipal museums of Venice, interview, May 1992; Uffizi: *Economist*, September 15, 1990; all art museums in Italy: *Art Newspaper*, April 1993. See also footnote 6.

austerely, and there are many more of them than could be seen in the same space in a conventional gallery. This is done in the Rijksmuseum, the Toledo (Ohio) Museum of Art which has one the largest collections of glass in the world, and by the Metropolitan which at times has also had a study gallery, something between open storage and a conventional gallery.

Few museums inform the visitor of what is in the collection. There are of course catalogues, guides, handbooks, maps, floor plans, and the like, but they are not complete or current. Here a comparison of a museum and a library is instructive. One would be astonished if on visiting a library one found it had no public catalogue, that its records were incomplete or that there were none, that information about what was on the open shelves was furnished by ladies who volunteered their time for a few hours each week. Equally astonished would be a collector who called at a commercial gallery and was told that information was not presently available about the painting he was interested in and would he kindly put the question in writing and allow a suitable time for reply.

(e) De-accessioning. Museologists believe the size of the collection should never be reduced and should if possible be increased continually. They are opposed to de-accessioning – a euphemism for disposal which in its day was a euphemism for selling – except if the proceeds from the sale of one work are used to buy another (an implicit acknowledgment that the size of the collection is to be measured in money). A business firm would regard this practice as unusual; it would sell an asset in order to acquire another of the same kind only if the latter yielded a higher rate of return than the former and a higher return than an asset of any other kind including cash.

In the U.S. the museums are so strongly opposed to net de-accessioning (selling for any purpose other than buying) that a director who does sell without buying can be expelled from the AAMD. That means his museum can be excluded from loan exhibitions, the fees from them, can be denied borrowing privileges, and the director can find himself in coventry. A museum that cannot meet its operating expenses except by net de-accessioning is advised to close and make its collection available to museums that can meet their expenses in the way the AAMD says is proper. It has been defied occasionally, and its policy is no longer at one with the policy of the American Association of Museums, which comprises museums of all kinds. It now advises but no longer requires its members to buy when they sell.[4]

In Italy the Solicitor-General of the government's auditing office in 1990 proposed that museums sell duplicates and other works they did not consider "precious" and use the proceeds to catalogue their holdings, to conserve and restore them, and to protect them from theft. The museums objected and were supported by art historians upon which show of force the Solicitor-General withdrew. In Britain the Minister of Arts in 1987 said museums should be permitted to sell what they wanted less, in order to buy what they wanted more. The museums objected, the Minister reconsidered, said they could use the proceeds in part for administration, and the museums' objections diminished but were not withdrawn.[5]

(f) Record keeping. The inventory and other records of the collection are often inadequate, often inaccurate, may not be attended to for long periods or may not be attended to at all. In Britain the Audit Office of the government in 1988 reported that "stock-taking" (compiling an inventory) was deficient in three of the large museums of London: the Victoria and Albert, the British Museum, and the Tate (which makes one ask how the Tate knows it rotates 70 percent of the works on exhibition). The British Museum, in its record keeping, is superior to any other museum in Europe, perhaps in the world, according to David Wilson. But it does not have a complete inventory, does not periodically verify the inventory it has, or is it able to if it wanted. An inquiry into the record keeping of the non-national museums of all kinds of Scotland (209 of them including those holding fine and decorative art) reported that two thirds had an inventory of half or more of their holdings while one fifth had no inventory at all. Half had a catalogue of some kind of half or more of their holdings but only an eighth used a recognizable system of cataloguing. The Dutch government in 1988 inquired into the record keeping of the museums and archives of the country. The report concluded that the records were not properly kept and that the system or method in which they were kept was understood by two people in The Netherlands. In the U.S. the inventory procedures are such that many museums, although they know what should be in the collection, do not know if it is actually there. The Art Institute of Chicago looked for a Georgia O' Keeffe that was recorded

[4]See *ARTnews*, Summer 1992.

[5]See *Financial Times*, May 21, 1988.

as being in the collection, could not find it, and after 10 years declared it "missing." "It could have been taken out with the garbage," the director of the Art Institute said to the press.[6]

(g) Admission charges. The admission charge, if there is one, is not fixed in order to maximize income or to increase attendance or to reduce congestion. Museums may levy a charge for special exhibitions and consider its effect on revenue but do so regretfully. This charge is usually the same for exhibitions that interest the many (Impressionism) as for those that do not (Masterpieces from the National Gallery of Ireland), and it is the same on Sunday afternoon as on Monday morning. A business firm, if the demand for its services varied according to the time of the day, week, or year, would consider varying its prices. Airlines, hotels, and resorts do, and commercial theaters vary ticket prices according to the popularity of what is being performed as well as the time of performance. (Non-profit theaters could do the same but instead leave that function to scalpers.)

Museums prefer not to make the admission charge an important source of revenue. They would like it to be an incidental source and some would like to make it no source at all, as it is none in most of the major museums of London and in all of the federal museums in Washington. When they must rely on it for revenue, they do so with regret. The Metropolitan from 1968 to 1988, according to its administrative head (a position different from that of director), "seemed" to mount exhibitions in order to secure revenue. A good year, he said, came to be one with a popular exhibition and a bad year one without it. The museum regretted that this should be so and after 1988 took "a more balanced approach." One feature of the approach was to require the visitor to buy his ticket to a special exhibition at the museum door instead of making it available to him at a commercial ticket agency as the museum previously had done. In the early nineties when it held two exhibitions of distinction, one of the works of Velazquez and the other of Canaletto, there was no appreciable decrease in the number of visitors passing through the main entrance of the Metropolitan where they paid the customary admission charge, but there was a decrease in total admission

[6]United Kingdom: *Burlington Magazine*, November 1986, Clarke (1991, p. 303) and Wilson (1989, pp. 48-50); The Netherlands: *Journal of Art*, January 1991; United States: *Chicago Sun Times*, August 14, 1990.

income which included the income from special exhibitions. There must then have been fewer visitors who came to see the special exhibitions and more who came to see the permanent collection. The explanation could be a change in taste – a decrease in the demand for what Velazquez and Canaletto provide and an increase in the demand for the objects the Met that year chose to exhibit from among the three million or so in its collection at that time. A more plausible explanation is that the effective price of a ticket to the special exhibitions increased because it took more time and trouble to buy. Visitors then were worse off, both those who bought a ticket and those who did not, and the revenue of the museum decreased. It did however have the satisfaction of turning its back on a marketing device.

The director of the Fine Arts Museums of San Francisco expressed the same aversion to relying on admission charges for revenue. He reported that in the early eighties when the city government reduced its subsidy the museums turned to popular exhibitions. The income from them, while it compensated for some of the reduction, nevertheless "masked an underlying structural deficit," meaning presumably that securing income from admissions is inconsistent with a sound financial structure while securing a subsidy is consistent. The administration of the museums changed in 1987 and made its first objective the balancing of the budget without relying on popular exhibitions. One change was to increase the standard admission charge. That, together with abolishing the additional charge for special exhibitions, meant eliminating the variation in the admission charge according to variations in demand. A flexible admission charge might have increased the income of the museum and have made visiting it more convenient by reducing the length of queues.

Yet museologists are not the economic innocents their conduct at times makes one believe they are. This needs to be said because economists have lectured them as if they were toddlers who must be taught the first steps into the world of supply and demand. They have been told that when considering whether to change the admission charge they should ask, what could the museum do with the extra revenue?[7] They cannot be that innocent. People in museums know as much as other people that every little makes a mickle. When museums cannot rely on their traditional and preferred sources of income, which are gifts and subsidies, they turn to others. The most common

[7] See Feldstein (1991, p. 9).

is the admission charge. The revenue it yields, museums know very well, depends on what is popular. Impressionism, or what passes for it, is. The Art Institute of Chicago expected its 1995 exhibition of Monet (Impressionism *tout court*) would help to pay the museum's future operating expenses. The museum store was enlarged to display things that are associated with Monet and things that are not, and all were meant to catch the fancy of the large number of visitors who were expected and came. The exhibition was advertised extensively, in the theater and arts section of the newspapers as one would expect, and also on billboards along the expressways which one does not expect. In preparing and staging it the museum employed the devices of what on other occasions has been called "the dreaded m-word," which (at the Metropolitan) is marketing. At the apex of the Chicago affair was the admission fee, and it was smartly higher than that of other special exhibitions. When it was over, the museum's director of public affairs said "We will be able to stay in the black for years to come."[8]

(h) Hours. The hours when museums are open – and the days, weeks, and years – have no discernible relation, if they have any relation at all, to the use of their resources and the desire of the public to use them, which is to say museum hours have no relation to the supply and demand of museum services (to their marginal cost and revenue). The hours of a commercial gallery do have that relation. Its manager would set them so that the cost of being open would be met by the income it received, and he would consider what being open a little more or less would add or deduct from its cost and income, not minute by minute of course but over time.

No such calculation is to be noticed among museums. What is noticeable is how often they are closed. Given their excessive fixed cost, which is the result of their ignoring the opportunity cost of their art, they would make better use of it if they were open more. A perverse effect of their not considering art to be capital is that they make too little use of what they have too much of.

A museum that is open every day is a rarity. One that is open every evening is a greater rarity. Some are open four or five hours each day, some from morning to evening but are closed at midday which is just the time some people would use a portion of their lunch hour to visit them.

---

[8]See Luers (1991, p. 68) and *The Chicago Tribune*, October 11, 1995.

When museums are open, some of the galleries may not be because not all of the guards have reported for work. The Louvre in the early eighties would open if a certain number of guards reported, and it would close the galleries that could not be looked after. If fewer than the minimum number reported, the entire museum would be closed. In 1993 in Italy, 42 percent of the state museums were entirely closed as were an unreported number of other museums.[9]

Italy is not unique. Museums in other countries have been closed for extended periods. The Louvre was closed for a time during the renovation associated with the Pyramid. A commercial gallery in such circumstances would move its stock to another location and carry on there. The idea of temporary quarters for the Louvre seems ludicrous and is if taken to mean the transfer of everything on exhibit from one venue to another. But it need not mean that. In The Netherlands when the Mauritshuis was done over in the eighties, its major works were exhibited in another building in The Hague. The Louvre could have done this simply with what it says are its most popular works, as well as the greatest among the national treasures of France (none oddly by a French artist): the Mona Lisa, the Venus de Milo, the Winged Victory of Samothrace, Michelangelo's Slaves, and the Egyptian Seated Scribe. The museum public would have been better off and so would the Louvre, this on the plausible assumption that the cost of the temporary exhibition was no greater than the return.

When a museum is closed there is a loss of utility to the people who would have visited it if it had been open. If the value of their utility would have been no less than the cost of keeping the museum open at that time, there is a net welfare loss. But museums do not see things this way. Just how they do see them must be guessed since the impartial spectator is not privy to their accounting. They appear to be guided by the effect of opening hours on their operating (variable) costs. These costs increase if hours are increased. However looking at things in this way is to look only at the supply side, and that is only half of what should be noticed. The other half is the additional satisfaction visitors would receive if hours were longer; that is the demand side. In the for-profit section of the economy it is indicated by the price buyers are willing to pay. In the non-profit section which is the land of art museums, price or the admission charge is not supposed to guide the

[9]See *ARTnews*, April 1993.

decisions about hours (or anything else). When price is in fact a guiding force it is so to the regret of the museum profession. Its notions about opening hours complement those about admission charges.

(i) Conservation. The art in museums does not receive the care and protection which it requires and which cultural authorities would have the world believe it does receive.

The audit that deplored the poor record keeping of museums in Britain also reported that works in need of conservation did not receive it, that they were stored in conditions that damaged them, and exhibited in those conditions as well. Of the regional museums in Scotland in the eighties, five sixths did not have environmental controls. The condition of the regional museums in England and Wales was "not dissimilar," the audit continued. In The Netherlands, the director of the government's Office for Fine arts stated the museums neglected conservation to the extent that the objects were in grave danger of deteriorating. The Office declared the conditions to be alarming and initiated a program it compared to the Delta project that was undertaken after the disastrous floods of the 1950's. In Florence, after the flood of 1966, the reserves of the museums were distributed throughout the city, and some found their way into places that would be filled with water by a subsequent flood. In 1986, twenty years later, "hundreds of frescoes, panel paintings and canvases, thousands of liturgical furnishing [continue] to languish," according to the *Burlington Magazine* which usually hastens to the defense of museums but on this occasion reproved them.[10]

In the U.S., the *Belmont Report* of 1968 said "most museums [cannot] cope with their problems of conservation and restoration." How literally that is to be taken is uncertain since the document in addition to reporting the state of affairs was also a brief on behalf of federal subsidies to museums.[11] That the art in American museums is now better cared for is possible. That it still does not receive all the care it should is probable, and the probability is indicated by the fact that there continue to be reports of negligence.

Along with the losses a museum incurs because its conservation is inadequate are the losses from theft. Which is the greater is an interesting question but is not to be answered until museums disclose the money value

[10]See *Burlington Magazine*, November 1986.

[11]See *America's Museums: The Belmont Report*, Washington, 1968, p. 57.

of their collections, the rate of depreciation of objects that are not conserved properly and also those that are, and the value of what is stolen. The information is not likely to be available soon. But, the impartial spectator will note, there is a difference between the two losses. What museums lose when a work of art deteriorates physically is a loss both to them and to the world that would like to see it. What they lose by theft is a loss only to them so long as what is stolen passes into the possession of people who value it (leaving out the transactions cost of theft). Most stolen art does go to people who value it if, as is believed, it gets to market and is bought by collectors.[12] The impartial spectator, in a droll mood, could observe that art which is stolen may be better cared for than if it remained in the museums (except if they themselves buy it, as has happened).

The police on their part take a prosaic view. They offer this advice to museums: – Do keep the burglar alarm on at all times as the van Gogh Museum in Amsterdam did not and lost several paintings. – Do tell the night guards not to turn off the alarm however much they would like to doze off as they did at the Gallery of Modern Art in Milan which lost 28 paintings. – Do store paintings in a more secure place than a broom closet as the Art Institute of Chicago did and lost several Impressionist works (later recovered, fortunately). – Do keep a record of holdings so that the museum will know if a work is missing, as the Victoria and Albert did not until its Tenier was found by the police and returned to it. – Do not broadcast the price paid for a major acquisition, as museums are known to do despite their disdain for the cash nexus. – Do report a theft promptly as the Guggenheim did not when a mail room employe made off with a Chagall that turned up 20 years later at Sotheby's whereupon the Guggenheim demanded its return.[13]

2 The partial spectator replies

A museologist on seeing this register of what an economist calls inefficiency, and a moralist would call improvidence, could reply with observations of the following order as in fact museologists have. (Or could: Some of what follows in the museologist's reply has been inserted by the economist in the spirit

[12]See [Cannon-Brookes] (1992).

[13]Tillotson (1977, p. 118) and Solomon R. Guggenheim Fund v. Lubell, 569 N.E. 2d 426 (N.Y. 1991).

of devil's advocacy and with the chivalrous intent of strengthening an opponent's case.) The replies are in the order in which the observations of the impartial spectator were made, with *(aa)* referring to *(a)*, etc.

(aa) Acquisitions. When museums acquire a work of art they do so because it enhances the aesthetic, scholarly, or historic value of the collection. They do not ask if it will pay for itself in a monetary sense. That would misconceive how art should be valued and moreover would be impractical because the immeasurable cannot be measured. Museums do consider whether one work or another is the more suitable acquisition, and this implies they do consider which would add more to the value of the collection. The economist may take comfort in this because it is, if not a marginal, then an incremental comparison. But it is not a comparison of things that are to be measured in money.

(bb) Capital costs. The works of art in a museum are not capital in any sensible meaning of the word. They are not the kind of thing the world prices, compares, and exchanges. They are not and should not be regarded as goods, capital or otherwise. Art is of a different order from what passes in the ordinary business of life and which is the proper study of economists, as, they should know, their mentor Alfred Marshall said. The point restated is that the value of art cannot be expressed in money, therefore it cannot be capital. To think it is, quite apart from being conceptually wrong, can be harmful. It can turn the museum visitor away from what he should be attending to, which is aesthetics, scholarship, and history, to what has nothing to do with art which is its price.

(cc) Financial reporting. True, museums do not, on the balance sheet, report the value of their art, and the reason should be clear by now. The value cannot be expressed in money. To do so is impractical as well as wrongheaded. If such a measurement were attempted, the information would lead the untutored and the un-serious to suppose the art in museums is for sale. It decidedly is not, the director of the Cleveland Museum of Art said when asked why its art had no place on the balance sheet. The same was meant by a functionary of the Louvre when he said "The price of La Joconde? – That is not an interesting question." The same was meant by the administrative head of the Metropolitan when he said "We never refer to works of art as

assets – because to do so would suggest we intend to trade in them as assets – which we most certainly do not."[14] In still other ways the information could be harmful. It could invite theft. It also could dissuade the public from giving to museums, dissuade not just the benefactors who give in the thousands and millions, but also the visitors to museums that have no fixed admission charge and instead suggest a donation of, say, seven dollars, to which the informed visitor might respond with 25 cents. The information could also lead people, whether they visit museums or not, to believe subsidies and other government assistance are not necessary. These public effects were cited by representatives of American art museums in the early sixties when they were reluctant to reveal to the National Bureau of Economic Research the money value of their collections.[15]

(dd) Exhibition/collection ratio. True, museums do exhibit only a portion of their collection, and there are good reasons why. (1) They do not have enough space to exhibit more and they continually seek additional space. (2) The number of works that can be exhibited is less than in the past because museum practice today calls for allowing each work more space. There is still less space today if the museum wishes to bring together in a single gallery examples of the painting, sculpture, and decorative arts of a period which earlier in this century many museums did and some still do. To hang a single tapestry means consigning three or four paintings to storage. (3) What is in reserve is exhibited from time to time, that is, the collection is rotated. (4) Not everything in the collection that is not exhibited is in storage. Some is on loan to other museums, is consigned to government offices, or is exhibited in embassies abroad. (5) What is in storage is accessible to scholars and people with a serious interest in art. Others have access to it by interactive VDU's and reproductions. (6) There are works in the collection that are too fragile to be exhibited, e.g., works on paper. (7) Some of what is in storage is in too poor a condition to be shown or is not worth showing or is pornographic (this being what the director of the Louvre has said of the 5,000 paintings that will remain in storage when the remodeling is completed).

To be noted as well is the fact that the art in the private sector is not all of it on view at all times, not even to the owners. A commercial gallery keeps

[14] Luers (1991, p. 68).

[15] NBER (1964, pp. 788-90).

some of its inventory in the back room, and that is not a sign of inefficiency. Private collectors, if they have a number of paintings (and the number need not be large), must keep some of them in storage simply because they have not enough space to hang them.

(ee) De-accessioning. About de-accessioning this is to be said. In some civil law countries, among them countries with important art, the collections of museums and the museums themselves, are state property, and as such are inalienable. The museums could not sell anything even if they wished to. Where state property may be sold, it may nevertheless be regulated by the government, and museums that wanted to dispose of works could be prevented from doing so. They could also be prevented from doing so by the terms of a bequest which prohibits a museum from selling a work that has been donated to it. Where a museum is not restrained by law or contract, it can be restrained by prudence. For it to sell something that has been given to it in the past can diminish what it will be given in the future.

The control of museum collections by government is a part of cultural policy. One of the purposes of policy is to direct art into public collections. When museums say they are opposed to net de-accessioning and when they say the collection should grow, they are simply doing what cultural policy directs them to do. The U.S. appears to be an exception because it has no cultural policy of the scope of that elsewhere in the world. The AAMD nevertheless believes museums are bound by an ethical principle to prevent their collections from decreasing. The continual effort to increase them, whether or not it is an ethical principle, is in keeping with what cultural authorities around the world believe should be done.

Then there are reasons of an aesthetic, historical, and scholarly nature for a museum's amassing reserves. Michel Levey, once the director of the National Gallery of London, has explained why duplicates, why works of unsuitable quality, and why works that are damaged should not be disposed of. Few works are literally duplicates, that is, are identical, he said, citing the view paintings of Canaletto that are similar. Works that now are considered unsuitable for exhibition can become suitable if aesthetic opinion changes. Damaged works can be repaired.

(ff) Record keeping. The recording and inventory practices of museums are as adequate as their incomes allow. Museums have numerous and expensive

responsibilities. Primary among them are to conserve and exhibit their art, to inform and educate the public about it, and to undertake scholarly inquiry into their collections. The keeping of records, while important, should not draw resources away from still more important responsibilities.

(gg) Admission charges. There are good reasons why admission charges should not be relied on for revenue. If they were raised in order to cover the present operating expenses per visitor and if the number of visitors was constant, the charges would have to be many times what they are. The Cleveland Museum in the early eighties estimated the charges would have to be 10 dollars per visitor which at 1996 prices is about 19 dollars. The number of visitors would of course decrease, and the admission charge that would equal the operating cost per visitor would have to be more than 19 dollars. American museums in 1994 received about 16 percent of their operating income from admission charges and membership fees.[16]

There are other reasons for not relying on admission income. From their origin to the present day, museums have been supported mainly by government subsidies or by private gifts or, as in the U.S. and the U.K., by both. To rely on admission income is not in keeping with the historically validated forms of support. Where museums do expect a visitor to pay something they have, many of them, tried to keep within tradition by avoiding a fixed charge and instead asking the visitor to donate an amount of his choosing.

To calculate and fix a charge for the purpose of maximizing revenue would turn museums away from fostering the visual culture of a people and would have them act as a business enterprise does, that is, would subject them to direction by the price system. The reason the Metropolitan discontinued using commercial agencies to sell tickets to special exhibitions is that the agencies are associated in the public mind with profit making activities such as professional athletics.[17]

Another reason why museums should not rely on admission income can be drawn from economic theory, and it would hold if none of the other reasons did. It is that there are economies of size (scale) in the operation of a museum, and if they are to be realized the admission charge should be less than the cost per visitor. If the admission charge was equal to the cost per

[16] Association of Art Museum Directors (1995a, pp. 43, 76, 89).

[17] See Luers (1991, p. 69).

visitor, the number of visitors would be less than the number the museum can properly accommodate, with the result that its facilities would not be used as completely as they should be.

(hh) Hours. The hours a museum are open are determined by what the public expects of it and by what it can afford. It might be open more often if guards were docents and volunteered their time, if lighting were a trivial expense and heating none at all. Apart from what museums can afford is what the public expects. It does not expect them to be open every evening; they are not, after all, movie houses or super-markets. That most museums are closed one day each week is of course true and is simply explained. There must be a time for cleaning up. There is in addition a saving to be had by closing once a week; it often is Monday when the number of visitors would be small. The few hours each day that museums in some countries are open can be explained by union contracts and labor legislation. The long periods when museums are closed for renovation are to be explained by their not having enough money to set up temporary quarters.

(ii) Conservation. The art in museums is under the care of skilled and dedicated professionals. If the storage area is crowded the reason is that the museum has too little space for its reserves. Many, probably most, would like to have more, and they provide for it when they enlarge their quarters.

The conservation of art is a delicate, time consuming, and expensive kind of work. It can also be controversial and usually is if the work is familiar. There is scarcely a single undertaking, if there is one at all, from the cleaning of the ceiling of the Sistine Chapel to the repainting of the Barnett Newman in the Stedelijk museum, that has not been objected to by one authority or another, and they are authorities a museum must take note of.

The protection of art from theft is admittedly not complete in museums. But neither is it in commercial galleries, private collections, or in public collections outside of museums such as churches where art appears to be in greatest danger of all. In Italy in the 1980's, a painting was stolen from a church every four minutes, according to IFAR (the International Foundation for Art Research, a clearing house of information about theft).[18] In museums the security arrangements are continually reviewed and new arrangements are

[18]See [Cannon-Brookes] (1992).

installed as they become available and can be afforded. The system in the new Louvre brings guards to the scene of a theft within seconds. But even that can be too long as a theft in 1995 demonstrated. A picture was cut from the frame, guards arrived within four seconds, did not find the thief, searched visitors as they left the building, but did not recover the painting. The director of the Louvre stated that theft can be prevented completely only if there is a guard in every gallery, and that is too expensive. Other museum directors would concur.

3 The impartial spectator rejoins

The economist would not concur, not on this point or on the others made by the museologist, and would rejoin to each of them in the following way, with *(aaa)* being the rejoinder to *(aa)*, etc.

(aaa) Acquisitions. Everyone agrees that a museum director would consider whether a dollar (or a million) spent on an object would enhance the value of the collection more or less than the same amount spent on another object. That is simply the way decisions are made and is the only way they can be, whether in a museum or in the kitchen. What is at issue is whether the director's evaluation is equal to the evaluation of the people who provide the dollar or the million. They are the museum's visitors, its benefactors, and beyond them the public that supports the museum by its taxes or by doing without other government services. The evaluation of the first two would be taken into account to some extent by the director. He would give some thought to how an acquisition would interest visitors and please benefactors. The evaluation of the third group would not be considered or could it be since the payments it makes are not voluntarily made in the sense that the payments of the other two are voluntary.

(bb) Capital costs. A work of art is capital in the same sense that anything is capital which yields utility over time and is scarce, hence is priced and can be exchanged. To believe something is capital only if it is for sale is mistaken. Most of the capital in the world is *not* for sale in the sense that it is at all times on the market in search of buyers; and all of the capital of the world *is* for sale at all times in the sense that there is a price at which its owners

are willing to sell it.

Would a museum visitor get everything he should from the art he sees if he knew it is capital and knew its price? Or would the utility he receives be less? An economist would say the question should be left to the visitor, and he can answer it only if the information is available to him to use or not as his interest inclines him. The art world is quite interested, as its publications indicate. This leaves one to wonder if the more a man knows about art the more important its price becomes to him.

To claim that art is different from what passes in the ordinary business of life (whatever Marshall meant by that) does not take it out of economics. It includes much that is out of the ordinary (health, learning, wisdom) and some that is extraordinary (faith, hope, and charity). They have a common feature that brings them within the scope of economics. If they are to be experienced, acquired, exercised, expressed, believed, or provided, they must use resources that are valuable and scarce, hence have a price and can be compared. On this point, the descendants of Marshall are a better guide than he is.

(ccc) Financial reporting. For a museum to say the value of art cannot be measured and so cannot be reported on its balance sheet is for it to claim what is conceptually wrong, for the reasons just given, and is also to claim it cannot do what in fact it does. That is to put a money value on museum holdings. It does that when it monitors the de-accessioning of other museums in order to determine whether they have bought as much art as they have sold, hence whether or not the value of the collection has decreased. If its money value had nothing to do with its merit as art, the monitoring would be pointless.

Still, museums are correct when they say the reporting of the value of their art could have practical effects which are harmful to their interests, defining their interests to be those of the professional staff. If the public knew the value of museum capital, it probably would make fewer gifts and would question the need of museums for government assistance.

(ddd) Exhibition/collection ratio. Museums do not have a convincing explanation of why they exhibit only a small amount of their art. (1) If they do not have enough space to exhibit everything, as they obviously have not, why when they enlarge their premises do they usually increase storage space

as much as exhibition space and increase the space used for administrative and service purposes more than that used for exhibition? The new wing of the National Gallery in London has five floors, only one of which is used for exhibition. Why do museums believe their collections must grow which, given the way they allocate space, results in an ever smaller proportion of the collection on exhibit? (2) If good design calls for using more space to exhibit an object than was used in the past, why when museums enlarge their premises do they not allow more space for exhibition than for storage (if any at all is called for)? (3) The rotating of reserves is hardly ever described in a way that allows a judgment to be made of it. Museums do not report the period of time over which the entire collection is exhibited. That there is such a period is implied by their claim that the reserves are rotated. They do occasionally say what fraction of the collection is on exhibit, but that says nothing about how long the objects on view have been there or does it signify they will be replaced by others. (4) If museums place art in government offices, it is not being used as it is meant to be, namely, seen by the public. If the government office is an embassy, the art, if it is seen by the public at all, is not being seen by the people for whom it was placed in a public collection in order to make their cultural heritage known to them. If the cultural authorities of Britain believe a painting by Hogarth is a part of its heritage, the painting should not be in the British embassy in Tokyo or anywhere except on the walls of a museum in Britain. On the other hand, art that is drawn from the reserves of one museum and is exhibited by another is art that can ben seen by the public and its doing what museum art is meant to do. But if the borrowing museum must take something off its walls and place it in storage in order to exhibit what it has borrowed, the net effect is zero on the amount of art that is visible. (5) For a museum to say its reserves are accessible to people with a serious interest in art is curious. Does that mean the museum has visitors who are not serious? Is what they see, which is the art on exhibit, art that is not serious? Or is it art that is interesting to both the serious and the unserious? (6) While there are works that are too fragile to be exhibited, they do not comprise everything in a museum's reserves. What part they do comprise is never reported. Moreover some fragile works can be exhibited and are, e.g., drawings. (7) If there are works in a museum' s reserves that are not worth exhibiting, what are they doing there? Why are they not sold to another museum or to a collector and the money used to buy what is worth exhibiting? If no one would buy them why are they not discarded since storing them has a cost?

Then there is the statement that not all of the art in the private sector is to be seen. That is true but is not all of the truth. The art which a collector places in storage yields a return of some kind. It is the satisfaction of ownership and takes various forms. The art in a museum's reserves also yields a return, not to visitors of course, but to someone in the museum, a member of the curatorial staff, say. But there is a difference, and it is of a major order. The collector paid for his art, and the satisfaction it yields is (at the margin) proportional to its cost. The museum people did not directly pay anything for the art that yields them a return. Conceivably their money income is less because they receive a non-monetary return from being in the presence of art, which gives them a taste of what being a collector is like. But their money income could not be low enough to cover the entire cost of the art without their income being negative. The result is the inefficiency that comes of the prices of goods not being proportional to the satisfaction they give the people who pay the prices (i.e., the ratio of price to marginal utility of art in museum reserves is less than that of art in private collections).

(eee) De-accessioning. What museums say about de-accessioning cannot all of it be meant. They cannot mean that unimportant art should be kept because it may become important. If they believe this they must also believe that art which is now important may become unimportant. That implies museums should collect at random and also that art which the world has thought to be timeless (because it has been important for so long) is really not timeless.

Should duplicates be kept because they never are identical? They probably are not identical, most of them, but that is hardly a reason for never parting with them. Or do museums think it is? If a museum had a Canaletto of the Grand Canal at the Rialto and was offered a duplicate that differed in having one less gondolier and one more wavelet, or alternatively the museum was offered a quite different Canaletto or was offered a painting that had nothing to do with Canaletto, say a portrait by Hogarth containing a pug, is one to believe that the museum, if it was English, would choose the duplicate Canaletto?

About damaged art one would like to know if museums ever consider the opportunity cost of leaving it unrepaired. Do they consider how much the value of the art would increase if it was restored and compare the increase with the cost of restoration? A commercial gallery would consider that.

But there is more to the argument museums make against de-accessioning. They are correct when they say that in some countries the collections are the property of the state and as such may not be sold. The prohibition is not absolute, no more than other categorical acts of state are, but is a substantial obstacle to de-accessioning. What should be added is that the museums do not object to it. On the contrary, they favor it. It assures them that their collections will never diminish. They are also in favor, as one would expect them to be, of laws that increase their collections, for example, laws that authorize the state to pre-empt the sale of a work of art or to appropriate it from a private collection.

Where de-accessioning is not prohibited by law (and it is not in the U.S.) or where the prohibition is not complete (as it is not in the U.K.) the museums argue against it in much the same way, which is additional evidence that the case against it is not made outside of the museums by the state and imposed on them as something they must accept, willingly or not, but is a case made by the museums themselves.

A work that is donated to a museum can carry restrictions (about lending and exhibiting as well as selling it) but they are difficult to enforce. When museums sell – as they certainly do or their de-accessioning "policies" are meaningless – they do not inform the world of donors who in any event cannot monitor the terms of their gifts indefinitely.

(fff) Record-keeping. Whether the record-keeping of museums is adequate has in the end to be decided by its effect on the value of museum capital, including its art of course, or alternatively its effect on the rate of return to its capital. Would more or less spent on keeping records increase or decrease the value of the capital or its return? The information needed to answer the question is not available and is not likely to be as long as museums refuse to assign money values to all of their capital and to what they do with it, that is, to their services or output.

But the question is not insuperable. A few observations can be made. A museum that has no records at all does not know what its capital is and cannot be expected to make the best use of it. The same can be said of museums that have not reviewed their records for many years. Museums with records that are incomplete or inaccurate or unintelligible are probably not using their capital well.

(ggg) Admission charge. One must agree with the museums when they say their admission charge would have to be much higher if it was to equal the operating costs per visitor. Also one would expect that at the higher charge there would be fewer visitors and one would add that admission income might be and probably would be less (since the price elasticity of demand now is near unity). There may be no admission charge that would cover the museum's cost (that is, at every output, as measured by the number of visitors, the demand price would be less than average cost). Moreover, the costs of museums are larger than they now report because they do not acknowledge the cost of their capital. If they did, the excess of average cost over the present admission charge would be greater than is now reported and would be still greater if museums had to pay the taxes a for-profit firm must pay.

These observations assume the demand (function) of visitors is constant. If it increased, the revenue from the present admission charges might equal operating costs as they now are measured. A number of museums believe this to be so. But they do not care to do what will increase the demand, and that is to mount popular exhibitions. They will do it out of necessity, reluctantly, regretfully, even apologetically. Popular exhibitions, they say, interfere with their proper work which is to exhibit, conserve, and study the art that in the opinion of museum professionals is most deserving of attention.[19] That art appears not to be the art the public believes is most deserving of its attention.

How much the public is willing to pay in order to see what it wants, or what museologists believe it should see, is a question which is relevant to the claim that the admission charge should be less than the cost per visitor in order that the museum will have all of the visitors it can accommodate properly (the claim that museums have increasing returns to scale). There are three assumptions implied by this claim, and none (so far as I know) has yet been shown to be a fact.

One is that there is a minimum size for a museum and that if the museum is less than that size it cannot do what it is meant to do. How that size is measured – whether by the number or value of the objects in the collection, the number of visitors, the museum's endowment, number of employes,

[19]See *Art in America*, June 1986.

operating expenses, physical dimensions, or in some other way – is never explained. Or is there a ı explanation of why there are in fact museums of many different sizes as measured in any of these ways. Or is there an explanation of why, whatever its size and however measured, the museum is always larger than the number of visitors who, at a given admission charge, would provide the museum with an income equal to its expenses.

The second is that when the museum has the proper (optimal) number of visitors, the value they place on what the museum provides them is equal to the cost to the museum of providing it.

The third is that the cost is borne entirely by the visitors in a way (e.g., by price discrimination) that makes the charge each pays proportional to the value each places on his visit. (This is the Lindahl principle of just taxation applied to price discrimination.) This signifies that if a museum cannot meet its costs by charging all visitors the same amount, it may be able to meet them by charging them different amounts, for example, by varying the charge according to the day of the week, time of the day, or season of the year, or by using a multiple pricing system in which some visitors pay in advance for an unlimited number of visits in a fixed time and others pay for fewer visits or only one.

To be noticed is that even if museums must be large that is no reason for subsidizing them. If what they provide visitors is worth its cost, they can support themselves. If they cannot support themselves because price discrimination would not yield enough or because it is not practical, the reason is that what they provide costs more than it is worth.

(hhh) Hours. The hours the public expects museums to be open are probably the hours to which it has become accustomed to their being open. Those hours may or may not be the hours that are most convenient to visitors and that are within the means of museums. The former could be discovered by looking into the preferences of the public, via a demand function that includes time as well as admission charges, and the latter by a supply function that would include the opportunity cost of the art in the museum as well as all other costs. To say an organization should have some notion of the demand and supply of what it provides is not a counsel of perfection or even of approximate perfection. It is information which commercial enterprises look for constantly and to the extent that it is worth the cost of gathering it. Without it they could not maximize the return to their capital, or even try.

If museums had this information they would know when to be open. They would know what hours of the day and days of the week were most suitable. They also would know if they should close while the building was being done over and if so whether to open temporary quarters. They would also know what was the rate of return to their capital. If they were fearless, they would compare their rate with the return on art in private collections (a market rate of interest), and that would tell them, whether they want to know or not, if they should be open at all.

(iii) Conservation. The care of art should be guided by costs and returns as should the other things a museum does. The skill and dedication of the professional staff does not in itself tell one how well the collection is cared for, and they are relevant only as they affect the cost of care. The returns are indicated by how the care of a work affects its market value.

Suppose that a painting if it was in mint condition would have a market value of $100 and that in its present condition its market value is $90. If it was in the stock of a commercial gallery, it would be "restored" (put in mint condition) if the cost of restoration was no more than $10. So it would be if it was held by a collector. He might have it restored even if the cost was more than $10 but no more than the difference between the market value of the unrestored painting and what the restored painting would be worth to him, say $105, that being the lowest price at which he would be willing to sell it.

Alternatively, suppose the painting is in the collection of a museum. It would be averse to inquiring into the market value (except if the painting was to be insured) because museums believe the value of art is not something the market can or should determine. One would like to know what guides their skilled and dedicated conservators.

4 The colloquy turns to political economy

At this stage, the museologist could shake his head and say what he has said before, that museums are not commercial enterprises and should not be judged as if they were. The economist could rejoin with what he too has said, that the standards of efficiency apply to organizations of all kinds. But the exchange would not take the inquiry forward. What can do that is to ask how the behavior of museums is to be explained. Or, what are they trying to do?

They obviously are not trying to exhibit all of the art they have since they keep most of it in storage, continually increase the size of their collection, hence exhibit a continually smaller proportion of it. How well they take care of their art and protect it from theft can be questioned and has been. So too is how much influence museums have had in bringing about a greater appreciation of the visual arts; the proportion of the population interested in them has always been small and still is.[20] Thus the museums cannot claim they have achieved their stated purposes of exhibition, conservation, and education. What, then, have they achieved?

Consider whether the way they are conducted is consistent with the interests of the professional staff. Museum people, one may suppose without intending offense, are like everyone else. They know what they want and know reasonably well how to get it. They probably want a comfortable income, interesting work, a secure position, a respected place, congenial co-workers, pleasant surroundings, and other things bright and beautiful. They don't get all of them of course or does the rest of the world, scarcity being, as it is, a fact of life.

What sets museum professionals apart is that they are not exposed to all of the harshness of the market. Nowhere in the world is there a major museum that is a commercial enterprise, and if any minor museums are, they are inconspicuous. Moreover there are no major museums that want to become anything but what they are, this despite the talk of privatization (as in The Netherlands) which on examination is seen to be only a change in administrative procedure and not the sale of museum capital to a commercial enterprise.

There must be reasons why museums are non-profit organizations. One could be that in their present form they serve the interests of the professional staff better than its interests could be served if museums were commercial enterprises. This of course is not the common explanation which is that the market is unable to do what should be done and what museums in their present form do (produce a public good or a good with positive externalities). But, as has already been said, the explanation is no more than an assertion or claim.

[20]See Grampp (1989, pp. 54-55).

If museums were commercial enterprises there would be fewer of them, this because, given their number and size at present, the rate of return to their capital is almost certainly negative. There not only would be fewer of them. They probably would be smaller because they could not afford to hold the large collections they now have. Fewer museums and smaller museums would obviously mean a smaller museum profession. How this would affect salaries depends on the difficulty of becoming a professional (i.e., on the elasticity of supply of that kind of labor). One certainty is that salaries would not increase.

A museologist cannot be expected to look with favor on the position he would occupy in a world of commercial, hence self-supporting, museums. One is not surprised to hear him say an art museum is not and cannot be a commercial organization. One then is not surprised that museologists believe that the art in their charge is not capital, that they do not report its money value, and that when adding to it they do not consider whether it will pay for itself. These remarks have to do with observations (b), (c), and (a) above in that order. To the impartial spectator the facts they report denote inefficient behavior. But the behavior is consistent with the interest of the people who engage in it.

Also consistent with their interest is what they do about admission charges (g) and opening hours (h). It is not done in order to maximize income except in unusual circumstances and then it is not fully acknowledged. Fixing price and quantity to maximize museum income is not done by people who want to keep themselves as far as possible from the market. Another reason for their not doing it is that it could invite the public to consider if museums might manage with fewer private gifts and government subsidies, a thought that could also occur if the public knew the value of museum collections.

The position of museum professionals among their peers is influenced by the stature of the museum that employs them. That in turn is indicated by the quality and size of the collection, the endowment, number of employes, attendance, the architectural distinction of the building and its size, and the museum's operating expense. In the U.S. the common measure of size is operating expense, which is the output of the museum valued at cost excluding the cost of capital. Operating expense, in the judgment of Rosett (1991, p. 159.), is proportional to the money value of the collection. Net de-accessioning reduces the size of the collection as measured in money while acquisitions increase it. One is not surprised that museum professionals are opposed to net de-accessioning and that they believe the collection should grow (observation e).

The salaries of museum professionals appear to be related to the size of their museum. One must say "appear" because the information is incomplete. The AAMD reports salaries according to the population of the area where museums are located. It does not report them by the name of the museum that pays them. It does report the operating expenses of museums by name. Their location is common knowledge. The largest museums are most of them in the largest cities, and there salaries are highest.[21] To put the point plainly, the salaries of museum professionals appear to be higher in large museums than in small. One would expect the professionals of museums to look with favor, as in fact they do, on the measures that would, if effective, increase the stock of art in public collections while reducing that in private.

Museum people may wish they could exhibit a larger proportion of the collection, but if they look closely at their interest they cannot be unduly disturbed by not being able to do so. If a museum exhibits what in its collection are the works of highest quality (as one would suppose it does), then for it to draw on its reserves and exhibit more would lessen the average quality of what is shown. That need not diminish the stature of the museum. It has not done so in the new Louvre even though what hitherto was in storage and now can be shown is some of it distinctly inferior. But most museums do not have the standing of the Louvre, and if one exhibited a large portion of its collection its standing in the world of museums probably would diminish. Of course that would not occur if all museums did so. Yet, again, doing so would draw on resources that could be used in a way that enhances stature more immediately and directly such as on acquisitions. The relatively small amount of art that museums exhibit (observation d) is not inconsistent with the interest of the professional staff.

There remain two other observations: the poor record-keeping of museums (f) and the inadequate care of their collections (i). Is there a self-interest explanation of them?

Extensive record keeping and intensive care of the collection are expensive. What they cost could be spent instead on what adds to the stature of the museum. Acquisitions do. Poor records and inadequate collection care

[21] Association of Art Museum Directors (1995b, pp. 17-53) and Association of Art Museum Directors (1995a, pp. 110-113).

seem not to diminish the standing of a museum. If they did, some names would not be as great in the world as they now are, among them the Victoria and Albert, the British Museum, the Rijksmuseum, the Hermitage, and the Art Institute of Chicago.

This all but brings the colloquy to an end. What remains is to consider why the agencies that supervise museums allow them to be inefficient.

In most countries, museums are the property of the state and are supervised by a department of government. To ask why the supervisors don' t take notice of the inefficiency of what is in their charge, is to ask why government is inefficient. One is tempted to dismiss the question by saying the answer is self-evident or to say the question is unanswerable. Actually something can be said. There are instances of a supervisory agency counseling museums to mend their ways. But the museums declined, indeed, dismissed the counsel and carried on as before. This occurred in Italy and Britain where the supervisory bodies advised the museums to sell some of their reserves, and the museums refused. Yet there are instances where a supervisory agency may have had some effect. This occurred in The Netherlands and again in Britain when the museums were reproved for their poor record-keeping or inadequate conservation or both. How effective the reproof was is not known but it did bring to the attention of the public a regrettable condition which the museums did not altogether deny and which they were directed to correct. The Italian minister of culture who came into office with the reform government of 1993 directed the state museums to extend their hours. The Accademia in Venice for years (decades, generations?) had been open from nine until two for six days each week except when it was closed altogether. Now it posted a hand-written sign stating hours had been extended until six in the evening, much to the gratification of tourists and of vendors to them because the day trippers would now remain until early evening. The following year the Accademia returned to its ancient tenor. In France the Ministry of Finance along with the Ministry of Culture has responsibility for the proper conduct of museums and in the past stated the reserves of the Louvre were excessive, citing among others the works of Claude, some eight or ten of the 12 or 13 being in storage. In the enlarged French galleries of the new Louvre, Claude is much in evidence.

In countries where museums are nominally private organizations, as in the U.S., they are supervised by a board of trustees. The museums are not entirely removed from government but its authority is limited, and that limited amount is used sparingly. It made itself known, or, more accurately, announced itself, when the Metropolitan in 1972 sold a number of works. The Attorney General of New York said he would investigate the matter. He did that and found no wrongdoing. The States Attorney of Illinois did more when he was prevailed upon to investigate the Harding collection of armor that had not been exhibited for years. The outcome was the transfer of the collection to another museum. The police from time to time admonish museums to be more careful about their collection, and the fire department cautions them about hazardous material.

However this interference (as the museums would call it) is unusual in the U.S. The customary governance is by trustees. They usually are successful business and professional people and they volunteer their services. This suggests an explanation of the inefficiency. The trustees are people whose time has a high opportunity cost, and they receive no monetary return. Ecco – they do not spend enough time with the affairs of their museum to notice how inefficient it is.

But that will not do. Surely there must be a trustee here and there who is familiar with how his museum manages its affairs. Some one at some time must have noticed that only a small portion of the collection is exhibited, that nevertheless the museum staff wants to add to it, that it is not stored in suitable conditions and that it is exposed to theft, that works in need of conservation do not receive it, that others which have not been displayed for years could be sold in order to improve the storage area or to repair the roof over the exhibition galleries or to control the humidity, and on and on.

Actually there is no reason to think that trustees are ignorant of the affairs of the museum they govern. Some are known to devote a substantial amount of time to it and to have a part in how it is managed. The Metropolitan is an example.[22] What the trustees know must not trouble them. If it did they would act differently.

If they approve of how their museum is conducted, as they certainly seem to, the reason must be that what is in the interest of the professional staff is also in their interest although theirs is an interest of a different kind. It is non-monetary. Just what the non-monetary return is can only be surmised. It could be the satisfaction they receive from being associated with a museum

[22]See Hoving (1993, passim).

that is celebrated for the size of its collection or the quality, or for holding particular works, or for the scholarship of its director, or his notoriety, or for its building, its endowment, or its history. Or the non-monetary return could be entirely different. Sociologists and psychologists have several descriptions on offer, most of them uncomplimentary to the trustees. Whatever it is that the trustees receive, they value it highly. They usually are major benefactors of their museum and they stand ready to assist it in time of need. What they provide it may express their gratitude for what it provides them or may be the price they pay for a place on the board of trustees which they find is a reward in itself. What they do not find rewarding, the impartial spectator observes with regret, is to direct their museum along the path of efficiency.

5 References

Association of Art Museum Directors (1995a), *1994 Statistical Survey*, New York.

Association of Art Museum Directors (1995b), *1994 Salary Survey*, New York.

[Cannon-Brookes, P.] (1992), The movement, location and tracing of cultural property, *Museum Management and Curatorship*, 11, 3-18.

Clarke, R. (1991), Government policy and art museums in the United Kingdom, in M. Feldstein, ed., *The Economics of Art Museums*, Chicago: The University of Chicago Press.

Feldstein, M. (1991), Introduction, in M. Feldstein, ed., *The Economics of Art Museums*, Chicago: The University of Chicago Press.

Grampp, W.D. (1989), *Pricing the Priceless: Art, Artists, and Economics*, New York: Basic Books Inc.

Hoving, T. (1993), *Making the Mummies Dance*, New York: Simon and Schuster.

Lord, B., G.D. Lord and J. Nicks (1989), *The Cost of Collecting: Collections Management in the UK Museums*, London: H.M.S.O.

Luers, W.H. (1991), Museum finances, in M. Feldstein, ed., *The Economics of Art Museums*, Chicago: The University of Chicago Press.

NBER (1964), *Measuring the Nation's Wealth*, Washington: National Bureau of Economic Research.

Rosett, R.N. (1991), Art museums in the United States: a financial portrait, in M. Feldstein, ed., *The Economics of Art Museums*, Chicago: The University of Chicago Press.

Tillotson, R. (1977), *Museum Security*, Paris: International Commission on Museums.

Wilson, D. (1989), *The British Museum: Purposes and Policies*, London: British Museum Publications.

Economics of the Arts - Selected Essays
V.A. Ginsburgh and P.-M. Menger (Editors)

10

Cultural-Economic Analyses of Art Museums: a British Curator's Viewpoint

Peter Cannon-Brookes
Museum Management and Curatorship

1 Introduction

Cultural-economic analyses of art museums have been bedevilled by a lack of understanding of the functional basis of museums within the community and by the growth of 'cultural recreation' and idea-based institutions often calling themselves museums. The historical background to this confusion is reviewed, together with the Humanist basis of object-based museums and the intellectual foundations of their core functions. Fundamental differences between the legal and cultural environments of the common-law countries and those administered under civil law are identified, together with the more pragmatic common-law traditions of the U.S. in interpreting trust law and the deaccessioning of collections. The uncertain legal status of many collections in the U.K. is analysed, together with the potential impact of Purpose Theory, in relation to historic commitments entered into by the community for the preservation of specific chattels in perpetuity, and the dangers inherent in using attendance figures as a measure of 'output'. Market-driven management systems threaten the physical and intellectual integrity of museums as these object-based institutions are forced to increase their cash flow, and thereby trading profits, by searching for new mass publics uninterested in their core functions.

2 Background

When Alan Peacock and Christine Godfrey, in their seminal 1974 paper, set out "to review the activities of a gallery or museum as a 'firm' producing an unusual type of product and with a rather complex 'objective function'," they were questioning the rationale of public financial support for museums and galleries in the U.K. This was undertaken in the aftermath of the decision of the U.K. Government to charge entrance fees for the museums and galleries funded by it – announced in October 1970 but not introduced until January 1974 – and a lively debate concerning "major issues of principle in public policy towards the support of cultural recreation."[1] Sir Alan Peacock, then Professor of Economics at the University of York, was currently on leave as Chief Economic Adviser at the Department of Trade and Industry, and although this limited economic analysis of the U.K. national museums and galleries was strictly undertaken in relation to entrance charges, the subsequent influence of its ways of thinking, on both Government and Conservative Party policies, has been critical.

Unfortunately, the linking of "museums and galleries" with "cultural recreation" in the introduction to the article and its formal summary of intent, coupled with the omission of all national and international definitions of such institutions, based on function, invited the adoption of grotesque distortions in the public perceptions of the role of museums and galleries within the community. During the last two decades the massive, and often unjustified, expansion of what is now euphemistically termed 'the museum industry' has been undertaken increasingly within Peacock and Godfrey's "cultural recreation," until the museum and gallery foundations upon which the whole fragile card-castle has been erected have all but withered away.

Their idiosyncratic economic analysis was undertaken without any commensurate understanding of the core functions of museums and galleries, as against those more visible "cultural recreation" activities which directly involve the general public, and attempts made then by the present author to counter this flawed analysis were rebuffed. Indeed, with the wisdom of hindsight, Peacock and Godfrey's important study is now seen to be a key component in the unholy hotchpotch of misunderstandings, partial truths, political opportunism and naked individual ambition which has been developed in the U.K. during the last two decades. This process has been facilitated by an increasingly careless use of language whereby the precision

[1]Peacock and Godfrey (1974). Davies (1994, p.15), in his analysis of market forces, concluded that "one cannot simply transpose the concept of a market (as developed in the commercial world) on to museums and art galleries. Their market is dysfunctional and they need to develop marketing strategies appropriate to their particular situation."

of words is progressively blunted and intellectual constructs are corrupted for political expediency and the purposes of market-driven pseudo-populism. Part of the semantic dimension of the problem lies in the different usages of English and, for example, the reckless importation of concepts expressed in American English for dissemination within a U.K. environment. Peacock and Godfrey used in their paper the words "gallery or museum" to indicate – within standard U.K. usage – institutions which were non-commercial, while 'art gallery' in American usage generally implies a commercial establishment trading in works of art. Consequently American non-profit art institutions tend to adopt the title of 'art museums' and this paper will use, except in the context of quotations, the word 'museum' alone to describe those institutions which are, at least in theory, non-commercial.

Peacock and Godfrey recognized that museums "are not designed to operate as private concerns or as public utilities charging for their products and services" but they went on to postulate that "this is not to say that it is not useful to apply standard economic analysis normally used to explain the operation of commercial concerns, in order to elucidate the economic problems of the gallery/museum, although somehow such an approach always encounters emotional resistance!" This experience alone should have recommended caution, but Peacock and Godfrey pressed on to characterise the 'output' side as "a range of products in the form of exhibits which satisfy a desire for visual enjoyment or for instruction." They identified, on the 'input side', the labour as consisting of "a combination of highly specialised skills – art experts, restorers of pictures and exhibits, historians and cataloguers – and relatively unskilled (but responsible) staff in the form of attendants, cleaners and sales staff," while "the *stock* of capital inputs in the form of pictures, exhibits, etc., has three important characteristics: it is normally large in relation to the additions to stock; frequently a large part of it has been gifted, although maintaining the stock intact will require an annual provision for restoring, repairing, cleaning, etc.; although the situation varies from one museum to another and is inordinately complex, a large proportion of stock may have been gifted on condition that it is not to be sold, i.e. alteration in the composition of the structure of assets may be severely constrained. A museum/gallery may produce a range of alternative outputs requiring different input 'mixes'. Thus if the main concern is the general public's desire to see exhibits, resources will be devoted much more to preserving and mounting exhibits than in the case where the main concern is to help researchers who are more interested in an efficient cataloguing service."

3 Product v. function

This analysis draws attention to a whole raft of fundamental misunderstandings, not least those concerning the role of museum collections within the institutions possessing them and the legal environments in which they are held, and it is not entirely surprising that Peacock and Godfrey (1974) admitted subsequently that "it is clearly extremely difficult to specify the relation between the outputs and inputs by some kind of production function, principally because of the difficulty of defining output." In the event they effectively ignored the latter and plumped for attendance figures as a rough measure of output, concluding, correctly, that attendance figures tend to reflect what is on display rather than the collections which cannot be placed on permanent display, such as textiles and works on paper, or are held in study or reserve collections. They also observed that their speculations were "bound to enter the realm of fantasy in discussion of the 'objective function' of museums and galleries" and, having missed the point, they posed a series of rhetorical questions about the objectives being pursued and the relative importance of different functions commonly carried out by museums. Out of fairness, however, it should be noted that they stated: "Our investigations have not yet reached the stage at which we are certain what questions to ask and to whom they should be put," though this is no way impeded the momentum rapidly gained by the economic bandwagon, and they went on to note that "one thing is certain: 'maximizing' the relevant objective function is subject to one major constraint in the form of the 'frozen' nature of the capital stock. If collections cannot be broken up because of the contractual conditions of bequests, it is impossible, for example, to buy artistic treasures by the sale of assets. The situation is now under review and it will be interesting to observe how far policy will be affected by modification of such a constraint." From the pen of the Chief Economic Adviser at the Department of Trade and Industry, such confused signals deserved much more careful critical attention than was accorded to them at the time by the U.K. museum profession.

Furthermore, Peacock and Godfrey's speculative identification of "the 'frozen' nature of the capital stock of museums" as a major constraint on them was potentially very dangerous for the future maintenance of the physical integrity of their collections and, in the U.K. at least, laid the foundations for a series of important constructive misunderstandings of the long-term role generally undertaken by museums within the community. Indeed, Peacock and Godfrey went on to state that the "analysis above shows that there is no particular *technical* characteristic of museums and galleries which precludes their operation like ordinary commercial concerns. Those who are not prepared to pay for the 'product' could be excluded from enjoying it by denying them admission." It may seem unreasonable, in 1996, to subject a article published in 1974 to such severe criticism so long after the event, but the misunderstandings embodied in it, and the authority of Alan Peacock, have permeated subsequent cultural-economic analysis of museums and galleries in the U.K., and, more important, the advice given formally and informally by economists to successive British Governments. One of the hazards to be encountered in publishing a seminal paper is that the subtle blunting of meaning adopted by authors to indicate a lack of certainty tends to be ignored by subsequent writers for their own reasons and many of the significant misunderstandings embodied in Peacock and Godfrey's paper are only to be experienced in their full glory in the statements made later by others, less scrupulous. For example, the Audit Commission Report (1991), *The Road to Wigan Pier?*, published in 1991, is unthinkable without this background of cultural-economic speculation. As Appendix B of that document, the "objectives in supporting museums" are listed – presumably in order of importance for its authors – as "quality of life," "promote tourism," "encourage economic development," "support for scholarship and education" and lastly "to conserve the heritage and protect primary evidence of local history, etc." In "cultural recreation" the recreation had by 1991 evidently taken precedence over the culture.

The key to any cultural-economic analysis of museums based on function must lie in a clear understanding of the role of their collections within the community and the legal environment in which they are held. Notwithstanding the growing corruption of the word 'museum' in recent decades, the historic meaning is clear and the identifying characteristics of museum collections – objects assembled and maintained within a specific intellectual environment – separate them from other valued accumulations of objects, including household goods, votive offerings and commercial stock. Despite a certain cynicism expressed by critics of museums, this position is not entirely theoretical and although most museums will admit to having acquired objects in the past for which there would appear to be little justification today, the rationale applied at the time to their acquisition may not be fully comprehensible to us today. Very few museum collections are mindless, rather than quirky or just unfashionable, and like defence of the right to free speech, the right of such collections to survive and continue to put forward their views of the world is an obligation placed upon any democratic society. On the other hand, a museum cannot exist without collections of objects, and temporary exhibition facilities which grace themselves with the title of museum (such as the Museum of Modern Art in Oxford) are misnomers, admirably though they may perform their own particular functions.

4 The humanist tradition

The intellectual environment which has provided the essential framework for the assembly of museum collections is Renaissance Humanism, and although the first organised collections were formed in the Greek and Roman worlds, the fundamental Humanist concept that Man could be understood better through his creations and Nature through the systematic study of her manifestations, positive demanded, for the first time, the systematic formation of collections for study purposes.[2] For the fifteenth-century Humanist the collecting of the surviving remains of Classical antiquity – sculpture, coins, architectural fragments, inscriptions and so on, as well as the texts of the ancient authors – fulfilled an important function and these objects provided a potent insight into the vanished civilizations they sought to emulate and became a powerful stimulus to scholars and creative artists alike. Thus the formation of collections for study purposes, from the fifteenth century, was a concomitant of both the rebirth of Classical rationalism and the beginnings of experimental science, and in this context the processes of collecting cannot be considered separately from the cultural characteristics of the society undertaking them. Indeed, the widely differing geographical pattern of distribution of museum collections world wide is by no means accidental. As noted by Taborsky (1982), the great majority of societies, past and present, including the Celts, Bedouin, Bushmen and others are predominantly 'concept-centred' and for these the individual object is of very limited significance, while the long-term transmission of cultural traditions is mainly through sequential

[2] Cannon-Brookes (1992).

repetition of production and oral communication. However, for the minority – the 'object-centred' societies, above all the heirs to Greece and Rome, the Chinese and the Japanese – the retention of selected representative objects and their careful preservation has for centuries been of crucial importance in the transmission of their cultural traditions, and although museum collections have been particularly relevant to the majority of Western societies since the Renaissance, they have not been equally important to most other societies in the world prior to the creation of the United Nations and dissemination of the notion that the possession of relevant collections is an essential component of nationhood.[3]

Setting aside claims for restitution and debates concerning colonialism and the legitimacy of possessing certain collections and classes of objects, the museum in Western societies is the intellectual construct which has been evolved to collect objects, preserve them, research them and make them and knowledge about them available as part of the processes of transmission of their cultural traditions. This fundamental role emphasizes that museums are traditionally storehouses of knowledge as well as storehouses of objects, and that the whole exercise is likely to be futile unless the process of collecting of objects is strictly rational. This does not mean that selection of the objects is to be limited to any one single cultural or other agenda, unless the museum's stated function is limited to the documentation of one particular view of the world, and thus great catholicity in the processes of selection and subsequent conservation is to be desired so that the collections will in due course be able to support as many different interpretations as possible. In practice this fundamental role is coupled with other factors which reflect the legal and social environments in which the museum is established. In the common-law countries, for example, the holding of cultural property for its preservation (be it movable – a chattel – or fixed property – a building or land) is traditionally not an acceptable object for a charitable trust. Consequently, if the cultural property is to benefit from being held by a charitable trust, the objects of that trust must include objects acceptable to the Court, generally education. In civil-law countries (and also, incidentally, in Scotland) this problem does not arise and apart from the core function of collecting, preserving, researching and making available specific items on behalf of the public, the founding fathers have been at liberty to include

[3]Taborsky (1982).

whatever social and other objectives that seemed to them appropriate at the time.

The process of selection for inclusion in a museum collection is dependent upon the associated knowledge which has been accumulated by the institution and its staff, and new acquisitions will cast fresh light on previous acquisitions, leading to a constant revision of ideas. This feedback process can only take place if both the material integrity of the collections, and their intellectual integrity, are scrupulously maintained. It provides not only the intellectual lifeblood of the institution, but also one of the basic elements in the formulation and evolution of its collecting policy. For static collections, such as the Wallace Collection in London or the Isabella Stewart Gardner Museum in Boston, the processes of selection have already been undertaken by the private collectors who formed them, but those processes have been confirmed by the community in accepting responsibility for preserving those collections as discreet entities, in perpetuity. For certain collections, such as those formed by Isabella Stewart Gardner and Dr. Albert C. Barnes in the U.S., and Sir William Burrell in Scotland, their installation is on occasion as important as the individual works included and the terms of the bequests place clear obligations upon the community to respect those installations or specified components of them.

5 Legal environments

At this point the different legal environments in which museum collections are held provide clear expressions of the varying cultural traditions which have given birth to them. The common-law countries, including the U.K., the nations of the British Commonwealth and the U.S., have well-developed concepts of trusteeship whereby objects are entrusted to the care of groups of individuals for specific purposes, while in the civil-law countries whose legal systems have evolved from Napoleonic law generally treat museum collections as public property and as such inalienable, except *in extremis*. It is in consequence not entirely surprising that the equivalent of the American-English word 'deaccessioning' does not exist in many European languages, largely because the concept is entirely alien to their cultural traditions. Nevertheless, within the common-law countries the attitudes adopted towards the concepts of preservation in perpetuity and deaccessioning have diverged widely to the extent that it has to be asked whether, by virtue of their actions, certain institutions have ceased to be museums, at least when viewed from continental Europe.

Although closely modelled on the great European museums founded in the nineteenth century, the Metropolitan Museum, New York, decided as early as 1885 that "the Museum could in all propriety exchange duplicates of which it had no use, for others which would prove important and valuable additions to the collection." The Metropolitan Museum in this respect, as in many others, has proved to be an important innovator and in the U.S. has led the way in explaining to a wide public both its philosophy and techniques of collecting.[4] In its *Annual Report* published in October 1970 the Trustees announced formally their change of emphasis towards the upgrading of the Museum's holdings, rather than simple accumulation, which was in part based on their commitment to stabilize the overall extent of their collections. After confirming their strategic intention to pursue rare masterpieces of the highest quality, the Trustees stated: "Refinement of the collections also involves the disposal, whenever legally and professionally permissible, of those objects that for any one of a number of reasons are no longer appropriate for the Museum." Thomas Hoving (1973) – the then Director of the Metropolitan Museum – reissued the relevant sections of the above *Annual Report* when he added: "It is important to emphasize that it is aesthetic gain, not financial gain, that ultimately determines the Metropolitan Museum's programme of deaccessioning and acquisition."

6 Deaccessioning

Without attempting to summarise the long-running museum debate about the desirability of deaccessioning, or indeed its ethical justification, it may be noted in this context that attitudes in the U.S. and in the U.K. differ considerably and that most British curators deprecate the practice of 'trading up' as carried out in many museum institutions in the U.S., while continental European curators find it difficult to reconcile such practices with membership of the museum community. The institutionalized schizophrenia involved is reflected in the ambivalent attitude adopted by the International Council

[4] Hoving (1974).

of Museums (ICOM), and through it UNESCO, but possibly more significant is the relatively recent division in the museum world between those institutions which are object-based and the growing number of institutions which see themselves as concept-based. The former epitomize the traditional role of museums as archives of objects, collected for their information value and conserved, researched and made available for study by the community. The latter – once more often encountered in association with totalitarian regimes – are more concerned with ideas formulated outside the institution, and for them the main value of objects lies in their ability to illustrate those ideas. For the object-based museum its collections are its *raison d'être* and its intellectual history is embodied in them to the extent that deaccessioning is liable to compromise its integrity and falsify the record. Such museums make a conscious effort to document what has happened, by collecting objects (the 'products') as dispassionately as possible, while seeking to avoid becoming directly involved in the 'processes' which created them. The impossibility of fully achieving these ends does not in any way invalidate them as ideal strategic goals, although ICOM, at its Triennial Congress held in The Hague (1989) chose to adopt a proactive stance when it endorsed a policy of developing museums as "Creators of Culture."

7 Concept-based institutions

On the other hand, the concept-based museum – if a museum it be – exploits a very different relationship with its collections and if it changes its role, by altering its mission statement, it can discard whole sections of its existing collections, or indeed deaccession its entire collections in order to provide funds and make room for new, more relevant exhibits. The Walker Art Center in Minneapolis has recently completed the deaccessioning of its entire foundation collections, a process begun in the late 1950s when the institution, driven by an ambitious director, was entirely reconfigured as, at first, an innovative centre for fostering the Modern Movement and displaying contemporary art exhibitions. Since then a considerable number of 'contemporary' works of art have been acquired to form a new collection, but these have a strong 1970s focus and the question now arises as to whether they too should be deaccessioned when the Trustees have revised their Mission

Statement once again and identified another new role?[5]

From an American viewpoint, Conforti (1995) has identified four stabilising mechanisms, or "constraints," in museums: (1) the charters and founding mission statements which define the value system embraced by each museum at the time of its formation; (2) the system of governance and professional structure, including the codes for professional practice and ethics governing them; (3) the body of permanent collections which inhibits the museum's freedom of action and requires special allocations of resources for their conservation, research and display; and (4) the limitations imposed by their existing buildings; and any cultural-economic analysis of an art museum has to take cognisance of all four mechanisms. The pragmatic approach favoured in the U.S. facilitates the revision of mission statements and changes in systems of governance, while adhering firmly to the codes for professional practice and ethics evolved by its professional bodies, such as the American Association of Museums, not least in respect of the deaccessioning of collections following the revision of a museum's mission statement. From a U.K. viewpoint, the weakness of the American pragmatic approach is that in reality it positively encourages trustees to treat their collections as working capital, and recent developments with regard to the Guggenheim Museum's use of its collections as collateral for loans, and to the ruthless commercial exploitation of the Barnes Collection by its university trustees, do not exactly inspire confidence in the future there.

8 Trust law in the United Kingdom

In the U.K., unless specific provision otherwise has been made in the formal act of acquisition (deed of gift, committee minute, etc.), the normal presumption is that the object entering a museum has been acquired in perpetuity. The Cottesloe Committee Report (1964) states:

> The basic principle upon which the law rests is that when private persons give property for public purposes the Crown undertakes to see that it is devoted to the purposes intended by the donor, and to no others. When a work of art is given to a museum or gallery for general exhibition, the public thereby acquires rights in the object concerned and these rights cannot be set aside. The authorities of the museum or gallery are not the owners of such

[5]Conforti (1995).

> an object in the ordinary sense of the word: they are merely responsible, under the authority of the Courts, for carrying out the intentions of the donor. They cannot sell the object unless authorised to do so by the Courts or by the Charity Commissioners or the Minister of Education on behalf of the Courts because they have themselves nothing to sell. If they attempt a sale in breach of trust it is the function of the Attorney General to enforce the trust and protect the rights of the public in the object by taking proceedings in the 'Chancery Division'.

Although the public acquires rights in the object, the individual citizen in England and Wales, unlike Scotland, acquires no legal rights. Thus no individual in the U.K. can, for example, demand access to a museum object, be it on display or in store, merely by virtue of its ownership by a museum for public benefit.

The Museums Association's *Code of Practice for Museum Authorities* (1995) defines a museum as "an institution which collects, documents, preserves, exhibits and interprets material evidence and associated information for the public benefit" and in respect of disposal of collections reaffirms that "it is a key function of a museum or art gallery to acquire objects and/or works of art and to keep them for posterity. Consequently there must be a strong presumption against the disposal of any items in the collections of a museum." Furthermore, "any monies received by a governing body from the disposal of specimens or works of art should be applied solely for the purchase of additions to the museum or art gallery collections." The Registration Scheme for Museums in the U.K. established and administered by the Museums & Galleries Commission effectively imposes the same conditions, and in respect of collections states that "in no circumstances should those items be mortgaged or in any way held as security for any loan." Unfortunately, the recommendation in the *Code*, that "objects should be offered first by exchange, gift or private treaty sale, to other museums before sale by public auction is considered" is potentially flawed in that, when any trustees dispose of property deemed to be an asset, by sale, unless released from so doing by the terms of the trust, they are legally obliged to use their best endeavours to obtain the highest price for that asset. This general obligation placed on trustees applies throughout the common-law countries and each case has to be assessed on its own merits, not least the terms under which the trust has been established or subsequently modified.

If the object of the trust is solely the preservation of specific chattels (movable property) in perpetuity (i.e. in a museum environment) they cannot be deemed to be part of the trust fund. They are thus not assets and are unable to be treated as working capital, convertible on demand. Since the seventeenth century there have been many gifts or bequests of chattels to charities for their preservation and continued enjoyment in kind by the community, but their legal status today is the cause of growing concern. At the *University & Foundation Collections and the Law* seminar held in London in 1994 the organisers asked the round tables *inter alia* to address the implications of distinguishing between gifts or bequests of chattels to an established charity to further the pre-existing objects of that charity, as against gifts or bequests to an established charity which were intended to extend the pre-existing objects of that charity to the preservation of those specific chattels in perpetuity. The first is the unencumbered gift of an asset which is freely convertible, while the second is more akin to conferring custodianship in perpetuity.[6] The *Code of Practice for Museum Authorities* adopts the latter position, quoting in full the important advice provided by the Cottesloe Committee.

Nevertheless, the protection afforded is largely illusory and certain auditors have, for example, advised that chattels in the possession of local authorities and included in their museum collections, unless protected by specific provisions, form part of the general collateral of those bodies. Objects in many university collections are similarly exposed. The present situation is deeply unsatisfactory and the bankruptcy of the Chatterly Whitfield Museum and the subsequent auction by the liquidators of part of its collections, in April 1994, despite their being vested in a charitable trust, has sent tremors through the U.K. museum community.

It has, however, been the policy of successive Governments in the U.K. to encourage museums to increase their cash flow by trading, but if their collections are to be sacrosanct and only convertible *in extremis*, and then with the consent of the Courts, those collections are presumably not available for use as collateral. Indeed the conditions for acceptance in the Registration Scheme for Museums in the United Kingdom, administered by the Museums & Galleries Commission and approved by H.M. Government, specifically precludes the mortgaging of museum collections or their use as collateral. Conse-

[6] Cannon-Brookes (1994).

quently, in the case of local authority and university museums, it is presumed that the formal act of applying for registration and maintaining registered status has signalled the withdrawal of their museum collections from the general collateral employed by them. Both classes of museum authorities have other substantial assets which they can employ as collateral, but many collections vested in small foundations and voluntary associations funded by modest trading companies have virtually no trading capital as such and a single, relatively small trading misadventure can, under the Companies Act, result in an immediate inability to continue trading legally, thereby hazarding the future of the collection funded by it. The trading company will have been set up to support the museum and its collection, not vice versa, and today there are strong arguments in favour of a total separation between the trading company and the body in which ownership of the collections is vested, notwithstanding the problem of inadequate trading capital.

9 Purpose theory

A more drastic change in attitudes towards collections is put forward by those attracted to the so-called Purpose Theory which postulates that under certain circumstances the property which forms the object of a trust belongs not to the trustees as individuals but to the purpose which animated the person who set up the trust. The Courts tend to attach great weight to the original purpose as fundamental and unvariable, but according to the Theory purposes change over time and the cultural conventions which formed the purposes established by the person who set up the trust will not always be shared fully by succeeding generations. If this view of changing cultural conventions, and of the roles to be performed by the trustees to change with time, is taken to its logical conclusion, the original objects can legitimately be set aside in due course or ignored when addressing new conventions. It is very tempting for cash-strapped universities in the U.K. to adopt this philosophy today in response to their financial difficulties, but whereas in Scotland any aggrieved citizen can by an *actio popularis* in the Courts oppose the breach of a trustor's intentions, in England and Wales few persons can demonstrate the necessary proprietary *locus standi* to apply to the Courts in respect of alleged 'wrongful interference with goods'.

10 Attendance as a measure of 'output'

At this point it is useful to return to basic principles and the archival role of the object-based museum, as against the very different agendas adopted by the concept-based institutions possessing collections. The object-based museum collects, conserves, researches and makes available to the community those objects and knowledge about them by means of displays, publications and other object-based activities. These are the core functions of the object-based museum and, to take the economic model proposed by Peacock and Godfrey, their main 'output' as measured by cost, etc., is in reality the secure accommodation of those collections and the reduction of the rate of their decay to a minimum while facilitating access by the community. By comparison the cost of research and visible storage (i.e. basic display) can be relatively modest, while all the other activities based on secure, adequately conserved and researched collections, such as educational programmes and temporary exhibitions, are desirable but not essential, and thus secondary.

Historic commitments have been entered into by the community, in various guises, to accept responsibility for preserving in perpetuity various chattels within the intellectual environment we have come to identify as the object-based museum. These commitments have until recently been limited to the funding of the core functions of object-based museums and it may be that such a museum is able to discharge its specific obligations very efficiently with virtually no general public visitors. Hence the perniciousness of settling for attendance figures as even a rough measure of 'output' when high attendance figures are liable to increase the cost of the core functions without actually improving performance except in terms of achieving a higher take-up of information. However, the general presumption that increased attendance can automatically be equated with demonstrable increased total benefit to the community is open to question and, taken to an extreme position, the increased attendance can soon lead to such congestion and disagreeable visiting conditions that the overall benefit actually declines. Heavy marketing has ensured that many high-profile blockbuster art exhibitions have been huge commercial successes, but the overcrowding experienced has detracted greatly from their educational and cultural value and all too often rendered them useless for individual scholarly study.

11 The commercialisation of museums

Before the 1970s the cost of funding historic commitments to maintain the core-functions of object-based museums was generally accepted as a legitimate charge on the public purse, like public reference libraries and archives, for the long-term benefit of the community. However, during the last two decades, the secondary functions have increasingly hijacked the institutions to the extent that the huge increases in staffing and other overheads required to undertake the ever broader range of secondary activities, can no longer be funded from the public purse alone. This political imperative can be met by either reducing the secondary activities and thus the operating funds required, or by further expansion which is designed to increase cash flow through trading, sponsorship, raised entry charges, etc., though few institutions have to date taken the decision to adopt the creed of voluntary simplicity and not only offer, relatively speaking, less, but to justify their stand. Consequently, all cultural institutions competing for limited public subsidies must be able to demonstrate to the lowest common denominator the success of their particular activities, and the market-driven funding of those object-based museums following this route inevitably depends more on their range of secondary activities than the core functions on which the whole fragile structure is based. These pressures produce increasingly serious distortions as the object-based museum is driven to attract new visitor groups regardless of whether those visitors have any sympathy for its core functions.

Today all cultural institutions are exhorted to study carefully their customers, be they real or only potential. McLean (1993) has asked many of the key questions:

> For a museum to operate successfully it needs to have more refined notions of the general public. To what end is a museum communicating? To what extent can experience be embodied in communication? How can experience be determined? To whom is the museum communicating? Evaluation of what is provided needs to be be very specifically tailored. This involves a conscious policy decision on whether the museum is operating for less than the whole public's benefit. Why does a museum confine its communication to targeted visitors? When is a decision made that the museum is operating for a chosen public? Does the nature of the collection determine this? Access is also a critical factor in this debate. The degree of access reflects the museum's attitude to the public by determining the profile of the visiting public.

The answers are not simple and Prentice (1994) has analysed the perceptual deterrents to visiting museums and other heritage attractions. His conclusions do not make happy reading for traditional object-based museums seeking to increase their cash flow and thereby trading profits, though he desists from spelling out the mindlessness of an alarmingly high proportion of those interviewed. But apart from identifying the motivation of visitors one must also ask how are the demands of the tax-paying local community to be reconciled with those of the more freely spending cultural tourists from outside? A display calculated to assist local school children in fulfilling the requirements of the National Curriculum will not detain international cultural tourists for long or encourage repeat visits.

12 The role of temporary exhibitions

On the other hand, high profile temporary exhibitions – not necessarily blockbusters – can do wonders for the trade in local pubs and restaurants, and even boost the museum's short-term cash flow, but they can also consume a disproportionate amount of the resources needed by the museum to discharge adequately its core functions. Temporary exhibition entrance changes may be relatively high since few cultural tourists who have travelled specially to see it will be deterred at the last moment, but local inhabitants will compare them unfavourably with the much more modest entrance charges which are able to be levied throughout the year in respect of the permanent collections, and public resentment in this sector is not conducive to continued public subsidies. Furthermore, these temporary exhibitions depend upon reciprocity of loans and mutual trust between lenders and borrowers as to the motives of the exhibition organizers. Increased local tourism will generally be welcomed by a lender when it is an incidental benefit, but few lenders will contemplate loans to an exhibition organised primarily for that or any other non-museum purpose. The example set by the series of blockbuster exhibitions mounted in Memphis, Tennessee, from which the profits have been creamed off to subsidise local housing programmes, has encouraged lenders to ask much more searching questions of potential borrowers, and Tübingen may find it more difficult to obtain its loans when it becomes more generally known that most of the substantial profits made by the 1993 Cézanne Exhibition have been appropriated by the town council for non-museum purposes.

The strangulation at birth of all but a few serious scholarly art exhibitions in museums other than the very largest has been an inevitable corollary of the largely frustrated search for new mass publics, but the organization of blockbuster exhibitions has long been seized upon by ambitious individuals for personal career enhancement, incidentally drawing attention away from neglected core functions. Indeed, the pursuit of high attendance figures through high-profile displays, hyped temporary exhibitions, socially-orientated educational programmes, and the like, is driven by political or social agendas, not economic, because in the cold light of dawn it is recognised that more often than not they cost the institution more than the increased funding which they attract. The overall result of over-dependance upon market forces will be to drive object-based museums progressively out of business, in both common law and civil law countries. After all, empty barrels make most noise!, or, in the terms of economics, bad money drives out good.

13 Conclusions

To return to the institutional 'constraints' identified by Conforti, it becomes clear that the concept-based institution, which is at liberty to revise its mission statement repeatedly and deaccession its collections accordingly, is in a considerably stronger position to adapt to each change in its financial circumstances and those of the supporting community. Until the reconfigured Walker Art Center acquired new collections it had effectively ceased to be a museum and it was in a position to direct all its resources to its highly successful programme of temporary exhibitions, but today its freedom of action is again greatly constrained by its collections and its building, an important example of the Modern Movement. Consequently, in this increasingly messy environment, any attempt to undertake cultural-economic analyses of the range of institutions identifying themselves as museums is doomed to failure if it does not recognise the differences in attitudes towards collections evident within the common law countries, from the pragmatic traditions of the U.S. to the much tighter legal controls which in theory operate in the U.K., let alone the inalienability of collections in the civil-law countries. Experience gained within one environment will not necessarily be applicable within the others, and while the hypothetical pecuniary values of the collections currently held by a concept-based institution might logically be included on the balance sheet of its operating accounts, those in the possession of an object-based museum cannot. However, within the common law countries, the law has yet to distinguish between the object-based museums and the concept-based institutions on the basis of the differences between the objects (purposes) of their respective governing charitable trusts, and since the collections in the possession of all 'museums' provide such a major constraint on their activities, clarification of their legal status is an essential prerequisite to any cultural-economic analysis. Meanwhile, the continued erosion of the intellectual consensus, above all in the common law countries, as to what precisely constitutes a museum and distinguishes it from a wide variety of superficially similar activities, also has to be addressed and separated from political dogma and the opportunism of ambitious individuals.

14 References

Audit Commission Local Government Report (1991), London: HMSO.

Cannon-Brookes, P. (1992), The nature of museum collections, in J.M.A. Thomson, ed., *Manual of Curatorship. A Guide to Museum Practice*, Oxford: Butterworth.

Cannon-Brookes, P., ed. (1994), The proceedings of the seminar held at the Courtauld Institute of Art, *Museum Management and Curatorship*, 13, 340-407.

Conforti, M. (1995), Museums past and museums present: some thoughts on institutional survival, *Museum Management and Curatorship*, 14, 339-355.

[The Cottesloe Committee Report] (1964), Report of the Committee of Enquiry into the Sale of Works of Art by Public Bodies, London: HMSO.

Davies, S. (1994), *By Popular Demand: A Strategic Analysis of the Market Potential for Museums and Art Galleries in the U.K.*, London: Museums and Galleries Commission.

Hoving, T.P.F. (1973), A policy statement from the Met, *Museum News*, 51, 43-45.

Hoving, T.P.F. (1974), The Chase, the Capture: Collecting at the Metropolitan, paper presented to a meeting of the College Art Association of America.

McLean, F.C. (1993), Marketing in museums: a contextual analysis, *Museum Management and Curatorship*, 12, 11-27.

Museums Association, Code of practice for museum authorities, printed in each issue of *Museums Yearbook*, London: Museums Association.

Peacock, A. and C. Godfrey (1974), The economics of museums and galleries, *Lloyds Bank Review*, 111, 17-28.

Prentice, R. (1993), Perceptual deterrents to visiting museums and other heritage attractions, *Museum Management and Curatorship*, 12, 264-279.

Taborsky, E. (1982), The socio-structural role of the museum, *The International Journal of Museum Management and Curatorship*, 1, 339-345.

Economics of the Arts - Selected Essays
V.A. Ginsburgh and P.-M. Menger (Editors)

11

Special Exhibitions and Festivals: Culture's Booming Path to Glory*

Bruno S. Frey and Isabelle Busenhart
University of Zürich

1 The boom

There is hardly an art museum not running or at least preparing a special exhibition of some sort. Such an exhibition may feature one particular artist (often in commemoration of birth or death), or a group of artists, may focus on a period or a genre of paintings, or may establish a connection to some historical event (see Belcher (1991, p. 49)).

Table 1 shows how more than 1,100 exhibitions of various types are distributed among European museums for the years 1994-95 as collected by the "International Exhibition Guide." Dominating are exhibitions devoted to one particular artist (solo exhibitions), modern and contemporary thematic, and classical fine arts exhibitions. This guide only takes into account a rather limited number of museums and exhibitions (it is based on a voluntary survey with a substantial number of non-respondents). Concerning our own town (Zurich), for instance, only two museums are listed (Museum Rietberg and Schweizerisches Landesmuseum with two exhibitions each in 1994-95), whereas there were at least 38 museums with 34 exhibitions in August 1994.[1]

*We are grateful to Iris Bohnet, Nicola Dischinger, Reiner Eichenberger, René L. Frey, Trine Bille Hansen, Alexander Hunziker and Jürg de Spindler for helpful discussions. Part of the paper was presented at a joint research seminar of the Universities of Basle and Zurich, at the 1994 ICARE Summer Workshop in Venice and at the 8th international congress of Cultural Economics in Witten-Herdecke 1994.

[1]Obviously, the same applies for other countries. The "International Exhibition Guide" lists 231 exhibitions in Germany for the years 1994-95 whereas, alone in 1991, as many as 1,600 exhibitions took place according to data from the German Institut für Museumskunde (1992).

Table 1
Exhibitions according to Theme
in 300 Museums in Europe, 1994-95

Regional, Religious and Archeological		**Other Art**	
African Art	11	Architecture	32
Archeology	11	Cinema, Video, New Techn.	19
Asian Art	19	Photography	71
Egyptian and Oriental Art	4	Design	22
Greek and Roman Art	12	Fashion	17
Islamic Art	1	Graphic Arts	13
Latin American Art	2	Jewelry, Ceramics, etc.	20
Visual Arts (Modern and Contemporary)		**Ethnology and History**	
Solo Exhibitions	352	Ethnology	22
Exhibitions featuring two or more Artists	15	History	33
Thematic Exhibitions	153	Literature and Music	18
Decorative and Fine Arts		Society Museum	34
Art Object, Decorative Art	38	**Nature**	
Fine Arts	169	Natural Sciences	13
		Technology	23
		Total	1,124

Source: International Exhibition Guide, Grunfeld (1994); own calculations.

Table 2 shows the distribution of art exhibitions organized by museums in various countries based on the "calendrier des arts" of the *Journal des Arts* (July-August 1994). This enumeration is rather doubtful, especially for France, where many exhibitions by private galleries are included. Indeed, the Italian *Giornale dell'Arte* (June 1994) lists for the same period only 79 exhibitions in France, but 306 in Italy (while the *Journal des Arts* counts only 63 for that country.)

Some special exhibitions are composed solely of paintings from the holdings of the organizing museum, but most such special shows bring together works of art from different museums and private collections. Once put together, large temporary exhibitions frequently travel to other museums cooperating with the organizer. Some exhibitions indeed are already designed to be sent to various countries. Not infrequently, important museums simultaneously display several shows which they have either mounted themselves or taken over from other organizers.

Table 2
Art Exhibitions July-August 1994 according to Countries

	July	August		July	August
Austria	26	23	Argentina	2	3
Belgium	48	36	Brazil	2	1
Czech Republic	12	13	Chile	1	2
Denmark	5	6			
Finland	5	5	Canada	15	14
France	629	476	USA	167	148
Germany	102	92			
Great Britain	56	51	South Africa	2	2
Hungary	2	2			
Italy	63	50	Japan	7	6
Netherlands	23	20	Singapore	1	1
Portugal	16	13			
Slovakia	1	1	Australia	9	9
Spain	22	11	New Zealand	3	5
Switzerland	103	107			
			Total:	1,322	1,097

Note: The same exhibition may figure both in July and August.
Source: Le calendrier des arts, publication of *Le Journal des Arts*, August 1994.

Due to problems of definition, it is impossible to determine precisely how many special exhibitions museums run, but it is unquestionably a booming industry.[2] The example of Germany shows that the phenomenon is not only due to the increasing number of museums: while the number of art museums has grown by 35% between 1982 and 1991 the exhibitions held by these museums have almost doubled (Institut für Museumskunde (1992)). A similar picture is presented in Feldstein (1991, p. 80). Five major urban museums

[2]Our analysis is restricted to temporary special exhibitions at art museums, neglecting similar events taking place in other types of museums. It must be noted that exhibitions come in many different forms and are therefore ill-defined (see Velardo (1988) and Belcher (1991) who develop an extensive classification of modes and types of special exhibitions).

are considered, where large scale exhibitions increase by 100% between 1980 and 1987.

Most noticeable are the "blockbuster exhibitions" attracting huge crowds and enjoying considerable media attention. Examples are the "Emperor's Warriors" in Edinburgh, 1985 (220,000 visitors); "Monet in the 90s" in the Royal Academy, 1990 (650,000 visitors); the Cézanne-Retrospective in Tübingen, 1993 (430,000 visitors); Matisse in New York, 1993 (900,000 visitors) and the Klimt Exhibition in Zurich, 1993 (250,000 visitors)[3] – just to name a few recent shows.

Museum exhibitions do, however, not always meet with enthusiasm. Thus, the director of the Metropolitan Museum of Art, Philippe de Montebello, complained that, whenever he meets people, they ask him what show he is presently preparing, to which he retorts that he is the director of the Metropolitan *art museum* and not of the Metropolitan Opera (Montebello (1981)).

A similar development can be observed for the performing arts. Virtually every city or at least region in Europe has its own festival of serious music. While the festivals at Bayreuth, Salzburg, Glyndebourne, or Spoleto may be older and more in the limelight than others, there are many thousands of music festivals today.[4] Due to the problem of how to define a music festival, no precise counts exist; guessed estimates range from one thousand (Pahlen (1978), Dümling (1992)) to at least two thousand (Galeotti (1992)). Merin and Burdick (1979) list no less than 83 musical festivals for former Yugoslavia, for West Germany 46, Spain 42, Portugal 38, Austria 25, Italy 22 and Switzerland 16. This list is certainly not exhaustive because, for instance for the United Kingdom, Merin and Burdick name 70 festivals, while the more detailed study of Rolfe (1992, p. 2) lists no less than 529. Even in tiny Denmark, roughly 45 festivals take place every year. A recent enumeration for France counts 864 festivals of which 40 percent are devoted to serious music (Maillard (1994, p. 65)), another one lists 600 festivals of which 450

[3] Attendance figures are quite important, though this is often disputed by the art people involved. According to one museum expert "Attendance figures still constitute an index of the popularity of museums and exhibitions..." (Belcher (1991, p. 197)).

[4] In this paper we only consider festivals devoted to serious music and operas but even so, it is difficult to define what a music festival exactly is. There are, of course, many other types of "festivals" ranging from country music, jazz, theatre, circus to films. A classification is e.g. provided in Getz and Frisby (1988).

are devoted to serious art (*L'Expansion* (1994, p. 32)). An official publication by the French Ministère de la Culture comes up with 245 festivals of serious music and opera for 1994.

Festivals became a significant part of the serious music and opera scene in the 1920s, but the boom took place within the last twenty years. In its special issue on musical events, *L'Expansion* (1994, p. 32) estimates, for example, that 6 out of 10 festivals in France have been founded in the 80s. Festivals usually take place in the summer and are often very popular. Some festivals are permanently sold out and entry tickets can then be acquired only by good connections, or on the black market.

The boom in special exhibitions and music festivals poses a challenge to art economists because of the glaring contrast to the financial depression in which opera houses, orchestras and art museums find themselves. Many opera and concert houses are under such intense financial strain that they are forced to cut down their activities, dismiss artists and workers (if they are legally allowed to do so), or risk closing down completely.[5] Art museums are also confronted with serious financial difficulties (only France seems to be an exception; see Menger (1983)). In many of the world's leading museums, some wings are temporarily closed, and opening hours are reduced in order to save money. Curators are concerned that they have less and less money available for the restoration and conservation of their collections. The museum people's complaints about dwindling financial resources are not immediately obvious, at least not to economists. Over the last decades, the value of their holdings has greatly increased in real terms[6] and in this sense art museums are richer than ever. The fact that they are short of current income is no counterargument, because the financial position of many museums would dramatically improve if they sold a tiny part of their holdings, in particular that share stacked in their cellars which is rarely if ever exhibited. However, most European art museums are public and are not allowed nor willing to sell any part of their holdings for a variety of other reasons (Frey (1994a)). It follows that as things are today, both art performed and exhib-

[5] "Baumol's Law" is one of the reasons for this demise (Baumol and Bowen (1966)). For a general analysis of the performing arts see e.g. Throsby and Withers (1979), Baumol and Baumol (1984), Frey and Pommerehne (1989).

[6] See the literature on the rate of return of paintings and other collectibles by Baumol (1986), Stein (1977), Anderson (1974), Frey and Pommerehne (1988), and the surveys in Rouget, Sagot-Duvauroux and Pflieger (1991) and Frey and Eichenberger (1995).

ited in the traditional venues are faced with serious financial problems – but at the same time musical festivals and special exhibitions are thriving.

2 Special exhibitions and festivals: similar features

Special exhibitions and festivals are closely related in various important respects. This section discusses similarities in demand (subsection 2.1) and in supply (subsection 2.2).

2.1 Demand

On the demand side, the similarities are particularly strong with respect to seven features.

High income effect

Consumers tend to spend an increasing share of rising income on visiting music performances and art exhibitions. Scattered empirical evidence exists showing that econometrically estimated income elasticities of demand are larger than one for both types of art. Throsby and Withers (1979, p. 113), for example, find an income elasticity for performing arts services of 1.55 for the United States 1949-73, and of 1.4 for Australia 1964-74 (full income). The rise in attendance to performing art events is also documented in Baumol and Baumol (1984). In a survey on cultural audiences in the Netherlands, Ganzeboom (1987) finds a positive and slightly increasing influence of income on museum visits for the period of 1962-83. Special exhibitions and festivals thus find themselves in the comfortable position of being in a growing market. This does, however, not explain the growth in the number of special events as opposed to regular arts venues.

Attracting new visitor groups

As has been well documented in cultural sociology,[7] social factors may lead to a feeling of uneasiness of some groups towards attending certain cultural events. A large share of the population rarely, if ever, attends cultural events in opera and concert houses, or visits art museums.[8] Many people are overawed by the "temples of culture," feel insecure and unwelcome, and therefore do not even consider attending an opera performance or visiting the local art museum. This applies, in particular, to population groups with below average education, which are also short of cultural tradition (see Blau (1989) and DiMaggio and Useem (1989)). The situation is clearly different for special cultural events which are broadly advertised, and which are made attractive to new groups. This holds in particular for music festivals taking place in "public spaces," thus being more amenable to the great mass of the population, and less prohibitive than the established temples of culture (see e.g. Rolfe (1992, p. 82)). Indeed, many festivals make a strong effort to "go to the people" by e.g. playing in sport stadiums or popular meeting places (such as inner-city parks).[9] As special exhibitions normally take place in museum premises – exceptions are, for instance, the Biennale in Venice or the Documenta in Kassel –, they still face the difficulty of attracting new groups. This is partly overcome by "dressing-up the museum" (see also Elsen (1986)): special exhibitions are without exception marked by huge banners and other advertising gags, and even the museum entrances (which to non-museum goers otherwise look menacing) are virtually opened up and made welcom-

[7]Klein (1990) provides extensive empirical evidence on the socio-demographic background of the "museum visitor." Data refer mainly to the Federal Republic of Germany. For the sociology of arts in general see Foster and Blau (1989).

[8]The situation is quite different for museums of technology or of transport. Especially automobile and railway museums are very popular. In Switzerland, for instance, which boasts many fine museums of art, the museum with by far the largest attendance is the Verkehrsmuseum in Lucerne. In 1993 it attracted over 547,000 visitors while the (famous) collection at the Basle Kunstmuseum was visited only by 103,000 persons.

[9]A good example is the "Opera Spectacular" which tours the whole world. Its production of Aida is normally performed in sports stadiums, and has so far attracted almost 2 million visitors. Open air performances have attendances of up to 45,000 people (in Montreal); this can be attributed to concrete visual elements (e.g. a sphinx 15 metres high, live elephants and camels), a large number of performers (roughly 600 supernumeraries), as well as to the extraordinary emphasis on high technical tone quality.

ing. The "Emperor's Warriors" Exhibition in Edinburgh 1985 is such an example of opening up the museum. Extensive promotion also plays a role. Coutts (1986) relates in his article "Profile of a Blockbuster" the success story of that exhibition. It attracted over 200,000 visitors; when questioned, a considerable part (15%) reported that they normally do not visit museums.

Focusing attention

A festival and an exhibition seek to attract consumers by presenting some extraordinary cultural experience. They specialize on some particular artist (e.g. Bach with festivals, Rembrandt with exhibitions), some period (e.g. renaissance music or renaissance paintings), some topic (e.g. courtly music or courtly paintings), some genre (e.g. mannerist music or mannerist paintings), or some type of presentation (e.g. original musical instruments or portrait paintings). As a result, the visitors interested in such particular forms of art come together, often from far away locations (which is, of course, supported by low and secularly falling travel cost). Special exhibitions, in particular the "blockbusters," are in this respect not different from festivals, and may even be compared with major sports events such as Olympic games or world championships. In both cases, public attention is drawn away from the regular activity – showing the permanent collection and pursuing the normal sport schedule – towards a special and unique (or at least rare) event. Special exhibitions and festivals share common features with pilgrimages (Börsch-Supan (1993, p. 73)), which also have an aura of mysticism, and are surrounded by much commercial activity.

Newsworthiness

Festivals and special exhibitions are news, and attract the attention of television, radio and the print media which, otherwise, is impossible to get to the same degree and, especially, free of charge. It is easy to get media people to report on a special exhibition, while the permanent collection is hardly any news (see e.g. Bayart and Benghozi (1993, p. 210)). Large exhibitions devoted to mythified artists such as Rembrandt, Van Gogh or Picasso, or to a far away, magic culture mobilize the press and throw the organizing museum people into the limelight (see also Elsen (1986, p. 20)). The publicity not only attracts larger crowds of viewers, but also improves the museum directorate's position vis-à-vis politicians, sponsors and donors.

Operatic and musical performers get some media attention on opening nights but with few exceptions, i.e. short of a scandal, the respective reports are digested by only a small share of the population, while the rest does not bother. Festivals offer much better opportunities to get media attention, as they present themselves every year as new (even if, in practice, some of them repeat performances, Verona's "Aida" being a case in point).

Closely connected to novelty is the limited duration of both festivals and special exhibitions. The restricted time raises prospective visitors' incentives to really attend, while a visit to the local opera or concert house, or to the museum, is easily put off in the expectation that nothing is thereby lost.

Low cost to visitors

Festivals and special exhibitions are closely connected to tourism (see e.g. Getz (1989), O'Hagan (1992, p. 65)). The French characteristically like to name them "estivals," in order to indicate that they normally take place in the summer tourist season. It has, for instance, been econometrically estimated that as tourists have their income situation improve back home, they increase their vacation expenditure and correspondingly demand more cultural experiences during their stay abroad (Gapinski (1988)). A considerable share of visitors comes from out of town, from another region, and often from a foreign country.

Special exhibitions also strongly rely on tourist visitors but as they are mostly organized by major museums which are located in large cities, the period outside summer holidays is more attractive. Winter is a good season for special art exhibitions as the prospective visitors are prepared to travel to these centres, thus combining holidays with a cultural experience (for the Basle Holbein exhibition, see Schenker (1988)).

The combination of a cultural event with tourism lowers individuals' cost of attending in various respects. In the case of increasingly popular package tours, consumers only have to take the initial decision and all the rest is taken care of by the travel agent. In the case of culture where it is often burdensome to acquire the tickets from outside, this reduction of decision and transaction cost is substantial. Festivals and special exhibitions should thus be considered as one input into a consumption production function (Becker (1976)). The total cost of the output consumed is made up of the cost of the various inputs which comprise, among other, the travel costs which have been secularly declining (especially if one takes into account the reduced time input required). This argumeht, however, also holds to some extent for a combination of tourism with regular art venues.

Low price elasticity of demand

The strong attraction of special exhibitions and festivals to tourists and people from out of town paying day-visits, also affects the price elasticity of demand. Tourists do not relate an increase in the ticket price (within reasonable bounds) to the previous entry price, but rather to expenditures for the trip as a whole. A given price rise is then in comparison perceived to be small only and does not have much impact on demand (for the general argument, see Thaler (1980); for museum admission fees, see Blattberg and Broderick (1991)). This effect is supported by empirical evidence. Attendance figures at the Museum of the Palazzo Ducale in Venice, for example, have been fairly stable although admission fees for the exhibitions presented in the last years have increased by more than 10 percent on average. In fact, the number of visitors to the Palazzo Ducale seems to be in direct proportion to the number of people visiting the centre of Venice (ICARE (1994)).

The low price elasticity of demand compared to the permanent venues gives the managers of festivals and special exhibitions more leeway to increase their revenue by increasing entry fees. It may indeed be commonly observed that the entry prices for special exhibitions are often much higher than for the permanent collection (even if they are located in the same house). The same is true for many festivals, compared to traditional performances. This suggests that entry fees are more fully used as an income source, when tourist demand is higher.

High demand by business

Festivals and special exhibitions offer many opportunities to make money. Indeed, there is a large literature documenting the monetary profitability of such cultural events.[10] They do not only extend to the tourist industry,

[10] For art exhibitions see Börsch-Supan (1993), Feldstein (1991), Fronville (1985), DiMaggio (1985); for festivals see Frey (1986) and O'Hagan (1992).

but also to firms catering for the production of the festivals and exhibitions. There is also a benefit to the recording industry in the case of festivals, and to book publishers in the case of special exhibitions. They benefit from the interest raised by glamorous cultural events.

2.2 Supply

There are five major determinants of supply which are similar, if not identical, for music festivals and special exhibitions. They contrast with the conditions faced by the permanent venues and contribute to the boom of festivals and special exhibitions.

Low production cost

The absolute cost of many festivals and special exhibitions is certainly high, but it is low compared to the sum they would require if all the resource inputs used were attributed to them. In the case of both art forms, important resources are taken from the permanent venues and only marginal (additional) cost is covered by the special artistic event. Museum employees are taken on to organize and run special exhibitions but the corresponding cost is not attributed to the special events (Montebello (1981)). In real terms, the costs are substantial but often appear in disguised and long-term form only. One such cost is the neglect of cataloguing and keeping-up the permanent collection (see Börsch-Supan (1993) for several pertinent examples). But also the museum rooms where the special exhibitions take place do not enter the accounts, as the opportunities forgone are not part of bookkeeping. The cost of mounting a special exhibition are also significantly lowered, because the art works shown do not have to be rented at a market price. Extensive inquiries with museum administrators, private collectors and a variety of art experts, have revealed that a rental market for art objects only exists under very exceptional conditions, and is of little importance (see also Frey and Eichenberger (1995)). Rather, the exhibits are lent free of charge; the organizing museum at best has to cover the insurance and transport cost (which may be substantial). The cost of this lending "free of charge" shows up in a non-monetary form. The whole system of special exhibitions is built on mutual exchange or on the principle of reciprocity. Only those museum directors who are prepared to also lend art objects from their own permanent collection, are able to participate in this exchange system. The (indirect) cost of being able to show the treasures of other museums at one's own special exhibitions consists in the temporary losses of treasures of one's own collection. But again, these are opportunity costs which are nowhere accounted for, at least not in monetary form. The productivity cost can be further lessened by arranging travelling, circulating or touring exhibitions where they can be shared by those museums which are to show the exhibition (see more fully Belcher (1991, pp. 51-55)).

Festivals taking place outside the permanent venue have to carry a higher share of total cost in monetary form than museums. However, as festivals are predominantly organized during the summer holidays, they can hire much of the artistic and technical staff at marginal cost as these persons are otherwise not employed.[11] They can also, to a considerable extent, draw on volunteers. In the United Kingdom, for instance, almost 40 percent of the over 500 arts festivals are run by unpaid staff (Rolfe (1992, p. 1)), but that source of labour is also important in virtually all festivals (see e.g. Curtis (1990, p. 4) or O'Hagan (1993, p. 161)). The locations at which the festivals play are often "public" (they belong to the state or the church); they can be rented at a nominal charge, and are often free (Rolfe (1992, p. 62); Galeotti (1992, p. 133)).

More scope for artistic creativity

Permanent opera houses and orchestras are strongly bound by the clientele they have to cater for. They often find it impossible to interpret classical plays in a new form, and even more so to perform modern and/or unknown plays, because they risk losing their regular customers.[12] The holders of season tickets with mostly conservative taste are moreover strongly interested in what is presented; they form a powerful lobby which can exert considerable pressure on the managers and the subsidy-giving politicians if they are dissatisfied with "their" opera house or orchestras. As a consequence, the directors have little possibility to fulfil their artistic conceptions of originality.

[11] At the festival of La Roque-d'Anthéron (France), for example, artists accept to perform for sometimes half the fee they get on other occasions (*L'Expansion* (1994, p. 35)).

[12] As Baumol and Bowen (1992) point out, this was not always so. In Mozart's time "audiences generally were prepared to listen only to *new* music, usually to works written no more than a decade earlier."

Independently organized festivals provide an opportunity to exhibit artistic creativity. Festivals may well cater for an audience honouring unorthodoxy, excellence and special tastes. While a permanent opera house or orchestra only performing contemporary plays and music comes under heavy pressure from its established clientele and is quickly forced by the subsidizing politicians to conform to broader tastes, a festival exclusively devoted to such contemporary art may well prosper, as the festivals at Donaueschingen and Lockenhaus demonstrate.

Museum directors are similarly bound by artistic conventions. The particular hanging of pictures at many museums has become part of the cultural heritage, and it is next to impossible to rearrange the permanent collection to any significant extent. Special exhibitions offer a chance to evade such historical restrictions. One of the major tasks and potentials of an art exhibition is to arrange the art object in a way which creates new insights and effects. In addition, the assembly of art objects coming from many different permanent collections, provides a much-sought challenge to the museum directors, curators, exhibition and graphic designers, conservators, editors and managing officers, to exert their artistic creativity and sense of innovation, and possibly to raise controversy – these aspects are highly valued by museum people for their own sake, but also because it is beneficial for their career.

Evading government and trade union regulations

Cultural institutions' freedom to act is restricted by two major institutions, government and trade unions.[13]

In continental Europe, both establishments of serious music and art museums are to a large extent either directly part of the public administration, or at least have to follow the administrative rules of the public sector as they are heavily subsidized by it. In particular, they are subject to the "non-affectation principle" according to which all expenditures are covered by the public budget, and, in return, all the revenue goes to the public treasury.

[13]This argument especially applies for Europe. In the United States, where generally less regulations are imposed on cultural institutions (at least compared to other institutions), the incentive to evade regulations is lower. For the case of festivals, the empirical picture is consistent with that observation: fewer festivals take place in the U. S. than in Europe (see Frey (1994b)).

All revenue thereby gained is "taxed" by the public treasury at one hundred percent, as the subsidy is correspondingly reduced. Indeed, the effort to gain own revenues is taxed at more than one hundred percent in the longer run, because the budgetary authorities become aware of such possibilities and correspondingly reduce future subsidies. As a result, art institutions (as well as all other governmental units) have no incentive to gain revenue by own efforts, e.g. by ticket sales or income from auxiliary activities, such as selling goods in the museum store or recordings of opera and musical performances. The director of the highly subsidized Wiener Burgtheater, for instance, categorically refuses to include advertisments in the theatre program "for esthetic and artistic reasons" (Österreichischer Rechnungshof (1994, p. 28)) without mentioning that this is routinely done elsewhere. A major reason why museums do not charge for loaning out works to special exhibitions, but rather rely on exchanges, is that non-monetary activities are extra-budgetary, and are therefore more likely to escape the intervention by the ministry in charge of museums.

Government restrictions go much beyond budgetary affairs. They hinder the art institutions' way to act and to perform in a myriad of ways. Thus, the pricing policy is strongly restricted, as well as opening and performing days and hours (for many examples see e.g. Börsch-Supan (1993, pp. 11, 15)). In view of the strong hand of the government, and its persistence due to a long tradition, the major possibility of evading these regulations is to engage in special events.

Festivals are, with very few exceptions, organized as private enterprises in which public bodies are, at best, one of several members. As a consequence, the directors of music festivals do not have to conform to administrative regulations and, in particular, do not have to transfer surpluses to the public treasury but can use them in a way they find sensible, above all to invest them into innovative features of their festival.[14] The directors risk losing their degree of freedom to the extent they accept, and become dependent on, public subsidies, in which case the festival's possibility to engage in artistic originality is reduced to the low level corresponding to established opera

[14]Abundant evidence exists showing that festivals enjoy greater financial freedom than normal music establishments. A good example is the Schleswig-Holstein Musikfestspiele, where the originator and promoter, Justus Frantz, enjoyed more leeway than he would ever have had at an established venue. While he received public subsidies, he kept his independence by relying on financial support from many different sponsors.

houses and orchestras.

Special exhibitions provide a good opportunity for directors of art museums to appropriate at least part of the extra revenue generated. Since they are extraordinary events, museum directors are in a good bargaining position vis-à-vis the public budgetary authorities to keep some discretion over the funds, and not to be fully "punished" by a reduction in future budget allocations. A pertinent example is the Cézanne exhibition held in Tübingen in 1993. The organizing museum (Kunsthalle) being public, its expenditures and revenues form part of the budget of the town of Tübingen. Eventual profits are normally absorbed by the public budget. However, things looked different in the case of the Cézanne-Retrospective, which unexpectedly accounted for a profit of 4.5 mio DM. This surprisingly good result made it possible for the museum director to bargain with the town authorities. In the end, the museum was allowed to keep more than a million of the profits, for the purpose of organizing more such special exhibitions.[15]

A few art exhibitions are at least formally outside the public sector, such as the Documenta in Kassel or the Biennale in Venice, but the organizers are in constant danger of being invaded by government regulations. Of course, financial independence strengthens the organizers' position vis-à-vis the state.

One of the most stringent public regulations imposed on art institutions pertains to government sector employment. The virtual impossibility of dismissing inefficient or downright destructive employees, to promote and pay employees according to performance, and to adjust working hours to needs, are major factors reducing creative endeavours and to turn art institutions into mere bureaucracies. Additional regulations have been pushed through by trade unions, and are often fully supported by the government. Festivals and special exhibitions make it possible to evade at least some employment restrictions, especially as most of the employees are only part-time and temporary,[16] are not union members, and are therefore not legally bound by trade union regulations.

In the case of both government and trade union restrictions, festivals and special exhibitions only provide relief as long as they do not occur in a

[15]Personal communication by the director of the Kunsthalle Tübingen, Professor Götz Adriani, to the authors, 20 June, 1994.

[16]Many museums employ part of their personnel only temporarily when they have an exhibition on display (Bayart and Benghozi (1993, p. 199)). For an analysis of temporary work contracts in the performing arts, see Menger (1991).

too regular sequence. A museum which organizes yearly exhibitions with a large surplus, risks losing the special status relative to other governmental units. One therefore observes that museum directorates stress the extraordinary nature of each exhibition. They moreover purposely feature exhibitions meeting their own criteria of a "good" exception (and therewith attract the attention and admiration of their reference group, i.e. of art critics and of other museum directors) but which are due to produce a substantial deficit. That festivals are on average more independently organized than special exhibitions, may be attributed to the fact that, as (mostly) yearly events, they are under greater danger to be subjected to outside regulations.

More sponsoring

Politicians and public officials have a pronounced interest in festivals and grand special exhibitions. They not only respond to the respective demands of the arts world and the local business community, but they are also given an excellent opportunity to appear in the media as "patrons of the arts" (with tax payers' money). The fact that some festivals initially made profit until the politicians seized the chance to intervene, suggests a causality which is reverse to the accepted one: subsidies are not offered because deficits must be covered, but deficits appear because politicians offer subsidies.[17]

Business is also more prepared to sponsor festivals and special exhibitions than regular activities[18] where legal provisions often hinder sponsoring. The most important reason, certainly, is the higher media attention of these events and of their particular contribution; moreover, an individual firm has more control over the funds contributed, and sees less of it wasted by an inefficient bureaucracy, as may be the case in opera houses or art museums. Sponsors "want a well-defined, high quality event aimed at specific audience" (*The Economist*, 5 Aug. 1989).[19] For the reasons given above, the corporate

[17] DiMaggio (1985) confirms that in the U.S. it is possible to obtain government subsidies to cover the cost of mounting an exhibition. See also Frey (1986) for the reverse causality of deficits, in the case of the Salzburg Festival.

[18] Data from the Ifo-Institute Munich suggest that enterprises do more often sponsor special art events than regular art institutions (Hummel (1992)). For examples of business sponsorship in the arts, see Tweedy (1991) and Perrot (1992).

[19] The car producer BMW provides an example of a firm sponsoring special events. The firm is the major contributor to the Münchner Biennale (an international festival for

sponsors also feel that their contributions add to cultural output, and do not simply induce the government to provide less subsidies.

Career enhancement

As a result of increased internationalization particularly going with European unification, many of the top positions in opera houses, orchestras and art museums are opened to foreign competition. The normal career pattern has thus changed from staying all one's life in one house, and reaching a senior position by internal promotion. The change has been especially marked in the case of art museums (see Schouten (1989, p. 113)).

In order to successfully compete in this changed setting, (potential) curators and directors have to make themselves internationally known. An excellent means is to actively participate in festivals, and even more so to mount a special exhibition.[20] Such an event also opens the possibility of editing an exhibition catalogue whose scientific value is often quite limited (see Börsch-Supan (1993, pp. 56-60)), but which receives outside attention. Newspapers are much more likely to review, or at least to prominently mention, such a catalogue than a documentation of the museum's holdings. As a result, the chance of participating in a special exhibition reduces the quantity and quality of regular documentation, and many museums are rather uncertain about what holdings they actually have (Börsch-Supan (1993, pp. 54-55)). Art museum directors are increasingly chosen from, and transform themselves into, exhibition organizers ("Ausstellungsmacher" is the apt German expression), and move further and further away from being respected experts. This change in the museums' career system may run into problems in the long run. Some museum specialists argue that special exhibitions will run into diminishing returns because most attractive topics have been exploited, and repeating them only yields little prestige and recognition to the organizers.[21] Moreover, there is a rising perception that travel tends to

---

Musical Theatre) and finances yearly Musical Theatre Prizes.

[20]Through exhibitions, curators and organizers may get known internationally within their profession, as the event gives them the opportunity to write about it in professional journals (see Elsen (1986, p. 25)).

[21]An example is the Cranach exhibition in Kronach in 1994 which, according to the *Neue Zürcher Zeitung* (25-26 June 1994), is less interesting and of a lower standard than the 1974 Cranach exhibition in Basel.

reduce, and sometimes outrightly damages, the quality of art works; this makes it increasingly difficult to collect the objects necessary to mount an attractive exhibition.

3 Differences between festivals and special exhibitions

The paper has so far focused on the similarities between festivals and special exhibitions. It is instructive to also discuss the dissimilarities between the two. They refer to location, the relationship to normal activities, and to exchange.

3.1 Location

Festivals typically take place in locations outside established opera and concert houses. As most of them play during the summer season, they often are outdoors. The most famous and oldest festivals have managed to have their own houses, examples being Bayreuth, Salzburg and Glyndebourne.

In contrast, special exhibitions normally take place in the premises of the organizing museum. Rooms outside the museum must meet specific security and climatic requirements and are expensive to rent, as they can also be used for other purposes, in particular for commercial exhibitions of all sorts. Rooms in the museum are used free of charge. To hold an exhibition in the museum premises has the further advantage of being able to use the museum staff, including the guardians, for the special exhibition. It is simply considered a part of the museum activities.

3.2 Relationship to regular activities

As festivals tend to take place away from the home base and outside the regular playing season, the two art forms are quite different. In particular, festivals are unlikely to draw visitors away from the performances of the established opera and orchestra company. If anything, a glamorous and highly advertised festival raises people's interest in serious music and may induce them to also attend the local art performing venues.[22] A side-effect is that the visitors have higher expectations concerning quality and professionality of the local performers. They may realize that they are sometimes far from top class, which tends to reduce attendance.[23]

Special exhibitions, in contrast, tend to reduce visits to the museum's collection. People flock to the extraordinary event and often disregard the masterpieces of the permanent collection, probably because they think that they can visit it at some (unspecified) later date. Montebello (1981) describes this kind of competition from his own experience. In the long run, however, blockbuster and other grand exhibitions are likely to raise interest in art (see Conforti (1986)). Again, the publicity by the media plays a significant role.[24] Another contributing factor is that persons who are unfamiliar with culture lose their fear of entering a museum, i.e. the social barriers are reduced by the more welcoming special exhibitions. Again, the special event may have raised visitors' expectations to such an extent that the quality of the local permanent collection is a disappointment to them. This is not necessarily to the organizers' disadvantage, because it may serve as an argument to get additional funds for purchases from the government.

3.3 Exchange

Music festivals are able to get their administrative and technical staff as well as the artists from the open market, and can therefore organize themselves quite independently of the regular house. The organizers of special exhibitions, on the other hand, must for the reasons given above, be embedded in a system of exchange. This is a major reason why special exhibitions must be closely attached to art museums, because the latter's collection is

[22]There exists a similar complementary relationship with special sports events. A football world championship makes many people interested in this sport who would otherwise not care. Empirical evidence suggests that TV-reporting of football plays raises, rather than reduces attendance in subsequent games, i.e. complementarity outweighs the substitution effect (Gärtner and Pommerehne (1978)).

[23]High expectations are also produced by phonograph, radio and TV recordings and are therefore difficult to distinguish from the effect produced by the local festival. In any case, the raise in expectations enhances the "superstar effect." See Rosen (1981), Horowitz (1983), Adler (1985).

[24]The 1993 report on museums and galleries of the National Audit Office mentions exhibitions as activities promoting the interests of these institutions.

needed to offer art works in exchange. If a special exhibition were arranged independently of an art museum, it would be impossible to get the exhibits from other museums, as they do not lend their treasures on the open market. The only source for exhibits would then be from private collectors, who are generally averse to such "commercialization," or would ask high renting prices. Private collectors are, in contrast, prepared to rent to special exhibitions arranged by major museums because the art objects lent take part in the museum's prestige, and their authenticity is raised.

4 Concluding remarks

This paper endeavours to explain the boom in the number of music festivals and special exhibitions to a common set of factors amenable to economic analysis. On the demand side, the major factors identified were: the rising interest in cultural events in general (a positive and sizeable income elasticity of demand); the opening up of such events to groups of persons so far not patronizing the arts; providing for specialized cultural tastes (i.e. exploiting niches of demand); newsworthiness and publicity – going with rising importance of the electronic and print media; lowering of consumption cost, due to an efficient combination of art with tourism; the possibility to raise revenue by asking higher entry prices, because of the low price elasticity of demand due to tourists; and the increasing awareness of local business that festivals and special exhibitions can be commercially exploited. On the supply side, the major factors supporting the rise in festivals and special exhibitions are: the possibility of staging these events at lower cost than in the established venues (essentially, no fixed cost have to be carried); the larger scope for artistic creativity; increased possibilities to evade conventions of taste and government and trade union restrictions; the increasing role of corporate sponsoring; and the change in the career patterns in art institutions, favouring cultural events receiving outside attention and publicity.

Does this mean that festivals and special exhibitions are going to dominate cultural events completely in the future? There are various reasons why this is not to be expected. Certainly, these special cultural events are here to stay, but they will become less and less "special." As a result, the gap now existing between traditional venues and special events is due to narrow in the future. The brunt of the demand for festivals and special exhibitions will be carried by an increasing share of the population attending such events, which were earlier the province of the select few. Closely related, the cost of attending special cultural occasions will be further lowered by an increasingly efficient merging of tourism and art consumption. There will also be some leeway to care for niches of special tastes, but it will be increasingly difficult to mount original new art exhibitions – especially large ones – and music festivals. However, it is to be expected that new, so far unknown, forms of art presentation will be invented not least as a result of the changed career patterns of art producers.

The major factors curbing on the rapid future growth in festivals and special exhibitions is likely to come from the supply side. The advantage of comparatively low production cost is lost, the larger the number of such special cultural events is. They are no longer able to draw on the resources of the traditional venues at low or even nominal cost, because an increasing share of artistic performers have become free lance as a result of the great opportunities offered by festivals and special events. Even more importantly, as these special events become a regular feature, the supervisors of established opera houses, concert halls and art museums react and will force the organizers of special cultural events to participate in the fixed cost. Many of the best known and most prestigious festivals have become fully established: they often have buildings of their own and an increasing number of permanent staff. They now share many features with conventional opera and concert houses: they have to cope with increasing government and trade union regulations and interferences, and they rely ever more on a fixed set of visitors with expectations shaped by the respective festival's tradition. As a result, many of the "old" festivals have become victims of their own success, and find it difficult or impossible to engage in new artistic endeavours. Not surprisingly, some of the "old" festivals have given birth to new festivals, trying to evade the conventions and bureaucratic restrictions, and to break new artistic ground.[25]

The situation is similar with art museums. As special exhibitions become the rule rather than the exception, there is pressure to have them carry the whole cost, and to subject them to the same government and trade union

[25]Examples are the "incontri musicali fuori programma" existing since 1978 in the context of the Spoleto festival (Galeotti (1992, p. 128)), or the various "Fringes" at the Edinburgh festival. However, it seems that even part of the Fringe in Edinburgh has already become established again.

regulations as the other museum activities. The supervising ministries have already started to interfere in the exchange lending of art objects and have restricted it. Corporate sponsoring which, in the past, has been one of the major factors supporting festivals and special exhibitions, is also due to be of lesser importance. With the large increase in the number of special cultural events, each particular effort is less likely to receive substantial sums. Moreover, the more special events become regular, the smaller is media attention. The influence of sponsors will be reduced the more government and trade union regulations intrude, so that prospective sponsors have an incentive to look for new ways to gain publicity. This may be the new, yet unknown, forms of art presentation, but also of other activities such as, recently, the support of meetings of homosexuals or of other minorities (often called "festivals") .

Even if the rapid rise in festivals and special exhibitions cannot be expected to persist, they have had a strong and lasting impact on the art world. On the demand side, it has opened up art to an increasing share of the population. This "popularization" may not be in the interest of some art suppliers and art lovers, but from the point of view of caring for individual preferences, it is a considerable achievement. On the supply side, the increased competition between producers of art has transformed career patterns at (European) opera houses, orchestras and art museums, and has led to a new attitude towards potential and actual art consumers. By subjecting art producers at least partly to the market, it has also favoured more efficient forms of organization and production in the world of art.

5 References

Adler, M. (1985), Stardom and talent, *American Economic Review*, 75, 208-12.

Anderson, R.C. (1974), Paintings as an investment, *Economic Inquiry*, 12, 13-26.

Baumol, H. and W.J. Baumol (1984), The mass media and the cost disease, in W.S. Hendon, N. Grant and D.V. Shaw (eds.), *The Economics of Cultural Industries*, Akron: Association for Cultural Economics.

Baumol, W.J. and H. Baumol (1992), On the economics of musical composition in Mozart's Vienna, C.V. Starr Center for Applied Economics, New York University.

Baumol, W.J. (1986), Unnatural value: or art investment as floating crap game, *American Economic Review*, 76, 10-14.

Baumol, W.J. and W.G. Bowen (1966), *Performing Arts. The Economic Dilemma*, Cambridge, Mass.: Twentieth Century Fund.

Bayart, D. and P.-J. Benghozi (1993), *Le Tournant Commercial des Musées en France et à l'Etranger*, Paris: La Documentation Française.

Becker, G.S. (1976), *The Economic Approach to Human Behavior*, Chicago: Chicago University Press.

Belcher, M. (1991), *Exhibitions in Museums*, Leicester and Washington D.C.: Leicester University Press and Smithsonian Institution Press.

Blau, J.R. (1989), Culture as mass culture, in A.W. Foster and J.R. Blau (eds.), *Art and Society. Readings in the Sociology of the Arts*, Albany, N.Y.: State University of New York.

Blattberg, R.C. and C.J. Broderick (1991), Marketing of art museums, in M. Feldstein, (ed.), *The Economics of Art Museums*, Chicago and London: University of Chicago Press.

Börsch-Supan, H. (1993), *Kunstmuseen in der Krise. Chancen, Gefährdungen, Aufgaben in Mageren Jahren*, Nördlingen: Deutscher Kunstverlag.

Conforti, M. (1986), Hoving's legacy reconsidered, (Special Section: Museum Blockbusters), *Art in America*, June, 1986.

Coutts, H. (1986), Profile of a blockbuster, *Museum Journal*, 86, 23-26.

Curtis, R. (1990), Community and small scale festivals, National Arts and Media Strategy Unit, Arts Council. London, 1-10.

DiMaggio, P. (1985), When the profit is quality. Cultural institutions in the marketplace, *Museum News*, 63, 28-35.

DiMaggio, P. and M. Useem (1989), Cultural democracy in a period of cultural expansion: The social composition of arts audiences in the United States, in A.W. Foster and J.R. Blau (eds.), *Art and Society. Readings in the Sociology of the Arts*, Albany, N.Y.: State University of New York.

Dümling, A. (1992), Vorsicht Kommerz! Musikfestivals am Scheideweg, *Neue Zeitschrift für Musikwissenschaft*, 7/8, 8-12.

Elsen, A. (1986), Assessing the pros and cons. (Special Section: Museum Blockbusters), *Art in America*, June, 1986.

Feldstein, M. (ed.) (1991), *The Economics of Art Museums*, Chicago: University of Chicago Press.

Foster, A.W. and J.R. Blau (eds.) (1989), *Art and Society. Readings in the Sociology of the Arts*, Albany, N.Y.: State University of New York.

Frey, B.S. (1986), The Salzburg Festival. An economic point of view, *Journal of Cultural Economics*, 10, 27-44.

Frey, B.S. (1994a), Museum behaviour. The question of storage, *Scottish Journal of Political Economy*, 41, 325-335.

Frey, B.S. (1994b), The economics of music festivals, *Journal of Cultural Economics*, 18, 29-39.

Frey, B.S. and R. Eichenberger (1995), Returns on art. Critical evaluation and psychic benefits, *European Economic Review*, 39, 528-537.

Frey, B.S. and W.W. Pommerehne (1988), Is art such a good investment? *Public Interest*, 91, 79-86.

Frey, B.S. and W.W. Pommerehne (1989), *Muses and Markets: Explorations in the Economics of the Arts*, Oxford: Blackwell.

Fronville, C.L. (1985), Marketing for museums: for profit techniques in the non-profit-world, *Curator*, 28, 169-182.

Galeotti, G. (1992), Riflettori sull'iposcenio: elementi per un'analisi economica del Festival di Spoleto, in G. Brosio and W. Santagata (eds.), *Rapporto sull'economia delle arti e dello spettacolo in Italia*, Torino: Fondazione Agnelli.

Ganzeboom, H.B.G. (1987), Cultural audience formation in the Netherlands between 1962 and 1983, in D.W. Shaw, W.S. Hendon, C.R. Waits (eds.), *Artists and Cultural Consumers*, Association for Cultural Economics.

Gapinski, J.H. (1988), Tourism's contribution to the demand for London's lively arts, *Applied Economics*, 20, 957-968.

Gärtner, M. and W.W. Pommerehne (1978), Der Fussballzuschauer – ein homo oeconomicus? *Jahrbuch für Sozialwissenschaft*, 29, 88-107.

Getz, D. (1989), Special events. Defining the product, *Tourism Management*, June, 125-137.

Getz, D. and W. Frisby (1988), Evaluating management effectiveness in community-run festivals, *Journal of Travel Research*, 27, 22-27.

Grunfeld, J.F. (ed.) (1994), *International Exhibition Guide*, Paris: Editions Parama.

Hendon, W.S., N. Grant and D.V. Shaw (eds.) (1984), *The Economics of Cultural Industries*, Akron: Association for Cultural Economics.

Horowitz, H. (1983), Work and earnings of artists in the media fields, *Journal of Cultural Economics*, 7, 69-89.

Hummel, M. (1992), *Neuere Entwicklungen bei der Finanzierung von Kunst und Kultur durch Unternehmen*, Ifo Studien zu Kultur und Wirtschaft, Munich: Ifo Institut für Wirtschaftsforschung.

ICARE International Centre of Studies on the Economics of the Arts (1994), *I musei Veneziani. Indagine sulle strutture permanenti e temporanee*, Offerta culturale della città di Venezia, secondo rapporto, Venezia.

Institut für Museumskunde (ed.) (1992), *Erhebung der Besucherzahlen an den Museen der Bundesrepublik Deutschland für das Jahr 1991*, Heft 36, Berlin: Institut für Museumskunde, Staatliche Museen Preussischer Kulturbesitz.

Klein, H.J. (1990), *Der gläserne Besucher. Publikumsstrukturen einer Museumslandschaft*, Berliner Schriften der Museumskunde, Band 8. Berlin: Gebr. Mann Verlag.

L'Expansion (1994), En avant la musique, Special été, 481, 32-35.

Mai, E. (1986), *Expositionen: Geschichte und Kritik des Ausstellungswesens*, München, Berlin: Deutscher Kunstverlag.

Maillard, C. (1994), A quoi servent les festivals? *Grandes Lignes TGV*, 18, 65-66.

Merin, J. and E.B. Burdick (1979), *International Directory of Theatre, Dance and Folklore Festivals*, Westport, Conn.: Greenwood Press.

Menger, P.-M. (1983), *Le Paradoxe du Musicien; le Compositeur, le Mélomane et l'Etat dans la Société Contemporaine*, Paris: Flammarion.

Menger, P.-M. (1991), Marché du travail artistique et socialisation du risque. Le cas des arts du spectacle, *Revue Française de Sociologie*, 32, 61-74.

Ministère de la Culture et de la Francophonie (ed.) (1994), *Festivals et Expositions. Le Guide Culturel de l'Eté*, Paris: Ministère de la Culture.

de Montebello, P. (1981), Exhibitions and permanent museum collections. Competition or correspondence? in Institut für Museumskunde (Hrsg.), *Ausstellungen - Mittel der Politik?*, Berlin: Gebr. Mann Verlag.

National Audit Office, Department of National Heritage (1993), *National Museums and Galleries: Quality of Service to the Public*, London: HMO.

O'Hagan, J. (1992), The Wexford Opera Festival: A case for public funding? in R. Towse and A. Khakee (eds.), *Cultural Economics*, Berlin: Springer.

O'Hagan, J. and M. Purdy (1993), The theory of non-profit organisations: an application to a performing arts enterprise, *Economic and Social Review*, 24, 155-167.

Österreichischer Rechnungshof (1994), *Burgtheater*, Vienna.

Pahlen, K. (1978), *Erster Europäischer Festspielführer 1978*, München: Goldmann.

Perrot, P. (1992), Funding, sponsorship and corporate support, in P. Boylan (ed.), *Museums 2000. Politics, People, Professionals and Profit*, London: Routledge.

Rolfe, H. (1992), *Arts Festivals in the U.K.*, London: Policy Studies Institute.

Rosen, S. (1981), The economics of superstars, *American Economic Review*, 71, 845-858.

Rosenthal, N. (1981), Loan exhibitions at the royal academy of art, in Institut für Museumskunde (Hrsg.), *Ausstellungen – Mittel der Politik?*, Berlin: Gebr. Mann Verlag.

Rouget, B., D. Sagot-Duvauroux and S. Pflieger (1991), *Le Marché de l'Art Contemporain en France. Prix et Stratégies*, Paris: La Documentation Française.

Schenker, P. (1988), Die Holbein-Sonderausstellung. Besucher und Meinungen zu ökonomischen Fragen, *WWZ-Studien*, 5, University of Basle.

Schouten, F. (1989), Trends and the future, in P. Van Mensch (ed.), *Professionalising the Muses*, Amsterdam: AHA Books.

Stein, J.P. (1977), The monetary appreciation of paintings, *Journal of Political Economy*, 85, 1021-1035.

Thaler, R. (1980), Toward a positive theory of consumer choice, *Journal of Economic Behaviour and Organization*, 1, 39-60.

Throsby, D.C. and G.A. Withers (1979), *The Economics of the Performing Arts*, London and Melbourne: Arnold.

Tweedy, C. (1991), Sponsorship of the arts. An outdated fashion or the model of the future? *Museum Management and Curatorship*, 10, 161-166.

Velardo, G. (1988), *Designing Exhibitions*, London: Design Council.

Economics of the Arts - Selected Essays
V.A. Ginsburgh and P.-M. Menger (Editors)

12

Economics of Training Artists

Ruth Towse
University of Exeter

I was at the Royal College of Art and 10 years later they asked me, would I go and give them some advice about things. Well I gave them advice. Ten year later they asked me again and I gave the same advice. I notice they never took any notice of it. The problem was they made it into an academic institution. My advice was to get rid of the GCE qualifications, take in people who want to use their hand and eyes. But they need a bit of paper. When I was at the Royal College of Art they said to me: "You've failed the course". They said that to me because I hadn't attended enough lectures. I said, well that's OK, I won't say anything, and if I don't say anything nobody will know I didn't get a diploma because in painting nobody is going to ask for one, and if you're an accountant I would rely on one. But in painting people would ask to see the paintings, not the degree. They don't even look at the paintings these days. (David Hockney, Interview in the *Independent*, 7-11-95.)

1 Introduction

A long-running concern of cultural economics has been the question of state support for the arts. One aspect of arts policy which has received little attention in the literature, however, is the training of artists, and this despite the fact that, in most European countries at least, it is heavily subsidised. The economics of training has, of course, been extensively studied by economists of education and by labour economists but artistic training has not been singled out. There is now a body of work on artists' labour markets which includes artistic training among other variables in artists' labour supply and earnings functions but so far there have only been two attempts (Santos (1976) and Towse (1993)) to evaluate policy on artistic training by means of a rate-of-return study.

Economic analysis of artistic training is relevant to two questions which have attracted the attention of policy-makers lately: the status of the artist, and concern about the oversupply of artists. In so far as status (in any profession) is associated with earning power, there is an obvious link between the two. Training comes into the story because it is perceived by policy-makers as a solution to the problem of low status; raise the length and quality of training, it is argued, and this will raise the status of artists on the one hand, and, somehow mysteriously raise their earnings (because they are now "worth more") on the other. This type of thinking is not limited to the arts; we hear it said on every side. But it is even less persuasive in the arts than in other sectors of the economy. Contrary to what happens in other occupations, the earnings of artists are not related to formal training. Moreover, artists typically earn less than other full-time non-manual workers, regardless of educational qualifications (Towse (1995)). A second point is that upgrading artistic training has nearly always meant that it is formalised and moved into the higher education system; this encourages even more entrants into artistic professions because they receive virtually free training; that in turn increases the already existing oversupply and exerts a downward pressure on earnings. A third aspect is that training becomes more expensive both to society and to the individual on account of the indirect costs of forgone earnings.

In this paper I argue that the main problem for the status of artists is oversupply; more artists are trained than the market can absorb. These issues are discussed by looking at the costs and benefits of artistic training using rate-of-return analysis. Section 2 briefly sets the scene. In Section 3, I discuss training and its role in artists' labour markets, drawing on survey evidence. Section 4 contains rate-of-return analysis of artist training, and considers data from Britain. The question of why oversupply of artists persists is considered in Section 5. Section 6 is a brief conclusion. Detailed data which are used as the basis for the rate-of-return calculations are presented in the Appendix.

2 The status of the artist

In 1980, UNESCO designated 1988-1997 as the World Decade for Cultural Development and published its Recommendation on the Status of the Artist. The vocation and training of artists was seen as an integral part of artistic status. At the time, however, there had been little work done on artists' labour markets and data on artists' employment, earnings, educational qualifications etc. were sporadic or non-existent. Indeed, it was not clear how artists should be defined.[1] Several countries took the UNESCO Recommendation so seriously that they undertook major surveys of artists, which in Australia and Canada led to the adoption of specific policies on the Status of the Artist.[2] In Finland, a series of in-depth studies of every artistic occupation was started by the Finnish Arts Council.[3] Other studies, too numerous to list, of various groups of artists in various countries took place, and the EEC also commissioned overviews of specific areas.[4] In the USA, information on artists' earnings and employment was available from Census data and the National Endowment of the Arts has regularly published the figures over the last 15 or so years.[5] Economic analysis using these data has been undertaken by Filer (1986, 1990), Waits and McNertney (1980, 1983, 1989) and by Wassall and Alper (1984, 1985, 1992). Thus began what we might dub the decade of research on the status of the artist.

In 1992, half way through the Decade, the Finnish National Commission for UNESCO organised its European Symposium on the Status of the Artist. Information from 17 European countries on a list of items including training, earnings and employment was specially collected (Irjala (1992)). This revealed that professional artistic training provision was expanding in volume in most countries, as well as being upgraded and standardised, but also that entry for students into training institutions was difficult, with only ten per cent of applicants typically being able to enrol (Irjala (1992, pp. 228-234)), thus building up pressure for more places to be provided to meet increasing demand.

A recent statement of artistic policy in Britain stressed the need for increased training in the arts (Arts Council of Great Britain (1993)); the Eu-

[1]UNESCO adopted a very broad definition of artists. Researchers have often adopted a rather narrower one, usually dictated by pragmatic considerations. The definition used, however, can crucially determine research results. For discussion of these points, see Wassall and Alper (1985), Mitchell and Karttunen (1992), Towse (1992c, 1995).

[2]There have been several publications by the Australia Council (1983), Throsby (1986), Throsby and Mills (1989), Prosser (1989), Throsby and Thompson (1994), and by the Canada Council – see Canada Council (1984), Siren and Gélinas (1986) and Ekos (1987).

[3]See, for example, Mitchell and Karttunen (1992), Heikinnen (1995).

[4]See Moulin (1981, 1988), Leroy (1982), Vessillier (1988).

[5]They are summarised in National Endowment for the Arts (1990).

ropean Parliament has also called on member states to ensure that all young people who wish to enter training in the arts are encouraged to do so. So training has come to be high on the current agenda in the arts. The view is beginning to prevail, however, that the value of training to artists cannot be seen in isolation from conditions in artists' labour markets; increasing opportunities for training leads to an increasing supply of artists and this probably in fact, has the opposite of the desired effect if, as seems to be the case, it results in lower earnings for artists (ILO (1992); Towse (1993), (1995)).

Work by O'Brien and Feist (1995) in Britain on the 1991 Census illustrates these issues. There were almost 180,000 economically active artists, designers, actors, entertainers, stage managers, producers, directors and musicians in cultural occupations in 1991, of whom only 28 per cent had obtained a qualification after the age of 18. On the other hand, 190,000 individuals held qualifications at degree level or above in visual arts and design, music, drama and combined arts, of whom over three-quarters were aged between 30 and 34. Between the 1981 and 1991 Census, employment of individuals in cultural occupations rose by 12 percent and self-employment rose by 81 percent (O'Brien and Feist (1995)), there being a growing proportion of cultural sector work in the economy. Figures on the number of students undertaking training and on state subsidy to training in England are published by the Higher Education Funding Council for England. In 1992 there were over 53,000 full-time (and nearly 5,000 part-time) taught students doing courses in music, drama, art and design in state-funded higher education in England; by 1994 these figures had risen to nearly 67,000 full-time (and over 6,000 part-time) students, a growth of 26 percent. This spectacular increase in only two years took place during a massive expansion of higher education and at a time when public funding per student place in British higher education was being cut, and while a policy of gradually replacing state student maintenance grants by loans was introduced. The increase in student numbers caused a rise on average of nearly 20 percent of the outlay on arts training in England between 1992-3 and 1994-5 (see Table A1 in the Appendix, where details of the funding system are also provided). But this is an average figure for all types of higher education institutions; the cost per place in many specialist arts training colleges was considerably higher (see Table A2).

One way of tackling the question of the value of increased provision of artistic training is to look at rates of return to expenditure on training using the standard human capital model: the private rate-of-return to the individual and the social rate-of-return to society at large. Studies of rates of return to artistic training are, however, few and far between. Apart from my own study of classically-trained singers in Britain in the 1980s (Towse (1993)), the only other one I know of, on singers and dancers, was done by Santos (1976). Santos found that the private rate-of-return to training for singers and dancers was negative. I found that the rates of return to a "notional" singer were low but positive:[6] the private rate-of-return in the 1980's was 4 per cent with the social rate-of-return being 1.7 per cent (Towse (1993, p. 227)); that compared with a private rate-of-return taken over all higher education in Britain in the early 1980s of 20 per cent, and social rates of return varying from 12 per cent to below zero, depending on the subject studied (see Clark and Tarsh (1987)).

3 Training and artists' labour markets

The aptly named "Diploma Disease" is becoming increasingly prevalent in the arts. Historically, artists usually undertook some form of apprenticeship or on-the-job training. It is really only with the growth of state-subsidised higher education in the last few decades that training has become formal, off-the-job, and provided in institutions of higher education – universities, drama, music and art colleges, ballet and film schools etc. The upgrading of artists' training, such as that called for by UNESCO and the European Parliament, usually implies that training becomes academicised and carries increasingly prestigious paper qualifications.

There is now a considerable body of evidence on the role of training in artists' labour markets. That suggests: first, that significant numbers of practising professional artists and craftspeople do not actually have formal qualifications in their artistic field; secondly, that the "screening hypothesis" does not work in artists' labour markets, partly because many artists, partic-

[6] The "notional" singer was so designated because I lacked true survey data on individual singers' length of study and earnings; what I had were the "typical" duration professional training for singers, data on earnings, and a lot of anecdotal evidence on career length. Despite the shortcomings, I am confident that I obtained a reasonable accurate picture of singers' earnings. I use the term "notional" artist in this paper in the same way.

ularly creative artists and craftspeople are self-employed, and partly because talent anyway cannot be measured by paper qualifications; and thirdly, that artists' earnings from their work in the arts are not determined by either the length of training, the level of educational attainment, nor years of acquired experience. Fourthly, artists' earnings from art work do not rise with age. In short, the human capital model does not apply in the arts. These points are discussed in more detail in Throsby and Towse (1994) and Towse (1995). However, artists' earnings from arts-related work (such as teaching) and non-arts work do rise with educational attainment, and, given that many artists are multiple-job holders, they have an incentive to acquire paper qualifications for that other work (Throsby (1992)). But it is only for arts-related work that they need formal *artistic* training; for non-arts work, any type of higher education leading to a qualification would suffice. Indeed, in a few artistic professions, particularly dance, longer training is actually correlated with *lower* earnings (Filer (1990)). This looks like a case of "those that can do, and those that can't go in for longer training," to paraphrase George Bernard Shaw.

All these findings point to a low private rate-of-return to training in the arts. The question then naturally arises; why do so many young people want to undertake formal artistic training? They do so to such an extent that the great majority do not even succeed in gaining admission. Those who do succeed enter overcrowded occupations where their chances of earning a living wage are low. To which the corollary question is, why are governments so willing to finance places for training in the arts, given that there is virtually no efficiency argument for so doing? These questions are analysed by way of the private and social rates of return.

Progress has also been made in understanding the various features of artists' supply behaviour: what artists earn, how many hours they work, how they allocate their time between their (preferred) art work and their need to earn a living (see Throsby (1994a)). It seems to be the case in most countries in which studies have been undertaken that professional artists earn on average less than other workers with comparable years of higher education/training and of similar age. However, I have pointed out elsewhere that while this finding is valid for male artists and craftspeople in several countries, there are cases where female artists in fact do better financially speaking than their sisters in other occupations (see Towse (1993), (1995)). That this is due to persistently lower earnings for women than for men all around is not the point. I found that two-thirds of all students studying singing in universities and conservatoires were female in 1988 and that far more women than men were seeking work singing. It would be interesting to know if this is the case in other artistic occupations and in other countries.

The gender breakdown of trainees and practitioners is important because it may prove rather vital information in the quest for the "rational" artist. For the overwhelming problem that we face as economists when analysing artists' labour markets is that we are far from understanding the motivations of artists, which like the formation of tastes themselves, are outside the realm of conventional economics. We know that there is some evidence of rationality in the economic sense without having to resort to the old chestnut of psychic income. Throsby (1992) showed that artists' labour market behaviour can be explained by conventional labour economics if dual working is taken into account. Inevitably, the kind of study he did aggregates different artist occupations together. That may mask some of the particular features of each group, e.g. that dancers are mostly young and female; that composers are mostly older and male, etc. It may be that with more data, statistical estimation will become possible at greater levels of desegregation, yielding better explanation. Throsby's systematic surveys of Australian artists over the last decade have certainly proved their worth, and it is clear that important information on artist behaviour can be gleaned from surveys which could not be obtained from census or other such official data sources.

4 Rate-of-return analysis

Rates-of-return are calculated from the costs of training and lifetime earnings. The internal rate-of-return, r, is found by solving:

$$\sum_{t=a}^{R}(E_t - C_t)/(1+r)^t = 0 \tag{1}$$

where E are earnings, C the cost of training and t the number of years devoted to training and work; a is the age at which training commences and R is retirement age. C may represent private or social costs, depending on whether it is the private or social rate-of-return that is to be calculated; later on, C_P is used to denote private costs and C_S social costs. In many areas of work, R is usually 60 or 65; in the arts there is no set retirement age so

R could be larger or smaller than 60; a is normally 18 when training takes place in an institution of higher education.

4.1 The private rate-of-return

Human capital theory tells us that individuals have an incentive to invest in training up to the point at which the private rate-of-return of the benefits over the costs of training is at least equal to the going interest rate, or some other measure of the return on capital. In a perfect world, rates of return to different types of training would equalise with the duration and costs of training, wage rates and other returns adjusting. The market would sort people into occupations according to the principle of equal net advantage. Oversupply is a disequilibrium outcome. Although labour markets are far indeed from being perfect, age earnings profiles are nevertheless generally well-behaved, showing higher incomes awarded to those with a greater investment in training. Not so in the arts. The theory recognises the consumption benefits of training which, indeed, may be considerably higher in the arts than in other fields. Moreover, trainees may gain utility from simply trying their hand in the arts, even if they know that their chance of success is small. I come back to these points later.

Private Benefits. Pecuniary benefits are measured by lifetime earnings. The difference between the earnings of people with higher education and the earnings of people who left school at 18 and went to work straightaway is a measure of the benefits of higher education. Non-pecuniary consumption benefits, or psychic benefits as they are sometimes called, cannot be measured directly.[7] In the case of artists, data are needed on earnings by age

[7]They are sometime measured by the gap between artists' earnings and those of comparably educated workers in other occupations. Withers (1985) has pointed out that this definition of psychic benefits is tantamount to an ex post rationalisation. Some economists make a virtue of that approach to the puzzles posed for economics by artist supply behaviour. If one asserts through thick and thin that markets work, that market outcomes are efficient and that all agents are rational maximisers, there seems little left to discuss. Defining artists by a market test of who succeeds in making a living as an artist is like "assuming we have a can opener." Filer is the leading exponent of this Panglossian view of artists' labour markets (Filer (1995)); to Filer there is no artist oversupply, just too many people who call themselves artists but aren't really, just as for Lucas there is no problem of involuntary unemployment.

and by level of educational attainment and also, given extensive multiple-job holding, on total arts and non-arts earnings.

Here we have to rely on survey data in Britain because there are no published earnings data for artists. These are sketchy but, at the same time, they show a consistent pattern (Towse (1995)). A ballpark figure for 1990 was £10,000. Women artists typically earned about three-quarters of male artists' earnings, a figure that is consistent with the gender differential in other occupations. Average earnings of all full-time male adult employees in Britain rose by eight percent and those of full-time female adults by ten percent between 1990 and 1991. If artists' earnings had risen at the same rate as earnings in general (a not very safe assumption – they are likely to have risen by less, or indeed not at all), the ballpark figure for artists' earnings 1991 would be approximately £11,000. That is the figure used for lifetime earnings of artists in the rate-of-return calculation. As already stated, survey data show that earnings do not rise with age or educational attainment, and it is therefore reasonable to use the same figure throughout.

Direct Costs of Training. In most European countries, higher education is virtually free, i.e. students pay only a small tuition fee. In Britain, students normally do not pay tuition fees themselves as they are paid to the university or other institution of higher education by the local education authority; in addition, the majority of students receive a means-tested (on parental income) maintenance grant. (This is explained in more detail in the Appendix). We can therefore ignore the direct costs of training artists in calculating the private rate of return in Britain (the student grant is included as "earnings" for the four years of training). This procedure would vary in other countries, depending upon the system of subsidy to higher education.

Indirect Costs of Training. The indirect costs of undertaking training are measured in terms of the opportunity cost of forgone earnings. Most countries collect data on average earnings by age. Ideally, they should be standardised for level of educational attainment. Data on male gross earnings by age for Britain are shown in Table A3 in the Appendix. These are used to calculate the indirect costs of training from a starting age of 18 and for the subsequent four years, the duration of an arts training course (results do not differ if we take three years as the duration of the course).

In countries where education is effectively provided free of charge, the private costs of training consist mainly of the value of earnings forgone, E_F, during the study period, with B representing the cost of books and study materials. Thus:

$$C_P = E_F + B \tag{2}$$

where

$$E_F = E_F(a, d, L) \tag{3}$$

Equation (3) shows that earnings forgone are determined by the age at which training commences (since, on average, earnings rise with age), the duration of study, d, and the level of previous education attainment, L. All first derivatives are positive. The effect of changing these variables by a policy of upgrading arts training which increased the duration of the course of training and raised entry requirements can therefore be found by solving for the value of $\partial r/\partial d$ and $\partial r/\partial L$ which will be negative, unless artists' earnings rise significantly as a result of the policy.

4.2 The social rate-of-return

In countries with free or very low fee higher education, the social rate-of-return is the relevant decision variable for assessing the effects of a policy of increasing training provision and upgrading quality adopted in order to improve the status of artists.

The social rate-of-return, in the absence of strong (and measurable) external benefits, must be lower than the private rate-of-return because the state bears the direct cost of provision. If quality of training is raised, say, by having smaller class sizes or by improving buildings and equipment, that raises the cost per student and *ceteris paribus* lowers the social rate-of-return. Any change that lowers the private rate also reduces the social rate-of-return. The effect of training more students would enter the calculation via lower (private) earnings which we may expect to result from the subsequent reduction in earnings due to an excess supply of artists.

Social Benefits. Social benefits from training in the arts are much the same as externalities from higher education in general – social cohesion, civic awareness etc. – with the addition of the benefits of taste formation for the arts,[8] the encouragement of a creative, vibrant and critical group of people who enliven social debate as well as being a force for change in product and process innovation; a large and well-trained artistic workforce also maximises the quality and choice of artists available to audiences. While it is not difficult to list these external benefits, it is extremely hard to assign a monetary value to them. The question is how much these outcomes are worth at the margin; what extra public expenditure on arts training is necessary to achieve them? The problems of measuring social benefits in education have long been discussed, though not resolved, in the economics of education.[9]

Social Costs. The output forgone by society while students train is conventionally measured by what they would have earned, i.e. E_F. The direct costs of training must be added to that, as they are paid for by the state. In England, direct costs consist of the subsidy to higher education institutions and tuition fees. Fees are set by a national body and are standardised across all institutions. However, the cost of a place varies according to the type of institution – university, conservatory, drama college etc. – and according to the type of course offered. Fees do not nearly cover the cost of a place, and the balance of the full cost is paid by the state. A more detailed explanation is given the Appendix.

To calculate the social cost of training an art student, the direct cost of providing the place, C_D, is added to C_P:

$$C_S = C_P + C_D \tag{4}$$

where

$$C_D = C_D(Q, D) \tag{5}$$

with Q being an index of the quality of provision and D the direct cost of formal training per student place. In the calculation that follows, D is measured by the average unit of funding (AUCF) plus the fee; student maintenance grants are ignored because they are transfer payments.[10] There may

[8]Morrison and West (1986) and Dobson and West (1989) have persuasively argued the case for subsidy to the arts on this ground in relation to school children; I am extending the argument to students of higher education.

[9]See, for example, Blaug (1987, pp. 129-140) and McMahon (1987).

[10]It is, however, correct to add them into the calculation of the amount of public funds spent on training students, Filer (1995) notwithstanding.

or may not be economies of scale underlying D, but we expect $\partial C_D/\partial Q$ to be positive.

The social rate-of-return is calculated from equation (1) using social costs and benefits. As with the private rate, $\partial r/\partial d$ and $\partial r/\partial L$ show the effect of increasing the duration of training and raising entry requirements; $\partial r/\partial Q$ shows the effect of raising the quality of provision on the rate of return.

4.3 Rates-of-return to artist training in England

Table 1 sums up the data needed to calculate private and social rates of return to training artists in England.

Table 1
Costs and Benefits (in £) of Training Artists in England, 1991:
Notional Graduate Artist Compared with Male with 'A' Level

Age	C_D	E_F	Gross earnings	Net *private* benefit	Net *social* benefit
(1)	(2)	(3)[a]	(4)[b]	(5)[c]	(6)[d]
18	3,900	4,332	2,000	−2,332	−8,232
19	3,900	4,332	2,000	−2,332	−8,232
20	3,900	9,755	2,000	−7,755	−13,655
21	3,900	9,755	2,000	−7,755	−13,655
22	–	12,403	11,000	−1,403	−1,403
23	–	12,403	11,000	−1,403	−1,403
24	–	12,403	11,000	−1,403	−1,403
25-9	–	17,141 × 5	11,000 × 5	−6,141 × 5	−6,141 × 5
30-9	–	22,855 × 10	11,000 × 10	−11,885 × 10	−11,855 × 10
40-9	–	26,399 × 10	11,000 × 10	−15,339 × 10	−15,399 × 10
50-9	–	25,503 × 10	11,000 × 10	−14,503 × 10	−14,503 × 10
60-9	–	25,503 × 10	11,000 × 10	−14,503 × 10	−14,503 × 10

[a]Data on male earnings by age and level of educational attainment from the General Household Survey (seeTable A3 Appendix).

[b]Students are assumed to have received a £2,000 maintenance grant for all four years. The other figures are earnings of a notional artist.

[c]Column 5 is calculated from Columns 3 and 4. In the private rate of return calculationit is assumed that students' fees are paid by the local authority.

[d]For the social rate of return student maintenance grants are ignored as they are a state transfer payment. Column 6 is calculated from columns 2, 3 and 4.

Sources: see Appendix.

In Table 1, column 2 is an estimated figure for the direct cost of formal training in 1991. It has had to be estimated by extrapolation back from the 1992-3 and 1993-4 data (Table A1 in the Appendix) because actual data in that year were collected on a completely different basis (the earnings data are all for 1991 and that necessitated this manoeuvre). Average earnings of males with 'A' levels as their highest educational qualification are presented in column 3; they measure forgone earnings/output. Column 4 shows that students received a grant during their four years of training, and after that they worked as artists typically earning £11,000. Column 5 shows the difference in earnings between the typical artists and the median man with 'A' levels; as artists typically earn less than male earnings for those who left school at 18 with the 'A' level qualification, all the figures are negative. That is the basis for the private rate-of-return calculation. Column 6, the basis for social rate-of-return, includes the cost of subsidy to training artists with output forgone by society, as measured by average male earnings. Taxes are ignored in all the calculations.

Since all the figures in columns 5 and 6 in Table 1 are negative, both the private and social rates of return are negative and thus need not be calculated. They are negative because artists' earnings, even after training, fail to equal those of other workers who have not undertaken higher education. $\partial r/\partial d$, $\partial r/\partial L$ and $\partial r/\partial Q$ could in principle be calculated using cost and earnings data for artists with different duration of training and varying previous levels of educational qualifications, but those data are not available.

4.4 Policy implications

The fact that rates of return are negative for training in the arts does not mean that there is no economic case to be made for artistic training at all. Although training in the arts is often thought of as vocational, there is in fact, a considerable element of general training to it, which may be utilised outside the arts sector. It is clear from the results of Throsby's labour supply analysis that artists' non-arts earnings are raised by their length of training (Throsby (1992)). Many jobs for graduates require only the possession of a degree or diploma regardless of the subject studied. A training in the arts does not therefore penalise students for work in other occupations.[11] So there is a

[11]Filer (1987) has shown that even after they began a career in the arts, artists are mostly able to switch to other occupations without an excessive earnings penalty.

private benefit to artistic training in the economy *outside* the arts sector, as for other types of training; artistic training is not a waste in that sense. The problem for the social rate-of-return is that it costs more to train students in the arts rather than in other subjects, and they subsequently earn less, and so pay lower taxes, than graduates of other subjects. If the cost differential were reduced, individuals and society would be indifferent between putting students through arts and non-arts higher education. While that differential persists, the argument for arts training only as general training cannot be sustained. Although average costs have fallen in arts training in England (as shown in Table A2 in the Appendix) that was true also of all other subject areas.

The type of information provided by rate-of-return studies is needed if conflicting views about the value of different types of education are to be resolved. In Britain, it has always been claimed by the science and engineering lobby that the main reason for the slow growth of the economy is because there is not enough investment in science and engineering training. On the other side, the arts lobby claims that future growth depends upon the service sector in which the cultural industries are the fastest growing component, and that more training in the arts is not only necessary for improving the status of the artist, but also to raise productivity. Rate-of-return studies of different types of training are one way of addressing this question. They could also be used to assess the economic consequences of raising the quality or duration of formal training courses as indicated above if appropriate data were available.

5 Oversupply of artists: why does the market not clear?

A huge literature in economics is devoted to the question of why labour markets do not clear. If they did, rates of return to different types of training would equalise at the margin, with social rates lower than private rates to take account of the role of the state in correcting for under-investment in training by subsidising it.

The persistent presence of an oversupply of artists – the cause of negative rates of return – testifies to the existence of the problem in artists' labour markets. The standard arguments for labour market disequilibrium are adapted here to the particular features of the labour market in the arts. They are:

1. Institutionalisation and formalisation of training
2. Barriers to entry: occupational licensing, trade union activity
3. Information problems
4. Rent seeking on the part of the higher education sector.
5. The role of regulation and subsidy.

I discussed these points in detail in relation to the market for singers (Towse (1993)). They apply in every art form in one way or the other.

1. Institutionalisation and formalisation of training in the arts. As mentioned earlier, in virtually every art form and in most developed countries, formal training takes place in institutions of higher education, which academicise vocational subjects (sometimes even excluding talented artists who lack formal entry qualifications). In Europe, these institutions are low cost or free and heavily subsidised by the state. In some countries a *numerus clausus* operates but in others student demand is accommodated. Students may or may not be given maintenance awards. Such conditions provide obvious incentives to students to undertake training for consumption purposes as well as for investment reasons, and certainly increase the number of people wishing to enter arts occupations.

2. Barriers to entry. In general, longer courses of study for artist training would be expected to act as a form of barrier to entry, even in the absence of occupational licensing. That is not common in the arts, though it does occur in certain areas such as stage lighting and technical work in TV and film. Those occupations for which there is no training and costs of entry are low are probably more overcrowded than others e.g. pop singing (for which, however, there are capital constraints for entry into recording work, if not for live performance).

Trade Unions are strong in the performing arts, film and TV,[12] and there is a *de facto* closed shop in several countries. This is usually achieved through

[12]In Britain, however the BBC (British Broadcasting Corporation) has undergone considerable organisational changes in the last few years which have casualised the labour force and weakened the role of the unions. This is one cause of the increase in self-employment in the cultural sector reported in the Introduction of this paper.

negotiated agreements between trade union and employers' federations and results in a host of restrictive practices on the one hand and adherence to minimum rates of pay for all but the stars on the other. The barrier to entry is that some trade unions set demanding conditions for joining. This is true of the actors' union Equity in Britain and the US.

3. Information problems. We now recognise that information problems pervade every area of economic life, causing market failure. Those relevant to the training of artists are uncertainty about the future in a capricious market (Santos (1975), Waits and McNertney (1980), Menger (1989, 1996)); the difficulty of setting objective standards for gauging talent (Towse (1992b), (1993)); asymmetry in the labour market, with "employers" (theatre and orchestral managers, art dealers, publishers etc.) being better informed than young artists. Students may only learn about their ability and how useful training is during the training process itself; survey evidence in the UK shows that significant numbers of students do not complete formal training courses (Towse (1995)). Training may be useful not for its inherent value but because it fulfils a sorting function, rather than the human capital or screening role, though students may use training to signal to employers that they are professionalised (Throsby and Towse (1994)). Students may also use their time at college for networking (Kadushin (1989), Strauss (1970), Moulin (1992)).[13] These problems occur in other areas of higher education and in relation to occupational choice in general. However, they are probably more serious in artists' labour markets. In the arts, trainees must discover how talented they are; it is not enough to be able. By providing formal, off-the-job training, colleges insulate students from the full rigours of competition. It is the cry of many graduates trained in the performing and visual arts that they were given no inkling of how to set about managing their careers (Towse (1995)). Ultimately, young artists may only be able to obtain information by exposure to the labour market (MacDonald (1988)). This could be called "learning-by-trying." All these factors would lead to oversupply of artists.

4. Rent-seeking. I have argued elsewhere (Towse (1993)) that institutions of higher education in the UK in the 1980s had a financial incentive to supply

---

[13] I am grateful to Pierre-Michel Menger for these references. His chapter in this volume deals with these questions, too.

more training places to students; if that was true of non-profit, state-funded universities (and it was acknowledged policy), how much more true it must be of privately provided training! Rent-seeking is pursued by the "training lobby," which advocates increasing formal qualifications provided by the further and higher education sector, thereby promoting its size and claim on state funds. Regulation of qualifications is also part of this process. Rent-seeking is rife in the arts, too. Indeed, the Arts Council in Britain, whose role is the "arms-length" disbursement of central government funds the arts, specifically included acting as "an advocate for the arts," i.e.. lobbying for greater funding, in its manifesto for the next decade (Arts Council (1993)). The promotion of more training for artists was one facet of this policy of advocacy.

5. The role of regulation and subsidy. In some countries there are other institutional incentives to undertake training because it confers certain rights to social security benefits. In France and Belgium, for example, unemployment and maternity benefits are organised on an occupational basis via the relevant professional association.[14] Membership of the association depends on having received a recognised professional training, and therefore access to social security protection is obtained via formal educational qualifications. In the Netherlands at one time, visual and plastic artists – identified as such by their qualifications – had the right to sell a work to the state authorities after graduation. Another variation on this theme is that graduates of accredited drama schools in Britain automatically obtain provisional membership of the stage performers' union, Equity. As Equity has a monopsony, that is indispensable to a young actor. Wherever artists' trade unions or professional associations are monopoly suppliers of artists' services and membership depends on a training qualification, the incentive to undertake formal training is very strong.[15] These institutional incentives and constraints have hardly been mentioned in the English language literature on artists' labour markets and there has, to my knowledge, been no systematic work on them. That

[14]Carpiau has advocated that this format be adopted for artists throughout the European Union. Menger (1996) in this volume provides details for France.

[15]Equity membership in Britain does not depend on formal qualifications except in the case cited. Membership is open to anyone who has completed the required number of weeks work at the recognised minimum rate of pay. Provisional membership, however, is almost the only way of getting started in acting, which is seriously overcrowded.

would be an important contribution to this line of study. The European Symposium on the Status of the Artist touched on these points here and there but the final publication does not elaborate on them (Irjala (1992)). The labour markets for artists that have been studied most, viz. those in Australia, Canada, Britain and the USA are in countries which do not have this type of social security system and such incentives to undertake formal training are therefore not relevant. It would be interesting to hear more from Continental Europeans about this topic.

The role of subsidy to higher education as an incentive on the supply side has already been argued in this paper. The demand side of the labour market is also affected by the level of subsidy to the arts. Usually subsidy is granted to arts organisations only on condition that negotiated minimum agreed rates of pay are adhered to (Towse (1993), (1995)), which are usually higher than the market would bear.

Altogether, then, there is considerable intervention in the working of artists' labour markets, with each of the points argued above stimulating oversupply. Artists may act rationally but markets cannot clear given these circumstances. The labour market therefore fails to sort artists as efficiently as other workers, and signals are distorted.

What of the role of middlemen – artists' agents, art dealers, impresarios and the like? They are certainly a significant force in artists' labour markets (see Towse (1993)), and it is interesting to ask whether or not they fulfil the same role as their equivalents in sports.[16] The main difference is probably that sports training is less institutionalised, at least in Western Europe, with provision being independent of the higher education system and formal qualifications. In arts labour markets, the middlemen wait to see how recent entrants fare before contracting them. It may be that talent is easier to measure objectively in sports (running speeds can be timed etc.) than in the arts. Ballet is the only example I can think of where children are trained-up for the profession in a school connected to the ballet company. This is another topic that could be explored more. Middlemen overcome some of the sorting problems in the arts, particularly in relation to established artists, but their role is limited because they only have dealings with a fairly small proportion of the artist labour force.

[16] An anonymous referee raised this question which certainly is an interesting one but probably more so in the American context.

6 Conclusion

The main argument of this paper is that those who wish to improve the status of the artist, which they often seek to achieve through more and better training, fail to distinguish symptom and cause. Oversupply is a cause of low earnings and they cannot be improved miraculously by training more artists and somehow shifting demand outwards. Too many people want to work in artistic occupations; they do so for various reasons – the chance of success, fame and fortune, because they value job satisfaction highly, because their training was subsidised – all good economic motives. The focus on training led us to look at private and social rates of return to training to see how they would be altered by policy that increased the length and quality of training. Rates-of-return to training artists in England turn out to be negative because artists' earnings are lower than those of other workers. The position would presumably be worsened by policies which extended academic, off-the-job training and raised entry requirements, as they would simply increase costs without improving returns. Low or negative private rates-of-return appear to have done nothing to reduce the demand for and supply of artistic training in Britain in recent years, however. With cultural sector workers now running to over one in 40 in the workforce of the UK, we should regard this as an important issue.

The finding that rates-of-return to arts training in England are negative in the arts raises questions not only about higher education policy but also about the validity of the human capital model that has dominated economic analysis of labour markets for the last 30 years. What are the implications for that theory of such a result? One that immediately springs to mind is that artists are not rational economic agents. Another line of argument regards artists as rational maximising agents faced with serious information problems about the supposed value of training and about their chances of success in an artistic career. Even if artists are not risk-takers *per se*, they are in occupations in which risk is endemic. They may not realise that fully before they enter the labour market. Even if they are told as much, they may well believe so strongly in their own talent that they are prepared to risk a great deal for the chance of success. Formal, off-the-job, academicised higher education/training fails to fully persuade them of the true risks involved. These factors would also lead to oversupply, and combine with other institutional influences to reinforce that tendency.

Concern about artistic oversupply has been expressed by the ILO and at the Finnish UNESCO meeting (Irjala (1992)). It may be that talk about upgrading training is really a euphemism for restricting supply. However, if raised standards of training are subsidised by the state as part of its policy on the arts or higher education (a more likely scenario in Europe, I would say), that simply exacerbates the problem. If, in addition, artists' pay were to be raised by state regulated arts organisations in recognition of improved training and status of artists, a kind of dynamic Baumol's disease could be set in motion. This may strike some readers as a wild fantasy. I assure you that such policies have been seriously advocated in one form or another in several countries.

7 References

Arts Council of Great Britain (1993), *A Creative Future*, London: Her Majesty's Stationery Office.

Australia Council (1983), *The Artist in Australia Today*, Sydney: Australia Council.

Blaug, M. (1987), *The Economics of Education and the Education of an Economist*, Aldershot: Edward Elgar.

Canada Council (1984), Profile of arts employment, Working Document 525, Research and Evaluation, Ottawa: Canada Council.

Carpiau, S. (1989), *La Qualification et la Variabilité des Revenus des Artistes*, Brussels: European Commission.

Clark, A. and J. Tarsh (1987), How much is a degree worth?, in J. Gretton and J. Harrison, eds., *Education and Training UK 1987*, London: Policy Journals.

Dobson, L. and E. West (1989), Performing arts subsidies and future generations, in H. Hillman-Chartrand et al, eds., *Cultural Economics 88: A Canadian Perspective*, Akron: Association for Cultural Economics.

EKOS (1987), *The Status of the Artist*, Toronto: Canada Council.

Filer, R. (1986), The 'starving artist' – myth or reality? Earnings of artists in the United States, *Journal of Political Economy*, 94, 56-75.

Filer, R. (1987), The price of failure: incomes of former artists, in D. Shaw et al., eds., *Artists and Cultural Consumers*, Akron: Association for Cultural Economics.

Filer, R. (1990), The arts and academe: the effect of education on earnings of artists, *Journal of Cultural Economics*, 14, 15-40.

Filer, R. (1995), Book review of 'Singers in the Marketplace,' *Journal of Economic Literature*, XXXIII, 253-5.

Higher Education Funding Council for England (1993, 1995), *Average Units of Council Funding*, Bristol: HEFCE.

International Labour Office (1992), *Conditions of Employment and Work of Performers*, Geneva: ILO.

Irjala, A. (1992), *European Symposium on the Status of the Artist*, Helsinki: Finnish National Commission for UNESCO.

Heikkinen, M. (1995), Evaluation of the effect of direct support on the economic situation of artists, *Journal of Cultural Economics*, 19, 261-272.

Kadushin (1989), The self-concept of music students, *American Journal of Sociology*, 389-404.

Karhunen, P. (1994), The interaction between artists' professional training and employment in the field of theatre, Paper presented at the 8th International Congress on Cultural Economics at the University of Witten/Herdecke.

Leroy, D. (1982), *La Formation Professionelle des Travailleurs Culturels du Spectacle et de l'Interprétation Musicale dans les Pays de la Communauté*, Bruxelles: Commission Européenne.

MacDonald, G. (1988), The economics of rising stars, *American Economic Review*, 78, 155-66.

McMahon, W. (1987), Expected rates of return to education in G. Psacharopolous, ed., *Economics of Education: Research and Studies*, Oxford: Pergamon.

Menger, P.-M. (1989), Rationalité et incertitude de la vie d'artiste, *L'Année Sociologique*, 39, 111-151.

Menger, P.-M. (1996), Work and compensated unemployment in the performing arts. Endogenous and exogenous uncertainty in the artistic labour market, this volume.

Mitchell, R. and S. Karttunen (1992), Why and how to define an artist: types of definitions and their implications for empirical research results, in R. Towse and A. Khakee, eds., *Cultural Economics*, Heidelberg: Springer.

Morrison, W. and E. West (1986), Child exposure to the performing arts: the implications for adult demand, *Journal of Cultural Economics*, 10, 17-24.

Moulin, R., ed. (1988), *A Handbook for Plastic Artists*, Brussels: European Commission.

Moulin R. (1992), *L'Artiste, l'Institution et le Marché*, Paris: Flammarion.

National Endowment for the Arts (1990), Research Division Note 53, Washington DC: National Endowment of the Arts.

Office of Population Censuses and Survey (1993), General Household Survey, London: HMSO.

Prosser, G. (1989), *Visual and Craft Artists*, Sydney: Australia Council.

Santos, F. (1976), Risk, uncertainty and the performing arts, in M. Blaug, ed., *Economics of the Arts*, London: Martin Robertson.

Siren, P. and G. Gélinas (1986), *The Status of the Artist*, Ottawa: Ministry of Supply and Services.

Throsby, D. (1986), *Occupational and Employment Characteristics of Artists*, Sydney: Australia Council.

Throsby, D. (1992), Artists as workers, in R. Towse and A. Khakee, eds., *Cultural Economics*, Heidelberg: Springer.

Throsby, D. (1994), A work-preference model of artist behaviour, in A. Peacock and I. Rizzo, eds., *Cultural Economics and Cultural Policies*, Boston: Kluwer Academic Publishers.

Throsby, D. and D. Mills (1989), *When Are You Going To Get a Real Job?*, Sydney: Australia Council.

Throsby, D. and B. Thompson (1994), *But What Do You Do for a Living? A New Economic Study of Australian Artists*, Sydney: Australia Council.

Throsby, D. and R. Towse (1994), On labour markets in the arts: some unresolved issues, paper presented at the American Economic Association meeting.

Towse, R. (1992a), *Economic and Social Characteristics of Artists in Wales*, Cardiff: Welsh Arts Council.

Towse, R. (1992b), The earnings of singers: an economic analysis, in R. Towse and A. Khakee, eds., *Cultural Economics*, Heidelberg: Springer.

Towse, R. (1992c), The labour market for artists, *Richerche Economiche*, XLLVI, 53-73.

Towse, R. (1993), *Singers in the Marketplace: the Economics of the Singing Profession*, Oxford: Clarendon Press.

Towse, R. (1995), *Economics of Artists' Labour Markets*, London: Arts Council of England.

Vessillier, M. (1988), *La Situation Sociale des Travailleurs Culturels dans les Pays de la CEE*, Brussels: European Commission.

Waits, C. and E. McNertney (1980), Uncertainty and investment in human capital in the arts, in W. Hendon et al., eds., *Economic Policy for the Arts*, Cambridge: Abt Associates.

Waits, C. and E. McNertney (1983), Income incentives and the selection of artistic careers, in V. Shanahan et al., eds., *Markets for the Arts*, Akron: Association for Cultural Economics.

Waits, C. and E. McNertney (1989), The incomes of cultural providers: a review of current research, in D. Shaw et al., eds., *Cultural Economics 88: An American Perspective*, Akron: Association for Cultural Economics.

Wassall G. and N. Alper (1984), Determinants of artists' earnings, in W. Hendon et al., eds., *The Economics of Cultural Industries*, Akron: Association for Cultural Economics.

Wassall, G. and N. Alper (1985), Occupational characteristics of artists: a statistical analysis, *Journal of Cultural Economics*, 9, 13-34.

Wassall, G. and N. Alper (1992), Determinants of artists' earnings, in R. Towse and A. Khakee, eds., *Cultural Economics*, Heidelberg: Springer.

Withers, G. (1985), Artists' subsidy to the arts, *Australian Economic Papers*, December, 290-295.

Appendix

Direct Costs of Training Artists in England. Higher education is funded differently in each of the countries in the UK. In England all institutions of higher education are funded via a central body, the Higher Education Funding Council for England (HEFCE), which administers central government grants to the whole higher education sector. These institutions include universities, colleges of higher education and specialist colleges, such as music, drama and art colleges. The annual publications of the HEFCE "Average Units of Council Funding" (AUCF) have provided figures for every institution under eleven subject groupings, of which Art, Design and the Performing Arts is one, since 1993. These figures can be used to analyse the cost of public funding to training students in the arts. The AUCF is the amount per student granted by the HEFCE to the institution of higher education but it is not the whole amount of the subsidy because the institutions charge fees. The fee is set by the central government in different bands for each subject area. UK students are mostly eligible for a student grant paid by the local government authority of the student's place of residence; this automatically pays the fee, as well as giving the student a means-tested maintenance grant. Thus the annual average total cost of training consists of the HEFCE's AUCF plus the fee. Courses typically last three or four years, so the annual average total cost must be multiplied by that factor to estimate the total costs of training a student. Table A1 gives figures for the average Art, Design and Performing Arts AUCF and fees for 1992-93 and 1994-5 for all institutions of higher education in England. Average total cost for those courses, i.e. the subsidy to the institution per funded student, is the direct cost of training artists in England.

Table A1
Arts Training in England:
Costs (in £) and Number of Students

Year	Average AUCF	Fee	Average total cost	Number of full-time students
1992-3	1,232	2,770	4,002	53,199
1994-5	2,200	1,600	3,800	66,839

Source: HEFCE (1993, 1995).

By way of comparison in the academic year 1994-95 the average AUCF for Science subjects was £2,565 and for Humanities and Social Science subjects, £1,834. Fees were £1,600 and £750 respectively. Thus the average total cost of funding a place in a Science subject was £4,165 and £2,548 in Humanities and Social Science subjects in 1994-95. The average figures in Table A1 mask significantly higher than average costs in most of the specialist colleges, particularly those offering courses in the performing arts. These are shown in Table A2.

Table A2
Specialist Arts Training Colleges in England:[a]
Costs (£) and Number of Students, 1992-3, 1994-5

	Average total[b] cost		Student numbers		Total cost[c] (millions)	
	1992-3	1994-5	1992-3	1994-5	1992-3	1994-5
Royal Academy of Music	8,669	8,027	345	420	3.0	3.4
Royal College of Music	8,303	7,538	323	401	2.7	3.0
Royal Northern College of Music	7,190	7,395	528	499	3.8	3.7
Trinity College of Music	6,882	6,224	382	353	2.6	2.2
Northern School of Contemporary Dance	–	4,808	56	147	–	0.7
Rose Bruford College of Drama	5,273	4,964	260	337	1.4	1.7
Central School of Speech & Drama	4,822	4,594	225	324	1.1	1.5
Dartington College of Arts	4,954	4,643	316	417	1.6	1.9
Falmouth College of Arts	3,915	3,916	612	639	2.4	2.5
Kent Institute of Art & Design	4,241	4,276	984	1,124	4.2	4.8
Royal College of Art	10,188	10,134	481	485	4.9	4.9
Surrey Institute of Art & Design	3,662	3,578	1,241	1,906	4.5	6.8
Wimbledon School of Art	4,448	4,525	351	368	1.6	1.7
Winchester School of Art	3,993	3,804	406	574	1.6	2.2

[a] A selection of colleges specialising in training in one specific art form.
[b] AUCF plus fee.
[c] Average total cost multiplied by student numbers.
Source: HEFCE (1993, 1995) and author's calculation of total cost.

It can be seen from Table A2 that, apart from the Royal College of Art (David Hockney's alma mater), which has the highest unit of funding, the music conservatories are the most expensive institutions, followed by the dance, drama and art colleges. All these subjects are also taught in a total of 150 other institutions – universities and other types of colleges – but the aggregate AUCF published figures mask the cost of each study area. In general, the other colleges specialising in art and design (only a small sample is shown in Table A2) attract much lower funding per student. Detail apart, what is noticeable about practically every college is that student numbers have increased and it is this which led to the increase in total costs. By "Total Cost" is meant the AUCF plus the fee multiplied by the number of funded students. The total cost to the taxpayer is that figure plus the cost of student maintenance grant.

It would be useful to make cost comparisons of artist training with other countries but I am not aware of any study which present such data. Perhaps this paper will encourage others to do the same.

Indirect Costs – Forgone Earnings. In Britain, data on earnings by age and level of educational attainment are collected by the General Household Survey. The latest figures are for 1991.

Table A3
Median Gross Earnings (£) of Men[a] by Age
and Highest Qualification Level Attained, 1991

Age	Degree or equivalent	'A' level or equivalent	GCSE grade A - C or equivalent
16-19	–	4,332	4,303
20-24	12,403	9,755	9,616
25-29	17,141	13,657	11,985
30-39	22,855	16,863	14,354
40-49	26,339	17,002	15,608
50-69	25,503	16,026	13,518

[a]Data on women's earnings are not available for degree level because the sample is too small. They are published for 'A' level plus but are not reproduced here. 'A' Level, meaning Advanced Level, is the highest qualification attained by school leavers and it is normally taken at age 18. To get into university, students are required to have at least two (but often three) subjects at 'A' level. GCSE (General Certificate of Secondary Education) is normally taken at age 16. Five subjects are required for university entrance in addition to 'A' levels.
Source: General Household Survey (1993)

Economics of the Arts - Selected Essays
V.A. Ginsburgh and P.-M. Menger (Editors)
1996 Elsevier Science B.V.

13

Disaggregated Earnings Functions for Artists*

David Throsby
Macquarie University

1 Theoretical background

It is now generally recognised that in making their labour supply decisions, artists choose, subject to certain constraints, between two distinct labour markets, one in the arts and one outside the arts ("nonarts"). Working conditions and expected returns are markedly different between the two labour markets. Artists generally face insecurity of employment and low wages in the arts labour market, whereas the nonarts market can frequently offer greater regularity of work and relatively higher returns. In these circumstances, it has been argued, artists' multiple job-holding decisions will be influenced by their preferences for different types of work, relative wage rates, attitudes to risk, and their minimum income requirements (Wassall and Alper (1992), Throsby (1994) and Cowen and Tabarrok (1996)).

These considerations are also relevant to the specification of earnings functions for artists. Estimates of earnings functions which do not recognise the arts/nonarts earnings distinction, such as those of Filer (1986), provide only an incomplete picture of the determination of artists' incomes. Filer's study showed that artists' gross incomes from all sources were broadly comparable with those of other workers; however, this result sheds no light on how incomes specifically from artistic work are derived. Wassall and Alper (1984), in an earlier study, recognised the distinction between arts and nonarts earnings, but did not estimate separate earnings functions for each source of

* The empirical work in this paper is based on a survey funded by the Australia Council. I am grateful to Ghulam Badar for excellent research assistance, and to two anonymous referees for very helpful comments.

income; rather, they entered nonarts earnings as an explanatory variable in an equation for artistic income. More recently, Throsby (1992) obtained estimates of earnings functions for arts and nonarts labour markets separately.

Yet, despite the progress in recognising the distinction between arts and nonarts sources of income in studying the earnings of artists, there are grounds for believing that this two-way distinction does not go far enough. Consideration of artists' time allocation indicates that, for most artists, their "arts work" can be divided into two distinct types of labour. Firstly, there is the primary creative labour in pursuing their professional artistic practice: the writer sitting at the wordprocessor, the painter at the easel, the actor or dancer on stage, the musician in performance. Associated with this work, and in a sense inseparable from it, is the process of preparation for producing artistic output, including thinking, dreaming, hunting for ideas, searching for materials, rehearsing, practising, and so on. All of the above activities could be grouped together under the heading of "creative activity" in pursuit of the artist's primary artistic goals. Secondly, many artists also engage in work within their art form which is not directly related to producing creative output, but which is nevertheless associated with being a professional artist. The most common example of such work is teaching: many musicians, for instance, take private pupils in singing or in playing an instrument; visual artists teach in art schools; writers take group classes in creative writing; and so on. Other examples include artists who work in arts institutions or organisations as administrators of one sort or another. Mostly this is paid work, though occasionally artists may contribute such labour voluntarily, i.e. for no monetary reward.

Ample evidence has now accrued that this distinction between "creative artistic work" and "other arts-related work" is a valid one for most artists. For example, in a recent survey of artists in Australia reported in Throsby and Thompson (1994), artists were able to distinguish clearly, in specifying their time allocation between different types of labour, between these two types of work. The mean percentages of time spent at different occupations by artists across all artforms in that survey were the following:

Creative work: 54 percent
Other arts-related work: 28 percent
Nonarts work: 18 percent

It is clear from these figures that the "other arts-related work" category is not insignificant. Further, in terms of earnings functions, it could be hypothesised that the standard determinants of earnings are likely to influence the level of income from each source differently.

In this paper we propose a model of artists' earnings that disaggregates income into these three sources and we estimate the model using data from the Australian survey cited above.

2 Model

Although there has been a lengthy debate in the literature of labour economics concerning the relative merits of human capital theory and various versions of the screening hypothesis in the operation of labour markets, including some discussion of the relevance of this debate to the arts (Towse (1992) and (1993)), most attempts to estimate empirical earnings functions for artists have adopted an explicitly human capital approach. The results in general have been consistent with human capital theory, although it has been acknowledged that the traditional explanatory variables of education and on-the-job experience have a somewhat diminished role to play in a market where the unpredictable and largely unquantifiable influence of "talent" is a significant determinant of success.

In the present context, we accept the human capital orthodoxy as providing the foundations for our model. Two versions of the model are proposed. Firstly, a straightforward linear specification relates earnings from the three sources identified above (creative income, other arts income, and nonarts income) to standard human capital variables of education/training and experience, controlling for other influences such as time worked, gender, etc. Secondly, in view of the dominance of Mincer-type earnings functions in the labour market literature (see, e.g. Polachek and Siebert (1993, Chapter 4)), it is of interest to propose such a functional form in this case, to see whether the peculiar life-cycle characteristics inherent in the Mincer model are reflected in artists' earning patterns.

We define the following variables:

$CRINC$ = annual income from creative artistic work (\$);
$OAINC$ = annual income from other arts-related work (\$);

$NAINC$ = annual income from nonarts work ($);
$TINC$ = total annual income from all types of work ($);
$TIME$ = weekly hours spent at each type of work:

$CRTIME$: creative artistic work time;
$OATIME$: other arts-related work time;
$NATIME$: nonarts work time;

$TRAIN0$ = arts training dummy 0 (no professional qualification in artform obtained); omitted;
$TRAIN1$ = arts training dummy 1 (basic professional qualification in artform obtained = 1, otherwise = zero);
$TRAIN2$ = arts training dummy 2 (higher professional qualification in artform obtained = 1, otherwise = zero);
$EDUC0$ = general education dummy 0 (primary education only); omitted;
$EDUC1$ = general education dummy 1 (secondary education completed = 1, otherwise = zero);
$EDUC2$ = general education dummy 2 (post-secondary certificate or diploma or first degree completed = 1, otherwise = zero);
$EDUC3$ = general education dummy 3 (postgraduate diploma or degree completed = 1, otherwise = zero);
$EXPER$ = experience as a professional artist, measured as number of years since first began practising as a professional;
$EXPERSQ$ = square of experience ($EXPER^2$);
AGE = age in years;
$AGESQ$ = square of age (AGE^2);
$GENDER$ = dummy for gender (male = 1, female = zero).

In specifying the models, we hypothesise firstly that returns to both types of arts work will be influenced by the level of professional training in the arts, whereas returns to nonarts work are more likely to be related to the level of general education. Secondly, we postulate that the period spent on-the-job as an artist is the appropriate explanatory variable to measure experience in the creative earnings function and the other arts-related earnings function, whereas the person's age is the more relevant experience measure in the nonarts function.

In a simple specification of the model, the determination of the three income types might be regarded as independent of one another. However, more realistically, it would be appropriate to allow for substitution or complementarity relationships between different income sources, implying a simultaneous system with each equation containing the remaining two income sources amongst its explanatory variables.

We might therefore propose a four-equation system, containing three behavioural equations and one identity, specified as follows:

Model 1

$$CRINC = f(CRTIME, TRAIN1, TRAIN2, EXPER, GENDER, OAINC, NAINC),$$

$$OAINC = f(OATIME, TRAIN1, TRAIN2, EXPER, GENDER, CRINC, NAINC),$$

$$NAINC = f(NATIME, EDUC1, EDUC2, EDUC3, AGE, GENDER, CRINC, OAINC),$$

$$TINC = CRINC + OAINC + NAINC.$$

The order and rank conditions for identifiability of each of the behavioural equations in this model are satisfied. The model can be estimated using 2SLS.

A Mincerean semi-log form with quadratic polynomial terms on the right-hand side may also be proposed, as follows:

Model 2

$$lnCRINC = f(CRTIME, TRAIN1, TRAIN2, EXPER, EXPERSQ, GENDER),$$

$$lnOAINC = f(OATIME, TRAIN1, TRAIN2, EXPER, EXPERSQ, GENDER),$$

$$lnNAINC = f(NATIME, EDUC1, EDUC2, EDUC3, AGE, AGESQ, GENDER).$$

The equations of this model can be estimated independently using OLS.

In estimating these models, we make a distinction between types of artists. It would be expected that labour supply decisions and earnings determination will differ between types of artists in accordance with differences in the specific artistic labour markets in which they operate. A two-way distinction can be proposed between *initial creative artists* such as writers, visual artists, craftspeople and composers, and *performing artists* such as actors, dancers, musicians and singers. The former produce work for sale, such that in the market for their creative activity they are not paid a wage but rather they receive a lump-sum return (perhaps spread out over time) on sale of their creative output. Performing artists, on the other hand, generally work for wages or fees (when work is available). Both types of artists work for wages, fees and/or salaries in the other-arts-related and nonarts labour markets.

3 Data

The data for estimating the above models are taken from a nation-wide sample survey of artists across all artforms in Australia carried out in 1993 and reported in Throsby and Thompson (1994). The full sample comprised the following numbers of artists by artform:

Initial creative artists	
Writers	159
Visual artists	243
Craftspeople	112
Composers	61
Total	575
Performing artists	
Actors	118
Dancers	24
Musicians (incl. singers)	194
Total	336
All artists	911

However, not all artists furnished income data, and some observations on other variables were missing for particular respondents, hence the total numbers of observations for inclusion in regressions were somewhat smaller than indicated by the above figures.

Before presenting results, we provide some details of the survey and of the artists who are contained in the sample. The population of artists considered was that of practising professional artists in Australia, defined against certain criteria relating to externally specified standards of professional practice in each artform. The total size of the population thus defined was estimated at around 40 thousand. The sample of almost one thousand artists was stratified according to artform and location. The survey questionnaire was administered by interview. The income data and the work-time allocation data collected and used in estimating the models in this paper relate to the fiscal year 1992-93.

Bearing in mind the definitions of income sources and of types of artists noted earlier, we show in Table 1 the mean incomes of the sample artists as revealed by the survey. The distribution of incomes is strongly skewed towards the lower income ranges, and hence median incomes in all cases are substantially less than the means. For example, for all artists, the median income from creative work is \$5,000, from all arts work is \$9,400, and for income from all sources is \$20,000 (see Throsby and Thompson (1994, Tables 16 and 19, pp. 25-27)). These income figures may be compared with data for professional workers in other fields where the levels of training and experience are roughly comparable; in all cases the earnings of artists, even accounting for all sources of arts and nonarts revenue, are substantially below those of these other comparable workers, whose incomes in 1992-93 ranged between about \$30-40,000.

Table 2 shows cross-tabulations of artists earning or not earning creative income by the other income sources: other arts income and nonarts income. It can be seen that about 12 percent of all artists earned no creative income (though they were engaged in creative work) in 1992-93, and of these roughly one-third earned some other arts income and roughly one-half earned some nonarts income. Of those who did earn income from creative work (about 88 percent of the sample), a little more than half also earned some other arts income, and about 40 percent also earned some nonarts income. There are no substantial differences between the subgroups of artists identified in regard to these patterns.

Table 1
Mean Incomes of Artists
Australia 1992-1993[a]($A per year)

	Initial creative artists	Performing artists	All artists
Income from creative work	11,700	12,200	11,800
Income from other arts work	8,500	5,800	7,400
Total arts income	20,200	18,000	19,300
Nonarts income	6,500	6,200	6,400
Total income	26,700	24,200	25,800
Sample size	516	297	856[b]

[a]Minor differences in totals within table are due to rounding errors. Minor differences between these figures and those shown in Throsby and Thompson (1994), Table 15, are due to slightly different numbers of artists included in each case.
[b]Includes some artists not included in subgroups (e.g. community artists).

The characteristics of these artists in terms of what might be called the "human capital variables" – education and training, experience and age – are shown in Table 3. It can be seen that more than two-thirds of all artists have some formal training (including private training) in their art form, though it is noteworthy that it is as many as 30 percent who have no such training, and are practising as professional artists on the basis, essentially, of being self-taught and of learning on the job. It might be noted that the level of general education of artists is significantly greater than that of the workforce as a whole, with 72 percent of all artists holding some form of post-secondary qualification, compared with 52 percent having reached the same educational level in the labour force at large. A marked difference, however, is apparent between artist types: writers, visual artists, craftspeople and composers are significantly better educated than actors, dancers and musicians, and relatively larger numbers in the former group have had formal training in their artform as well.

Table 3 also indicates that whilst the mean number of years of experience is comparable between the two artist types, the mean ages of the samples show performing artists to be on average considerably younger than initial creative artists, reflecting the significantly lower entry ages for members of the former group: for example, the mean age of commencing professional work

Table 2
Combinations of Income Sources
(% of all artists within each group)

Creative income	Other art income Zero	Other art income Nonzero	Nonarts income Zero	Nonarts income Nonzero
Initial creative artists				
Zero	10.0	4.4	7.0	7.4
Nonzero	39.2	46.3	52.8	32.9
Performing artists				
Zero	5.0	3.7	5.4	3.0
Nonzero	50.0	41.3	54.5	37.0
All artists				
Zero	8.3	4.1	6.3	5.8
Nonzero	42.6	45.1	53.4	34.4

for writers is 34, whereas for dancers and musicians the mean entry ages are 19 and 20 respectively (see Throsby and Thompson (1994, Appendix I, Table 4.2, p. 61)). Finally, we note that the sample of artists showed a fairly even split between the genders (51 percent female), a larger proportion of women than in the labour force as a whole (42 per cent female). However, the mean proportion for artists overall conceals some marked differences in the gender distribution between artistic occupations. The highest proportions of women occur amongst dancers (80 percent) and craftspeople (68 percent) and the lowest amongst musicians (31 percent) and composers (18 percent).

4 Results and Implications

In estimating both models, only artists with non-zero work time in each work category (though not necessarily non-zero income) were included in the regressions for that category. This leads to different sample sizes for the estimation of each equation in each model. In the simultaneous equations model (Model 1), the inclusion of different sample sizes for different equations

Table 3
Human Capital Characteristics
of Australian Artists (in %)

	Initial creative artists	Performing artists	All artists
*TRAIN*0	27.1	38.0	30.9
*TRAIN*1	35.0	35.9	36.0
*TRAIN*2	37.9	26.1	33.1
Total	100.0	100.0	100.0
*EDUC*0	5.3	16.0	9.1
*EDUC*1	15.6	26.2	19.2
*EDUC*2	48.4	43.7	46.6
*EDUC*3	30.7	14.2	25.2
Total	100.0	100.0	100.0
EXPER (mean no. of years)	17	19	18
AGE (mean no. of years)	47	39	44

For explanation of the variables, see text.

of the system would not be possible with some estimation methods (e.g. 3SLS); however, it does not cause a problem with 2SLS, which treats each equation independently.

Table 4 shows the estimated earnings functions for Model 1. The model's explanatory power is reasonably good, with significant F ratios in all cases. However, the results for Model 2 were much less satisfactory, and only the results for initial creative artists are presented here, for illustrative purposes (Table 5); although a number of individual coefficients are significant and of the expected sign in the equations in Table 5, the overall goodness-of-fit tests are poor, with relatively low adjusted R^2 and F statistics. In both tables, t-statistics are shown in parentheses.

We can identify several implications of these results; given the generally inconclusive results for Model 2, most of the discussion in this section is based on Model 1.

Table 4
Estimates of Earnings Functions: Model 1

	Initial creative artists			Performing artists			All artists		
	Creative income	Oth.arts income	N.arts income	Creative income	Oth.arts income	N.arts income	Creative income	Oth.arts income	N.arts income
TIME	397.8	564.1	644.9	436.2	592.7	416.7	387.0	568.9	544.7
	(7.6)	(9.3)	(6.0)	(7.4)	(8.8)	(5.1)	(10.4)	(12.8)	(8.2)
*TRAIN*1	-465.6	6592.6	-	-2114.8	1852.4	-	-1247.2	5103.8	-
	(-0.2)	(2.6)		(-1.0)	(0.7)		(-0.8)	(2.8)	
*TRAIN*2	-2162.4	5889.3	-	-300.8	-1389.3	-	-1810.2	3753.8	-
	(-0.9)	(2.4)		(-0.1)	(-0.5)		(-1.1)	(2.1)	
*EDUC*1	-	-	7400.2	-	-	1090.6	-	-	2031.9
			(0.8)			(0.3)			(0.5)
*EDUC*2	-	-	15617.4	-	-	1775.9	-	-	7224.8
			(1.9)			(0.4)			(1.9)
*EDUC*3	-	-	15056.6	-	-	5844.3	-	-	9370.0
			(1.8)			(1.2)			(2.3)
EXPER	80.1	92.7	-	127.2	132.4	-	98.2	109.4	-
	(1.0)	(1.0)		(1.9)	(1.6)		(1.9)	(1.8)	
AGE	-	-	518.1	-	-	192.4	-	-	321.6
			(3.5)			(1.6)			3.6
GENDER	7116.4	6682.6	7355.5	1314.8	1491.0	711.4	5579.2	4642.2	4138.9
	(3.7)	(3.4)	(2.1)	(0.7)	(0.7)	(0.2)	(4.1)	(3.2)	(1.9)
CRINC	-	-0.147	0.069	-	-0.076	-0.084	-	-0.124	0.045
		(-2.2)	(0.3)		(-1.2)	(-0.5)		(-2.7)	(0.3)
OAINC	-0.091	-	0.393	0.002	-	-0.184	-0.079	-	0.244
	(-1.5)		(1.0)	(0.0)		(-0.5)	(-1.7)		(0.9)
NAINC	-0.117	-0.427	-	-0.184	-0.231	-	-0.144	-0.364	-
	(-1.7)	(-4.0)		(-2.2)	(-1.7)		(-2.8)	(-4.3)	
CONST	-1496.0	-1471.2	-34757.9	2402.4	-477.9	-3314.1	254.8	-1585.4	-16420.5
	(-0.5)	(-0.5)	(-3.2)	(0.9)	(-0.1)	(-0.5)	(0.1)	(-0.8)	(-3.0)
Corr. R^2	0.161	0.378	0.329	0.219	0.397	0.253	0.174	0.370	0.304
F	14.6	24.1	8.9	11.9	14.0	5.2	25.3	37.3	14.3
No. of obs.	495	268	130	275	140	101	810	433	244

Firstly, in regard to income from creative practice, it appears that arts training has little significant influence on an artist's financial returns, whereas there is a stronger positive relationship between creative income and experience, at least for the performing artist group. This finding is interesting in view of opinions expressed by artists in the course of the 1993 Artists' Survey concerning the importance of various training avenues to their professional careers. Less than half of all artists (40 percent) nominated "formal training" as the most important means of skilling in their careers, compared with 24 percent nominating "learning on the job", and 17 percent indicating "self teaching", with smaller percentages nominating other avenues including private teaching (Throsby and Thompson (1994, p. 16)). Our earnings functions are broadly consistent with this assessment. Note also that the results from Model 2 suggest that the relationship between earnings and experience is concave, i.e. earnings increase with experience at a diminishing rate.

Secondly, however, despite the lack of any apparent connection between arts training and creative earnings, there is a significant positive relationship in the All Artists equation between arts training and other arts-related earnings, with a further positive influence on these earnings deriving also from length of experience. This result is apparently driven principally by the relationship between arts training and other arts income that is evident amongst initial creative artists. Since the majority of these other arts earnings derive from teaching, these findings would seem to indicate that both formal arts training and experience are important in enabling artists to acquire the necessary skills to practice as teachers in the arts, or, equivalently, that artists without formal qualifications or experience are unlikely to obtain remunerative work as teachers either with private pupils or in institutions. Again, the Mincerean functions suggest that other arts-related income increases with experience but at a decreasing rate.

Thirdly, as might be expected, the nonarts earnings functions show general education to be a strong positive influence on earnings, with a rise in annual nonarts earnings of around \$2,000 for secondary school graduates compared to those with only primary education, a further \$5,200 thousand for tertiary graduates, with an additional \$2,200 thousand per annum for holders of postgraduate qualifications. Age is also a significant explanatory variable in the nonarts function in Model 1. These overall results for the nonarts earnings function accord with the human capital explanation of earnings in the general workforce.

Table 5
Estimates of Earnings Functions: Model 2
Initial Creative Artists

	Creative income	Other arts income	Nonarts income
TIME	0.0601	0.0821	0.0654
	(8.1)	(6.2)	(4.1)
*TRAIN*1	0.4000	0.9236	-
	(1.1)	(1.6)	
*TRAIN*2	0.3281	0.4809	-
	(1.0)	(0.9)	
*EDUC*1	-	-	0.1535
			(0.1)
*EDUC*2	-	-	0.5421
			(0.5)
*EDUC*3	-	-	1.2864
			(1.1)
EXPER	0.0636	0.0837	-
	(1.8)	(1.4)	
EXPERSQ	-0.0014	-0.0028	-
	(-2.1)	(-2.2)	
AGE	-	-	-0.1231
			(-0.9)
AGESQ	-	-	0.0017
			(1.1)
GENDER	0.3654	0.5006	0.2542
	(1.3)	(1.1)	(0.5)
CONST	4.6757	4.6918	8.1319
	(10.0)	(6.5)	(2.6)
Corr. R^2	0.123	0.162	0.137
F	12.7	9.8	3.9
No. of obs.	544	287	143

Fourthly, the coefficient on the time variable in these equations indicates the additional annual income to be gained from working an additional hour per week in each of the three labour markets. It can be seen from Model 1 that artists as a whole gain most at the margin if they can secure work outside their creative practice but within the arts. The marginal return to nonarts work is somewhat lower, suggesting that, whereas artists' other arts-related work demands specialist skills, their nonarts work does not. They are thus likely to take jobs outside the arts (waiters, taxi-drivers etc.) which are less skilled and hence pay lower wages. At the same time, as might be expected, returns to creative art practice are the lowest of all across the board. Yet, despite the fact that financial returns to creative output are so low, artists still continue to want to supply that labour market. These observations are consistent with a "work-preference" model of artist labour supply (see Throsby (1994)).

Fifthly, we note that the earnings of male artists are, other things being equal, consistently greater than those of females. Whilst these equations do not contain sufficient detail on their right-hand sides to control for all possible explanations of divergence between male and female earnings, they are at least consistent with the mass of evidence from other earnings studies in many fields (including the arts) which find a persistent differential in earnings between the genders, even after differential participation rates and human capital influences are accounted for.

Sixthly, the coefficients on the endogenous variables when they appear on the right-hand sides in Model 1 show (for all artists) significant negative coefficients on the other income sources in the creative income and nonarts income functions; however, these coefficients are not significantly different from zero in the nonarts income function. Translating these results, given fixed wage rates, to terms of time allocation, we might infer very broadly that an additional hour of nonarts work tends to displace work in the arts (whether creative or other arts-related work), whereas an additional hour of either type of arts work tends to have no effect on time allocations outside the arts. If this inference is valid, it would be consistent with a hypothesis that nonarts work is undertaken by artists essentially as a means of satisfying fixed minimum consumption requirements. Artists above this minimum constraint will tend to swap between creative and other arts work, leaving nonarts work unchanged as the source of meeting basic needs. On the other hand, artists who are able to lower their nonarts time (or are forced to raise it), for example as a result of changes in relative wage rates, can increase (or must decrease) their time spent working at the arts. These speculations are consistent with the "work preference" model of artists' behaviour referred to earlier.

Finally, turning to a comparison between results for initial creative and performing artists, we can observe that differences between the two groups are not particularly marked. Perhaps the most interesting observation is that training is more strongly related to other arts income for initial creative artists than for performers, as noted above, whereas experience may be more important in contributing to other arts income for performers (though the latter tendency cannot be clearly inferred from these results). Applying these suggested propositions to teaching, it seems that experienced actors and musicians may make more productive teachers than do experienced visual artists and writers, whereas better formal qualifications may be more important in providing skills for teaching writing, visual arts, crafts or music composition than for taking acting or dancing classes.

5 Conclusions

In this paper we have suggested that the simple arts/nonarts dichotomy in labour market studies involving artists may in some circumstances be insufficient to capture the full range of labour supply and earnings relationships experienced by artists. Whilst recognition of the basic arts/nonarts distinction has been a substantial step forward in theoretical and empirical work in this area, there may be occasions when it is not enough. We have suggested a three-way division of working time and earnings between creative practice, other arts-related activities, and nonarts work.

Earnings functions estimated for these three types of labour markets indicate significant differences between them in the nature and degree of influence of standard human capital variables in explaining earnings. The results suggest, amongst other things, that relationships between arts income and arts training may be strong in relation to arts-related activities such as teaching but considerably weaker in relation to primary creative practice, whereas income from the latter is more significantly influenced by the artist's on-the-job experience.

6 References

Cowen, T. and A. Tabarrok (1996), An economic theory of avant-garde and popular art, or high and low culture, Paper presented at Ninth International Conference on Cultural Economics, Boston, 8-11 May.

Filer, R.K. (1986), The 'starving artist' – myth or reality? Earnings of artists in the United States, *Journal of Political Economy*, 94, 56-75.

Polachek, S.W. and W.S. Siebert (1993), *The Economics of Earnings*, Cambridge: Cambridge University Press.

Throsby, D. (1992), Artists as workers, in R. Towse and A. Khakee, eds., *Cultural Economics*, Heidelberg: Springer Verlag.

Throsby, D. (1994), A work-preference model of artist behaviour, in A. Peacock and I. Rizzo, eds., *Cultural Economics and Cultural Policies*, Dordrecht: Kluwer.

Throsby, D. and B. Thompson (1994), *But What Do You Do For a Living? A New Economic Study of Australian Artists*, Sydney: Australia Council.

Towse, R. (1992), The earnings of singers: an economic analysis, in R. Towse and A. Khakee, eds., *Cultural Economics*, Heidelberg: Springer Verlag.

Towse, R. (1993), *Singers in the Marketplace: the Economics of the Singing Profession*, Oxford: Clarendon Press.

Towse, R. and A. Khakee, eds. (1992), *Cultural Economics*, Heidelberg: Springer Verlag.

Wassall, G.H. and N.O. Alper (1984), Determinants of artists' earnings, in W. Hendon et al., eds., *The Economics of Cultural Industries*, Akron: University of Akron Press.

Wassall, G.H. and N.O. Alper (1992), Toward a unified theory of the determinants of the earnings of artists, in R. Towse. and A. Khakee, eds., *Cultural Economics*, Heidelberg: Springer Verlag.

Economics of the Arts - Selected Essays
V.A. Ginsburgh and P.-M. Menger (Editors)

14

Work and Compensated Unemployment in the Performing Arts Exogenous and Endogenous Uncertainty in Artistic Labour Markets*

Pierre-Michel Menger and Marc Gurgand
Ecole des Hautes Etudes en Sciences Sociales and CNRS, Paris

1 Introduction

In the economics of artistic labour markets, some attention has been given (1) to the unbalanced growth of stable organizations employing workers on long-term contract and subject to the well-known Baumol disease and (2) to how individuals active as independent, self-employed workers have to be compensated for highly uncertain prospects in artistic occupations. It has also been observed that, like other sectors facing unstable demand and rapidly changing market conditions, the art world is in search of increasing flexibility, especially when teamwork is required. In the performing arts – the film industry, audio-visual productions, theatres, orchestras, etc. – both forms of jobs coexist: some workers sign long-term contracts, while others hold freelance jobs shaped by multiple short-term hirings with fee payments. Proportions vary greatly from one country to another, but everywhere workers

* We are grateful to Unedic and Griss for access to the data on which the research reported here is based. We owe special thanks to Philippe Cuéno, Jean-Louis Dayan, Jean-Paul Blouard and Danièle Schaeverbeke at Unedic and to M. Courboulay, Maurice Semblat and Jerome Borrel at the Griss. We also wish to thank Louis André Gérard-Varet, Victor Ginsburgh, David Throsby and Ruth Towse for their helpful comments on our first draft. Research assistance was provided by Stéphane Vari at the Laboratoire d'Informatique pour les Sciences de l'Homme (CNRS MSH). Financial support was provided by CNRS through the Groupement de recherches sur l'analyse comparée des arts en sociologie et en économie. We are of course responsible for remaining errors.

often hold multiple jobs, so that the employment status is blurred at the individual level. Multiple job-holding is not the only way of securing income. An original scheme is the French "intermittency" work scheme which combines features from both statuses. As is the case with the self-employed, intermittent workers receive fees and must build a network of contractual relationships. And as is the case with stable workers, they offer labour services entailing subordination to their successive employers; in return, they become equated with wage earners and they are eligible for unemployment compensation.

We study two large data bases on job opportunities and unemployment compensation in France between 1980 and 1992. We show (1) why a highly uncertain labour market attracts a number of job applicants that grows much more rapidly than the total labour demand; (2) how agents in the industry may shed their professional risk; (3) how agents, constrained by job rationing, learn to optimize the use of the unemployment compensation program, specific to that industry.

2 Casual work in the artistic labour market

A core distinction with respect to employment strategies contrasts firms that operate with casual workers and short-term contractual ties and firms that emphasize low turnover and high productivity, bear costs of screening, trying out and training and use optimal reward schemes based on long-term contracts and tenured jobs. The former category of workers seems to be most appealing in firms where jobs are simple and easy to routinize: since workers are indeed mainly untrained and unskilled, wages are low and productivity differences between individuals are small. This corresponds to the secondary labour market where workers are highly mobile and wages are much more flexible than for tenured jobs.

Describing this type of labour force, Okun (1981, pp.82-83) notes however that:

> these weak employer-worker attachments also seem to apply to certain types of blue collar craftsmen who have relatively high skills and earn high pay - construction and dock workers, workers in the printing industry, and so on. These characteristics seem to arise most prominently when (1) an industry has many firms within a locality; (2) a firm has extremely variable demands

> for labour; (3) the worker's skill is 'general' in Gary Becker's sense, that is, readily transferable across firms within an industry; and (4) the individual worker's degree of skill categorized by conventions that develop among employers or unions or through government-sponsored occupational licensing. Carpenters thus may be classed as apprentices, journeymen, or masters; and references from one employer to the next carry weight. In such cases, workers develop an attachment to a local industry rather than to an individual employer.

Okun should have mentioned artists as well as technicians and other workers involved in artistic production. Employment and work organization features in the arts meet reasonably well the paradoxical picture combining highly skilled, highly mobile and well-paid workers moving from one employer to the next while accumulating experience through on-the-job training and highly diversified jobs.

This is especially true of the performing arts, on which we focus our study. Of course, casual work is not the only form of employment. Large organizations operating on a pluriannual basis – permanent organizations like symphony orchestras, opera houses or radio and television broadcasting companies – hire workers on long-term as well as short-term contracts. By contrast, temporary organizations or small organizations use mainly or exclusively short-term contracts. It should also be noted that most artists work under the latter employment form and that non-artistic workers are increasingly hired on that basis, as shown below. People may combine the different contractual forms: for example, musicians in orchestras can also be hired as freelancers for some studio recording jobs, so that the distinction is somewhat blurred at the individual level. In fact, the range of contractual arrangements offers many opportunities.

Okun does not explain why this paradoxical type of casual labour occurs in certain industries. We shall refer to the organizational characteristics of artistic production. Casual employment structure and the corresponding search for flexibility are a core feature of artistic work, due to the "high rate of change over time of the content of activities," according to Stinchcombe's (1968) phrasing in his pioneering work on craft administration of production and structures of activities. This occurs for at least three reasons. First, artistic products are often designed as prototypes and their market value builds on originality and on more or less pronounced differentiation. Secondly, the combination of activities needed to produce a movie, play or opera involves a large number of different artistic occupations and crafts, and each participant shifts to a new project a few hours, days or weeks after the initial one, with some new requirements and challenges. Thirdly, tastes (especially in the most speculative parts of the art markets such as musical hits, contemporary painting, blockbuster novels, mass audience designed movies and serials) undergo unpredictable shifts. Finally, uncertainty can be seen as a built-in characteristic of the creative process. On the supply side, it makes artistic work highly attractive, since predictable outcomes would lead to routine work (Menger (1989)). On the demand side, consumer versatility and taste for novelty give social and economic value to newness and originality as far as these are unpredictable. Uncertainty must be considered as the true condition of the breakthrough innovation that opens to its author a new (temporary) monopoly and, simultaneously, as the threat contained in the destructive aspect of every true innovation.

Far from meeting the canonical dual labour market criteria, casual work in the performing arts therefore allows producers to meet organizational constaints. But as fiercer competition takes place among a larger number of producers and as increasing variance in activity levels requires more and more flexibility, short-term contracts tend to be substituted for long-term ones mainly as a device for reducing overheads. In that sense, work casualization in the performing arts may be similar to that observed elsewhere in the economy.

As stated by Stinchcombe (1968, pp. 260-262), flexibility needed in industries like construction, shipbuilding, ladies'garments, research and development activities or the movie industry, can be reached through three main social requirements:

> (a) a system of performance contracts and subcontracts, rather than stable employment contracts, for subsets of activities. (...) Rather than provide stable job descriptions for permanent roles, one wants to specify the objectives to be reached and let people adapt their own roles to the requirements of the objectives. (...) One requires a larger repertoire of skills in each worker and delegates much more responsibility to him to decide which activity from his repertoire is appropriate;
>
> (b) a system for transmitting information about performance capacities of people between productive groups – a system of certification of competence. The requirement of a larger repertoire of skills and a greater degree of discretion in the workforce implies

> that the workforce must be highly skilled. But the rapid reconstruction of social systems implies that skill cannot be tested and developed in long employment. This combination requires supra-firm institutions for training and certifying workers as skilled;
>
> (c) a minimization of the fixed overhead costs, especially administrative and capital costs. (...) A great deal of reduction of fixed administrative overhead is achieved by subcontracting.

The performing arts turn out to be a good example: for each project – film, opera or theater performance, musical show, etc. – new teams are formed and then dispersed. Networks help to build the stable relationships that are needed to lower transaction costs. They facilitate hiring procedures through patronage and trustworthy ties among peers, and they convey reliable information about skills and talents quite rapidly, since formal screening and hiring processes would often be inefficient and too costly in a casual work scheme.

Okun's characterization deserves attention for one more reason: it suggests that the distinction between short contractual arrangements (at firm level) and employment processes (at industry level) is blurred by the multisided activities of each worker as well as by the dense formal or informal relations between employers. Indeed artistic production is based on three components: (a) a nexus of ties between firms involved in the different parts of the production process and between the many employers who draw from the artistic labour pool, (b) an original way of processing information through this network in order to minimize the costs and length of the sorting and hiring operations and (c) conventional industry-wide negotiations and arrangements regarding wage and fringe benefit schemes. An effective way to overcome the complexities of the disintegration of the production process is to rely on spatial concentration. Storper and Walker (1989) point out that "where transactional relationships between production units are especially dense, those relationships can have geographically-sensitive cost structures. The greater the costs per transaction, the greater the probability that firms will agglomerate in order to reduce them." Again, the prototype character of artistic production meets the criteria of high distance-sensitivity of transactions mentioned by Storper and Walker (1989, p. 139):

> Three types of transactions are especially affected by distance: those that cannot be standardized - that is, are unforeseeable -

> and require frequent search and recognition (these appear where markets and product designs change frequently); small-scale linkages which cannot enjoy volume discounts on transport costs; and problematic linkages that must be resolved through personal contacts or renegotiation.

Artistic activities show a very high level of spatial concentration in a few locations or even in one dominant city in each country. It is also remarkable that even in the presence of active decentralization of cultural public policy, the concentration rate of artists and art professionals does not decline. The Parisian case is perhaps the most striking: during the 1980s, the population of artists and professionals involved in cultural production expanded rather rapidly in France (+ 55% between 1982 and 1991) but the share of artists living and working in Paris and Ile-de-France also increased (from a 45.8% to a 54.1% rate; see Menger (1993)).

3 Short-term labour contracts and the excess numbers of workers

Under perfect competition conditions, labour allocation would not be biased by individual characteristics since labour is perfectly homogeneous: each unit of labour demanded can be supplied by any worker in an auction type market. Actually, spot labour markets with perfect substitutability among workers are most likely to be found wherever simple and routine work performed by unskilled workers prevails. But the artistic labour market highly values individual differences in productivity. Although substitutability among artists and among other personnel involved in a teamwork of course exists, skill and ability differences among professionals are highly rated both for the main creative functions and for less visible collaborations (e.g. film editor, director of photography, sound mixer) to the production.

How can such a paradoxical situation (heterogeneous workers combined with an auction type labour market) work? Our answer takes into account the double-sided – functional and cost saving – requirement of flexibility: employers want to draw from a large pool of artists and personnel in order to build efficient and well-matched teams, to reduce overheads and because they may gain from the variety of talents and skills at hand. However, they do not want to bear the cost of securing workers from risks of unemployment.

This leads to a steady excess supply of workers. Christopherson and Storper (1989), Menger (1994a), Rannou and Vari (1995) show that with the extension of disintegrated production and subcontracting practices, the number of workers grows much more rapidly than the quantity of work in demand. As a result, although the labour market expands, the number of hours worked per head diminishes. Several factors act as disequilibrium forces.

There are no barriers to entry which limit access to jobs as under labour institutions regulating access to jobs like the roster system, nor is there any powerful licensing system to deter untrained candidates from jobbing. Cultural entrepreneurs are increasingly in search of new talents, in order to get high returns from speculative bets on young artists: usually not well-paid, but highly committed to their work, young talents meet the market demand wherever this demand is shaped by fashion and by age-sensitive tastes. Short-term contracts facilitate these bets since employers are free to hire and fire at will and leave aside all the aspects of career building. Thus employers need an oversupply of candidates among which they can sort, once they have an idea about the expected market value of the work of each candidate.

This is the reason why "the artists' labour market will seemingly always be prone to shortages of talented workers while at the same time there may be an excess supply of less talented workers" (Towse (1992)). One should note however that "talent" should be considered not only as an exogenous factor of market success but also as an endogenous factor shaped by competition through innovation. The more competition raises the rate of innovation or, at least, of differentiation between prototype-like works, exploiting and stimulating consumer demand for novelty, the more the sorting mechanism will be based on shifts in specification and search for new talents.

To mention scarcity of talent does not tell us the whole story of disequilibrium in artistic labour markets. Talent needs time to be revealed and assessed; moreover, talent does not refer only to innate, very unequally distributed abilities.

First, professionalization and success in artistic occupations depend only partly on initial training: although there is considerable variation between the various forms of art (writing or acting obviously require shorter and less specific formal training than classical dance or music), an on-the-job learning process that extends over the whole lifetime is a common feature, especially in creative activities, where the hallmark of highly valued artistic work is variety, originality and novelty.

Secondly, even if one were to assume that innate abilities command success much more than formal training, talent could express itself only by meeting training and work situations that reveal the multiple characteristics of what artistic achievement really is and that confront the artist to public evaluations. Therefore we can think of a dynamic model in which workers accumulate skills through experience and learning by doing; at the same time, they accumulate information on how their endowment in skills and talent is rated; this allows them to continuously assess which class of workers they probably belong to (for theoretical contributions along these lines, see Mac Donald (1982), Miller (1984), Rosen (1986)).

If only non-routine work is demanding enough and provides enough information about one's capacities to reveal how well-suited one is to an artistic occupation, the non-routine aspect also helps to explain why people can remain for some time in artistic occupations without major financial or reputational successes. If innate talent were the sole determinant of success and if talent could be detected rapidly, then quit rates in artistic professions would be much higher. Uncertainty concerns not only the first part of career building but extends over the whole span of the professional lifetime. One can never be sure whether one's next picture will be a hit or will at least be held in high esteem by peers. Just because the only certainty in work is that its course always faces discontinuities and a high rate of change in content, one can expect that success will come with the next project one gets involved in. The only certainty is that one will steadily experience considerable variation in and uncertainty about the amount of work one is offered from time to time.

In a casual work set-up, the variety of work experiences, which is highly formative and informative, must be balanced against the risk of unemployment and against the highly uncertain prospects of career continuity. We cannot simply assume that on average people in the artistic freelance labour market are true risk-lovers; nor can we assume that they are mainly moved by such a love for the arts that they could even earn much less without quitting, provided that psychic income is always secured. Therefore we have to explain how workers can be induced to face uncertainty and how they can manage such risky careers.

According to conventional economic theory, a labour contract is mutually advantageous when it provides both parts with insurance against misbehaviour and uncertain prospects. Several theoretical models have tried to capture the informational and temporal dimensions of the mutual insurance built-in property of the contractual relationship. Most of them show that only long-term contracts can meet such requirements to capture intertemporal aspects missing in short-term relationships – incentives to long-term productivity and insurance against wage fluctuations.

In the case of casual work, the risk of unemployment is pervasive and insurance devices through long-term contractual relationships are, by definition, missing. Since Adam Smith, economic theory has dealt with such situations, mainly in terms of compensating wage differentials (see Rosen (1986) and for a discussion of the application to the arts, Menger (1989)). The typical worker will view the risk of unemployment as something that must be compensated for by a higher pay. Greater risks in earnings prospects in an occupation should also reduce the supply of labour. As already noted by Adam Smith and by Alfred Marshall, some risk-prone workers who overestimate their chances of success may view it as an attractive gamble to enter an occupation where a few do very well while most do poorly, but the majority of workers will require a pay differential to compensate for uncertainty about lifetime earnings.

Compensation for uncertain labour prospects is in fact observed in the performing arts since intermittent artists and workers earn much higher hourly wages than those employed on a long-term basis. The wage premium is the price that employers must pay in order to draw on a reserve army of underemployed individuals whose availability has to be secured: a loss of flexibility in employment decisions would be more costly for firms. But, as noted especially by Christopherson and Storper (1989), this compensating differential scheme operates only partly, since hourly wages are not higher for greatly underemployed workers than for their more successful fellows who are frequently rehired and who can build continuity in their career.

Compensating wage differentials therefore play their role mainly at industry level: in industries like television or motion pictures, where contracts are, on average, very short, workers are better paid than in the live performing arts where spells of intermittent work are longer. But individual differences in hiring probabilities are not subject to compensation: here is another kind of risk at stake. That is simply to say that casual work in the performing arts stems from the freelance status of employment, and that artists as well as other skilled workers in the performing arts do build their career on the basis of their reputation. In such a context, accumulation of hiring records acts as a reputation signal in a self-reinforcing process: hiring calls for hiring. As in professional careers (Kanter (1989)), the key organizing factor for a freelance career is the whole community of employers and fellows, but the reputation-based market value of each member in this community determines his individual probability of moving upward or downward. Building a career in the freelance system indeed means that work opportunities are frequent enough and involve the chance to accept more demanding or rewarding assignments: this is the only way for artists as well as for craft workers to acquire greater or new skills and therefore increase their reputation.

Now, as the intermittent working system expands, it generates more competition among a growing number of performers and workers for a less rapidly increasing number of workhours. At any time the number of job candidates exceeds the supply of full-time jobs and the quantity of work allocated varies considerably among the workforce. Since job allocation takes place on an individual basis and involves on-the-job accumulation of skills and reputation, experienced and network-building artists and workers are constantly hired; by contrast, younger or less skilled individuals, loosely connected with the most active entrepreneurs, form a peripheral population facing discontinuous employment and longer spells without work. Christopherson and Storper (1989) have found that, in the U.S. motion picture industry, differences in annual earnings of workers reflect differences in hours worked more than in wage rates. The situation is different for artists, since praise and public recognition of creative talent lead to much wider earning inequalities, based on individual market value and not only on the amount of work supplied.

4 Risk diversification

From studies on artistic occupations we know that income sources can be diversified in three main ways, which are not incompatible and may be combined: artists can be supported by private sources (working spouse, family or friends) or by public sources (subsidies, grants and commissions from the state, sponsorship from foundations or corporations); they can work in cooperative-like associations by pooling and sharing their income and by designing a sort of mutual insurance scheme; and finally, they can hold multiple jobs. This last possibility forms a means of diversifying occupational risk that seems unusual in labour markets. As noted by Meade (1972) (quoted by Drèze (1987, pp. 349-350)):

> While property owners can spread their risks by putting small bits of their property into a large number of concerns, a worker cannot put small bits of his efforts into a large number of different jobs. This presumably is a main reason why we find risk-bearing capital hiring labour rather than risk-bearing labour hiring capital.

Now casual workers in the arts just put "small bits of their efforts into a large number of different jobs," since they contract with various employers for short periods. In facing a highly unpredictable labour demand and intense competition with their fellow workers, artists as well as other intermittent workers have to learn how to build a career by spreading their occupational risks. In a highly suggestive study on freelance composers working for the Hollywood film industry, Faulkner (1983) and Faulkner and Anderson (1987) describe how career portfolios can be formed by mixing one-shot ties, which are the normal feature of a loosely coupled hiring system, and recurrent, "bread and butter" accounts with a few producers: Faulkner (1983, pp. 202-203) shows that such a spreading of accounts allows the artist to hedge his bets, to get information about a wider environment and to accumulate credits as an optimal human capital investment program:

> Accumulating credits is of course crucial but it is advantageous to accumulate those credits through a multiplicity of ties. Quantitative data show us there is advantage in strong and weak ties, and the structure of success is partially defined by that. (...)
>
> First, a career portfolio mixed with one-shot and recurrent ties renders freelancers less vulnerable to the downswings in the fortunes of their producer-employers, let alone the liability of dependence on a strong tie to a single filmaker. Second, visibility and multiple connections combined reassure other film producers. They see their colleagues placing their 'bets' and resources on certain film composers. This commitment is a kind of 'cultural insurance,' drawn upon and imitated by producers when they are deciding which composers they are going to try to hire for their own films. Third, a diversity of film work increases the chances that a composer will face challenges and perhaps arrive at novel solutions for dramatic problems.

This observation has been recently supported by our findings on performing artists in France: with a portfolio of mixed ties as well as with a sectoral diversification of hirings, artists are financially better off and can survive longer on a highly risky labour market (Menger (1994b), Menger, Rannou and Vari (1996)).

Another way to secure a livelihood – that of multiple job-holding inside or outside the arts – is better known, although it may be difficult to gather reliable information on the different categories of earnings combined by artists to make a living (see Throsby and Mills (1989), Throsby (1996), Towse (1996), and, for monographs on artistic occupations, Moulin (1992) and Peacock and Weir (1975)). Such combinations are more or less efficient according to the kind of additional jobs held by artists: human capital considerations militate for arts-related jobs (as demonstrated by Throsby) and portfolio choice considerations for salaried side-jobs, namely teaching positions, to mention one of the most frequent arts-related income source for artists.

The last way of shedding one's professional risks – that of unemployment insurance – is designed to insure salaried workers. In many countries it is beyond the reach of the freelancers who are numerous in artistic professions; in some countries however, freelancing can be equated with a wage-earning position, as we shall see. For those eligible to unemployment benefits, the resulting combination of security and independence at work may play two different roles: (1) that of providing earnings replacements, which reduce the compensating pay differential associated with the risk of unemployment and the uncertainty about lifetime earnings. Actually the position on that casual labour market may be optimized so that each individual permanently combines fees and unemployment benefits; (2) that of subsidizing non-working time which can be used as leisure time, or as training time for a future demanding job, or as searching spell for new jobs.

In the former function, unemployment is seen as a constraint on individual behaviour along a theoretic demand approach whereas in a labour supply explanation, unemployment can be interpreted as the outcome of a worker's choice with regard to job search. Ambiguity also arises from the way uncertainty itself is interpreted: as observed by Drèze (1987, p. 349), "in the case of the self-employed, the distinction between endogenous and exogenous economic uncertainties is not always clear-cut." Should a lack of jobs and an unsuccessful career be attibuted to insufficient ability or to low demand for the kind of ability the artist is endowed with? Consequently, insurance against career failures does raise questions, as we shall show by studying how the French Insurance scheme has operated between 1980 and 1992.

5 The performing arts labour market, 1980-1992

Employment in France during the 1980s rose sharply in the performing arts. Labour demand was enhanced by the growth of the audio-visual industry as well as by the dramatic increase in public fundings for culture provided by the State and by the Local Authorities (Menger (1993)). This demand could lead to two different forms of employment: long-term jobs, or short-term hirings. The latter may typically spread the available work amount among a growing number of agents whose career expectations are shaped by the cultural boom situation. Since the French official labour statistics apparatus does not provide detailed data on employment in the performing arts nor on the two distinct employment forms, one needs other sources to measure this trend.

Our investigation is based on administrative sources. Data on employment in the performing arts come from the Groupement des Institutions Sociales du Spectacle, a health insurance and pension complementary fund which keeps the employment and payment records transmitted by each employer for every hiring period. The data base which we have built out of these records provides extensive information on the bulk of the labour force.[1] As already mentioned, a core distinction has to be drawn between those who are hired on a "permanent" contract basis by only one employer – a full-time job or a part-time job during at least several months – and those who work as casual, or "intermittent" workers and who are successively hired by several employers for extremely variable but mainly very short durations.

Most artistic jobs are intermittent ones; the only true exception is in the classical music sphere, where one finds long-term jobs in orchestras and opera houses (largely financed by state subsidies in France). In contrast, executives, technicians and clerical workers employed in the performing arts fall into both types of employment status. We do not take into account permanent artistic jobs in our data on employment and its trend in the performing arts since

[1] We have no detailed statistical information on artists, craftspeople and administratives working in a few large organizations (symphony orchestras, opera houses, TV and radio companies) since the health insurance and pension fund set up by these organisations is not managed by the Griss. For 1992, this amounts to about 13,000 employed workers, that is, less than 10% of the entire population we are concerned with.

our source does not cover this small part of the artistic workforce; anyway these are a minority in the performing arts.

Tables 1 and 2 show how the labour market for both types of employment status has expanded over the period 1980-1992. The total amount of work, measured in days, has increased by 50% and total wage payments have almost doubled in real terms. The share of intermittent work has increased from 24% in 1980 to 33% in 1992. Since hourly earnings are higher for intermittent work, the share of casual workers in total wage earnings amounts to 53.3% in 1992 against 41.5% in 1980. The case of non-artists is especially striking: hirings have increasingly shifted from long-term contracts to intermittent ones. Wage earnings provided by intermittent work contracts represented 23.8% of the whole amount of non-artists' earnings in 1980, but 40.3% in 1992.

During the 1980s, the number of intermittent workers doubled, contrasting with the rather moderate increase of the workforce employed on a long-term (so-called "permanent") basis. Although they are, in 1992, nearly twice as numerous as permanent workers (100,000 against 55,000), they account for only one half of the total amount of working days (6.7 millions against 13.7 millions). Thus the average annual duration of work is four times lower for casual than for permanent workers. In addition, the activity of the former is increasingly fragmented: on average, a casual worker signs 4.9 contracts in 1992, against 3.9 in 1980.

Competition turned out to be fiercer among growing numbers of producers and workers during the 1980's. Increasing search for flexibility in this highly competitive industry led to shorter labour contracts. Again, artists and non-artistic personnel differ in the way they could adapt to this situation: artists, whose number grew less rapidly, did maintain their average annual work duration by being hired on shorter terms but more often whereas others, who are three times as numerous in 1992 as 12 years earlier, are hired as often but for shorter durations. For the latter, work under an intermittent employment status means an increasing unemployment risk.

In order to understand how a work life can be managed under such conditions, we shall explore the compensating role of a key device, the unemployment insurance program that operates in the performing arts. Since unemployment periods are compensated for eligible workers, the two factors (increase in numbers of workers and decrease in working time per individual) may trigger a growing use of the Unemployment Insurance (UI for short)

Table 1
Characteristics of Indidivual Activity
according to Employment Status

	Type of personnel[a]	No. of agents	No. of employment contracts	No. of contracts/ agent	Length of contract (days)	Length of activity/ agent (days)
1980	Permanent[b]	43,966	51,367	1.2	207.6	244.3
	Intermittent[c]	50,780	200,619	3.9	16.5	63.7
	artists	39,154	163,989	4.2	13.4	55.0
	non-artists	11,626	36,630	3.1	30.2	93.1
1985	Permanent	50,765	59,561	1.2	220.9	261.0
	Intermittent	69,197	285,995	4.1	17.0	69.4
	artists	44,573	208,942	4.7	12.9	60.3
	non-artists	24,624	77,053	3.1	28.2	85.9
1990	Permanent	55,633	63,401	1.1	217.9	250.8
	Intermittent	95,603	462,215	4.8	13.9	66.2
	artists	52,827	327,120	6.2	8.9	54.6
	non-artists	42,776	135,095	3.1	26.1	80.6
1992	Permanent	55,081	62,222	1.1	219.0	249.4
	Intermittent	99,867	489,781	4.9	13.8	66.8
	artists	53,804	349,385	6.5	8.8	56.8
	non artists	46,063	140,396	3.0	26.1	78.5

[a]Since workers can have more than one employment status in a year, we classify agents according to the employment status under which they have spent most time each year.
[b]Permanent workers are those who are hired on longer (fixed or unfixed term) contracts by only one employer. A distinction is made between three kinds of workers in the film industry, the audio-visual industry and the live performing arts, according to conventional agreements: "cadres", or executives (e.g. film director, director of photography), technicians (e.g. sound engineer, lighting technician, stuntman) and blue collar workers (e.g. stage-hand).
[c]Intermittent workers are those who are hired successively on shorter fixed term contracts by several employers. Artists in our data (e.g. musicians, actors, dancers, choreographers) are only those hired on such an intermittency basis.
Source: GRISS.

Table 2
Trends in Activity: 1980-1992
(increases in %)

Type of personnel	No. of wordays	Total wages	No. of agents	No. of contracts
Permanent	28	59	25	21
Intermittent	106	153	97	144
artists	42	86	37	113
non artists	234	241	296	283
Total population	46	97	64	119

Source: GRISS.

compensation system as well as changes in the way work and compensated unemployment periods may be interlinked optimally.

6 Unemployment insurance and its uses

As mentioned above, the situation of the workers who are employed on short-term jobs in the performing arts industry in France differs from that prevailing elsewhere. Except if they opt for a self-employed status, intermittent workers are equated with salaried workers, since they work, even for a few hours, under contractual relationships that provide each actual employer with decision-making authority. The so-called "lien de subordination" that characterizes the position of a salaried employee in the French law is therefore taken for granted, although artists and skilled workers very often show in their work an autonomy that brings them close to independent workers. Like for other temporary or intermittent workers hired under fixed term contract, intermittent employment in the performing arts provides entitlement for UI compensation. However, within the French general UI system, a specific UI Scheme – hereafter called Performing Arts Unemployement Insurance Scheme, in short PAUIS – was settled in 1969: specific rules were designed so as to deal with the pecularities of the hiring process in the arts and to allow workers to alternate work with non-work spells over a compensation entitlement period. Note that this PAUIS consists of two UI programs: non-artistic intermittent workers employed in the film industry (their specific UI program is called hereafter "Program 28") are compensated differently from those who work in the audio-visual industry and in the live performing arts and from artists ("Program 29") (see Appendix for a detailed presentation).

We want to know not only how that specific UI program has evolved as the number of workers increased but also if agents make a different use of it as they are better informed and experienced. The data on the Performing Arts UI compensations and benefit claimants we study come from the French UI Fund (UNEDIC). Our empirical investigation is based on administrative records that provide the unemployment insurance history of all claimants between 1980 and 1992. About 8% of initial compensation entitlement periods (hereafter called CEP) have been dropped out, because of inconsistencies; nevertheless the data set registers nearly 80,000 individuals with more than 250,000 CEPs.

Within each CEP, every period of unemployment compensation is recorded, along with periods during which no compensation is paid ("carence"). The first and last day of each period are known as well as the amounts of daily allowances. Identification and characterization of the individual and information on the employment contract supporting the CEP are also given.

As shown in Figure 1, every CEP (A-B, C-D and D-E) can be divided into three main types of situations: compensation, "carence" and short-term employment during which compensation is cut off (some interruptions are reported but not as working time and will hereafter be called "other interruptions"). We have no information on the working periods (except for their duration); information on occupation between CEPs (B-C and E-... on the figure) is also missing. The vertical bar indicates that the data are truncated (on December 31, 1992).

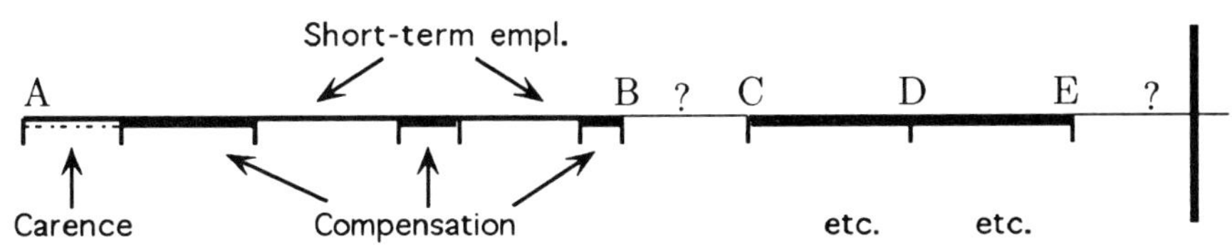

Figure 1: Lifetime structure of an artist

6.1 Total spending and population growth

Table 3 gives the amount of compensation spent every year over the two programs 28 and 29 (values are in constant French Francs 1993). Compensation is multiplied by 8.2 between 1980 and 1992. Both the level and the growth rate are lower for program 28 than for program 29. The annual cost of program 28 is multiplied by 5.2 while that of program 29, by11.1. Between 1990 and 1992 alone, compensation in program 29 increased by 171%.

Growth has not been steady, however. It was lower during the period 1982-85 and increased afterwards, with a slow down in the year 1990. During the late 1980s-early 1990s, annual growth rates reached 19% in program 28 and 24% in program 29.

The number of beneficiaries also increased dramatically (Table 3). This trend partly results from the increasing proportion of potential applicants who actually get benefits. In 1992, 91% of the workers who met the eligibility criteria (i.e. who worked more than 50 days over a year) were covered by UI against only 34% in 1980. The growing number of beneficiaries, however, explains only partly the rise in spending: it accounts for some two thirds of the total growth. The remainder results from increased spending per individual. This, in turn, was generated by two mechanisms: (1) a rise in daily remittances and (2) an increased share of compensation periods over an individual's lifetime.

6.2 Rise in daily remittances

In constant terms, average daily remittances follow different patterns in the two programs (Figure 2). In program 28, the 1980 and 1992 averages are similar (FF 281) although a small decrease occurred between these two dates. Program 29, however, basically shows a significant increase from FF 165 in 1980 to FF 258 in 1992. This accounts to a large extent for the differences between the two programs; but it should be interpreted with care, since remittances are indexed on daily wages. A change in either indexing rules or wages may thus explain the observed pattern.

Average wages have grown by 96% in the two programs, but this may reflect changes in employment and population structure rather than actual increases in wage rates. The wages considered here are averaged over all contracts giving right to compensation, and they may have been truncated if higher than a given ceiling.

Table 3
Total Spending, Number of Beneficiaries and of Days, 1980-1992

Year	Program 28[a]	Program 29[a]	Total compensation[a]	No. of beneficiaries	No. of days compensated[b]
1980	178	185	363	7,089	1,751
1981	255	302	557	9,044	2,562
1982	272	358	630	10,457	2,813
1983	268	381	649	11,968	2,999
1984	270	431	701	12,989	3,384
1985	280	420	700	14,268	3,442
1986	334	464	798	16,286	3,760
1987	370	610	980	18,339	4,558
1988	444	785	1,229	22,153	5,574
1989	568	1,013	1,581	26,323	6,851
1990	616	1,200	1,816	28,940	7,478
1991	760	1,606	2,366	34,394	9,176
1992	934	2,049	2,983	38,250	11,264

[a]In million 1993 FF.
[b]In thousands.

We now turn to the rules governing benefit rates, and denote by RW the reference wage and by DB the daily benefit. Table 4 presents the estimates of coefficients a and b, assuming the following rule:

$$DB = a + bRW.$$

This equation reproduces exactly administrative rules for program 29 but things are more complicated for program 28 so that it should be viewed as an approximation. Ordinary least squares adjustments are run separately for every CEP starting year. The coefficients show that, in the context of strongly asymmetric information, the PAUIS' main line of action has been to adjust administrative rules in order to contain spending. This occurred during the years 1984-86, when the system was still on the edge of explosion.

Table 4
Coefficients of the Wage-Benefit Relations

Year	Program 28		Program 29	
	a	*b*	*a*	*b*
1980	194	20.1	56	43.2
1982	168	20.5	50	43.7
1984	200	8.0	54	33.0
1986	201	8.5	55	31.3
1988	205	7.9	56	31.0
1990	205	7.7	55	31.6
1992	214	7.4	52	31.0
No. of obs.	95,017		159,996	

Coefficients are strongly significant.

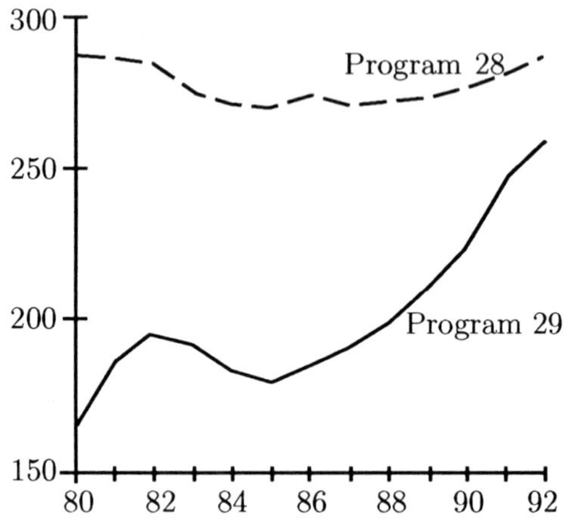

Figure 2: Average daily remittances

Table 5
Changes in the Structure of CEPs

Year	Share of employment time (%)	Share of compensation time (%)	No. of employment periods	CEP length (in days)	No. of obs.
1980	4.7	82.9	4.4	418	8,668
1982	6.7	80.5	4.5	338	10,303
1984	9.7	78.2	6.5	302	13,591
1986	9.8	75.8	8.0	311	19,436
1988	12.3	75.1	9.9	309	25,648
1990	11.2	74.7	10.7	314	25,450
1992	18.7	68.8	15.5	352	37,909

6.3 Lifetime structure

A claimant's lifetime consists of CEPs, split mainly into compensation spells, short-term employment spells, and periods between CEPs during which anything can occur *but compensation.* If, on average, individuals spend more and more time getting compensation over a year, annual spending per head will increase. As a matter of fact, the average benefiting artist received remittances for 247 days in 1980 and 294.5 days in 1992 (see Table 3).

The underlying changes in behaviour are of particular interest. From Table 5, it is clear that there has been a significant reduction in the share of compensation time, made up by increased short-term employment time ("carence" and "other interruptions" show little change).

Employment represented 4.7% of time in CEPs started in 1980 and 18.7% in those started in 1992, with figures slightly higher in program 28 (once again, more rapid changes took place during the 1990-92 period). A closer look at the distributions brings out a very important feature. In 1980 only 36% of CEPs included *some* employment time. This figure rises to 60% in 1985 and to 90% in 1992. Therefore, inclusion of some working time into CEPs has generalized over the period to *become the norm.* This points to a significant change in behaviour, whereby the flexibility of the system has been exploited more and more intensively.

An additional way to measure this phenomenon is to look at the number of employment periods. These rise from 4.4 to 15.5, indicating an increased fragmentation of CEP time (Table 5). Thus, the growing share of employment time does not result from longer employment periods, but from *more employment contracts of shorter average length.*

A specific incentive to report short employment contracts is provided in program 29. In this program, one is credited with 8 hours per working day when the contract lasts at least 5 days long, but one benefits 12 hours credit a day when it is less than 5 days long. Since this is absent from program 28, there is a simple way to show that this feature affects individual behaviour. Consider the average length of employment periods is each program: except in 1980, it is more than 5 days in program 28 while, except in 1981 and 1983, it is lower than 5 days in program 29. There is no time trend in either program, but growing homogeneity is attested by steadily decreasing variance of the statistics (from more than 20 in 1980 to 10 or less in 1992, in both programs).

As the share of compensation within CEP time decreases, growing compensation time per year and per person results in shorter periods *between* CEPs. Take all individuals who had at least one CEP in a given year and consider the number of different CEPs each of them underwent during that same year (Table 6). If total CEP length is subject to little change, this gives a measure of how close CEPs are one to another. On average, an individual had 1.07 CEPs in 1980, 1.36 in 1986, 1.35 in 1990 and 1.42 in 1992. In fact, average CEP length decreased during the early 80's, but increased afterwards, implying stronger reduction in "time between CEPs" than suggested by these ratios.[2]

Measuring the length of time between two consecutive CEPs of the same individual (typically, period B-C in Figure 1) provides a different assessment of this pattern. This is reported in Table 6 by year of beginning of the period (year-end of the first CEP, thus point B in Figure 1). Coupled with our previous findings on CEP structure, results reveal that, in the early 1980s, a typical career consisted of CEPs with no interruption for employment, separated by nearly a year. In the late 1980s, CEPs would be separated by

---

[2]CEP length is determined by administrative rules so that its change is not readily interpretable in terms of individual behaviour. Generally, however, longer CEPs may be related to enhanced job opportunities.

Table 6
Time Between Consecutive CEPs

Year	No. of CEPs per year	CEP length (in days)	No. of days between CEPs[a]
1980	1.07	418	346
1982	1.25	338	279
1984	1.32	302	233
1986	1.36	311	172
1988	1.44	309	140
1990	1.35	314	195
1992	1.42	352	11

[a]By year-end of first CEP.

less than 200 days, and interrupted by numerous short periods of employment. The picture is that of fragmented time, with intricate working and compensation periods and, maybe, less secure situations.

The sharp reduction in "time between CEPs" in the later years results to a large extent from a selectivity mechanism. Consider a CEP that takes place towards the end of our sample period; the following CEP is observed only when "between-CEP time" is short enough (so that it ends before December 31, 1992). In other cases, the potential following CEP will fall out of our available period of observation and the "time between two CEPs" is not observed. The later the year, the more acute the problem, so that the 1992 figure is not meaningful and early 1990s figures should be interpreted with care. This difficulty can be partly overcome when estimating survival rates, that is probabilities that the period between two consecutive CEPs lasts at least a given length of time. When a CEP is not followed by an (observed) second CEP, we consider the length to be truncated on December 31, 1992.

Non-parametric estimates of the survival function can be computed using the Kaplan-Meier estimator (see Kiefer (1988)). As evidenced by Figure 3, the probability that a "between-CEP period" lasts at least t days is always smaller if the period started in 1989 than it is if it started in 1980, for all values of t for which the survival function is defined.[3] The problem with

[3]Other years can be included, but they are not presented in order to keep the figure readable.

this computation is that we cannot distinguish individuals who have left the system for good from those who are potentially part of it and will reappear at some point with a new CEP. For this reason, survival rates do not tend towards zero as t becomes large. Yet comparisons are meaningful for a limited range (t between 0 and 1,500 days in 1989). The result that "between CEPs periods" get shorter is thus confirmed.

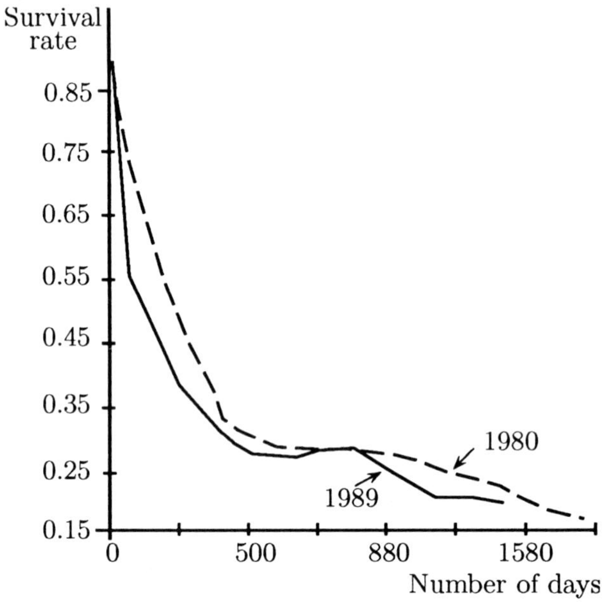

Figure 3: Survival rates for "between-CEP duration" (by starting year of CEP)

6.4 Core population behaviour

The changing pattern of aggregate behaviour may be viewed as the outcome of a time trend affecting the whole system. An alternative would be to assume learning mechanisms: individuals with sufficient experience in the system make a more efficient use of available opportunities. In order to assess this hypothesis, we define as a core population those who were first

Table 7
CEP Structure and "Between-CEP Time" in Core and Total Population

Year	Share of employment time (%)		Share of compensation time (%)		Between-CEP time (in days)	
	Total	Core	Total	Core	Total	Core
1980	4.7	5.0	82.9	83.0	346	705
1982	6.7	10.3	80.5	76.1	279	481
1984	9.7	10.4	78.2	74.7	233	210
1986	9.8	9.9	75.8	73.7	172	151
1988	12.3	11.9	75.1	71.9	140	132
1990	11.2	11.7	74.7	72.8	195	199
1992	18.7	19.1	68.8	66.2	11	18

observed in 1980 and who remained in the system (whether in CEPs or not) until 1992.

It is important to make sure that they are not significantly different in terms of characteristics, other than experience in the system. Statistics reveal that there are less program 28 individuals in the core population and more of them are employed in small firms (1 to 4 employees) and in the Paris area, but the differences are small and the two populations are similar with respect to other characteristics (age, sex, qualification, etc.).

Table 7 indicates that the behaviour of the core population did not differ from that of the total population in terms of CEP composition, except in 1982-84. As for "between-CEP time", it is clear that core and total population follow the same trend although absolute duration is slightly different (longer for core until 1982, comparable afterwards).

6.5 Returns to fragmenting CEP time

Organizational constraints in artistic production provide an obvious demand-side explanation for the observed fragmentation of working time and its frequent alternation with compensation spells. In view of the growing pressure and competition on the labour market for performing arts it is worth considering also a supply-side interpretation. It can be expected that employment periods will act as experience variables and will positively affect wages and the amount of daily compensation. In contrast, long periods of unemployment may be interpreted by potential employers as a negative signal and explain why, in a competitive environment, maximizing agents would tend to break unemployment periods with work.

There are three additional possible supply-side interpretations. First, reputation effects and personal networks may be an important determinant of employment opportunities and higher wages. They may depend more on frequency than on total duration of employment contracts. The second interpretation derives from the fact that eligible artists and workers spend a large share of their lifetime receiving unemployment remittances. According to a job-search approach, assume that an agent has to choose between a short-term and a long-term contract, carrying the same daily wage. If he chooses the first, he will soon be available for a possibly more interesting offer; but there may also be no offer before long or only poorly paid ones. Thus, choosing the long-term contract may reveal insurance securing behaviour. However, things are more complicated in our setup: expected compensation is also a determinant of his choice, and the benefit depends not on total wage income, but on some index of the *wage rates* obtained over a series of employments. In this respect, it will be optimal for a risk-averse agent to seek for many short-term contracts rather than for a few long-term ones: in doing this, his average wage rate will get closer to the expected wage rate. This standard "diversification" behaviour may have to be arbitraged with the insurance strategy first presented, and the outcome will depend on various parameters. But job fragmentation may happen to be globally optimal.

A last reason why fragmentation may lead to higher wages and benefits has been discussed above: employers may declare a smaller number of working days than actually performed, in order for the employees to report a higher wage rate (and receive larger benefits). Since we do not observe actual but only reported wage rates, these look larger if declared working periods are smaller.

A simple way to test these supply-side interpretations is to check whether the number of within-CEP work periods (holding the share of working time constant) during the previous CEP affects positively the wage index on which compensation is based in the current CEP. This would explain why, in addition to the constraints agents face on the labour market, it may be in their interest to have a fragmented working time. Our strategy is to run wage equations where the log of the wage index is regressed on age, sex, qualification, sector and type of occupation.[4] Shifts over time are accounted for by time dummies (referring to the beginning of the contract that gave rise to the current CEP). Three variables from the previous CEP are added: total CEP time, the share of CEP time devoted to short-term work and the number of work episodes. Because these variables and employment characteristics are determined simultaneously with wages, the estimates may suffer from an endogeneity bias. Moreover, as little information on individual characteristics (such as education) is available, there are unobserved individual effects that could be correlated with some explanatory variables, resulting in a further bias. For instance, individuals who, for some reason, tend to have many short employment contracts may be those who have, for the same unobserved reason, higher wages. We would then wrongly attribute high wages to fragmentation. Exploiting the panel dimension of the data will help solve one of these difficulties. If we restrict the sample to individuals with two CEPs or more, *Within* estimators can be computed in order to remove unobserved heterogeneity.[5] Lagged values are sometimes used as instruments to solve simultaneity problems, but they are valid instruments as long as there is no significant autocorrelation between the residuals of the equations, and there are good reasons to expect that shocks should be transmitted over an artist's career (unexpected success for instance). As there are no other possible instruments, they are nevertheless presented but Within estimates are preferred.

Coefficients obtained by OLS, instrumental estimation (2SLS) and Within estimation are presented in Table 8, where we report only parameters of interest. Programs 28 and 29 are presented separately and they reveal fairly contrasted patterns. Interpreting the negative effect of CEP length in all but one equation is difficult because, as already noted, it is to a large extent determined on an administrative basis. In contrast, the share of working time has an expected positive sign in program 28, which confirms its interpretation in terms of experience. The negative sign of the OLS and 2SLS estimates for program 29 is puzzling and the satisfactory Within coefficient confirms that the former two may be biased.

---

[4]The last three variables are based on the contract that gave rise to the current CEP.

[5]To obtain a within estimator, every variable X_{it} where i is an individual and t a period is replaced by $X_{it} - X_{i.}$ where $X_{i.}$ is the average of X_{it} over all periods. Deviations to the mean are thus considered instead of levels and individual heterogeneity is removed.

Table 8
Effects of Within-CEP Working Time and its Fragmentation on Reported Wage Rates

	Program 28			Program 29		
	OLS	2SLS	Within	OLS	2SLS	Within
No. of working periods	0.00119 (4.72)	0.00569 (5.10)	0.00106 (3.26)	0.00453 (23.02)	0.01884 (27.79)	0.00296 (16.47)
Share of working time	0.18372 (8.82)	1.27867 (11.17)	0.09295 (4.51)	-0.12643 (-6.14)	-1.00813 (-10.37)	0.14350 (8.18)
CEP length (in days)	-0.00003 (-2.47)	-0.00065 (-11.50)	0.00003 (1.74)	-0.00017 (-14.77)	0.00096 (-14.79)	-0.00010 (-8.11)
No. of obs.	48,032	48,032	33,728	71,269	71,269	46,629
R^2	0.12	0.11	0.10	0.15	0.14	0.15

The dependent variable is the log of the reference wage index.

Most interesting is the very significant positive effect of the number of working periods. This implies that not only total working time matters, but also the extent to which it is fragmented. Based on the Within estimates, splitting the same amount of working time into 5 periods instead of 1, for instance, would raise the wage by 0.4% in program 28 and 1.2% in program 29. Moving from the average 4 periods in 1980 to the average 15 periods in 1992 would increase the wage by 1.2% and 3.3% respectively. These increases are not extremely large, but it is striking that fragmentation should have an effect at all.

The above equations do not help to explain why the number of working periods (thus the time fragmentation) has increased over time. It would be more convincing to make it clear that the returns to fragmentation have been rising with time. To do this, we allow the coefficients to vary every year. OLS results are reported in Table 9. The positive effect starts in 1982-83, increasing slightly in 1990-92 in program 29. The effect appears later in program 28 (1988) and decreases. The effect is now sizeable in program 29 since in the years 1990-92, a shift from 1 to 5 working periods would

Table 9
Effects of the Number of Employment Periods
on Reported Wage Rates over Time

Starting year of CEP	Program 28	Program 29
1980	0.00203	-0.00071
1982	-0.00061	0.00294[a]
1984	-0.00011	0.00428[a]
1986	0.00139	0.00388[a]
1988	0.00243[a]	0.00305[a]
1990	0.00146[a]	0.00589[a]
1992	0.00158[a]	0.00558[a]
R^2	0.12	0.15

[a]Significantly different from zero.
The dependent variable is the log of the reference wage index.

raise wage rates by about 2.4%. Although the Within estimator is preferred to OLS in terms of consistency, identification of time dummies would be impossible due to collinearities.

A reasonable conclusion is that the effect of work fragmentation is very small in program 28 but significant in program 29. This may reflect the technical nature of labour in program 28, that may result in more standardized wage rates than for program 29, which concerns artists.

7 Conclusion

In the currently prevailing intermittent employment scheme, unemployment compensation turns out to be a more and more advantageously internalized benefit. The marginal cost is not borne by firms and workers in the sector but by the whole UI fund for salaried workers which absorbs the increasing deficits of the particular Performing Arts UI Scheme. It is well-known that where experience rating – under which an employer's UI tax rate depends upon the stability of employment he provides – does not exist (like in France) or is incomplete, the structure of UI financing systems subsidizes the benefit payments of some industries at the expense of others, provided that the aggregate UI system does balance. In our case, contributions paid by employers and workers to the UI fund represent a declining share of total allowance expenses: in 1984, the amount of spending was 1.8 times higher than that of collected contributions; in 1992, it is 6 times higher. The PAUIS is therefore not simply an individual insurance scheme, but represents also a growing subsidization of the performing arts industry. The condition of aggregate UI system balance being harder to satisfy in periods of steep increases in the general unemployement rate, the deficit of the PAUIS has on several occasions given rise to public controversy on the PAUIS' rules.

How did the UI fund administration react to the above-mentioned evolution? Through successive and limited disincentive modifications that made the UI compensation less generous or the eligibility criteria more selective. For example, in 1984, the income replacement rates decreased significantly as displayed in Table 4. But deficits did not stop increasing. In 1991 and again at the end of 1992, new modifications were negotiated, consisting mainly of a regressive compensation scheme and a slight increase in the length of the initial uncompensated period for each new UI spell. But as it is designed, the PAUIS' running can only partly escape its subsidizing role. Substantial moral hazard and adverse selection problems are pervasive, induced by the insurer's inability to distinguish unpredictable exogenous constraints on the hours intermittent workers are able to sell in the market, from the worker's choice with regard to job search or allocation of non-market time. Similarly, it is well-known that employers do exploit asymmetrical information about their work and job allocation agenda in order to include entitlement to UI benefits in the wage bargainings with their casual employees. Organizations may also collude with their employees by hiring them repeatedly for short periods, in order to secure a kind of internal labour market without bearing the total cost of long-term relationships.

In their survey of unemployment insurance, Topel and Welch (1980) noted that "to the extent that workers take future unemployment benefits into account when evaluating a job offer, this effect must be ambiguous. While workers will certainly be more selective with respect to job offers if benefits are increased, the value of any particular job must be comprised of both income from working and benefit income from contingent unemployment. The increase in benefits will allow firms to offer the same value of an employment contract with a lower wage." (See also the very useful critical review by

Atkinson and Micklewright (1991)). The effects on employers are much less ambiguous: through UI cross-subsidy, the industry with such an unstable demand and volatile employment did expand by having a larger part of the income required to attract workers paid through UI benefits. The subsidizing role of the PAUIS is striking at the end of the period since the amount of UI benefits paid to compensated intermittent workers represents in 1992 about half of the amount of wages and fees paid to the whole population of intermittent workers. The question it raises is whether short-term hirings are exogenously or endogenously determined. The specific unemployment compensation scheme appears to provide an incentive for both firm and worker to short-time working.

8 References

Atkinson, A.B. and J. Micklewright (1991), Unemployment compensation and labour market transitions: a critical review, *Journal of Economic Literature*, 29, 1679-1727.

Christopherson S. and M. Storpe (1989), The effects of flexible specialization on industrial politics and the labour market: the motion picture industry, *Industrial and Labour Relations Review*, 42, 331-347.

Drèze J., (1979), Human capital and risk-bearing, reprinted in J. Drèze (1987), *Essays on Economic Decisions under Uncertainty*, Cambridge: Cambridge University Press.

Faulkner R. (1983), *Music on Demand*, New Brunswick: Transaction Books.

Faulkner R. and A.B. Anderson (1987), Short-term projects and emergent careers: evidence from Hollywood, *American Journal of Sociology*, 92, 879-909.

Kanter R.M. (1989) Careers and the wealth of nations: a macro-perspective on the structure and implications for career forms, in M.B. Arthur, D.T. Hall and B.L. Lawrence, eds., *Handbook of Career Theory*, Cambridge: Cambridge University Press.

Kiefer N. (1988), Economic duration data and hazard functions, *Journal of Economic Literature*, 26, 646-679.

MacDonald G., (1982), A market equilibrium theory of job assignment and sequential accumulation of information, *American Economic Review*, 72, 1038-1055.

Meade J. (1972), The theory of labour-managed firms and of profit-sharing, *Economic Journal*, 82, 402-428.

Menger P.-M. (1989), Rationalité et incertitude de la vie d'artiste, *L'Année Sociologique*, 39, 111-151.

Menger P.-M. (1993), L'hégémonie parisienne. Economie et politique de la gravitation artistique, *Annales ESC*, 6, 1565-1600.

Menger P.-M. (1994a), Etre artiste par intermittence, *Travail et Emploi*, 60, 4-22.

Menger P.-M. (1994b), Appariement, risque et capital humain: l'emploi et la carrière dans les professions artistiques, in P.-M. Menger and J.-C. Passeron, eds., *L'art de la Recherche. Essais en l'Honneur de Raymonde Moulin*, Paris: La Documentation Française.

Menger P.-M., J. Rannou and S. Vari (1996), *Le Marché du Travail et l'Emploi dans les Arts du Spectacle*, Paris : La Documentation Française, forthcoming.

Menger P.-M. with S. Vari (1993), Le marché du travail et l'emploi intermittent dans les arts du spectacle, Paris, Centre de Sociologie des Arts et MIRE, mimeo.

Miller R.A. (1984), Job matching and occupational choice, *Journal of Political Economy*, 92, 1086-1120.

Moulin R. (1992), *L'Artiste, l'Institution et le Marché*, Paris: Flammarion.

Okun A.M. (1981), *Prices and Quantities*, Oxford: Basil Blackwell.

Peacock A. and R. Weir (1975), *The Composer in the Market Place*, London: Faber.

Rannou J. and S. Vari (1996), *Les Itinéraires d'Emploi des Ouvriers, Techniciens et Cadres Intermittents de l'Audiovisuel et des Spectacles*, Paris: La Documentation Française.

Rosen S. (1986), The theory of equalizing differences, in O. Ashenfelter and R. Layard, eds., *Handbook of Labour Economics*, Amsterdam: North-Holland.

Stinchcombe A.L., (1968), *Constructing Social Theories*, Chicago: The University of Chicago Press.

Storper M. and R. Walker (1989), *The Capitalist Imperative. Territory, Technology and Industrial Growth*, Oxford et New York: Basil Blackwell.

Throsby D., (1996), Disaggregated Earnings Functions for Artists, this volume.

Throsby D. and D. Mills (1989), *When Are You Going To Get A Real Job? An Economic Study of Artists in Australia*, Sydney: Australia Council.

Topel R. and F. Welch (1980), Unemployment insurance: survey and extensions, *Economica*, 47, 351-379.

Towse R., (1992), Market value and artists' earnings, paper presented at the ICARE Conference, Venice, 1992.

Towse, R. (1996), *The Economics of Artists' Labour Markets*, London: The Arts Council of England.

Appendix: The French Performing Arts Unemployment Insurance Scheme.

Unemployment insurance for the performing arts adapts the French general UI program to the casual work frame that prevails in these arts: each intermittent worker active in the field – whether an artist or a technician or an administrative – meets the UI eligibility criteria when he performs enough hours of work for employers considered (by conventional agreement) as belonging to the performing arts field. In a significant number of cases, people may be hired as artists for a particular job and as executives, technicians, clerical or even blue collar workers for the next. This refers to the multiple-job holding situation very common in the arts. Our convention is to regard as artists those who have more of 50% of their work time in jobs recorded as artistic ones.

Like for UI systems in most countries, eligibility conditions require a substantial amount of employment over a given period: this amount is computed by adding up all paid employment spells over the last 12 (or 24 or 36) months. Only those who have worked a minimum of 507 hours in a given twelve-month period (or 1014 hours in a twenty-four-month period and so on) qualify. Many workers fail to meet the qualification requirement. The more hours accumulated, the longer the duration of the entitlement to compensation. The record of past job applications helps to compute the level of daily UI benefits a worker will receive over the period. Two schemes of UI compensation exist:

- workers in the film industry come under the so-called "régime 28" or "annexe 8" ("program 28" in our text). That scheme consists of a compensation based on the minimum daily payment for each category of job according to conventional agreements in that industry;

- workers employed in the audio-visual industry and in the live performing arts and artists wherever they work in the performing arts come under the "régime 29" or "annexe 10" (called "program 29" in our text). In that case, one is entitled to receive a proportion of the average amount of previous earnings: the taxable wages obtained by each eligible applicant during his different work spells are taken into consideration, up to a certain ceiling; the benefit payment is a given proportion of the average hourly wage earned plus a daily fixed payment.

There is no benefit during an initial period – called "carence" – the length of which varies with the number of accumulated workhours.

During the spells of compensated unemployment, an eligible worker can work on short-time contracts and nevertheless stay in the UI system: during these workdays, he gets of course no UI benefits. Each of these working periods is taken into consideration so that the worker, if accumulating enough of these job records, is allowed to requalify for the next compensation entitlement period (called CEP in our text), as soon as his current entitlement ends.

The Performing Arts Unemployment Insurance Scheme is financed through contributions from employees as well as from employers. Since it belongs to the whole French UI program, the deficits it has shown for several years are made up by the general UI Fund. So it may be said that the whole community of workers and employers subsidizes, through its UI contributions, the performing arts industry.